Xiuwu R. Liu

Wandering from China to America

A Life Straddling Different Worlds

Xiuwu R. Liu

WANDERING FROM CHINA TO AMERICA

A Life Straddling Different Worlds

Bibliografische Information der Deutschen Nationalbibliothek
Die Deutsche Nationalbibliothek verzeichnet diese Publikation in der Deutschen Nationalbibliografie; detaillierte bibliografische Daten sind im Internet über http://dnb.d-nb.de abrufbar.

Bibliographic information published by the Deutsche Nationalbibliothek
Die Deutsche Nationalbibliothek lists this publication in the Deutsche Nationalbibliografie; detailed bibliographic data are available in the Internet at http://dnb.d-nb.de.

A bamboo grove in the author's home province, Hunan. Photo by Chen Jingdong.

Second, amended edition. The first edition was published in 2006 by Zip Publishing, Ohio.

ISBN-13: 978-3-8382-1071-1

Printed in the EU

For Haiyan,
the freest spirit with the kindest heart

Contents

Author's Note on the 2nd Edition

It's been sixteen years since the publication of this life story. Meanwhile, I've discovered some errors in spelling and punctuation. (About the latter, adopting an informal tone, in the 1st edition I often omitted the comma after an adverbial phrase at the beginning of a sentence. In revising the text for this edition, I saw many of these places flagged by MS Word and so added a comma, sometimes reluctantly.) Going through my old files uncovered factual inaccuracies, too. Altogether, I've made over five hundred changes to the 1st edition, including corrections, deletions, additions and wordsmithing. The subtitle is new. Besides, I thought it would be informative to include some historical documents related to the story for readers of Chinese. I present these as appendices in photocopies, displaying the authors' drafts with their own revisions for authenticity's sake. Three English documents are also appended. For word divisions in *pinyin* I've followed *Xiandai hanyu cidian* (Modern Chinese Dictionary), 7th edition (2016), which differs from the *ABC Chinese-English Comprehensive Dictionary* (2003), especially in idioms. A brief coda brings you up to date.

I'm grateful to my former teacher mentor Richard Quantz for the permission to include his letter from 1999 as an appendix. If you enjoy the book, the credit goes to Jakob Horstmann, commissioning editor at ***ibidem*** Press's London Office. If not, and if you think your taste isn't to blame, then it's all my fault.

Author's Note on the 1st Edition

Chinese names are transcribed the Chinese way, i.e., family name first, given name second.

Three consonants in *pinyin* are confusing to English speakers. Their approximate pronunciations follow: C is similar to "ts" as in "rats," Q is similar to "Ch" as in "Chinese," X is similar to a relaxed "sh" as in "shop."

Friends, colleagues, former teachers, former students, and editors gave me encouragement, advice, and feedback, and a peer reviewer's comments led me to cut out a third of the manuscript. I thank them all.

Nancy Nicholson, M. P. P. D. W. (Model Poor Peasant Digital Worker), was responsible for the book's appearance.

1. A Family Both Red and Black . . .

I was born in March 1957 according to the Chinese traditional calendar, whose dates are about a month apart from those of the Western or Gregorian calendar, so the birth date on my driver's license or the forms I filled out for the Immigration and Naturalization Service is not what it seems. It wasn't until 1997 that I bothered to find out my birth date on the Gregorian calendar, April 21, 1957.

When I was six months old, my mom took me from Hubei to her parents in Hunan to be raised as their "adopted" (*guoji*) grandson. They wanted to raise me so that when they grew old, I would help them with housework and care for them. But since my maternal grandparents' only son went to Taiwan before Liberation, continuing my grandpa's family line might also have been behind the decision to adopt me. Anyhow, I got my maternal grandpa's family name, and my generation name, the "Xiu" in "Xiuwu," came from his lineage. "Xiu" means "to cultivate," and "Wu," martial or military (arts). Obviously, I didn't live up to my name, as I ended up cultivating literary or cultural arts (*wen*). As if to make the connection between word and essence (following Karl Kraus), later on my middle school classmates gave me the nickname "Xiuzi" (with "zi" meaning both person and master), and my factory pals gave me the nickname "Ink." (In China, "middle school" included grades 7 through 10 or grades 6 through 9 in my time.)

My grandma was born in 1900 into a "middle-peasant" family, that is, one with just about enough land to support itself. She had some private schooling in the old style called *sishu*. After marrying Grandpa in 1931 (second marriage for both), she had an unsettled life as Grandpa lost and obtained various positions in the Nationalist Army and moved from one city to another. Grandma remained a housewife her entire adult life.

Grandpa was born in 1899. When his grandma, an able matriarch of a large family in the country, died, the family waned in wealth and luster. Still, Grandpa studied thirteen-and-a-half years with private tutors before sojourning to Changsha to attend a school with a strange name—Hunan Special Prison School, where he studied law and military affairs. After the prison school he returned to his native place, where he helped organize a local militia to deal with bandits. In 1926 and 1927 he participated as a company commander in the Northern Expedition, the northward campaign to rid China of the blight of warlords. In 1928 and 1929 he received more military training in Nanjing. In the next two decades he served the Nationalists or KMT mostly as a noncombat officer and was unemployed several times. In 1949, through a friend's recommendation he became a deputy commander of the 63rd Division. By this time the Nationalist Army had suffered one defeat after another; while a lot of troops had fled to the island of Taiwan, others had risen in revolt. Due to the intervention of Bai Chongxi's troops, Grandpa's first attempt to surrender to the People's Liberation Army in Shaoyang, Hunan, failed. He was forced to seek another appointment in Chongqing, Sichuan. After a month's service in the Defense Ministry, he was assigned to the 144th Division, stationed at Jiangyou, Sichuan. When his troops moved to Mianzhu, General Pei Changhui, commander in chief of the Seventh Army (*bingtuan*), secretly ordered his officers to revolt. Grandpa agonized all night (on December 4, 1949) in part because the division's commander, who had been a protégé of General Hu Zongnan, was reluctant to betray Hu. The next day, with coercion and persuasion, Grandpa and the chief of staff managed to make the commander and another deputy commander agree to revolt and go over to the People's Liberation Army (see app. 1). Grandpa wrote about the insurrection in his autobiography, which was mostly a confession of his service under the Nationalists, especially his misdeeds (see app. 2). I asked him in the early 1970s when I read a revised version of his confession why he hadn't gone to Taiwan. He said, "Falling leaves return to their roots." I wondered: "Had he gone to Taiwan, what would have become of me?"

Demobilization and reeducation followed his revolt (see app. 3). When he was transferred to civilian work in 1952, given his rank he could have gone to Changsha, the capital of Hunan Province. But a hundred and fifty kilometers was still too far from his roots, so he returned to Yueyang, an ancient city by Lake Dongting, only sixty *li* (a li is half a kilometer or about a third of a mile) from his native village (even though he rarely visited it). After clerking for a couple of years in a salt company, he was made resident member of the Standing Committee of Yueyang County's Chinese People's Political Consultative Conference, an organization (not a meeting) in charge of those who had worked for the Nationalists in the old society.

Grandpa was tall and handsome, the latter especially in his uniform. A good swimmer, in his youth he survived a shipwreck by swimming with a piece of the wreckage from morning till dusk in Lake Dongting. Having been a soldier in his prime, he kept a soldier's habits throughout his life: his gait was brisk, his posture erect, and his quilt always folded with straight edges and pointed corners. His handwriting was graceful—firm but not stiff, flowing yet not unsteady. For years it served as an exemplar as I practiced to improve my own. On occasion he composed *qilü*, an eight-line poem with seven characters to a line and a strict tonal pattern and rhyme scheme. He would pace back and forth while humming a particular line he was composing. Though I enjoyed reading classical poems (and see free verse as broken prose), the idea of learning how to write one never occurred to me.

If one has made something of oneself, it is customary for one's relatives to feel proud. Grandpa was on the wrong side of the Communist Revolution, but he left his native village, traveled far and wide within the country, and became a major general. So, when relatives from his village came to visit us in Yueyang, they would speak of Grandpa with pride and admiration. However, Grandpa's autobiography and his conduct after 1949 did not show him to be a man of great ambition, ability, or integrity. His promotion in the military was far from rapid and his career was punctuated with periods of unemployment. His conduct was characteristic of someone who had been brought up and lived in a society with an age-old oppressive atmosphere, with circumspection as his motto. For example, shortly after Liberation, he donated his big old house in the native village to the government as private property became ideologically suspect.

One target of the Cultural Revolution was the "four olds"—old ideas, old culture, old customs, and old habits. My grandparents had an old-style bed with painted glass and carved wood panels, a likely target of the Cultural Revolution. To show that he was with it, Grandpa smashed up the panels, leaving an unadorned bed, to Grandma's protest.

More revealing of Grandpa's circumspection were the series of requests he made during the Cultural Revolution. According to his personal documents in my collection, on September 3, 1966, he submitted a report to the United Front Department and the county's Committee of the Communist Party requesting early retirement. He said that he understood that the People's Political Consultative Conference was an outdated organization; besides, Red Guards from Yueyang No. 1 Middle School had ordered his organization to be disbanded. He added that he was already sixty-eight years old and should no longer occupy his post just to make up the number (*lanyu-chongshu*). Nine days later, on September 12, 1966, he submitted another report to have his salary cut so that the extra money he didn't deserve could be used for building up the country. Before Grandpa got any response from the authorities, for September 1966 he only took fifteen *yuan* (Chinese dollars) of his regular salary of 74.5 yuan. Because he and Grandma didn't have any savings, by October he had already borrowed forty yuan to cover their living expenses. Then on October 7, 1966, he submitted yet another report, in which he described his rather difficult financial situation but insisted on needing only forty yuan a month.

Soon the Political Consultative Conference was disbanded and his salary was cut more than once. To make ends meet, he sold the few possessions of his, including a serge army uniform he treasured. By 1970, the withheld salary added up to over one thousand yuan. On March 1, 1970, Grandpa submitted yet another report to the county's Revolutionary Committee, the body in charge of the county at this time. In that report he offered to donate the withheld salary to the state so that a world without exploitation could be built, etc., etc.

There are more examples of his circumspection. In the early 1970s, he would urge caution in sunning our smoked pork, which had been prepared over the Chinese New Year and was meant to last several months, in case our neighbors thought we were better off than they. Cultivating harmonious relationships in one's neighborhood and with one's colleagues and trying to be in the good graces of one's superiors were imperative to him. When Grandma and I protested against certain obsequious gestures of Grandpa's, such as giving New Year's gifts of smoked pork and fish to the Party official in charge of old folks like Grandpa, he would say, "*What* do you know?" A refrain of his and to a lesser extent, of Grandma's, was "How difficult it is to be a person" (*zuoren nan a*)! Indeed, how to *zuoren* or conduct oneself in life has been made into an art in Chinese society.

If Grandpa conducted himself as if he were always treading on thin ice, especially after 1949, his eldest daughter was bold and stubborn. My aunt was born in 1919. In 1936, she went to school in Changsha. Fired up by anti-Japanese sentiments, my aunt like numerous other educated young people went to Yan'an in 1937. Upon graduation from the Chinese People's Anti-Japanese Military and Political College or Kangda for short, she was assigned to work underground in southern Hubei, which was controlled by the Nationalists. She worked in various positions in parts of Hubei till 1945. In October 1945, she was assigned to Huanggang County together with three comrades. They traveled on foot. One day at noon, the group of four came to a small village next to a highway. My aunt was having her period. The coarse paper chafed her thighs so badly that she refused to walk on. She told her comrades to cross the highway to find a stretcher while she rested in the village. Her comrades insisted that they find a more secluded spot to rest. My aunt would not listen. When her comrades came back with a stretcher four hours later, local security forces had picked her up. Her comrades reported this incident to higher authorities. Her superior Zhang Tixue dispatched my aunt's husband to head a team carrying concealed pistols to find out where she was being held in prison and if possible, to rescue her. They found out that she had been transferred to a different location shortly after her arrest. She was tortured in prison. Just like the Communist heroes portrayed in post-1949 books and movies, she refused to betray her comrades and was shot (see app. 4).

As my grandpa had a career in the enemy camp, when my aunt saw him briefly in 1938, she didn't breathe a word about her education in Yan'an or her assignment to Hubei. In the 1950s, Grandpa asked around to find out what had happened to his daughter. One of my aunt's former comrades wrote a testimony that she had died for the revolution and should be given the status of martyr. Grandpa submitted a request with the supporting evidence he had gathered, but the government office in charge of this type of case was too busy with the Great Leap Forward. For a decade no progress was made in the case.

Then one day in November 1968, two strangers came to see Grandpa. It turned out that the two had been investigating my aunt's death for some time. They had come from Hubei and were looking for Aunt because she should know about the activities of another underground worker, who in the 1960s was the head of a county in Hubei Province and who was, like other Communist leaders, under investigation for possible misdeeds before 1949. The two investigators had collected several testimonies about Aunt's execution and a list of leads that might provide further confirmation. Grandpa filed more requests for official recognition of Aunt's martyr status, but it wasn't until another decade had passed that he was successful. The county government honored Aunt's martyr status and conferred "Martyr's Family" (*lieshu*) on my grandparents. As a result, they received a monthly pension of over thirty yuan and extra ration coupons for eggs, pig stomach, and lard at some festivals. Only that Grandpa was to die within a year and Grandma, in less than two.

When Aunt's case was sometimes talked about in the family, it was said that had she lived, she would have become a high-ranking official in the government and the family would have benefited. Maybe. But given her temperament, she would not have come away unscathed from the numerous political campaigns after Liberation.

For years I lived with my grandparents at 32 Tea Lane. Ours was part of an old house that had belonged to the Taos, who before 1949 had in fact owned the entire compound walled with gray bricks of the old kind—larger and thicker than the new red bricks. Stone steps led up to the entrance of the compound, which housed in the 1960s six to seven families. All the households except one had a small yard in front and the compound also had a large yard used by adults to sun their laundry and by children as a playground. A line of trees stood along the eastern wall of the big yard. Numerous trees also provided shade and fruits throughout the compound: fig, pomegranate, loquat, and date. The Taos still owned the trees and when the dates were harvested, they would share some with the families living in the compound. The oldest member of the Tao family was a private teacher. His son went to Taiwan before the Communist victory in 1949, leaving behind his wife and several children, one of whom was an actor in the next-door Baling Opera Troupe. There was another actor's family living in the compound, the Xiaos; both husband and wife were actors in the same theater troupe. Their eldest son was a year or so my senior and we were playmates from time to time. An outhouse stood in the back of the compound.

Our living quarters consisted of a spacious hall shared with another family that served as our dining area and my playground on rainy days, a front room that served as living room and Grandma's bedroom, a small backroom where I shared a bed with

Grandpa, and a narrow kitchen half the width of the hall. The front room had a wooden floor, while the hall was paved with large bricks. Both the backroom and the kitchen had dirt floors.

At first, across the hall lived an old couple with the woman having the same last name as my grandma, Peng. They became such good friends that they started treating each other as sisters. As a result, the woman became my grandaunt. The relationship lasted for years after they had moved elsewhere. Another old couple moved in, who were the in-laws of the eldest daughter of the Taos, whose family then moved in after her in-laws moved out.

Our street was paved with stone slabs, which covered the center of the street, leaving the unpaved parts muddy on rainy days. Several doors to the west lay a garbage box that was emptied by a garbage man who pulled a garbage cart. A couple of hundred meters to the east were the water faucets where people in the neighborhood bought water. Adults carried water in two large pails on a shoulder pole, while kids used pails half the size. Each household had a water vat and used alum to make the dirt in the water settle on the bottom of the vat.

The west end of our street ran into the south end of Dongting Avenue and north end of South Main Street. Right across lay Upper Fish Lane, a main vegetable market with an occasional fish seller. A steep slope led into Lake Dongting, while a perpendicular slope formed the Lower Fish Lane into which extra vegetable venders spilled from Upper Fish Lane. The city center formed the largest intersection with three stores and one fruit shop occupying the four corners. To the west stood a major pork and fish shop; to the east, a photo shop, Yueyang Restaurant, a hospital, and farther down the road, a bookstore. To the south, an uphill slope named Tianyueshan was lined on both sides with a variety of small shops and to its east was a movie theater. About a li to the south stood tall and upright the ignored Cishi Pagoda dating from the thirteenth century. Across the street was the main hospital, and the old train station stood a few hundred meters away.

Two to three li north of the city center stood the famed Yueyang Tower. It is said that at this site back in the Three Kingdoms period (220–280) Lu Su had built a platform to review his navy on Lake Dongting. Engravings of the immortal essay of the Song dynasty statesman, Fan Zhongyan (989–1052), "The Record of Yueyang Tower," (Yueyanglou ji) greeted visitors to the first and second floors.

I envy those who can remember their earliest childhood; the little I know of my early years in life came from the mouths of my grandparents, my grandaunt mentioned above, and a few neighbors. Since I lived away from my mother, I had no breast milk. At that time, early in the morning the milkman would carry a basketful of bottled ewe's milk to the households with a subscription, but I didn't like the smell of ewe's milk. Maybe in part due to the poor nutrition, I was a sickly baby. At one time my diarrhea was so bad that I was hospitalized for twelve days. Grandma stayed by my side the entire time, sleeping hardly a wink. Since everybody was saying I was beyond help, Grandpa would stand over me with tears in his eyes.

I was slow to learn to talk—I couldn't utter a word by the time I was eighteen months old, when most babies can say simple words or even sentences. The eighteen-month-old I would stand in the pen with my big eyes wide open; seeing the clattering cap dancing on the steaming tea kettle, all I could utter was "Haw, haw, haw!" When I got older, I would come to the gate of the compound and sat on the top step of the entrance, watching the activities in the street. Some adult would yell, "Xiuwu, your grandma is coming!" I would stand up immediately and beat the dust off my bottom with my little hands, only to turn to see no trace of Grandma. I was too dim-witted to learn the lesson and my neighbors' teasing would work every time.

It is now widely known that China experienced a savage famine in the late 1950s and early 1960s. I was two years old when the famine hit. Since I have heard and read reports of people stuffing their poor stomachs with wild plants or even red earth, I feel extremely fortunate in being spared hunger and the resultant illnesses. I do remember the following scene, though. Grandma used a steamer to heat up leftover rice. When Grandpa went for a second bowl, the rice scoop would make scratching noises when it went over the metal rack. Needing a second bowl myself and fearing there wouldn't be enough left, I would announce, "Xiuwu wants some more!" "There *is* enough for you!" Grandpa would assure me. With Grandpa as a government employee and us as city residents, I never suffered an empty stomach.

The Chinese have a saying, "Kids look forward to the New Year." The Chinese New Year or Spring Festival is the biggest holiday of the year, with tons of delicious dishes, spiffy new clothes, New Year's allowance (*yasuiqian*), piles of candy and other munchies, fire crackers, etc., etc., to delight children and adults alike. Every Spring Festival was more or less alike but I remember one in particular. With my New Year's allowance, I boarded a bus that went as far as the pagoda. When the bus reached its destination, whereas all the other passengers had gotten off, I just stood there. The ticket seller yelled at me, "Hey, kid, time to get off!" I said timidly, "but I need to go back home." It took her a few moments to realize I was there just for the ride. A few years later I would move to where my parents were living to attend grade school. The train ride was only nine minutes and I would envy those passengers headed for the train's final stop— Changsha, some three hundred li away. Who would have thought that decades later I would be taking the dreadfully long flights between China and the United States?

I was not an unruly or naughty boy, but that doesn't mean my grandparents thought I didn't need corporal punishment. After all, as the saying goes, "Smacking and scolding one's kids are signs of love" (*da shi teng, ma shi ai*). When a child—a boy much more often than a girl—is too naughty, people would blame his parents because the child's behavior showed a lack of proper domestic discipline or upbringing. A common form of corporal punishment was whipping with a bamboo strip, which had a delicious name—bamboo shoots stir-fried with meat. Upon seeing some unacceptable behavior, a parent would threaten the child, "Hey, you want some bamboo shoots fried with meat?" Another common form of punishment was making the guilty child kneel on the washing board, the toothed side for added effect. My grandparents both had a mild temper, so they didn't beat me that often. Two occasions left vivid memories, however. One Spring Festival I was given a new jacket and new pants. Before I went out to play, my grandparents repeatedly exhorted me to be careful, to keep my outfit clean, as it was slushy in the streets. "I will, of course!" I shot back, impatient that they were belaboring the obvious. An hour later I came back with one side of my body badly soiled, as I had slipped and fallen into a puddle. Although fearing it, I knew I deserved a beating. Grandpa took out the wide bench and tied me face down. My bottom and legs were deep-fried with bamboo shoots.

I don't remember the cause of the second punishment. At any rate, Grandma made me kneel on the washing board and think about my wrongdoing. As I was kneeling near the entrance to the hall, our neighborly old lady saw me. She went over to my grandma and said, "Xiuwu already knows he's wrong. Let him stand up." Grandma said OK. The old lady then came over to me and said, "Xiuwu, you can get up now." I didn't budge. She said again, "Xiuwu, your grandma has already said you can get up. Now get up." I kept kneeling there. The lady walked away muttering half to herself, half to Grandma, "Looks like Xiuwu wants his grandma to come and get him up." My stubbornness was already showing in early childhood.

Another saying of parents and grandparents was "One will not become a useful person without beating." I would receive much more beating in my grade school years. Nowadays, I sometimes joke with my American students about the need to bring back corporal punishment, as some of them are too lazy. But honestly, I can't vouch for its salutary effects. In fact, as I got older, I also became naughtier.

It is a custom in China to call one's parents' friends and colleagues of their generation aunts and uncles and those of one's grandparents' generation, Grandpa X or Grandma Y. My grandparents had a relative who was the gatekeeper of the Park of Yueyang Tower, an old lady friend who lived on a street near the river (i.e., Lake Dongting), and another relative who lived in the eastern suburb called Dongmao Ridge. To help me remember them, my grandparents made me call them by their place of work or residence. Thus, I would call the gatekeeper Grandma Yueyang Tower; the old lady by the river, Grandma Estuary Street; and the last, Grandpa Dongmao Ridge. (I didn't know any other kids using this nomenclature.) One exception was an old friend of my grandparents whose last name was Huang. I called him Grandpa Huang instead of Grandpa Guanyin Pavilion. For some years Grandpa Huang made a living writing letters for those who didn't know how to write. He had a desk not far from the city center; his office was the street itself. I would mosey over to his "office" and he would say, "As you like?" meaning "Something to eat?" This was because when I first went to see him, he had offered to buy me some candy or a Popsicle and I had answered, "As you like" (*suibian*, i.e., *sui ni de bian*). I was easy to please. This early casualness would later flourish into a grandiloquent view of life: Few things in life are truly important; hence, one should be easygoing and not take things too seriously. Which doesn't mean I can always match my conduct to my philosophy. I still worry too much.

2. Docile Country Boy

About fourteen li south of Yueyang stood the headquarters of a state-owned horticultural farm. Its main crops were fruits such as pears and peaches. Tea and peanuts were also abundant. And there were of course plenty of rice paddies. To the west lay the vast Lake Dongting, hence the name Lakeside Horticultural Farm. The farm had a grade school, where my dad was principal and mom a teacher of Chinese. The school had over four hundred students.

Mao's China had a rigid household registration system whereby the flow of population was tightly controlled. The two categories of this registration were urban resident and rural resident. Though my parents were rural residents, I was an urban resident by virtue of my adoption by my maternal grandparents as their paternal grandson. When I went to school where my parents were working, my residential status remained intact. My grandparents paid a monthly stipend to my parents to cover my living expenses and my rice ration coupons were good anywhere in the province. Whenever I reminisce about my childhood, I feel lucky that I spent almost all my grade school years in the country, because I got to be a country boy without really being one.

In the fall of 1963, I was six-and-a-half years old. As in the United States, children in China needed to be seven to enter first grade. But rules were not nearly as strict in the country as in the city and mentally I was no longer underdeveloped for my age. Besides, I had connections.

In Chinese schools of those days, country schools anyway, teachers' families often lived in rooms adjacent to or even between classrooms. For the first three years of my grade school, we lived in three different "apartments," all at the end of a row of classrooms. At first, the school was on the west side of the railroad tracks; later it moved to the top of the hill on the other side of the tracks.

Right on the shores of the lake and on the water was a lumberyard, where huge piles of lumber were stored and colossal rafts bound together by bamboo cables bobbed on the waves. Countless times, sometimes with my friends, sometimes all by myself, I jumped from one log to another, balancing my body like an acrobat as the logs rolled and bobbed. Not that I had that much playtime; in fact, I had little of it for a kid my age. Mom believed that a well-raised child was one made to learn to do all kinds of chores. At that time, firewood was our fuel for cooking and we never had too much of it, so onto the rafts I went, to collect scraps of wood and broken bamboo cables.

One source of firewood was the shavings from the railroad ties being cut by railroad workers whose sheds stood about two li from the school. These deeply tanned, muscular workers (who had no need for gyms or tanning booths) wielded their glistening axes; as the blade cut at an angle into a log, my eyes rolled downward, eager for the twirling shavings to fall to the ground. The pine logs occasionally oozed resin; that and the texture of the wood made for good firewood. As we put it, the shavings "stood burning." I would fill up my basket with shavings and walk barefoot along the railroad tracks back home. The tie cutting didn't last long, so I had to revert to the old ways of collecting firewood around the lumberyard.

It was in second grade that I got to cut firewood for the first time. Our neighbor's son, a boy much older than me, offered to take me on a bush-cutting trip. We each brought a knife, a round shoulder pole (with pointed ends for sticking into the bush bundle) but no rope. We walked across rafts after rafts and finally came to a small island. We jumped off the last raft and climbed uphill. There was no need to climb far—the island was completely covered with bamboo. We laid down our shoulder poles and started cutting right away. My guide, Xiangsheng, showed me how to cut and my two hands were moving in synch in no time. "I like this chore!" I thought to myself. It was more fun than a kids' game. It didn't take me long to cut enough for a bundle, but Xiangsheng had already cut enough for two big bundles. He then picked two pieces of bamboo and showed me how to make a tie. One bundle was just about the weight I could carry. Into the bundle the shoulder pole was thrust and up onto my back the bundle went, the pole resting on the shoulder pointing toward the ground at an angle. Xiangsheng balanced the two bundles on his shoulder and we went over the same rafts home. In later years I would spend much more time cutting firewood and become expert at it, too.

One afternoon in second grade, I went to collect firewood with a girl, a fellow student whose father worked at the lumberyard. After a couple of hours of walking around, we came to a small estuary, where a long log was floating a few meters from the shore with a broken bamboo cable straddling over it. Having not yet learned how to swim, I was afraid I might fall into the lake. Still, the cable scrap was too enticing. I waded into the water before gingerly stepping onto the log. Before I knew it, I fell into the water with a splash. Luckily, the water was shallow. I really should have floated the log over with one hand. As it was late afternoon, there wasn't enough time for my clothes to dry off. Experience told me that I could expect a beating from Mom. To my great surprise, after hearing my confession, instead of beating me she rewarded me with a treat—fried rice with eggs.

But Mom did have a hot temper. I was hardly a naughty boy and yet, "bamboo shoots fried with meat" was a frequent dish for me. Still, compared with Mom, a woman colleague of hers, Teacher Wu, was worse. Once I failed to complete a chore. Teacher Wu said that kneeling on the washing board was not enough to make me behave. She suggested that Mom use two small bowls turned upside down. As a result, I was made to kneel on the bottoms of two bowls well into the night with the bottom rims cut deeply into my knees despite my efforts to shift my weight away from them. Mom and Dad were sleeping inside the mosquito net and I was not rebellious enough to stand up. Harsh though this punishment and others were, I am not aware of any scars on my psyche, nor did I turn into a juvenile delinquent.

At Mom's urging, I learned to do not only a boy's chores but also a few of a girl's. In second grade I learned how to wash clothes using a washing board. Washing clothes wasn't my chore, however. It wasn't until I moved back to the city to live with my grandparents again that washing clothes and bed sheets became my responsibility.

Among the colorful personalities of the school was the chef. All Chinese schools (and factories, etc.) had a canteen where teachers and some students ate. Our chef, Grandpa Liu, had a favorite spice—fermented soybeans. Normally, this type of beans was fried with chilies, fried or steamed with pork, or steamed with fish. In other words, it might be called a "heavy" spice and goes with similar dishes. But not for Grandpa Liu. He would put fermented soybeans in almost every dish, including Chinese cabbage, a "light" dish. Unavoidably, the light dishes cooked with fermented soybeans would have a strange taste and teachers would talk about this odd habit of Grandpa Liu's. But strangely, nobody brought this up as a serious complaint and Grandpa Liu went on in his merry old ways.

Another memorable figure was Teacher Cheng. He had only one arm: he had lost his other arm (and his mother) during a Japanese bombing in WWII. It was a capable and powerful arm. He could ride a bike and drive a truck. When a student was unruly, he would grab his chest and lift him up in the air while staring at and scolding him. He often directed us in choruses. I still remember the first two lines of a propaganda song, a popularized expression of a rigid theory about the relationship between one's background and oneself. The lyrics went, "A heroic father breeds a brave son; a reactionary father breeds a skunk of a son." Too young to understand its meaning, I joined my fellow students in enthusiastic encore after encore as Teacher Cheng directed us with his forceful arm.

Those were the days of revolutionary songs. There were songs of praise and songs of abuse. Objects of praise and worship included the great Communist Party, the socialist new China, the heroic People's Liberation Army, workers, and above all, the great leader Chairman Mao. Songs of abuse were directed at reactionaries such as the U.S. imperialists and Chiang Kai-shek, and at old enemies such as the Japanese devils who had ravaged China during WWII. Dozens of Chairman Mao's sayings were turned into songs, called "quotation songs." There were frequent gatherings of the student body, where singing always preceded the proceedings. The gathered classes would compete with one another in singing. One class or even a whole grade would challenge another to sing a song, which challenge would then be returned. This would go on for several rounds, leaving everybody present in high spirits.

I was too young to fully experience the Cultural Revolution that began in 1966. Still, I need to jot down my limited experiences.

Almost all those in leadership positions were branded "people-in-power who took the capitalist road," stripped of their power, struggled against on stage, and paraded through streets. A grade school's principal held only a minor position of power, but as the head of a work unit Dad had to be "overthrown," along with leaders of the farm. Big-character posters were pasted everywhere that screamed "Down with so-and-so!" "So-and-so, confess your counterrevolutionary crimes right now or else!" "If reactionaries refuse to surrender, we'll wipe them out!" and "Carry the Great Proletarian Cultural Revolution through to the end!" One day, all the students were gathered in the auditorium of the lumberyard, where a struggle session was held. Former leaders of the horticultural farm were lined up in the front of the stage with my dad standing at the end, as he was the smallest fish. As usual, a placard was hung on the neck of each strugglee with his name crossed out (otherwise for criminals who were to be or had been executed). Teacher and student representatives went on stage one after another to denounce the strugglees' counterrevolutionary crimes. One of Dad's colleagues, who had a thick accent students liked to mimic, went on stage and made his denunciation. Then he raised his right arm, his hand forming a fist, and shouted at the top of his voice, "Down with Sun Zhenhua!" The students followed him in thunderous chorus. He repeated the slogan a few times. Being short, I sat in the front row. Gazing up at my dad wearing a placard, I was at a loss about how to conduct myself. He looked forward, expressionless. When a slogan was shouted, including the ones attacking him, I automatically raised my right arm like everybody else, even though my shouting was not as enthusiastic. Maybe the adults knew what they were doing; I was unable to make head or tail of the whole business. Long after the Cultural Revolution was over, when reminiscing about the period, Mom would tease me because I had waved as a toy the little paper pennants used at struggle sessions.

Not just officials were sacked during the Cultural Revolution; people with bad family backgrounds (e.g., those whose parents had worked for the Nationalists or owned too much land) were made to sit through criticism sessions and write confessions about their family's history and their own conduct in the early 1970s. Mom's father had been a reactionary military officer in the old society, so, of course, she wasn't spared. According to

Grandma, Mom insisted that she had done nothing wrong and didn't deserve the criticism sessions.

For us nine- or ten-year-olds the Cultural Revolution was more than struggle sessions or political speeches. Some activities were even fun. One summer weekend in 1966, a small group of us were scheduled to serve water to the passing Red Guards on their pilgrimage to some remote sacred place of the revolution. These teenagers wore army uniforms with a quilt bundle on their back, a red armband on their left arm, and an army water bottle slung across the shoulder. As they walked alongside the railroad tracks heading north, they greeted us while passing out quotations from Chairman Mao, printed on colored palm-sized pieces of paper. The hot sun was beating down on them, their faces sweaty and their uniforms dusty. They looked tired but pushed on.

Before long, our school moved to the hill across the railroad tracks. Our apartment was inside the classroom-building complex on a hillside. It was here that I spent my first sleepless night. One of the faculty, Teacher Du, was writing slogans with a brush one evening and I decided to help him. As each slogan was done, I would find an empty spot to lay it down on the floor to dry out. Soon the finished slogans spilled into the corridor. I called myself Captain of Transportation, even though I was the only one doing the transporting. I was having such a good time that I didn't feel drowsy the whole night. It seems unreal today that one could be so wrapped up in such an activity, but it is indicative of the kind of mindless enthusiasm the Red Guards felt during that heady period.

The violence of the Cultural Revolution rarely spread to the countryside. But the horticultural farm was under ten li away from Yueyang, so travelers to the city brought news of fights between rebel factions. One day in 1967, rumor had it that one faction was going to attack the farm, especially our school. Since our revolution had only been gentle slogan pasting and not-so-gentle struggle sessions, the threat of real violence scared us. We dared not go to sleep till midnight. My parents told me, "When they come, exit the back window and run into the fields." The back window opened onto the roof of a lower house on the hillside from which we could jump to the ground. The night passed without incident. It was either a false alarm or the rebels changed their course of action.

Shortly afterward, while Dad stayed in the main school of the horticultural farm, Mom was transferred to a one-classroom village school three to four li away, probably as a form of punishment due to her bad family background. From that point on I experienced no memorable events of the Cultural Revolution on the farm. But since I visited my grandparents frequently when school was in session and stayed with them during summer and winter breaks, I got to see a lot of action of the revolution in the city.

If lots of slogans were pasted in my school on the farm, the situation paled in comparison with that in Yueyang. Slogans were pasted or directly written on walls; even the ground of sections of the central streets was covered with them, written with broad brushes. Big-character posters denouncing Party and government officials hung from ropes and covered walls. Some posters attacked the enemy faction; others defended their own, including officials seen to be on their side. One poster pasted on a wall near the city center described the torture a woman had to suffer: a red-hot iron rod was thrust into her vagina. The authors of some posters protested that they had been wrongfully accused of some wrongdoing and cried for justice. On one of my weekend trips to the city, I saw two revolutionary rebels on a bike, the one sitting on the rear rack brandishing a pistol.

At night hordes of Red Guards poured onto the streets, sometimes in trucks. They would occupy a street corner, sometimes set up a stage, and put on a show consisting of dancing to revolutionary tunes and singing revolutionary songs, including songs whose lyrics were quotations from Chairman Mao. In front of the big hardware store on South Main Street, not far from the city center, swappers of Mao badges clustered into little circles comparing their collections. These were metal or porcelain badges of various shapes and sizes; they were exchanged for their perceived value. Prized collections were often pinned onto strips of velvet or arrayed in boxes. At one time a poster was shown in front of a shop on South Main Street that supposedly contained a furtive counterrevolutionary slogan. The explanation said that if one looked at the poster in a certain way, the slogan would become visible. I followed the instructions—eureka! The slogan was unmistakable. Did the designer of the poster really hide the slogan that way? Or was the slogan simply a coincidence? All I could think was marveling at the ingenuity of the decoder.

Closer to home was a particularly fierce fight between two rival factions of the revolutionary rebels. A stray bullet ricocheted off an eave of our house in the compound of the Taos. At dusk the mother of the Taos living next door started crying because her eldest son, the actor, had not come home and she feared he might have been killed in the gunfight. Later that night he did come home, shaken but not hurt.

The county's Political Consultative Conference was shut down and its long sign taken away. Posters covered the inside and outside walls of the building; denouncers included an old friend of Grandpa's. One evening Grandpa was taken away to be paraded through the streets with more important Party and government officials who had by now been deposed. I caught up with the procession on Liberation Road. Standing on a truck, Grandpa wore a placard on his neck but he didn't cower—maybe because he had been a soldier. Thunderous slogans erupted repeatedly from the procession, including "Down with reactionary officer Liu Youwen!" I felt neither fear nor humiliation, only a faint embarrassment.

The procession went by and turned north. I went home. A bit later the youngest son of the Taos said that I should go to the county's Party headquarters to meet Grandpa. I walked into the big room where paradees had been brought. A young man was abusing an official who was kneeling on the floor. The young man shouted at the bound official: "If you don't fess up, don't expect to go home tonight!" I felt a twinge of despair for the official, as the night seemed endless. Grandpa came out in a few minutes. He saw me, took my hand, and we walked out. We didn't say a word on the way home.

Grandma told me that the Red Guards had come to our home while I was in the country. They ransacked the place but found nothing they could confiscate. My grandparents had nothing of great value, nothing "feudal" or "bourgeois"—not even books. After the Red Guards had gone, Grandpa and Grandma put things back in place. In the unvarnished wooden box, which served as their armoire, was a gold band that had escaped the ransackers. It was the only article of some value in their possession. The next day the ever-dutiful Grandpa took the band to the Red Guards and got a receipt for it. (The band was returned to him later on. A bank receipt dated August 12, 1972, says that he got 28.30 yuan for it.)

As I mentioned in chapter 1, the Baling Opera Troupe was next door to our compound; we could see its stage over the wall dividing the theater and our compound when the theater's west side-door was open. Baling is an old name for Yueyang and Baling Opera a distinctive local opera with its own style of music, costumes, and dialect, the dialect of Yueyang. Since the old costumes and other theater gear were part of the four olds, they couldn't survive the vandalism of the Cultural Revolution. One early evening I was walking down Tianyueshan toward the city center. A boisterous procession was heading down South Main Street approaching the city center. The young actors and actresses of the Baling Opera Troupe were pushing and pulling cartloads of their embroidered costumes and glittering headgear to be burned. They reached the large intersection, dumped everything on the ground, and set it ablaze. Onlookers gathered around but kept their distance as the fire flared up. Too young to understand the significance of the event, I only thought to myself: "All these fantastic costumes are being burned; what a pity!" Witnessing this spectacle, I could hardly believe my eyes. The traditional repertoires of the various local operas came under fierce attack during the Cultural Revolution for being nothing but tales about emperors, kings, generals, and ministers; and gifted scholars and beautiful ladies (*diwang-jiangxiang, caizi-jiaren*). Instead, the ordinary laboring people should have been the protagonists. As a result, heroes of the Communist revolution, feats of the Communist army, exemplary workers and, above all, Chairman Mao, replaced the kings and princes, scholars and beauties.

But I'm getting ahead of the story. There's more to be told about the days before the school moved.

School was not particularly fascinating for me, though neither was it dreary. Where there are children, there's fun or mischief. One of the fun times was the break between classes in the winter. Because there was no heating, our toes would be numb from the cold and inactivity during a class period. The moment the bell rang and we were dismissed, we boys would throng into the corner and form a line along the back wall. The one standing at the end of the line would try to nudge out the one in front who would in turn attempt to nudge out the one in front of him, all the way to the first boy in line. Once a boy lost his position, he would go to the end of the line and start all over again. Yelling, cheering, taunting, and boasting would accompany the nudging; in a few minutes we would no longer be cold. Girls would pair up and clap each other's hands to a rhythmic ditty.

In every class there would be a few naughty students. Some would get into a fight at the slightest provocation; others played pranks on their classmates. In second grade I was the victim of a dirty prank. Summer was hot, often muggy, in Hunan, and we were required to take our early-afternoon siesta on top of our desks and stools. One such summer day, I was napping on the desks. In my shallow sleep I felt a faint movement of my fly. When I realized what was happening, it was too late: my fly had been unbuttoned and my little you-know-what was exposed. (The days of zippers and underwear were yet to come.) I didn't open my eyes for some seconds, feeling embarrassment then a novel sense of exhibitionist excitement. When I got up and looked around, nothing seemed to have happened: no shuffling, no snickering. I buttoned up my fly while muttering my displeasure at the prank and let the matter drop.

Although I didn't show any aptitude in school, I was a good student. And boy, was I conscientious. For a while we lived in a corner of a compound whose classrooms and walls formed a big yard, where movies were shown on Saturday evenings. Not only did we not have to buy tickets, we didn't even have to leave our room to see the movie screen in the distance. One Saturday I had some homework, which I insisted on finishing instead of watching the movie being shown outside the door. Mom urged me to finish the homework the next day but I wouldn't listen. Later on, Mom would praise me in front of my siblings because of this, but in retrospect it showed my obstinacy as much as it did my conscientiousness.

Americans like camping and sometimes I am asked whether I like it or not. Honestly, I don't know, because I never had a camping trip as a kid. But then again, if you spent a lot of time in the fields and hills and your school and village were surrounded by them, would you feel the urge to go camping? You might say the school or village *is* a big camp. Meanwhile, I remember one night spent outdoors that probably resembles one on a camping trip. What happened was the school had some watermelon fields that needed tending at night. A thatched shed on bamboo stilts stood in the middle of the fields serving as a watchtower. The watcher stayed in the shed all night through watching over the ripening melons. He carried a long torch and whenever he heard some noise, he would shine the torch in the direction of the noise and yell, "Who's there?" The night I was allowed to stay in the shed with the watcher, no thief came to steal our watermelons.

People living in the country are close to nature, but sometimes nature can get too close. One evening I was home alone and went to bed early. I lay in bed awake. In one corner of the room was a pile of sweet potatoes boxed in with red bricks. Suddenly, some noise came from that direction. I sat up and froze at the sight: A snake about the length of a shoulder pole was inching from the potato pile toward my bed! I didn't panic, didn't scream. I got out of bed, tiptoed out the door, went through the classrooms, and ran up to the compound to get help. In no time a teacher grabbed a hoe and came with me. Strangely enough, when we returned, the big snake had still not reached my bed. Maybe it was tired of a day's hunting in the wilderness. Maybe it was confused by the indoor environment. At any rate, the teacher aimed at the snake's "neck" and killed it with one strike. My parents came home from a meeting shortly afterward and we buried the dead snake in the overgrown basketball court.

In 1967 Mom was transferred to the one-classroom village school. By this time, I'd had two brothers, Huiwen and Huibin, but Mom and Dad were busy with their work and had sent them away to be taken care of by two old ladies in Yueyang. In fact, it was common practice for young and middle-aged couples to have their children taken care of by their own parents or some old nanny. It didn't seem that any psychological problems had developed among these children as a result of their living away from their parents.

The main part of the village had one row of apartments, with the sole classroom sticking out in the middle of the row, forming a short T. There was a big yard on both sides of the classroom, which had rickety desks and chairs. Our kitchen was in the back of the classroom. Smoke from the stove blackened the section of the dirt-brick wall next to it; bundles of firewood were stored on a rack overhanging the entrance. Our big living room-cum-bedroom was next to the classroom. In the front of the yard on the west side of the classroom stood a bare flagpole, which I loved climbing. I would go all the way to the top; with my legs wrapped around the pole and one hand holding the top I would wave my other arm and yell with joy.

Kids in the country would start helping out in the rice paddies in grade school. I had learned how to transplant rice seedlings in third grade, before Mom and I had moved to the small village. In early spring, rice is planted in fields called seeding beds. When seedlings are ready for transplanting, they are pulled out of their beds, bundled up with straw strings and carried in bamboo vessels to the rice fields that have been readied for transplanting. Bundles of seedlings are thrown into a field at appropriate intervals. They are then picked up, untied, and inserted into the earth. Transplanting rice seedlings is simple enough, but it takes dexterity and practice to become fast. It's also backbreaking work, because the laborer has to bend forward and walk backward all day long. During the double rush in the summer, the work gets even more toilsome with the scorching sun beating down on the laborer while heating up the water in the field.

Because timing is critical, peasants work hard during the spring planting season and even more so during the double rush, when the workday can be as long as sixteen hours. Partly for this reason, there were often informal competitions to see who among a group was better or best at transplanting rice seedlings. When one was passed by another on the outside, one would be "in a hole" and be teased. Similarly, there were rice-cutting competitions during the double rush, although somehow much less frequent. Cutting rice involves little skill but real danger in that the slightest slip can lead to injury—the sickle cutting one or more fingers of the hand holding the rice. The fingers on my left hand have five scars from rice cutting.

There was a flood in the summer of 1967. Water from the inner lake of Dongting came up to some of the rice fields of our village. The ripened rice must be rescued before it was lost. We rushed to the fields, where water came up to our calves. (The fields are supposed to be dry at harvest time.) Halfway through the afternoon, the sky suddenly changed face and down came big raindrops, making the scene "Water, water, every where." Luckily, it was a passing shower. Still, we were all turned into drenched chickens.

Getting firewood continued to be my duty. At this time, besides bushes, we found another source of firewood. Some of the hills were being reclaimed and as the earth was turned over, the roots of tree stumps and bamboo were dug out. The peasants doing the reclamation of course picked up most of these, but there were always plenty of remnants for us kids to collect. These roots were better firewood than bushes because they stood burning.

Then there was the old bush cutting. By now, I had become more proficient and being a bit stronger could carry a bit more at a time. We would go to a hill in twos or threes and come home with two small bundles of firewood on our shoulders. Especially fun was wading through the irrigation canals in the summer, where we could submerge our sweaty bodies in the cool water and splash around. One day, I went with a pal to tend a water buffalo (a common draft animal in southern Chinese countryside) along the shores of the inner lake of Dongting, a few li away from our villages. He let me ride the water buffalo and we also dug up an edible root called "lake roots." We scraped the dirt and skin off the roots with our blackened fingernails before eating the mildly sweet roots.

More substantial and sweeter were sweet potatoes. Another goody from the fields was peanuts. There were several hills planted with peanuts on my way to school. We weren't supposed to eat the peanuts, which belonged to the production team (the smallest administrative unit of Chinese countryside in those days). But could a ten-year-old keep away from such delicious things? Besides, it was said that raw peanuts were good for the lungs. Still, I did restrain my longing for peanuts and only occasionally stole into a peanut field. Sometimes, spotting a missed peanut plant in a harvested field, I would give out a cry of joy. But what about the pears everywhere? As a matter of fact, I behaved much better in the case of pears. Not that I didn't like them. And yet somehow being bigger and grown on trees made them look more forbidding and walking into a pear grove made me feel more like a thief. Indeed, I only stole into a pear grove a couple of times and plucked a few pears.

If planted fruits were off limits, wild ones were there for the picking. I learned about edible berries, the sweetest of which was raspberries. They grew on a thorny roselike bush and would be the high point of a bush-cutting trip. All these things we ate unwashed, and yet I didn't get sick once. Is country dirt cleaner than city dirt? Or were we used to it? It would seem that city dirt would contain much more germs.

In addition to spending summer and winter breaks in Yueyang with my grandparents, I also visited them quite often. I would take to my grandparents some firewood (they burned coal but needed kindling) or fresh vegetables and bring back some goodies from the city. One night I had a dream in which a big fish jumped out of the lake and landed on the bank. More than once when reaching the dam, I went down to the sluice on the east side hoping a fish would jump out. Once my dad went with me, and Grandma cooked some pork for us to bring back to the village. When we reached the dam, a gale blew off the cover of the little pot containing the dish. I was able to retrieve the lid only after chasing it for some distance.

Life got harder in the small village. Rice was of course our staple. Fresh and pickled vegetables were plentiful but we could rarely afford meat. Even flour was a treat. For breakfast, when there was not enough leftover rice, Mom would add plenty of water and Chinese cabbage before dropping clumps of flour into the rice porridge. When it was done, we would count the number of flour clumps each could have (Mom would always let me have a few more), and I would savor the texture of the inside of each clump because the inside had more body to it than the mushy outside.

The headquarters of the horticultural farm lay about five li southwest of our village. From time to time, Mom and Dad had conferences there. I liked going there partly because the food in the canteen was better than that at home. One dish stood out for me: a flat omelet sliced into narrow strips and then refried with chives or green onions. One day I discovered a peanut oil press at the back of the headquarters. I hung around the press and picked up bits of the peanut dregs squeezed out of it and popped them into my mouth. A bit gritty but tasty.

Mom's temper got worse during this period. For my slightest negligence, she would beat me with a piece of firewood and I would scream with pain. (The name "bamboo shoots fried with meat" no longer fit the dish.) Once she threatened to put nails into a strip of wood and whip me with it for bloodier effects, but I wasn't particularly scared of the prospect. I vaguely sensed it was a mere threat. One early morning the villagers were making dirt bricks in the yard on the east side of the classroom. I was fascinated and forgot to return to my chore. Mom called me inside. Seeing her with a home-made ruler in hand, I ran out to the yard on the west side. Mom chased me. I only ran halfheartedly so she caught up with me near the flagpole. She hit me on the head, where the ruler broke into two pieces. It left a big bump on my head.

When I visited my grandparents, they would see bruises on my legs. If Mom was present, they would scold her for beating me, but Mom said a naughty boy deserved beating. At some point I began to run away at the prospect of a beating. One evening I ran to my dad in the main school; not wanting Mom to worry, he escorted me back to the village. Then one night I had a pleasant surprise. I went to bed early. Hours later I was awakened by some noise. I opened my eyes and saw Mom and Dad sitting by the fire cooking something. Dad had come to visit us from the main school. Dad said to Mom, "You should go easier on Xiuwu." Mom replied, "Actually, Xiuwu isn't too intractable." A current of warmth invaded me and I fell back asleep right away.

When Mom was away at various meetings, I got to be home alone. I had my village pals, plenty of chores, and no problem being alone. Except for once when Grandpa came to see us. It was a sunny day. In the middle of the morning, Grandpa walked into my sight just like that! He looked around the village, the classroom, and our living quarters. As Mom was not home, he wanted to go back right away. Suddenly I had a strong urge to go with him, so I begged him to let me go with him to Yueyang. He said I was supposed to housesit. I wouldn't listen. He offered to give me ten cents if I stayed. (In the city, a plain Popsicle was three cents, while one with mung beans cost five cents.) I refused to accept the bribe. I don't remember what happened next: Did I see him off with tears in my eyes till his figure disappeared around the bend of the road, or did he finally soften up and agree to let me go with him?

Mom continued to beat me up. One day we all went to the farm's headquarters. Mom and Dad were at a meeting while I played around the building. I was also carrying a crock with which I was supposed to bring home some cooking oil. Mom told me to be careful with the jar. Before I bought the oil, I dropped the jar on the concrete ground. (At least I didn't break the jar *after* it was filled with oil!) It was still early in the afternoon so I roamed around the headquarters trying to think of a solution—I had been beaten up for a much smaller negligence. "Maybe I could mend the jar with some concrete mix?" I thought to myself. I searched the compound thoroughly for some concrete but found nothing. As the afternoon wore on, I became more and more anxious. Finally, I had to face my parents when they emerged from their meeting. I told them about the jar with apprehension. On the way home, Mom said repeatedly she would give me a good beating once we got home. "What shall I do? Run away!" I quickened my pace in order to reach home ahead of them. Mom was talking with Dad, so she didn't become suspicious of my intentions. I hurried home, put down the things I was carrying, and shot out the east door. I roamed round the hills until it was dark. "What now?" Dad was with Mom, while Yueyang was too far away. Then it occurred to me that I might be able to stay in a nearby village, so I went to the second village I would pass by on my way to school, where an older schoolmate let me stay with his family. He had been a student of my dad's and all the villagers knew my parents. They treated me to dinner. Around nine o'clock I was lying in bed when suddenly somebody yelled, "Xiuwu, your mom's coming!" "What shall I do?" "Quick, hide yourself!" I suspected it was just a tease. It was. I slept like a log that night.

I stayed there for several days. Meals were not a problem. I was even invited to a banquet: one of the families was having either a wedding or birthday celebration (the latter usually for old people), and dozens of guests had been invited to the banquet. Knowing that I was staying in the village, they also invited me. I had a feast.

And it happened to be the time to harvest peanuts. Peanut plants were pulled up and stacked up into tall cylinders on a hill to the southwest of the village. I rode a water buffalo and simply grabbed bunches of peanut plants from the heaps. I ate to my heart's content. In the evening, when the sun-dried peanuts had been pan-fried with sand, we feasted on fried peanuts. Leading such a carefree life, who would want to go home? But entirely carefree I was not. For villagers kept teasing me about my running away and I knew I couldn't stay away from home forever. I set my condition for returning home: When I did, Mom would not beat me up either for breaking the jar or for running away. Word came that Mom agreed. I ended my chore-free exile and returned home. By now Mom's anger had evaporated.

Mom's temper seemed to have gotten better from that point on. Did I bear any grudges against her? No. Mom was Mom. Reflecting on my life, I can't think of any long-term good or ill effects all that beating had on me. (What a waste!) Though beating was not good, spoiling would have been worse.

In contrast to the chore-filled school year in the country, summer and winter breaks in the city gave me plenty of time to play games. We played with marbles, buttons, Popsicle sticks, and scraps of metal.

It was a time of austerity, so when kids needed spending money, most of the time we had to rely on our own resourcefulness. Kids in my neighborhood had several ways to get money. First, there were cigarette butts lying on the ground everywhere. We would roam the streets, alone or in twos and threes, and pick up cigarette butts adults had thrown away. These were then torn apart and their contents shaken down onto a piece of paper. When enough tobacco had been collected, it was taken to a street peddler for some cash. The peddler would spruce up the tobacco bought from the kids and resell it to those who couldn't afford fresh cigarettes.

A second source of spending money was metals or other kinds of throwaways that could be sold to recycling shops. Sometimes, stray construction ties could be found near construction sites, which sold for two cents each. Broken glass and cardboard boxes were also cash trash. One would be extremely lucky if he found a piece of copper, as ordinary copper sold for 1.5 yuan a *jin* (about 1.1 pounds) and red copper, 2.2 yuan. A couple of my friends and I once went to a garbage dump of a factory in search of copper scraps. Frugal households didn't throw away their own cash trash, but the money went to the adults.

One day, I discovered a new source of income. I was loitering in the hardware store on South Main Street. Suddenly, I heard the dropping of a coin on the floor. Following the noise, I saw a coin roll under the counter. As the gap between the bottom of the counter and the floor was narrow and dark, the customer who had dropped the coin didn't even try to retrieve it. I was seized with a flash of insight: Many customers must have lost a coin that way! So, when that customer left the store, I also quickly left to look for a stick. In a few minutes I returned with a short stick and went straight to the counter where the coin had disappeared into the darkness. I inserted the stick into the crack and made a sweeping movement and out slid the nickel! To build on my booty, I went to the next counter then the next, in an inconspicuous manner so as not to arouse the suspicion of the shop attendants, who were as a rule lackadaisical. My gleanings were slim: only a few one-cents and two-cents. (The largest coin was a nickel.) Next, I went to the store on the southwest corner of the city center, where I mined a nickel and some smaller coins. I was disappointed by my booty and gave up the get-rich-quick operation. (All this might inspire an enterprising academic to do some research and then write a paper with a trendy title: "The Social Construction of Children's Spending Money in Modern China.")

In 1968, yet another change in government policy hit us. According to my dad, the local moves were instigated by an editorial in a Party newspaper. As a consequence, in September I moved with Mom to Dad's native village, the village of the Suns and Wangs, some seven li from where we had been living. This policy was called "returning to one's native place," apparently applicable to those who had been struck down during the Cultural Revolution and maybe also to those who had bad family backgrounds. In our case, Mom and I had to move because of Dad, though he only stayed with us for three months. The leaders in his home commune trusted him enough to ask him to head some school in another part of the commune, which left Mom and me living in his native village.

The village of the Suns and Wangs was small: A square complex formed the heart of the village with a few self-standing houses. A rectangular skylight stood in the middle of the common hall with a corresponding sky-well to receive rain and light. On rainy days, one or more turtles would crawl out into the open well from the depths of their dwellings. Typical of such villages, several of the families were relatives. In our case, besides other relatives Dad's elder brother also lived in the complex with his wife and several children, the eldest of whom was born in 1958 and got the name "Leap Forward."

We had three rooms in a row, with the front room facing the skylight and kitchen in the back. (Dad had gotten these rooms at the redistribution of property that occurred with the Communist revolution and had until then let his brother use them.) The kitchen had two cauldrons, one to cook rice and dishes for us, the other slop for the pig I raised. The latrine and the pigsty were in a separate, low building across from the kitchen. Both human waste and waste from the pig were valuable fertilizer for our vegetable plots located on a ridge facing the village. Below the plots was a clear stream where we cleaned vegetables and women washed clothes. Drinking water came from a well not far from the village. There was a verdant bamboo forest behind the village, a scene missing from the blessed American landscape.

Our diet continued to be almost fat-free, consisting of rice and fresh and preserved vegetables. However, what I remember best about the diet is not the longing for meat but the delectable *guoba* soaked in *mitang*. Guoba (rice crust) from the kind of cauldron used in the countryside was crispy and plentiful, while mitang (the extra water poured from the cooking rice) was available every time fresh rice was made. We would pour some mitang over pieces of guoba in a bowl, let the guoba soak just enough so that it wasn't too soggy, and eat it with relish. The scent of the mitang mixed with the body of the half-soaked guoba made for a yummy appetizer where none was needed. The physical labor and simple diet assured a good appetite.

Dad taught me how to use a hoe to prepare our vegetable plots for planting. We planted such common vegetables as string beans, chilies, eggplants, cucumbers, sponge gourd, water spinach, Chinese cabbage, amaranth, and pumpkins.

A peasant family's main source of meat was the pig they slaughtered around the Lunar New Year. The pork would be salted, dried in the sun, and smoked for consumption for the rest of the year. Whereas in the old society a rich family would have enough smoked pork to last till the next New Year, for most families in the old society and for practically all the families in the new society, the preserved pork would not last nearly that long. Going into town to buy fresh pork was a rare affair, usually only when there were rare guests (*xike*). Almost every family also raised cash pigs. Poorer families would sell all the pigs they had raised for cash. In the late 1960s, pigs were bought by the government when they weighed at least one hundred and fifty jin. If the pig raiser knew how to raise them, piglets could grow as much as one jin a day.

Shortly after we moved to Dad's village, we bought a piglet. I was responsible for raising it. Mom taught in the small grade school of the brigade, the administrative unit between the production team and the commune. Since there was no fifth or sixth grade in that school, I had no school nearby to attend. Nor did I insist on continuing my schooling. I rather enjoyed farming.

Gathering pig feed was my chore. I learned from village pals what plants were edible for pigs and would go out with a basket, alone or with my pals, to gather food for my piglet. Only the tender tops of the edible plants were picked. It would take a few hours to a half day to pick a basketful of pig feed. After the feed was cut up into little bits and pieces on a side tool, it was dumped into the cauldron to be cooked. Usually, some rice bran was added to enrich the swill so that the piglet would grow more quickly. Before pouring the swill into the trough, I would feel it to make sure it was not too hot.

One evening, Mom was mending clothes while I chopped pig feed. It was late; the light was dim. Mom said, "Be careful now." I was. Until the last stroke of the knife. The left hand fed the last bits of feed under the knife but the ring finger stuck out a bit too much. I could almost sense the oncoming accident—in an instant the right hand came down with the knife and chopped off the tip of the ring finger on the left hand. I was a bit embarrassed when Mom raised her head and saw blood dripping from my finger. She quickly found some gauze and dressed my wound. I was lucky: the knife had only nicked the very tip of the finger. When the wound healed, one couldn't tell by looking at the finger that it had once been injured. But fifty some years later, the quick still hurts when pressed—a bittersweet reminder of my days as a pig raiser.

The old chore of firewood cutting became more colorful. I learned how to make ropes out of the outer layers of rice stalks; where bamboo could be found, I continued to make bamboo ties; I learned that certain shrubs were elastic enough to make ties, too; and there were several kinds of vine. I would get up at daybreak, go to a hill, cut two bundles of firewood, and return to the village for breakfast. If it was a good spot, I would go back after breakfast. In winter and early spring, it was difficult to find bushes to cut. To cut the thorny bushes left behind by earlier cutters, we would wear a thick glove on the left hand to handle the bush. Two or three of us would roam a hill looking for thorny groves. Once a bush was spotted, one of us would yell out, "That one's mine." We never quarreled over the "ownership" of a thorny bush.

Once, the peasants in my village wanted to avenge themselves on another village for some wrong that village had done us. They decided to cut firewood on their back hill, which, as a rule, was off limits to firewood cutters. They planned to set out round midnight, steal onto the back hill, and cut firewood to hurt the rival village. I was exhilarated at this clandestine operation. But when the time came to leave, they didn't include me in their ranks for my age. The next day I heard the operation was successful.

About four to five li from my village lay Mount Gan, the largest mountain in the area. In the early 1950s, tigers still roamed the mountain and the surrounding area. Dad told me that one day when he was coming home from Yueyang, he saw a tiger crossing a hillside above a pond. He quickly hid himself in the bushes, afraid to make any noise. The tiger sauntered by without noticing him. I also heard a well-known story about an old man living in a hut all by himself. One summer evening, he was cooling himself off on a bamboo bed outside his hut. Suddenly, he sensed a tiger approaching him. Knowing that a tiger normally would not eat a dead body, the old man lay motionless, playing dead. The tiger came up, flipped him over a few times, smelled him, and decided he was too dead for dinner. The old man held his breath till he heard the tiger walk away.

Because there was a ban on woodcutting and bush cutting on Mount Gan, the bushes there were luxuriant. But the mountain was several li long so the chances of being caught by the mountain watcher were slim. I would go to the foot of the mountain, climb a short distance, and start cutting. I justified my act to myself by thinking that cutting bushes would do no harm to the forest.

Mount Gan was after all a bit too far for us, so when we couldn't find bushes to cut, we would cut the small branches of trees. A conscientious cutter would use his judgment and not cut a tree so bare as to threaten its life, but due to the difficulty in finding firewood, some cutters would cut a tree's branches all the way to the top. Larger trees had more branches to spare and we would cut the branches the knife could handle. Once I climbed up a medium-sized tree. I had been cutting firewood for several hours, so the knife was getting dull. I cut into a branch several times but made little progress. Then swinging the knife with all my strength, I cut off the branch. Unfortunately, I had used too much force—after cutting through the branch, the knife kept going, right into my kneecap. The pant was cut through, so was the thin skin on my right kneecap. I limped home; nobody was there. I put some mud over the wound and ignored it. Luckily, the wound healed without inflammation.

I had heard that, like people, water buffalos have feelings, but I didn't witness this till one day when someone came running to the village and announced that a water buffalo had caught himself in a ditch and was now dying. I hastened to follow a few others to the site of the accident. By the time we got there, the old water buffalo had been dragged out of the ditch and was now lying by the road, panting. Uncle Chunsheng, a leader of the production team, held a long knife in his right hand. He kneeled by the water buffalo, ready to plunge the knife into the poor thing. At this moment, the water buffalo seemed to sense his imminent death: large balls of tear rolled out of his eyes. I felt like crying. In his late 30s or early 40s, Uncle Chunsheng proceeded with the act without any expression of pity.

It was during this period that a macho toughness developed in me, a toughness that smacked of a peculiar vanity and sometimes bordered on foolishness. One day, I came home from a trip barefoot. A few pals were leaving to cut firewood. I ran indoors but somehow couldn't find my shoes. Grabbing my knife and shoulder pole I went with them to a hill. I secretly gloated over my toughness in going bush cutting barefoot but actually had to tread carefully—it wouldn't be fun if a bamboo stump punctured a sole. Another manifestation of this toughness was working in the wilting summer sun without wearing a straw hat. Everybody else did, but I thought I was tougher. When Mom asked me to wear one, I would say, "Unnecessary." Peasants wore straw hats not because they were afraid of skin cancer—indeed, I had never heard of the disease till I came to the U.S.—but because the summer sun in Hunan is pitiless. Luckily, all I got was a great tan, albeit a tan that produced no vanity of an American kind.

During spring planting and the double rush, I also worked as a member of the production team, earning labor credits. The highest daily credit was ten points, earned by the stronger and more skilful men. Women earned six or seven credits. Certain tasks were always done by men, for example, plowing, and then usually by men in their thirties or older, probably because they had more physical strength as compared to women and more skill as compared to younger men. Also, an older man, often the team leader, always checked the irrigation routes of the rice paddies. However, women performed some tasks at least as well as men, for example, rice transplanting, but they still only got six or seven points. I got five points. Nobody asked me to work for the production team; it just seemed natural that I should help out.

In the spring planting season we would get up early, sometimes before 5 a.m., and pull up rice seedlings from the seeding beds. Coming to the edge of the field, I would hesitate for a second before stepping into the icy water. In a minute the mud around the feet would be warmed up a bit. Alas, we couldn't stay in the same spot for long. When the rising sun started shining on our backs, it would be time to go back to the village for breakfast. Spring is a time of rain in Hunan. Older peasants would wear a palm-bark rain cape, while the younger ones would sport a plastic poncho. Both would be wearing a large bamboo rain hat stuffed with reed leaves.

If cold early mornings were the bane in spring, the sweltering summer days were long and exhausting. We would get up before dawn, work for a few hours before breakfast, have lunch in the early afternoon, take a nap when the sun was the hottest, and work till dusk. Occasionally, a large field needed to be finished, and we would go home even later.

Manure was vital to the crops. Chemical fertilizer was scarce and too expensive, anyway. Human waste and waste from animals were the main sources of manure. Water buffalo dung was picked up. Human waste was carried all the way from the city and stored in a cesspool. The carrier would go to a latrine in the city and fill up two big pails with night soil. The pails were hung from a shoulder pole and the carrier would walk the entire distance from the city to the village. When I shuttled between Yueyang and my village, I would see a lone carrier on the road with two pails of night soil filled to the rim, his shoulder pole bouncing under the weight of the pails, making rhythmic squeaks. He would get twelve points for the trip.

One spring afternoon the animal waste pool was to be emptied and the manure carried in bamboo vessels to the fields. Several peasants jumped barefoot into the pool and loaded the manure into the vessels. Thinking I couldn't shrink from such a task, I also jumped into the pool. Before long the waste pool was empty again. If you think this is too much, I heard that the head of our brigade had used his bare hands to break up clumps of human waste floating in a pail so that crops could better absorb the manure. Even fellow peasants shook their heads at this act. But then again, in that era leaders were supposed to "be the first to suffer hardships and the last to enjoy ease and comfort," echoing Fan Zhongyan's improbable ideal.

Even during the busy season it wasn't all work and no play, at least not for us kids. One of my happy memories is of a summer night when the three neighboring villages had a big eat-out in the village next to ours. It was a cloudless evening with stars twinkling high above in the blue sky. All of us, adults and children alike, gathered in front of the village overlooking a row of rice paddies. Hot steam curled upward from the rice porridge. Tables and chairs had been laid out. Adults talked and laughed loudly while children darted about, chasing one another. I had one big bowl of the hot porridge. Then another. Dishes and other goodies were also served. By the time we streamed back to our own village, it was already late at night.

Another happy memory related to eating is when lotus roots were harvested. After adults had gone through the field, we kids would walk around in the mushy earth looking for missed lotus roots. Once a section was dug up, we would clean it in the muddy water and enjoy it to the last bite, with big smiles on our faces.

Even work could be fun. Once, my uncle needed to replace the old tiles on the roof of his pigsty. Neighbors came to help. The new tiles were thrown from the ground up to the roof seven to ten in a deck. It was such fun. I was impressed by the fact that the deck didn't come apart when thrown upward. Working with peasants was also pleasant. Male peasants, young and middle-aged alike, loved to tell lewd jokes and tease female peasants. The woman would curse the man teasing her but the teasing would continue, with both of them and the others laughing all the while. Sometimes the teasing would even get physical. Rarely would a woman get mad at the teaser. And it wasn't unusual that a man would be teased or taunted by a woman, such as for being henpecked or slow in a task. As a result, the long day felt shorter and the drudgery became more bearable.

Sometime in the summer of 1969, Mom asked me, "Xiuwu, do you want to go back to school?" I answered, "As you like." Maybe my grandparents thought I shouldn't have stopped schooling at such a young age; maybe Mom thought I was having too hard a life and took pity on me. To me, going back to school or not was no big deal. I was content with life, with very few complaints, no desires, and no worldly ambition. Partly because I didn't share the burden of raising a family, I was carefree. But since I had said, "As you like," I did what the adults wished—I went back to school, in the city. My life was to change, although it would be some time before I discovered the world of books.

3. Budding Learner, Avocational Food Shopper

When I moved to the city in August 1969, my grandparents still lived in the compound of the Taos. Having not only visited them often in the years I'd lived in the country but also spent summer and winter breaks with them, I adapted to city life swimmingly.

During the Cultural Revolution, the beginning of the school year was changed from fall to spring. My cohort had either repeated a term to jibe with the new school year or in some cases, stopped schooling for a while. By the fall of '69, I had been a peasant for a year and forgotten much of what I had learned in fifth grade. I now faced the choice of either repeating the second term of fifth grade or going directly to the second term of sixth grade. My grandparents asked me about my intentions. I said of course I would go to sixth grade. My school was called "Red from Generation to Generation."

Each class had a teacher, usually one teaching Chinese or math, in charge of the class. Teacher Wang, our teacher-in-charge (*banzhuren*), was a soft-spoken young woman. At that time, students were encouraged to "do good deeds," i.e., do some volunteer work for one's collectivity or in society like the model soldier Lei Feng. Typically, students swept the classroom or the schoolyard on their own initiative. We also helped the cart-haulers get their heavy loads up the hill near the school. These were mostly women in their thirties and forties who pulled a cartload of coal through the streets, with the load weighing as much as half a ton. They inched along the road, their bodies bent forward, straw-sandaled feet almost digging into the ground, and dark-colored shirts wet through with sweat. Dongting Avenue was a long slope that reached its top near our school before going downhill. We students would on our way to school sometimes push the carts from behind to ease the load for the women cart-pullers and get a "thank you" or a smile in recognition of our help.

One day, seeing our class in need of a new eraser, I asked Grandma for the money to buy one. Teacher Wang praised me for it and went so far as to note it in my graduation evaluation.

In the beginning I had trouble with classes. On the first math test given a few weeks into the term I got thirteen points out of a hundred. But by the end of the term, I was doing well in all of my classes.

At home a tragedy struck. Like my two younger brothers, my little sister was in the care of an elderly nanny. She had a high fever that didn't get proper treatment. Then one day I came home from school at noon. Upon turning at the entrance of the compound I saw some boards in front of the entrance to the hall. I had an immediate premonition that something had happened to my three-month-old sister. My premonition was soon confirmed. The boards were for a coffin for her. She had died of dehydration. The boards were nailed into a box into which the flaccid little body was placed. We buried her on a hill outside the city.

Like many others of their generation, my parents always put their "revolutionary work" first, often at the expense of their personal well-being and that of their loved ones. In this connection, my parents would lament the mishap that my second younger brother had had: his hearing was damaged as a result of an overdose of an antibiotic in treating a high fever. Again, at the time my parents were busy with their work in the countryside. Huibin never learned to speak properly. Despite numerous efforts on the part of my parents to treat his condition, he remains hard of hearing. A smart young man, he is kindhearted and good with his hands. Above all, he is a happy person despite his bad luck. He does industrial painting for a living.

Now that my parents had lost their only daughter, they tried again. A year later, I had a sister, Xiaoling. I remember vividly the special way she came into this world. One day in July 1970, Mom came to visit us in the city with a big belly. We were eating lunch in the hall. Suddenly, her water broke. Mom was taken to the back room and an old woman in the neighborhood who knew how to handle births was immediately sent for. I waited in the yard while the adults busied themselves with the birthing. Though Mom lost a lot of blood, both she and the baby were OK.

Nineteen sixty-nine was the twentieth anniversary of the founding of the People's Republic of China, which called for elaborate National Day celebrations. We lined up into two long columns in the school auditorium, where we practiced *yangge*, a popular folk dance for a festivity. Being short for my age, I stood at the front of my column, while a girl headed the other column. I must have smiled to that girl more than I should have, because after the celebrations were over, some fellow students teased me about my carrying on with that girl. I wish. But no, I was a late bloomer in romance. In fact, I didn't have a girlfriend till I was twenty-three years old.

Otherwise, the last term of my grade school went by uneventfully. There were neither graduation examinations nor qualifying exams for middle school. I was to enter Yueyang No. 1 Middle School, the best middle school in the county, with a good reputation going back to pre-Liberation days.

Yueyang No. 1 Middle was located a few hundred meters beyond the Park of Yueyang Tower, about a twenty-minute walk from where I lived. Registration took place in a long meeting room behind the office building. The teacher-in-charge, Teacher Ren, sat at a desk in the front of the room with one or two student helpers. I got a registration form, which asked for some basic information about the student. One of the items was "family origin."

After the Communist victory in '49, everyone went through a process by which one's class status was determined according to a set of criteria set by the government. In fact, one had two classifications, "family origin" (*jiating chushen*) and "one's own status" (*geren chengfen*). The former was based on one's father's economic standing or occupation, while the latter was one's own occupation. In the countryside, the main categories included "landlord" (one who had owned much more land than needed to feed one's family), "rich peasant" (one who had owned less land than did a landlord but still more than one had needed), "middle peasant," "lower-middle peasant," and "poor peasant." In the city, the main categories were "capitalist," "small businessman," "clerk," and "worker," the last referring to factory workers. Then there were "revolutionary cadre," "revolutionary soldier," "reactionary officer," etc. The poorer one's background, the better one's family origin. But I didn't know the intricacy of the class classification system at the time, so there I was, at a loss for a category to put down under "family origin." I thought for a moment and remembered that I had heard that Grandpa's family origin was "landlord," so I put down "landlord."

When I got home, I told my grandparents what I had done. Grandpa scolded me gently for my obtuseness and told me to go back to the school to change my family origin to "poor peasant," my dad's family origin. Actually, the correct category should have been my grandpa's or my dad's own status, the former being "revolutionary soldier" (which came as a result of his revolt against the Nationalists and joining the People's Liberation Army) and the latter, "teacher." At any rate, I went back to the school immediately and saw Teacher Ren going through the forms with a few students standing around him. I walked over and watched as he looked through the registration forms. Seconds later they were looking at my form and one of the students said, "Who's this? 'Landlord.'" I took the form from the done pile and went over to another desk. They simply went on. I crossed out "landlord" and wrote down "poor peasant" above the space. I then casually inserted my form into the done pile and left. Mission accomplished. From then on, I used "poor peasant" as my family origin.

Although I had corrected my blunder at registration, forms at school usually asked for information about all of one's family members and close relatives. Thus, Grandpa's reactionary history couldn't escape the attention of the school, especially of those having direct authority over me, such as the teacher-in-charge and student organizations. One's performance on tests and exams determined one's academic record, but one's family background figured importantly in one's political status such as whether one would be chosen as a class cadre (i.e., a student leader in charge of an area of activity in a class of some fifty students) and especially, be considered good enough to be admitted to the Communist Youth League, a youth organization for politically active and well-behaved students. On my school forms Grandpa's background didn't look so good. To counterbalance this negativity, Grandpa told me to put my aunt down under "Relatives," because she had lost her life working as an underground Communist. In the first year of middle school, it was still too soon for students to establish a record of their political and academic performance in the new school; by the second year, because class membership remained the same, students would have formed their views of their classmates. Whereas my academic performance was above average, our new teacher-in-charge, Teacher Luo, placed a greater emphasis on a student's family origin than on academic performance. I was chosen the class leader in charge of physical labor by popular vote, but the Communist Youth League was closed to me. Meanwhile, my popularity hit an all-time high when my class voted to give me the only ticket allotted to the class for a song-and-dance show in the theater near the train station.

By 1970 when I entered Yueyang No. 1 Middle, the Cultural Revolution's worst violence and assault on human dignity had ended; only an occasional political spasm seized the students. One day, older students organized a meeting to denounce (surely for the nth time since '66) the dethroned principal, Wu Xiaoxia, for following a revisionist black line in education before the Cultural Revolution. Walking by the long meeting room, I heard loud noises and turned to see the place filled with students. I went over to one of its windows to find out what was going on inside. The principal stood in the front, head slightly lowered and his bespectacled face blank, as student leaders took turns verbally abusing him. After a student was done speaking, he would lead the crowd in shouting some slogans; fortunately, the fists were only thrust into the air, not upon him.

If politics in the form of denunciation meetings was coming to an end, the principle of "putting politics in command" continued to be implemented in all areas of school life. All the textbooks opened with quotations from Chairman Mao. Lesson One in our English textbook was "Long Live Chairman Mao!" with the following three lessons being "Long Live the Chinese Communist Party!" "Long Live the People's Republic of China!" and "Long Live the People's Liberation Army!" Every classroom had a Mao portrait flanked by his admonition, "Study well and make progress every day." Revolutionary slogans decorated the walls. Every class had a "blackboard newspaper" carrying politically correct student writings and the school's Communist Youth League also had a big blackboard newspaper made up of several blackboards. At the end of a school year, each class wrote a report on its activities, many of which were of course political, as did each student. In my second year I wrote a report well over ten pages long, including a description of how recalling a quotation from Chairman Mao helped me overcome my fatigue in completing a task of physical labor, the recalling being an automatic embellishment expressing proper thinking and behavior. I suspect that even for adults such ritualistic incantation, even if done to provide an expedient cover, if repeated often enough and long enough, would impair their ability to see, feel, and express themselves authentically. For us impressionable early teenagers, that ability was never nurtured in the first place. Instead, for annual reports and classes in Chinese and in politics, we all learned to write those new revolutionary eight-part essays (*baguwen*). (An eight-part essay is a literary composition prescribed for the imperial civil service examinations in the Ming and Qing dynasties, known for its rigidity of form and poverty of thought.) Some Western leftist academics insist that everything is political in an attempt to debunk what they see as sham neutrality in academic discourse. To see a political dimension in things is one thing, whereas to politicize everything is another. To parrot Jack Nicholson's character in *A Few Good Men*, "You want politicization? You can't handle politicization!"

I'm not particularly embarrassed by what I wrote in those reports and essays for Chinese classes: I was too young to know better. I am, however, a bit ashamed at something else I did, or rather, failed to do. It happened in the second year of middle school. For the Chinese class we were asked to write an essay or a poem in praise of Chairman Mao and the Party. I told Grandpa about the assignment, which intrigued him because he was itching to write some poetry. Before long he had composed a pyramid with each succeeding line having one more character. He said not to tell anybody that he had written the poem. When the Chinese teacher returned the assignments, I was so dense as to be puzzled by the lack of markings in my exercise book. Teacher Zhou didn't change a word of the pyramid, nor did he give me a grade. He must have suspected that I had committed plagiarism, and yet he didn't talk to me about it.

The late '60s and early '70s was a time of educational experimentation, or "revolution in education," an important part of the Cultural Revolution. The practices of the seventeen years between '49 and '66 were severely attacked for their overemphasis on rote memory, book learning, and an overall emphasis on academics. Teachers were criticized for giving too many tests, especially pop quizzes, which were dubbed "surprise attacks." (In Chinese schools, the scope of an exam was not specified, anything within the textbook was fair game.) One result of the revolution in education was that in '71 we got to take home our tests: we got our test papers, worked on them at home, and then brought them back to the teacher for a grade. Another consequence was that middle school was shortened from six years to four. (Grade school was also shortened from six to five, so that fifth-graders went to middle school with us sixth-graders in early '70.) This was done because Chairman Mao had instructed, "Schooling must be shortened and education revolutionized." The old curriculum was simplified with some basic theory cut out and applied subjects added. In math, for example, the section on complex numbers was cut; examples were taken from problems encountered in industry and agriculture. Likewise, in physics and chemistry, applied subjects were taught together with and right after the basic principles. We learned how motors worked, how chemical fertilizers were manufactured, and how steel was made. One class taught foundations of agriculture in which we learned how to plant different crops and how to treat their common diseases. I liked both pure theory and its applications. Some of the ideas of the revolution in education make good sense. For example, in math the time spent solving hundreds of abstruse problems in preparation for the cutthroat exams might be better devoted to studying actual problems in science, or even in industry and agriculture.

In '71 Lin Biao, Mao's designated successor, died a scandalous death. The way we learned about Lin's fall left a vivid memory. Before his death we would begin the first class of the day with two chants: "We wish Chairman Mao a long, long life!" and "We wish Deputy Commander Lin eternal good health!" (The latter because Lin was in rather poor health, even though we common people didn't know about it at the time.) Then one morning we were told not to perform the daily ritual. There was a momentary unease in the classroom. I only had a faint suspicion that something was up but no clue as to what it might be. We didn't find out till a while later when we were made to sit through the longest meetings, at which lengthy documents of the Central Committee of the Party on the Lin Biao affair were read to us. The documents detailed the conspiracies of Lin's son's group, their attempted coup, and Lin's fatal crash in Mongolia. The event might have shaken many an adult's belief in the system, but we were still too young for it to have any serious impact on us. (A mystery surrounds the crash to this day.)

For me the best change from junior middle to senior middle (the second two years) was the teacher-in-charge. Zhang Anmin, a fresh college graduate who had majored in mathematics, became and remained our teacher-in-charge. Idealistic and energetic, Teacher Zhang came at the right time, because after Lin Biao died, the political climate cooled off somewhat and Deng Xiaoping was rehabilitated and made vice-premier. A student's family background didn't matter as much (not at all to Teacher Zhang); now what mattered more was a student's academic performance. As a result, I was admitted to the Communist Youth League and became the class leader in charge of academics (*xuexi weiyuan*) with the concurrent post of representative for English classes.

We had memorable teachers. Teacher Zhang taught math. To challenge us, he sometimes gave us extra problems to solve. Teacher Fang, our physics teacher, had a gifted hand. Her drawings on the board were true to life and she drew a better circle without a compass than any other teacher did. I also heard she knew how to use an English typewriter, a rare skill. Teacher Shen, a tall Shanghai native, succeeded Teacher Fang as our physics teacher. His accent was exotic. I remember a public lecture on astronomy given by him, in the same long meeting room where I had first registered at Yueyang No. 1 Middle and where I had witnessed the denunciation of the old principal. I had read in the popular science book series A Hundred Thousand Whys about stars, planets, the first cosmic velocity, the second cosmic velocity, etc., so I eagerly attended the lecture. I arrived early and sat in the front row of the right column of pews. The meeting room was soon packed, with students standing outside poking their noses through the front window. Teacher Shen's animated lecture was illustrated with chalk drawings on the board. As this was the first scholarly lecture after years of numbing political meetings, sweetened by a fascinating topic, Teacher Shen had a captivated audience.

Teacher Tang, one of the older teachers we had, taught chemistry. He was actually an acquaintance of Grandpa's and like Grandpa, wrote a good hand. I tried to copy some of his strokes and the ways he structured several Chinese characters. He would arrive a few minutes early and start writing things on the board right away. At the top of the board, he always wrote the same quotation from Chairman Mao on reviewing in a later study session what one has learned in a previous one. Below the quotation he summarized what he had covered in the last class before going on to new material. Another chemistry teacher, Teacher Lai, recited the periodic table of elements in a singsong tone, which left so deep an impression on me and a classmate (Chen Ruijun) that even today we can shoot out the table (the *s*-block and the *p*-block) without thinking. The last chemistry teacher, Teacher Lei, also had an accent that was sometimes mimicked outside class. I still remember how to say "chemical equilibrium" exactly as he did.

In our sophomore year our English teacher was Teacher Li. Though I wasn't aware of it at the time, she was the prettiest teacher I had ever seen. Once I saw on her desk a simplified version of an American novel. She quickly put it away, saying, "This is not a book for you students." When we had our English evening party in senior middle, she coached me in a few things.

Teacher Ding, our English teacher for the junior year, had been educated in an American missionary school before '49 and sported an American accent. Because our English textbook was full of political expressions, he would add some everyday vocabulary from time to time. He also took money out of his own pocket to buy sheets of paper for extra tests. He would begin a class by passing out strips of the paper he had bought and cut, and dictate ten to twenty words he had recently taught us. He was full of animation when he talked, of course in Chinese or we wouldn't have been able to understand him. Once he said, "Now some of us don't even know the word for *pingpongqiu pai* [i.e., bat or paddle]. Quickly close the door. Don't let others hear that we don't know the word. We'd lose face." Seeing that I was studying extra material, he brought the English version of

Chairman Mao's famous essay, "To Serve the People," and asked me to read it out loud after him. The English was beyond me but I received his attention with awe and excitement.

Sometime in our third year the old principal, now Teacher Wu, was considered safe enough to enter the classroom, and he was our substitute English teacher for a while. I did not know until then that Teacher Wu knew English; his specialty was education.

The last English teacher we had was Teacher Peng, whose English was considered the best at our school. If not for the Anti-Rightist Campaign of '57, Teacher Peng would have had a distinguished career, both politically and professionally. But he persisted in his studies and research. He put together a collection of essays and poems about Yueyang Tower and translated them into English, taught himself German, and even planned to translate Sima Qian's magnum opus into English. He also knew a lot about photography: he developed and printed photographs in his living room-cum-bedroom turned into darkroom. As student representative for English, I had more interactions with Teacher Peng than any other teacher except our teacher-in-charge, Teacher Zhang. In the two years after middle school, I was to have much more opportunities to work with and to borrow books, journals, and newspapers from him.

Teachers of politics? I don't remember any except my first teacher-in-charge, Teacher Ren.

As for teachers of Chinese, I have already mentioned Teacher Zhou. Once he told us that he had seen a sign on a garbage box that read, "Don't dump outside the box your garbage." He said the sign should have read, "Don't dump your garbage outside the box." The Chinese original of the sign with the inappropriate word order sounded awkward, and the change involved switching the two characters at the end of the sign. (At home, Grandpa told me the anecdote about a Tang poet who couldn't decide between *tui* [push] and *qiao* [knock] in composing a poem about a monk.) I began to develop a more acute sense of language, if only coincidentally. Then we had Teacher Liu, who had an expressive voice and wrote a good hand, too. Once I began an essay with a description of the street scene on Dongting Avenue. Her brief comment made me realize that I'd been carried away with the description, whose tone didn't fit the rest of the essay.

Our Chinese teacher for the senior year was Teacher Yuan. Teacher Yuan had once been editor in chief of a daily of another city. I heard that he had been demoted because he had refused to listen to the Party's advice against his decision to marry his future wife, who had a bad family background. His handwriting was strange: it looked like the unsteady scribbling of a child. But then we heard that it was a rare style of handwriting called baby style!

I opened one of my essays with what I thought was a clever scene that led into the real topic. He simply crossed out the whole beginning paragraph, noting it is better to come straight to the topic. There is a metaphor for this rule of composition: the door opens on a view of the mountain (*kaimen-jianshan*).

It's said that one's foundation for learning is laid in middle school. My own experience seems to bear this out. I was fortunate to have had some good teachers. I was equally lucky that a craving for book learning developed spontaneously in me, which coincided with a renewed emphasis on academics during my senior middle years. With the exception of English, I gave all the subjects equal attention. My scores in math, physics, and chemistry were always in the high 90s; sometimes they were perfect. In English the only time I didn't get a perfect score I got ninety-nine. I had added a definite article in front of "National Day" and lost one point. One day I was helping Teacher Zhang fill out grade reports when another teacher in the big office announced that one of his students had earned the highest total score in the school. She had gotten perfect scores in math, physics, and chemistry; and ninety-eights in politics, Chinese, and English; with an average of ninety-nine. "Wait a minute," Teacher Zhang said, "Our class has a Liu Xiuwu. His total score beats hers by one point."

Because I was in charge of my class's academics and my handwriting was good, Teacher Zhang asked me to help him fill out grade reports. (Privacy wasn't an issue; besides, unlike in this book, I wasn't a loudmouth.) On one occasion he brought me with him when he visited the homes of some students.

Several of my classmates were also good at one or more subjects. Though a poor test taker, Chen Huali went beyond our math textbooks, as did Liu Shuiping. Wen Youfang's essays were very good; more than once she wrote the annual report when the task was entrusted with us class leaders. Yan Xieliang was good at the sciences and alone wrote prose poems. Chen Ruijun was as good at any of the subjects as anybody else except English, and he had the amazing ability—which I lacked—to write an essay directly in the exercise book without doing a draft.

Inexplicably I began to go beyond our English textbooks. I found a textbook from the early '60s and started memorizing such everyday words as "apple" and "pear." I bought an English grammar book, the one by Bo Bin and Zhao Dexin, and read the whole book closely. It has served me well through all these years. Once a classmate asked me a grammar question. I happened to remember where exactly in the book the answer could be found and showed off. Since most of my classmates were not interested in English or found it difficult, I was asked to teach a tutoring session early in the morning before the regular classes began. One morning I was surprised to see our physics teacher, Teacher

Shen, sitting in the front row. For a while the school also put out an English magazine for which I cut the stencils. At the school's only English evening party, slides of the life of the model soldier Lei Feng were shown with the English captions read by us students. Teacher Peng did the translation.

In senior middle years, my after-school study group included Li Xinsheng, Fan Jinjun, and Zhou Jixin, and we studied at Xinsheng's place, whose family had moved into the compound of the Taos. Sometimes other classmates living nearby joined us. One day the four of us were sitting around a table, about to start studying. I had a newspaper in my hands. One of the news stories said that American bombers again bombed Vietnamese villages. I was suddenly seized by an overwhelming sadness, imagining myself living in one of those villages and running in panic from the explosions. Years later, I would read David Halberstam's *The Best and the Brightest* and writings on and by Henry Kissinger with professional calm, but from time to time I continued experiencing moments of sadness at the human misery I happened to read about or witness. As I grew older, increased exposure to human suffering increased my indifference. Meanwhile, I also grew more fragile and became easily outraged by acts of cruelty or even manifestations of folly.

Before I began reading philosophy in '74, I'd rarely been in a contemplative mood. I only remember having two philosophical, or quasi-philosophical, thoughts. The first occurred when I was in grade school. One day, sitting in the front room of our place in the compound of the Taos, I saw tiny particles of dust dancing in the beam of sunlight shining through the window onto the wooden floor. I thought, "I wouldn't be able to see the dust without the sunbeam, but that doesn't mean the dust isn't in the air." From that day on, sometimes I thought of holding, or did hold, my breath in a dusty room even when I couldn't see any dust in the air, imagining what I would see if a sunbeam shone through at that moment. I had the second thought during my middle school years. This had to do with the Chinese folk belief that somewhere there is a record of everybody's fate in this life: what's going to happen to you is predetermined by your fate and recorded in detail in that exhaustive compendium of human lives. "If that's the case," I thought, "how detailed is the record? For example, at this particular moment I'm standing here, and these other people are all going about their own activities, and the tree leaves are nodding in all directions: How can this record contain all these happenings? Even one person's record would load up an entire cart. And how many people are there in the world? Who can write that much?"

If I lay dormant philosophically, physically I grew increasingly active. Table tennis gave way to track and field and gymnastics. I wasn't a good sprinter, my endurance was only above average, and yet I liked running. For a while two of my classmates, Li Xinsheng and Chen Ruijun, and I got up early and ran around the school's sports field. I would first go to Yueyang Restaurant, where I got two "thousand-layer pancakes," or to the Muslim restaurant on Dongting Avenue to eat two sesame-seed cakes for breakfast. Once we ran all the way to the school's farm fifteen li east of the city, for which the principal praised us. I liked parallel bars and horizontal bars. At first, I couldn't get my body over the horizontal bar, but then on one try I learned to tuck in my stomach and I was euphoric. I immediately repeated the same move several times. I could also go up the climbing pole twice in a row solely on the strength of my arms. Once, I wrapped my legs around the pole on my way up and felt a sudden wave of pleasure in my groins. I didn't know what sensation it exactly was but was neither scared nor self-indulgent. When it happened again, I enjoyed the sensation. I didn't seek it.

There was hardly any interest in the opposite sex among us. In part this was because sex was a taboo subject. Students who were known to have a special friend of the opposite sex had a bad reputation, especially if a girl had a boyfriend. There was no sex education, so the little we knew about the opposite sex came from "naughtier" students. In my second year, while walking home from school one day, I heard one classmate say to another, "Did you know that girls bleed once a month?" I didn't have a clue what he was driving at. In the same year, we helped with the double rush in the country as urban students did in those days. One day, three of us went into a latrine to relieve ourselves. Pointing at the bloody sanitary napkin in the urine pail, a naughty student said it was so-and-so's and then laughed obscenely.

In '72 and '73, the revolution in education only slowed down; it didn't stop. We continued to "learn industrial skills and farming." An example of the former was a week spent in a pharmaceutical factory, where a technician gave us a talk on a popular method of optimization invented by the renowned mathematician Hua Luogeng. Several classmates and I helped out in the laboratory, washing test tubes and watching lab technicians do tests. One example of learning farming was spending a couple of weeks on the school's farm. We slept in bunk beds, all the boys in a big room. While my classmates worked in the fields, I was asked to lead a small group of boys in cutting firewood.

In the four years of middle school, except for one summer when I was asked to stay at school to perform another task, I participated in every spring planting and summer double rush. We would carry a small bundle—a quilt and a few changes of clothing—on our backs and walk to and from the production brigade that had been chosen for us. Now I cringe at the thought of going to the double rush again, but back then I took it all in stride. I remember once I was leaving for a double rush and Grandma said, "Be careful now!" Already outside the door, I answered with a mischievous smile on my face, "Going out alive, coming home dead!" When I got back, Grandma scolded me for saying such inauspicious words. She had worried about me while I was away, being a bit superstitious and all. But naughty or not, I got my treat I had been getting every time I returned from a double rush – a bowl of iced mung bean porridge at the cold drinks shop on South Main Street, which cost twelve cents. Swallowing the icy porridge at that time even beats the sensation of drinking well water brought to the middle of the field. Even my favorite American ice cream nowadays doesn't measure up. Not because the icy mung bean porridge beats well water and my favorite American ice cream, period, but because the state of mind is different for the former and the background of deprivation is different for the latter.

I grew up in an era of rations. As far back as I can remember, many basic food items and necessities were rationed: rice, cooking oil, flour, cotton cloth, sugar, tofu, and pork, though not all of these all the time. In the '70s, such durable goods as bicycles and sewing machines also required coupons.

My grandparents had adopted me in part so that I could help with the chores, and I was a good boy. Even before I moved back to the city, during summer and winter breaks spent with my grandparents, I'd begun my avocation as a food shopper. After I moved to the city to live with them in the fall of '69, food shopping became a daily routine. For rice there were long lines only during the week or two before the Lunar New Year. The same for rice poppers. Pop rice was eaten as a snack but for my family it was a must for the meatballs we made for the Spring Festival feast. Somehow corn was scarce and I would salivate at the popcorn when an occasional portion of corn burst out of the popper with a bang.

Fish was not rationed. Right before the Spring Festival, lines for fish were usually long. Getting wind of a shipment, I would hurry to the store to line up. Otherwise, Grandma told me to try my luck at one then another store just in case.

The most memorable lines were for tofu and pork. A section of the state-owned vegetable store on Fish Lane sold tofu. Throughout the year two kinds of tofu were available: tender or soft tofu and "aromatic dry tofu" (*xiangganzi*), a harder and smaller cake with a brownish-red skin. Occasionally, especially before the Spring Festival, "old tofu," a firmer and bigger cake than the soft kind, was sold. When we needed to buy tofu, Grandma would wake me up at or before dawn, sometimes as early as 5 a.m. (Years later, Xinsheng's mom, our neighbor, would tease me about hearing my grandma's call, "Xiuwu, get up to buy tofu!") I would rub my sleepy eyes while dragging my feet to the tofu line. Because the wait was long, someone came up with the ingenious idea of placing his or her basket at the tofu window the previous night. Others, having had their baskets stolen or thrown out of the line, placed a rock there to stand in for them, which was rarely honored by those standing there in person. Sometimes, a leader arose spontaneously from the ranks, usually a man from the middle of the line, and passed out slips of paper with numbers on them. Yet with or without numbers, some jostling couldn't be avoided when the tofu window opened at 6:30 or 7. Occasionally, a fight broke out between an unruly youth trying to jump the line and someone in the line. On cold winter mornings, children standing in line would jump up and down, breathe into their palms and then rub them against each other. Some would even light up a fire with the scraps of paper and twigs lying about. Standing in the snail line, I commiserated with the man selling tofu: there being no heating, his hands were red and swollen from handling the cold and wet tofu.

The meat lines were similar but somehow more orderly. Ribs, being not rationed, cheaper, and a delicacy, were a hot item. But there were only about one dozen sides of pork for sale any given morning, and one was never sure if there was a separate line for ribs or not, which were removed on the spot, not beforehand. When the store opened, though, ribs would have already been removed from several sides of pork, as the butchers started working very early. It helped if you knew the butcher, who could save some for you, which reminds me of a funny story about my mom buying ribs. It was the early '80s when things were still not as plentiful as they are now. One day Mom wanted to buy some ribs, but the line looked hopelessly long. On her previous visits to the shop, she had heard others call the old butcher Grandpa Wang, so she eased up to the counter and called him as if they had known each other for years. Miraculously the trick worked. Grandpa Wang mistook Mom for one of his acquaintances and gave Mom some ribs, to the mild protest of those standing in line.

Sometime in the early '70s, meat shops began selling pork that had been frozen in storage. At first, there was still some fresh pork, then only frozen pork. As a result, Grandma cooked her meatball soup only when I could find fresh pork; she said frozen pork wasn't fresh enough for the dish. At that time, a few private sellers sold fresh pork but its quality was usually under suspicion. The pork could have been from a pig that had died of a disease. It was also thought that one could get sick from eating a sow's meat. Knowing this, a seller could claim that the pork wasn't from a sow when it actually was, although an experienced shopper could tell the difference by the color and texture of the meat.

Because cooking oil was rationed, shoppers often begged butchers to give them as much fat as possible in order to extract oil out of it. Better yet, one could try to get lard, which, though not rationed, was even scarcer. Again, it helped if you knew the butcher. Nowadays, few customers want fat.

Xinsheng's mom was a noodle cook at the restaurant at the west end of our street, and Grandma often asked me to buy cooked meat at her place. This meat came from the bones that had been cooked over and over in a wok whose soup was used for noodles. At sixty cents a jin it was more affordable than raw meat. This meat went well with chilies and green onions.

I started helping Grandma cook when I entered middle school. To be more exact, I helped her prepare the vegetables, pork, and spices; she did all the cooking herself. Grandma was an excellent cook with half a century's experience. She summed up her craft with three simple words: *gun* (hot—a dish should be eaten hot), *dan* (bland—don't use too much salt), and *lan* (well done). Actually, she would utter these words when cooking a meat dish, especially a soup dish. To elaborate, a dish will lose much of its taste when cold or lukewarm (hence the saying, "Eat it when it's still hot"), a dish cannot be delicious if it's too salty, and the full flavor of a dish won't come out if undercooked though I suspect an undercooked dish just has a *different* flavor but was considered uncivilized. As with other simple answers to complex questions, Grandma's rules are not without exceptions. Vegetables, especially leafy ones, shouldn't be "well done," the way Americans cook their green beans—they are no longer green—and spinach. (How come vegetables are either uncooked or overcooked?) Fish should be saltier than meat dishes. Besides, all preserved dishes—though usually not cooked—are salty so that they'll last longer and they can certainly be tasty. Maybe the second rule, "bland," should be interpreted as "rather err on the side of blandness than saltiness."

Over the years, first from Grandma, then from Mom when I paid an occasional visit to my parents, but also elsewhere, I've heard numerous tidbits of wisdom about cooking. Too bad I didn't write them down as I did when Grandma uttered sayings about how to be a person. I do remember two maxims: a dish will be tasty if a lot of oil is used (its origin may be related to its scarcity in the past) and any vegetable dish will be tasty if pork is added to it (also related to the added oil but pork has its flavor, too). These pieces of advice and my grandma's rules may be difficult to apply elsewhere, for example, in the United States, my new homeland. First, vegetables are often eaten raw ("barbarian," as I used to call the practice). Second, roasted or baked meat is not eaten very hot, and besides "well done" a steak is also done "medium" or "rare." Third, health-conscious folks are leery of meat including pork, not to mention vegetarians or Muslims, who proscribe the eating of pork.

Of the above three obstacles to a delicious dish, a solution exists only for the third, and it is a qualified one at that: use plenty of vegetable oil. But then again, things change including diets. My grandma always used lard or fat when cooking a leafy vegetable or a soup, saying, "It won't do without it." Having stopped using fat myself in '95, now I find a vegetable cooked without fat is fine, too.

In writing the above, I don't mean to be a dietary imperialist. Not that I don't want to, but that it would be futile. Would that people in industrialized societies spent as much time cooking as the Chinese do. There would be less time left for the rat race and an improved quality of life for everybody. Failing that, I merely hope to promote a better understanding of Chinese food (or at least Hunan cuisine), if for no other reason, then because, as Fang Lizhi once said, food is the only aspect of culture in which China is outstanding in the world. (If he was not being hyperbolic, I am, as I think Chinese culture has three other outstanding contributions: classical poetry, idioms or sayings and Daoist philosophy.) Another reason for dwelling on Chinese food is I've found the food in Chinese restaurants in the United States uniformly bad. They are bad not only because they fail to satisfy the guidelines I've outlined above, but also because they use a brown sauce that eclipses the original flavor of a dish. And I can't praise the taste of the sauce, either. I consider this section one of the more important parts of this book, because most Americans and other Westerners haven't had the opportunity to taste Chinese food in a private Chinese home. Indeed, having spent seven months researching food and leisure activities in Yueyang in '97, I can say with only a slight overgeneralization that the food at large restaurants is not as good as that at smaller ones, while the latter is not as good as that at roadside one-room restaurants. And home-cooked food beats them all. If you haven't eaten at a Chinese home (with a good cook of course), you haven't had really good Chinese food.

The biggest meal of the year is the family banquet on the day before the Lunar New Year. Family members living far and near try to get together for the occasion. In Yueyang, some families eat it early in the morning, but most eat it at midday or in the evening on New Year's Eve. Preparations for the meal usually begin a week or two earlier and the food prepared for the meal should last several days. My grandparents' native villages were in Xitang, sixty li from the city, so the dishes of our big meal were prepared according to the ways they were done in that part of the countryside, even though they had spent much of their lives in various parts of China. Our family always ate the big meal at midday. Firecrackers were lit before the meal and doors were bolted so that the meal wouldn't be interrupted.

The most labor-intensive dish for the big meal was meatballs. Beginning in senior middle, I was responsible for that dish. Glutinous rice was first soaked for easy cooking and placed in a bamboo sieve. Minced pork (chopped on a cutting board, the most tedious part of the preparation), firm tofu, eggs, lots of pop rice, minced chestnut if available, minced ginger and garlic, salt and soy sauce were all kneaded to a paste in a large earthen bowl. The paste was made into balls, which then were rolled around in the glutinous rice so that they were covered with it. The finished meatballs were laid out on a tabletop or cutting board. To cook them, a steamer was needed. Because the dish was so time-consuming, we would prepare it the day before the banquet. Everybody in the family liked the dish. When my next brother, Huiwen, was small, he would sit in front of the dish. Occasionally the dishes were rearranged, and then he would switch his seat to the new location of the dish. We would tease him about it when he was a big boy.

A second major dish of the meal was chicken, which was rarely affordable during the year. The chicken was always made into a soup with dried dates; dried squid was added if available. Children were pampered and given a leg or some other big piece. Grandma would get the liver as it was thought to be a blood tonic. I would get the heart as we pretended it would make me smarter. I was no longer a dim wit, but one could hardly be too smart.

A third popular dish was steamed smoked pork. The best cut for smoked pork is streaky pork. When boiled in a soup, fat is too greasy, but smoked, it's sweet and less greasy. My grandparents thought lean pork by itself was "dead meat" or "dumb meat." Nowadays, when served smoked pork, I'll ignore any health hazard and charge ahead courageously.

A fourth dish was pork braised in soy sauce. Again, streaky pork was preferred. Lots of garlic, ginger, soy sauce, pieces of cinnamon, and fried tofu were cooked with pork in a crock over a slow fire. (For Westerners who want to try making this dish, you'll have to make do with metal cookware.) Frequent mixing is required to prevent the contents from sticking to the bottom and being burned.

A fifth dish was a fish: a common carp or grass carp or silver carp or crucian carp. Not that a carp was mandatory; a carp was what was normally available during those years. The fish was fried in shallow oil over a slow fire. Ginger, garlic, and soy sauce were required spices. Fish was an indispensable dish, because the character "fish" (*yu*) rhymes with the characters for "surplus" (*youyu*). The fish was served whole, but the head and tail were often left uneaten (though not in my family) so that the coming year would be one with surplus.

A sixth dish, not as essential as the first five, was "a thousand skins," also called "a hundred leaves," which was a tofu product made of thin layers. This dish was stir-fried with green onions.

A seventh dish, while available, was pigs' feet. This dish could be cooked as a soup or braised in soy sauce. It's a delicacy in part because of the skin, tendons and ligaments. The fat under the skin is not greasy, either.

Also indispensable was a vegetable dish, preferably a leafy one, stir-fried. It was thought a light dish must accompany so many meat dishes.

Lastly, for my family a dish whose importance ranked with meatballs and chicken was what in local dialect was called *hongguocai*, again popular in Xitang. This dish was Grandpa's favorite. He would insist that we cook a huge amount; as a result, it would go sour by the seventh day of the New Year. Four main ingredients went into this dish: clumps of pork, Chinese cabbage, hard tofu, and vermicelli made from bean starch.

The New Year's family banquet was an event children looked forward to and adults spent a lot of time and money on. Even poorer families would spend their meager savings or borrow money in order to have a bountiful banquet. It was not just a feast for the pallet; it was also a time of family reunion and celebration.

The Spring Festival was also a time of revelry for seven to eight of my classmates and me. For a couple of years, we gathered at Liu Shuiping's home for dinner on New Year's Eve. His mom was a most hospitable host. She would cook a whole table of dishes, at least ten, and we would eat and drink till our stomachs were about to burst. Before and after the meal, peanuts, various kinds of candy, cookies, and other goodies were served together with sweet tea or sesame-soybean-ginger-salt tea or both. Card games preceded and followed the meal and lasted throughout the night. At one time, Shuiping's stepfather told us Charlie Chan stories, which he had read a long time before and which kept us awake for hours. To welcome the New Year, staying up till midnight was enough, but we stayed up all night. Around two or three in the morning, we roamed the streets, screaming and yelling at intersections. Returning to Shuiping's place we continued drinking, eating, talking, and playing cards. Toward four or five, a few would be unable to keep their eyes open and crash on one of the beds.

On New Year's Day, Grandma prohibited the following activities: sweeping the floor, dumping the garbage, needlework, and using the scissors—all for good luck in the new year, symbolizing either the wish to prevent the loss of money or property, or the desire not to have to work too hard in the coming year. People were expected to pay a New Year's visit to their friends and relatives. My classmates and I would form a group and go from one classmate's home to the next, eating when it was time to eat, otherwise drinking tea, eating desserts, talking, and playing card games. We were all boys, but occasionally a few girls joined us. This carnival went on for days.

Shortly after I went to live with my grandparents, Mom moved to the small school not far from Dad's native village. I visited her on weekends sometimes, and when I did, I cut firewood or dug up brush roots as firewood for her. I would take the early evening train to the Lakeside stop, the first stop of the slow train to Changsha. It was about four li from the train stop to her school. By the time I went past the headquarters of the horticultural farm and reached the pear groves, it would be dark. A deep, wide ditch ran alongside the road (which had been a trench dug by Wu Sangui's army during his Three Feudatories rebellion against the Qing in the 1670s), whose cavernous depths evoked fears of ghosts and robbers. I would quicken my steps but didn't dare to make any loud noises. Thereafter the road threaded through an expanse of rice paddies. Lights from a village close to the school flickered in the distance, the hazy hills lying serenely against the night sky. To dispel my fears, I would sing at the top of my voice arias from the revolutionary Beijing Opera, *The Red Lantern*, which I had picked up from hearing it countless times over the loudspeaker. Not that I really believed in ghosts. But on a few summer nights when I lived in Dad's village, we children had gathered beside the skylight in the big hall, listening to eerie stories, stories about ghosts.

In '71, my grandparents were forced to sell our residence in the compound of the Taos for eight hundred yuan to the government, the official line being that private housing was being phased out. We moved to a smaller place across the street, where we got two rooms one on each side of the hallway. The rooms were so small that sliding doors were used. Soon we moved to an apartment next door. Here we also had two rooms, bigger ones. Grandma's bedroom still served as living room, while Grandpa's was also our kitchen and dining room. Another tiny room was a few steps down, but as Grandma grew older, she found it difficult to climb up and down to use it as kitchen. I continued to share a bed with Grandpa. I would remember with fondness and pleasure the days of the compound of the Taos, when in summer I relished the cool breeze generated by Grandpa's moving fan as he chased mosquitoes out of the mosquito net. In our new place, since Grandpa and I slept head to feet, I would straighten out his pajama pants and could almost feel the pleasurable sensation myself. Before going to sleep, he would talk about the heroes in the epic, *Romance of the Three Kingdoms*. I asked him who was the better fighter, Lord Guan or Zhao Zilong, and so on. I asked him about his military career, including whether he had fought on the battlefield but not if he had killed any enemy soldiers. Out of an adolescent sense of grandeur, I also asked him whether he had ever seen Chiang Kai-shek. Many times, I imagined the day when he would be gone and I would feel sorry because I hadn't asked him more about his life and the past. In '73 and '74, I copied his autobiography for him and learned much more about his life. However, I failed to do anything about the prescient regret.

Back in chapter 1 did you wonder why my parents had "given away" their firstborn to my grandparents? It turned out that my mom had been married to someone else when she gave birth to me, and she and my birth father had had a son and a daughter before they had me. My paternal grandfather and my maternal grandpa had been fellow students, which led to their arranging the marriage between my future birth father and mother. When my mom had me, she was teaching in the countryside in Yicheng of Hubei

Province. She nearly bled to death due to the difficult labor; for some reason, my father wasn't at her side. My mom's parents told me that her parents-in-law had been mean to her, and it seemed that my father also had not been an attentive husband. Shortly after I was born, the Anti-Rightist Campaign sent my father to prison. As a result, my mother divorced my father and moved to Hunan Province, though still teaching in the countryside, where she met my stepfather, who became my dad.

My mother never talked to me about any of this. My guess is it would have been painful for her to do so; maybe she thought it was a taboo to talk about it. My grandparents did so, however, in part because my sister had written them trying to find her mother. My sister even sent several pairs of hand-made cloth shoes, which sadly were returned to her because my mom didn't want to have anything to do with her former family. I remember holding the closely stitched soles in my hands, thinking how much feeling had gone into making the shoes and how sad my sister would be in receiving the returned shoes. But my timidity and confusion prevented me from asking my grandparents to keep the shoes, not that they would have listened to me. Still, my sister was persistent. In '72 or '73 she came to visit us in Yueyang. She only saw my grandparents and me. We took a walk through the city, and on the way back I was moved to buy her a roasted sweet potato with the little money in my pocket. On the same day I went to see her off at the train station. When the train was about to leave, I grabbed her hand and squeezed it with sadness while telling her to take care of herself. My grandparents told me to write a letter to that family, disowning any connections with them, but I don't remember whether it was before or after my sister's visit. I never heard from her again.

The knowledge about my real background didn't affect my feelings toward my current family. It did make me wonder what kind of person my birth father was and what his life had been like. I don't remember what my sister and I talked about on our walk some fifty years ago, but I know we didn't talk about our father, nor did I try to find out his side of the family's story. All I know is that his name was Ding Zhenghuan and his father's name was Ding Guanying, who according to my maternal grandpa had once been commander of the Wuhan garrison force (see app. 5). I wish I hadn't been so timid.

4. An Unwasted Youth

In January 1974 I graduated from Yueyang No. 1 Middle. Colleges were only admitting worker-peasant-soldier students with at least two years of work experience, while middle school graduates were being sent down to the countryside to be reeducated by peasants. They were thought to be too bourgeois with their book learning and lack of respect for the hard-working peasants. Not every middle school graduate had to go, though. For example, if one was stricken with some serious disease, one could stay. Also, single children didn't have to go in case their parents might need them. Families with more than one child could keep one in the city. After all, China is noted for its tradition of filial piety, that is, children are supposed to take care of their parents. Because I was the only child living with my aging grandparents, I got to stay in Yueyang. What was I to do with my life? I had not fancied any specific occupation, nor did I have any ambitions. In those days, you waited for a unit—mostly a factory—to come to your neighborhood to recruit workers and hoped your neighborhood committee would recommend you. The head of this committee was usually a young woman Party member sent by higher authorities, while its members were made up of politically reliable residents with good family origins.

I didn't look for work; work found me. One March afternoon, a mild-mannered young man came to see me. He was a math teacher at the school run by the Boat Transport Cooperative for the children of its employees. One of their English teachers was sick, and having heard my English was good, they would like me to be the substitute teacher of a sophomore class for a couple of months. I was delighted by this offer of my first job. The pay was thirty-six yuan, which I gave to Grandma as a filial child was supposed to. The school gave me a desk in an office shared with some ten colleagues. By this time, academics were again de-emphasized at schools and the idea of the uselessness of study was popular among students. Still, many of my students were intrigued by the presence of such a young teacher—I had not yet turned seventeen when I started teaching there and was just beginning to have my growth spurt. The classes proceeded without incident. In part this was because at my first appearance in front of the class, I took out an English translation of the Little Red Book and read a few quotations from it very quickly, then repeated the sayings in Chinese. As a result, the class seemed to have held me in an appropriate awe. My English teacher, Teacher Peng, who had done the same when he first came to teach us, had inspired me. Except that he had no need to impress us—his reputation had preceded him. Maybe he was merely trying to show he was both "red" and "expert."

One of the office mates, a young woman, was less lucky. She had a student who liked to pick fights with his classmates and was strong for his age. Once she had a hard time trying to break up a brawl by holding the raging young man from hurting his opponent.

I also stood in once for a colleague teaching a fifth-grade science class. As I was able to cover the material in less time than was allotted and couldn't dismiss the class early, I spent the remaining ten to fifteen minutes telling them a detective story having nothing to do with science. At that time, schools had factory workers as members of the school leadership because the Party line was "The working class must be the leader in every walk of life." Right in the middle of the story, the worker representative walked in and sat down in the back. I calmly continued my story. In due time the bell rang, and my inspector walked out with the students without questioning me.

During my stint as a substitute teacher at this school, I got another job. An acquaintance of Grandpa's, a retired professor of space physiology, came to me with a motor's manual in English. The motor had been imported from Romania and the factory owning it had asked the professor to translate the manual into Chinese. The retired professor didn't want to be trifled with the task and thought I might benefit from the exercise. There was no pay but I gladly accepted the task. The manual was printed on inferior paper, but the text was even worse. Two days later the job was done. I had found in the brochure over forty errors. I told Teacher Peng about it, who encouraged me to write a letter to the relevant authorities protesting against such an "insult." I felt a sense of self-importance but didn't know where I'd send the letter.

In May some factory asked Teacher Peng to translate two manuals for the Japanese truck it had imported, a user's manual and a maintenance manual. Teacher Peng did the translation but needed someone to copy in longhand the Chinese version. He thought of the jobless me. Again, I welcomed the opportunity. I also helped Teacher Peng print photographic illustrations for the copies. I got paid fifty yuan.

Soon fall came. My middle school, Yueyang No. 1 Middle, had a sick English teacher. Teacher Deng, the scribe in the dean's office, came to see me about substituting at my alma mater. I was thrilled by the offer, even though the pay was six yuan less than my pay at the boat cooperative's school. By this time, the idea of the uselessness of study was becoming rampant and discipline became a problem. Sometimes, when the teacher was writing something on the board with her back turned toward the class, one or two students would jump out of the window and run off to play, like a scene from a Hollywood comedy about high school life in the United States. I had no trick of controlling the few unruly students, so I resigned myself to teaching those who had the patience to sit there listening to and practicing with me.

The sick teacher recovered in a couple of months. Instead of discontinuing my employment, the school authorities assigned me to the general affairs office, where I worked under the director, Teacher Ren, who had been my freshman teacher-in-charge over four years before. My main responsibility was cutting stencils for the school's newsletter.

One day, a class of students was digging up and carrying dirt in the botanical garden, where an old house had stood. Suddenly, a student hit upon and broke an earthen jar, which contained a pile of old silver dollars. The teacher in charge quickly collected the treasure trove and brought it to the office. It was a bit short of one hundred coins. Some old rich family must have hidden the money underground at the time of Liberation or even during an earlier crisis. As was typically done about this sort of thing, the coins were submitted to higher authorities, and we heard nothing more of the find. I worked in the office till the end of the term.

The revolution in education became more radical. One important change was schools now began editing their own textbooks instead of having province-wide standard textbooks. Even the recent texts were thought to have too much basic theory in them, so that the science curriculum was being made thoroughly applied. In the spring of '75, Teacher Deng, the scribe who had asked me to substitute the previous fall, employed me as a scribe of the school's new physics textbook. This was to be cut on stencils, done with a stencil pen on mimeograph paper treated with wax against a stencil steel board. The paper had tiny squares fit for Chinese characters and some force was needed to cut through the wax. Some of the illustrations were hard to cut. One of these was the inside of a motor including its coil. I first traced the outline by placing the stencil over the original (taken from a published book) and then cut the figure on the stencil steel board. I cut long hours, fighting my strained eyes and pained fingers, but could only produce three stencils a day. Teacher Deng offered me forty cents a stencil. Altogether I cut sixty some stencils. Grandpa Fang then ran the cut stencils on a mimeograph machine. He told me that a stencil could make at best six hundred copies. He had worked at the school all his life, ringing the bell and running the mimeograph machine. I liked his earthiness and he was fond of me, too.

The summer vacation found the county's textbook compiling group busy at work at Yueyang No. 1 Middle. The group was made up of the county's best teachers. A large classroom served as the office, where desks were arranged in clusters for the mini-groups working on various texts. My job was to trace the illustrations for a math textbook. When they were done, a teacher and I took them to the Prefecture Printing House to have them made into molds. No more mimeographing: we needed to print enough copies for all the middle schools in the county. My stint with the group ended with a trip to the printing house of Xiangyin County, one of the six counties then belonging to Yueyang Prefecture.

Grandpa had a friend, Elder Uncle Yin, who was an official in the local branch of the county's tax bureau. In August '75, Uncle Yin got me a job as an assistant in the branch, where I worked for four months. Our group leader was Uncle Sun.

Our job was to collect business tax from fruit vendors, repairmen and repairwomen, and so on. The tax rate was 10 percent. Where the volume of business was unavailable, a flat rate was collected. We roamed the streets looking for mobile small business people from whom to collect tax. Here and there we stopped to chat with fruit vendors, who displayed their goods on a cart and who would offer us an apple, a pear or whatever, which we would politely turn down. When we stopped by a shoe repairperson's stand, she or he would offer to mend our shoes for free. Most of the time we would decline the offer.

Fruit vendors submitted their monthly receipts from a state-owned wholesaler to our branch, on which their business tax was calculated. One day Uncle Sun or some other veteran tax collector suspected that the vendors had not been honest about their volume of business, which was not based on actual sales but on purchases from the wholesaler. Uncle Sun took me to the wholesaler, where we spent two days checking its ledger against the receipts fruit vendors had submitted in previous months. The suspicion was borne out: A majority of the vendors had underreported their intake, ranging from 20 to 30 percent of the total. The delinquent vendors were called into the branch for a study session and criticism. The tax on the underreported portion was paid in arrears plus a fine. I went through the whole thing matter-of-factly, feeling neither exhilaration at having found out the vendors nor sympathy for them.

I did feel sympathy for a fisherman's family in another case. On an early winter morning, Uncle Sun and I boarded a motorboat not far from the branch office, going on a mission to catch a tax-dodging fisherman, which meant an exciting cruise on the vast Lake Dongting. The boat wound its way out of the harbor at the estuary, then headed west toward Junshan Island, a grayish hill in the middle of the lake famous for its tea and mottled bamboo with its ancient legends. In a few moments the boat picked up speed. I sat at the prow, ignoring the early wintry breeze, looking left then right, front then back, afraid I might miss a scenic view. A while later the boat turned slightly southward, clearing Junshan Island by some distance. In another ten minutes or so the Island was already far behind us, receding into a dot on the horizon. Before long we had come to the area where we were supposed to find the fisherman. In a matter of minutes, we spotted a lone boat floating ahead. Drawing near, we saw a family with several children, the father a deeply tanned tall man in his thirties. We jumped onto his small boat and found a heap of smart-looking nylon fishing nets. The fisherman seemed to know what we were up to and didn't resist when Uncle Sun confiscated his nets. Uncle Sun told the fisherman the overdue taxes would have to be paid before the nets could be returned to him. On the way home, I was no longer in the mood to enjoy the scenery, Fan Zhongyan's imaginative essay about Lake Dongting or not. "Where would the poor fisherman get the tax money to redeem his fishing nets? Without the nets, how would he feed his family?" I posed the first question in a matter-of-fact tone to Uncle Sun, who said, "Those sneaky fishermen, they've got plenty of dough," his tone suggesting that I was still green. He said the nets must be worth hundreds of yuan. We returned to the branch, where Uncle Sun dumped the nets in a dusty corner of his office.

Sometime in December I heard Yueyang Prefecture Nitrogen Fertilizer Plant was recruiting workers in my residential district. I had waited for two years without having been recommended once for a regular job. The fertilizer plant ran around the clock, which meant unpalatable night shifts. But it was a state enterprise with job security and was only about five li from home. If I got the job, I would still be able to help my grandparents with chores. But if I missed this opportunity, there was no guarantee a better job would come along any time soon. Besides, I was an "As you like" fellow, not at all picky about things. Having decided to try to get into the plant, I paid a visit to the official in charge of the old folks who belonged to the disbanded Political Consultative Conference. He graciously agreed to talk to the officials in my district about recommending me for a slot at the plant. A few days later, I filled out an application form and had my physical. Shortly after that I was hired with fifty-nine young men and women by the fertilizer plant. I had heard if one reported to work before the New Year, one's beginning year of service would be the old year, not the new. Everybody knew that rule, too. On December 30, 1975, I became a worker at the fertilizer plant, a card-carrying member of the working class, the leading class in socialist China.

Nineteen seventy-four and 1975 were years of physical and metaphysical growth for me. When I came out of middle school in January '74, I was less than 1.6 meters. By the time of my physical for the fertilizer plant at the end of '75, I had reached my current height, 1.76 meters or 5'9". By spring '74, I was seventeen years old. I didn't have a girlfriend. In fact, the concept was reserved for a girl with whom a boy was seriously "talking love." The two entered such a relationship with the intention to marry, even though not every relationship would end in marriage. There was of course no sexually explicit material for a seventeen-year-old boy to satisfy his curiosity about the opposite sex, which was burgeoning in me. It was difficult even to find a book on human physiology. But we teenage boys were not only curious about girls, but also attracted to descriptions of love between a boy and a girl or a man and a woman. For example, a chapter in the popular novel *Tracks in the Snowy Forest* described a young nurse who was attracted to the commanding officer but who wasn't sure if the feelings were mutual. It was an innocent scene of the kind typical of a revolutionary novel of that era; still, I would hear friends speak of the chapter title with a knowing smile.

By '74 I was savoring such passages myself. An extremely popular Soviet novel, *How the Steel Was Tempered,* had descriptions of the youthful friendship and puppy love between the male protagonist from a poor family and a girl from a well-to-do one. I read the relevant pages again and again. When I temped at Yueyang No. 1 Middle in '74, I borrowed a physiology book, not a technical one, but one about the life cycle, that had been published before the Cultural Revolution. The book described not only the differences between a man and a woman, but also the process of sexual intercourse. When I worked in the school's general affairs office, I had the opportunity to read part of a mildly pornographic novel. At that time there circulated among students handwritten copies of this novel about a young girl's sexual awakening, called *A Young Maiden's Heart,* which included a peek at a bathing scene and more. This book became a notorious item, and whoever was caught reading it was criticized and the copy confiscated. One day the director of the office gave me a notebook to store in my drawer; it contained part of *A Young Maiden's Heart.* I couldn't resist reading the notebook immediately, but to my disappointment it contained only the beginning of the novel; the copy stopped at the beginning of the bathing scene. Maybe the student copying it was caught red-handed. Another day, I was sitting at my desk, not doing anything in particular. Suddenly I felt an urge to make an obscene phone call. I picked up the phone and the operator answered. Right after I asked her the first question, she cursed me and said to her coworker, "He called me names." Having not anticipated such a response, I became flustered. I blurted out two more short questions and hung up. In 1990 when I was living in St. Paul, Minnesota, I received a woman's dirty phone call, which I had no desire to indulge. The call came sixteen years too late.

Sometime in '74 I stopped sharing a bed with Grandpa. I set up a bed in the attic above Grandma's room, which was hot as a steamer in the summer, but I was young and not pampered as I am now. More than once I dreamed that I was in the Ladies Room, and to my surprise and disappointment the women all had penises. More than once I had nocturnal emissions. Even the sight of a woman's hairy armpit could evoke a longing in me. On many a summer evening, I roamed the streets hoping to steal glimpses of exposed parts of the female body. I peeked through holes—made by more desperate voyeurs—in the partitions dividing the male section and the female section of latrines. In spite of all that sexual tension building up inside me, the idea of getting a girlfriend never occurred to me. I was too young to "talk love." Neither did I talk about love or sex with my friends. I don't know about others but I didn't learn to masturbate, either. (The Chinese expression is telling—*shouyin* or the hand is being lascivious—but at least there was no fear of going blind.)

During the two years after middle school, I did a lot of secretarial work for Grandpa, mainly copying and legwork. I had begun copying things for Grandpa in senior middle. In the early to mid-1970s, those who had lived in the old society were asked to write confessions about their backgrounds and doings before and after, but especially before, 1949. They were expected to report every little wrong thing they had done, such as a minor embezzlement, an affair, and so on. Grandpa, having been a reactionary officer in the KMT Army, had by this time already written such confessions more than once. Not only did Grandpa have to write a confession, so did Grandma for being guilty by association. Grandpa wrote Grandma's confession for her because she could read a little but couldn't write. Grandma's best friend, the one I called Grandma Estuary Street, had been married four times; two of her husbands had died early. She could neither read nor write, so Grandpa wrote down her life story for her, adding the obligatory confessional expressions. Grandpa was also asked to write a testimonial for an old acquaintance from time to time. Yet another case was my aunt's: there were letters, reports, etc. Grandpa wanted a copy for his own file every time he submitted a document to a government office, so he asked me to copy all these documents for him.

Another friend of Grandma's, a woman in her fifties, once came to me for help. In those days there were frequent political study sessions at which a Party document, a *People's Daily* editorial, or an essay by the Chairman would be read and discussed. Sometimes, people were required to write down what they had learned from the session. As this woman couldn't write, she asked me to write down whatever I could whip up. Knowing that she had been a child bride and suffered before '49, I wrote about her gratitude to the Party and Chairman Mao for founding a new society and rescuing her from her miserable life. I read to her what I had written and she liked it. But of course, after four years of practice in middle school, I had become a veteran writer of the new revolutionary eight-part essay (*baguwen*). (Over two decades later, in writing the *bagu* "Annual Report of Professional Activities" as a faculty member at an American university, I was so brief that the dean asked me to add details every year. The dean did it for my sake, to be sure, but prone to cross-cultural comparison, I can't help but wonder that back then in Mao's China we were required to sing paeans of the Party; now as an academic in the free U.S., I am expected to blow my own horn: Is this really an improvement? André Comte-Sponville shares my sentiment: "Why bother to stop believing in God if it is only to be so utterly self-deceived?")

The campaign to criticize Lin Biao and Confucius occurred in this period. Later, I would read that the movement was a veiled attempt by the Gang of Four to dethrone Premier Zhou Enlai, seen as a major obstacle on their way to the summit of power. But at the time to me it was just another political and ideological struggle or, as it was called back then, a line struggle. The People's Political Consultative Conference had been closed since the beginning of the Cultural Revolution, but by this time the county's Propaganda Department had appointed an official, a man in his thirties, to call together a group of old and would-be members for study sessions. Because there was no office space for the group and Grandpa had been the younger of the two resident officials of the old organization, the sessions were held in my home. A wall in Grandma's bedroom, now serving as the meeting room, was used for a wall newspaper, consisting of essays and poems written by members of the group. They met once a week. When there was a change in the schedule, Grandpa sent me on a tour of the homes of the members to notify them of the change. Occasionally I sat with them, listening to their discussions.

This group was a curiosity. The oldest member of the group, Grandpa Liao Xin (Shen in Mandarin), by then in his eighties, had been resident vice-chairman of the county's People's Political Consultative Conference. He had been the head of the county's Education Bureau before '49 and loved classical poetry. Due to his advanced age, he couldn't make the meeting every time, and when he came, he came with the help of a cane. Indeed, most group members walked with a cane. For a while, the youngest member happened to be Grandpa Liao Xin's oldest son, the retired professor of space physiology who had asked me to translate the motor's manual. He was sixty-three.

Another member of the study group was Grandpa Yuan Zhen. He was also a retired professor, one of physical education. An outstanding sprinter and swimmer in his youth, he had studied in Germany before '49.

Grandpa Kan Zhong, yet another member of the group, was a well-known retired doctor of Chinese medicine.

Grandpa Wang Qiu was an old teacher of Chinese who knew his classics. The campaign to criticize Lin Biao and Confucius required rereading of old texts and reinterpretation of ancient philosophical debates in terms of "the struggle between the Confucians and the Legalists," the former being seen as reactionary and the latter, progressive. At first, the group lacked primary texts, the old canon having long been out of print. Grandpa Wang Qiu went home and wrote down from memory the entire text of the Chinese primer, *The Three-Character Classic*, its original version dating from the Southern Song dynasty (1127–1279). His large, archaic-looking handwriting was an oddity even among his peers' (see app. 6).

The Three-Character Classic is a text on how to raise children and how to conduct oneself in life, drawing on exemplars from past centuries. Also canvassed in this concise verse is China's history, from antiquity to the Republican revolution of 1911, according to the latest emendation. Somebody else found a copy of *The Four-Character Classic for Females*, which gave women such antiquated instructions as "Do not show your teeth when smiling, do not raise your voice when speaking."

Lastly, there were Elder Uncle Xu, a store clerk, and Elder Uncle Deng, a pharmacist, both of whom joined the group later. Although members of the study group had lived much of their life in the old society, after over two decades of intensive ideological indoctrination and political browbeating, the old folks had by and large learned to adopt whatever views were deemed correct by the Party line or at least use the correct language. But occasionally, it showed that the indoctrination was incomplete. One day, Grandpa told Grandma and me the following incident. During the study session that morning, Grandpa Liao Xin the octogenarian said that he knew Confucius was reactionary but there was one thing he still failed to see: How could the teaching "Do not impose on others what you yourself do not desire" be wrong? Grandpa's tone and smile seemed to suggest that he was amused by Grandpa Liao Xin's obduracy, but in retrospect, Grandpa could also be interpreted as indirectly criticizing the undiscriminating attack on the entire Confucian tradition. It's a pity that I failed to ask him about his own views and the other group members' reactions to Grandpa Liao Xin's remark.

Grandpa annotated the historical allusions found in the *Illustrated Four-Character Classic for Females* (see app. 7) and the *Illustrated Improved Classic for Girls* (see app. 8). Grandpa Wang Qiu and another group member also contributed some annotations, all of which Grandpa again asked me to copy for him. As a result, I unintentionally memorized part of the latter verse and of *The Three-Character Classic*. I kept their handwritten copies and the poems written by Grandpa Liao Xin (see app. 9) as souvenirs.

In 1974 I became an avid reader, an obsessive notetaker and book copier, and a bookstore pilgrim.

I had started committing extra English words to memory in middle school. Now I got more methodical. First, I borrowed a small dictionary of some 2,500 basic words. My grandparents were smokers and the soft paper wrappers were unfolded and then crinkled as toilet paper. I would put a bunch of new words and expressions on a cigarette wrapper and take it out of my pocket to try to memorize a few at a time. I did this while standing in line for pork, especially early in the morning when we had to wait in line for a couple of hours before the store opened its doors. I would leave my basket in the line and stand under a street lamp to glance at the words on the cigarette wrapper. As time went by, I got more obsessive: I would look at my cigarette wrapper while walking on the street and a few times I was almost struck by a vehicle. Once I bumped into a tree. (But at least I didn't curse the tree or ask why it bumped into me.) After going through the small dictionary, I borrowed a larger one containing some 5,000 words, broken down into basic words and more advanced words. I told myself to memorize twenty words a day, but after about a month, I lost steam. I continued to plough through the dictionary, however. Russian experts of English had compiled both a while back.

Back in October '72 I had bought *A Concise English-Chinese Dictionary*, coedited by Zhang Qichun and Cai Wenyin. It had 26,150 words, so after I had worked my way through the second dictionary, though by no means memorized every word in it, I started memorizing words and phrases from my own dictionary. I would look at a word and think to myself, "A college student must know this word," or "Even a college student wouldn't need to know this word," even though I didn't fantasize about going to college at all—it was out of the question. College—literally "great learning" in Chinese—only meant a great deal of knowledge to me. I continued reading the dictionary; by the time I did go to college and then graduated, every one of the 1,180 pages of that dictionary had been marked up, though again that doesn't mean I had memorized every word in it.

I had been visiting my English teacher, Teacher Peng, since my senior year. In '74 I visited him more frequently. He had many old English books and past issues of the magazine, *English Monthly*, which carried informative and lively pieces on sundry aspects of the language. I borrowed several years' worth and read them avidly.

While working at Yueyang No. 1 Middle, I was able to borrow books from its excellent library, probably the best in the county. Among the English books I borrowed were simplified versions of works of literature, again done by Soviet experts and published earlier. I remember taking notes on *The Thousand and One Nights*, its fantastic stories greatly increasing the joy of learning the language.

Then I was seized with a mania for copying books, partly because there was next to nothing in the way of English books I could find in the local bookstore. Our living room-cum-Grandma's bedroom became my scriptorium. I first copied a book on how to translate Chinese idioms into English by Zhang Peiji, then the first two volumes of a four-volume set, *Essential English*. From December 11, 1974 through January 26, 1975, I copied volume one of *A Comprehensive Guide to Good English* by George Philip Krapp, originally published in 1927 and reprinted in '62. I had no idea, however, that this dictionary was already dated. When writing this paragraph, I opened the dusty copy randomly and saw this entry: "commiserate, v. *express pity or sympathy for*, followed directly by its object, as in *The officer commiserated his prisoners ironically*, not *commiserated with*." Contemporary dictionaries say exactly the opposite.

I also took to taking notes, using two types of notebooks. The regular pocket notebook had a plastic cover with designs on it. To economize, I cut the larger exercise books in two, made holes with Grandma's awl along the bound edge, and sewed together the two halves or even four halves into a thicker notebook. By the end of '75, I had some three dozen notebooks for English, literature, etc. For scholarly books, I stapled or sewed together the notes taken on loose sheets.

My mania went beyond books. I would go to a store and jot down the English trademarks on some merchandise. The pharmacy on South Main Street had bilingual descriptions of drugs pasted on the inside of a glass counter and I would copy the English descriptions in my notebook, too. Once, a movie about Chinese acrobats had bilingual captions. I saw it several times, a notebook and pen in hand. I jotted down as many of the captions as I could manage in the dark movie theater, oblivious of what I looked like to the other moviegoers.

There was a glaring gap in my language study, however: I was only learning how to read. I didn't have a radio, let alone a record player, with the help of which I might have been able to learn to speak the language, too. My listening comprehension was so poor that when Dad got me a ticket to a short movie in English, a story about a heartless landlord, I only understood one sentence: "Get up, you lazybones!"

I wasn't only obsessed with learning English; I also became a voracious reader. First, there were those new revolutionary novels, such as *Bright Sunny Skies* and *The Golden Road* (about class struggle in the countryside), *Gao Yubao* (about a boy growing up in the old society, part of which was made into the movie, *A Cock Crows at Midnight*), *The Seething Mountains* (about class struggle in a coal mine), and *Island Women Militia* (about—you guessed it—class struggle on an island). These books were available at the local bookstore, and though all about class struggle, enthralled me. Then there were older revolutionary novels and memoirs published before the Cultural Revolution, which had to be borrowed from friends or the library of Yueyang No. 1 Middle. These included *Red Crag* (about heroic Communist underground workers), *Fighting in the Heart of the Enemy* (about the exploits of a female undercover agent) and *Following Chairman Mao on the Long March* by Mao's one-time butler, Chen Changfeng. There were also old progressive novels such as Mao Dun's *Midnight*. Some old Soviet novels were popular, the most famous being, of course, *How the Steel Was Tempered*, about a young man who worked tirelessly for the revolution. Also popular was *The Gadfly*, about the life of a cardinal's illegitimate son. Like everybody else, I enjoyed the classic Chinese novels, *Three Kingdoms*, *Journey to the West* and *Water Margin*, reading more than one edition of the first and third. The tragic love story of *Liang Shanbo and Zhu Yingtai* was deeply mournful, as was Guo Moruo's *Qu Yuan* (in English translation), though in a different way. On the other hand, the famous

The Story of the Western Chamber left hardly a trace in my memory. (I'd read some of the above in middle school but don't remember which ones.)

As the campaign to criticize Lin Biao and Confucius raged on, Legalist readings of Chinese classics and Chinese history were published. The county's Propaganda Department also printed pamphlets introducing pre-Qin masters. (Qin was founded in 221 B.C.) I read every pamphlet in Grandpa's collection and some of the books I bought on my weekly pilgrimage to the bookstore.

What the bookstore didn't lack were books by Karl Marx and Friedrich Engels. The Translation Bureau of the Central Committee of the CCP had translated from Russian the complete works of the two authors, the first three volumes of which I bought. They included such pieces as *The Holy Family*, *The Condition of the Working-Class in England*, and *The German Ideology* plus short essays. I also read Plekhanov's book on the development of the monist view of history.

I loved reading biographies and memoirs. Among those whose life I read about were Marx, Engels, Lenin, Stalin, Mao, Zhou Enlai (a hand-copied volume), Chiang Kai-shek, a Japanese prime minister, Guo Moruo, Lu Xun, and Truman. What I admired most, both the book and the character, was Jawaharlal Nehru's autobiography. I was deeply impressed by his eloquence, his dedication, and his sustained analysis of India's socioeconomic conditions, especially its rural society. I filled one notebook with excerpts from Nehru's autobiography, then a third of another notebook. (Both Confucius and Laozi distrusted eloquence, especially in a politician. In her presidential address to the Eastern Division of the American Philosophical Association in December 1998, Mary Mothersill related the following anecdote that shows even great statesmen could be obviously phony sometimes. At a banquet honoring John Dewey on his ninetieth birthday, dignitaries galore made speeches. "Nehru, looking incredibly suave and distinguished, professed to have made it his practice to read a chapter of Dewey's work every day." She added that nobody believed him, at least she didn't.)

In Franz Mehring's biography of Marx, the author devoted a lot of space to summarizing and commenting on Marx's ideas, including a long section on *Capital*. Even though I had yet to read Marx's magnum opus, I had read enough of him to appreciate Mehring's summaries and comments. Again, I filled a notebook with excerpts.

History books borrowed from friends and the library of Yueyang No. 1 Middle both satisfied and whetted my curiosity about the past. One was a history of the Tang dynasty (618–906). Before long I saw a pattern in Chinese history: A major dynasty would last a long time, then decline and be replaced by a new one through war, treachery, chaos and much suffering. The new emperor would give the people a respite to recover from the ravages of war and calamity. But soon the emperor would itch for action, usually expansion. Taxes would increase, as would corvée. The glories of an empire were built on the corpses of the common people. However, I was yet to see Lenin's New Economic Policy and China's early 1950s in a similar light.

Also memorable was an eleven- or twelve-book series on history aimed at a youthful audience. The series introduced the vast span of Chinese history by telling the stories behind selected Chinese idioms. For example, *woxi-changdan* (sleep on the brushwood sticks and taste the gall) is based on a famous story from the end of the Spring and Autumn period (722–481 B.C.). It means undergoing self-imposed hardships so as to strengthen one's resolve to avenge a national humiliation, or more generally, to achieve a difficult goal. The idioms are condensed history; embedded in them are stories with a moral.

Foreign countries equally fascinated me. Teacher Peng subscribed to the newspaper featuring only translations of selected pieces from foreign news media, *Reference News*, which I borrowed regularly. I enjoyed small books introducing such Western countries as the United States, Great Britain, and France. These had been published in the 1940s. I drank in John Gunther's lively reports on Asian countries in *Inside Asia* and perused histories of World War II. A two-volume history of the French Revolution captivated me with its colorful characters and momentous events, as did a detailed history of the Paris Commune. On contemporary foreign affairs, I ran across a book on the Fourth War in the Middle East and another on the Sino-Indian War of 1962. *Is Soviet Union a Socialist Country?*, written by four Japanese students, contained some hilarious commentary.

As for foreign literature, Christian Anderson's fairy tales were not too simple for a youth of seventeen who hadn't grown up reading books, though more fitting for my age were Shakespeare's plays and the poetry of the Persian mathematician and astronomer Omar Khayyám.

It was also during this period that I began reading philosophy and scholarly books in other areas. The more memorable included "The Philosophy of Tables," an essay on whether the idea or the object came first; Gongsun Long's "On the White Horse," arguing that a white horse is not a horse; an orthodox textbook on dialectical materialism and historical materialism; a small volume on the thought of Saint-Simon; another on the physiocrats; a thicker one on d'Holbach, Helvétius, and other eighteenth-century French philosophes (from the observation that a person feels good about himself when he does a good deed I saw egoism in good deeds, but is that dopamine or serotonin?); a collection of Newton's writings on the philosophy of nature; Kant's *Universal Natural History and Theory of the Heavens*; Darwin's *The Origin of Species* and Huxley's defense of the theory of evolution; and Marx's doctoral dissertation comparing the natural philosophy of Democritus and Epicurus (all in Chinese translation).

In middle school I was equally interested in math and the natural sciences, social studies, and the humanities. But during the following two years when a pure fascination with the pursuit of knowledge developed in me, I spent almost all of my spare time reading in the latter two areas. My reading in the sciences was limited to natural philosophy and to the volumes in the popular-science book series, A Hundred Thousand Whys. I read randomly, whatever books I could find at the time, with no intention to master any body of knowledge.

I bought a few books in senior middle, but it wasn't until '74 that I began making a weekly visit to the local bookstore. I didn't really expect new books to arrive every week but I was like a small piece of metal attracted to a powerful magnet. The shelves being closed to customers, I would lean over the counter and look through the same titles from one end of a shelf to the other, then the next shelf, then the next. I would open a new book and bury my face in it for a few seconds just to get a whiff of fresh ink on clean paper.

While in senior middle, I saw on a shelf *Oxford Advanced Learner's Dictionary of Current English with Chinese Translation* and asked Grandpa to go to the bookstore with me to buy it. The clerk was a man in his fifties who reputedly knew some English. Grandpa asked to see the dictionary, but guessing I was the one who wanted the book, the clerk said it was for more advanced students of English, not a middle school student like me. Another time, an oral English text, *English 900*, books one through six bound in one thick volume, lay forbiddingly inside the glass counter. I looked at it with awe and didn't pluck up the courage to ask to see it.

By late '74 I was no longer the timid middle school student; I became a "social youth" with some work experience, though still a bit shy. With more spending money, I started buying more books, especially English dictionaries. I bought the bulky *A New English-Chinese Dictionary*, which contained twice as many words as did my favorite *A Concise English-Chinese Dictionary*. I also purchased *Webster's New World Dictionary of American English, Chambers Twentieth Century Dictionary*, Lin Yutang's *Chinese-English Dictionary* and English-Chinese dictionaries in math, chemical engineering, and meteorology. The last group was triggered by the experience of translating the motor's manual. Did I really need that many dictionaries? No. In fact, I hardly needed to consult any of them at all. The concise English-Chinese dictionary was sufficient most of the time. I was possessed.

For a while my morals gave way to my obsession with books. When I taught as a substitute at Yueyang No. 1 Middle, I had access to its library. Many of the books mentioned in the previous section were borrowed from that library. After I ended my stint there, the librarian was kind enough to let me continue borrowing books. But I unconscionably stole several dozen books from the library, in full knowledge of Lu Xun's satirical remark about book thieves not considering themselves to be stealing books but taking them. I was worse than Lu Xun's imaginary book thief: I needed no euphemism or rationalization.

At that time bookstores sold only orthodox books over the counter; unorthodox books such as translations of Western books on politics and society were marked "For internal distribution" and sold only to government and Party offices and libraries. I stood outside the backroom of my local bookstore many a time, salivating at the forbidden volumes. Then one day, I hit upon the idea of asking the Propaganda Department official to take me inside the backroom, because bookstores, as schools and theater troupes, fell under the jurisdiction of the department. I was thrilled when the official said he knew people at the bookstore and would take me there when he wasn't busy. After that I dreamed that I was taken into the backroom full of internal-distribution books. The day finally came. We sauntered over to the front counter, where the official spoke with a clerk. The answer was a crashing disappointment—the books were right there and I was free to look around. As if that were my first trip to the bookstore! But again, I was too shy to tell him that the backroom was where I wanted to go. Did I incorrectly assume that he knew internal-distribution books were what I wanted? Or did the official make the request but was told the rules could not be bent? The former seemed unlikely because I wouldn't have needed his help if I had only wanted to buy books over the counter. But the latter also seemed unlikely because their conversation was too brief. Whatever the case, I went home like a flattened balloon.

Yueyang was a small city compared to Changsha, the provincial capital. I had heard that He Guangyue, a local self-taught historian, had connections at Changsha's main secondhand bookstore. (Shouldn't it be secondhand-book store?) I had also learned that Elder Uncle Fan, the father of my old classmate Fan Jinjun, knew him. So I thought of asking Elder Uncle Fan to ask He Guangyue to write me a note of introduction to the secondhand-book store so that they would let me look at their stock at the back of the store. Then my friend Li Laya told me he was a friend of He Guangyue's and could procure a note from him for both of us. He did and we went to Changsha. We did get to look at the store's stock but again the trip fell far short of my expectations.

I also asked others who were traveling to other cities to buy English books for me. Once Grandpa Liao was going to Baotou, a city in the North, to see his son. Since he knew English, I asked him to check out the bookstores in that city, only to be disappointed later: Grandpa Liao didn't see anything good.

Another time I asked a neighbor's son-in-law to help me. A rare Portuguese who had grown up in China, Kaili had married the neighbor's daughter when both of them were sent-down youths at the Lakeside Horticultural Farm. He spoke perfect Chinese. I drew up a list of books for him to look for in Shanghai, China's largest metropolis. These were titles published before the Cultural Revolution and no longer in print in the 1970s, but I was so eager to get them I wanted to try my luck. Having been disappointed a few times, I sensed my list was unrealistic and too limiting. "What if Shanghai has books I don't know about?" So, I added on the back of the sheet this request: "Please buy all the English books you can find." Afraid that he might get some of the books I already had, I added "except for the following," under which I put down the titles of those on my shelf and desk. When Kaili went to a large bookstore in Shanghai, he simply followed the lists on both sides of the sheet, including the titles I wanted and those I didn't. He bought several on the list of books I already had. Back in his hotel he looked over my sheet again and realized he'd made a mistake. He took all but one small phrasebook back to the bookstore to return them. The bookstore as other stores in China had a no-return policy. Kaili insisted on returning the books, patiently explaining the situation. It was only because he had a big nose that the bookstore made an exception by letting him return the books. When he told me about his misadventure, we both laughed.

But my ardent quest for books was not all sorrow and no happiness. On more than one occasion I spotted an exciting book where I expected none. On my trip to Xiangyin to proofread the agriculture textbook with Teacher Cai, we stopped at Milo, a city that lay halfway between Yueyang and Changsha, which I couldn't pass through without checking out its bookstore. My eyes brightened up when I saw inside the counter the Chinese translation, in two volumes, of volume one of Joseph Needham's history of Chinese science and technology. When I temped at the tax bureau, Uncle Sun and I made a trip to Junshan Farm, where I couldn't even pass up the country store with its lone shelf of sparsely arranged books. Through the dim light I saw a thick volume on Marx, Engels, and other early generations of proletarian revolutionaries. After I returned to the hotel, it occurred to me that due to the poor lighting in the store I might have missed some other good book. I went back and looked through the row of books a few more times before giving up.

After middle school, besides socializing with my old classmates, I also made some new friends who liked to study and who were teaching themselves various subjects.

Li Laya had graduated from Yueyang No. 2 Middle, where his mother was an English teacher. A colleague of mine at the school of the Boat Transport Cooperative who'd been Laya's classmate in middle school introduced him to me. Two years older than me, Laya was ambitious. Whereas I was reading randomly, Laya was methodical in his studies. His main interest was political economy, but he was also studying math, English, and other subjects. Shortly after we met, Laya told me that he had just reviewed the outline of world history and drawn up time charts to help him memorize the important events. We became instant friends, visiting each other often, despite the differences in our interests and approaches. Four years later he would enter a teachers' college, majoring in mathematics, and eight years later he would pass the entrance examinations in political economy of the Institute of Economics of the Chinese Academy of Social Sciences. In his memorable words, "Everything I taught myself in those years became useful later."

Chen Huali was another friend with whom I spent a lot of time. He was an old classmate. Though a poor test taker in middle school, he had studied more math than any other classmate. Seeing that I was copying English books like a madman, he also started copying a book, of course a math book. It was one of the famous five-volume advanced mathematics textbooks written by Russian mathematicians published before the Cultural Revolution and unavailable in bookstores in the '70s. Huali had an idiosyncratic father who had a self-sewn notebook that looked like an English dictionary. Was he compiling a dictionary of some kind? But there were no English books in their home; neither did he show he knew the language on my numerous visits with them. He was a man of few words. Later Huali was hired to run water pumps in an oil refinery in Linxiang County, where I once visited him for two days.

Another friend was Fei Wenhan. A few years my senior and a worker in a small unit, he was also teaching himself English. Several years later he was able to get into Hunan Teachers' College in Changsha.

Yet another friend I made during this period was Master Shen. A man in his thirties, he held the highest grade in welding in Yueyang, the fifth. (The highest possible grade was the eighth.) He was a friend of Teacher Peng's and was also teaching himself English. We visited each other sometimes. Doctor Wu, a physician, became a friend, too. He would say to his acquaintances that my English was so good that as a senior middle graduate I taught senior middle classes. I didn't bother to correct him that I only taught junior middle classes, just as two decades later I wouldn't bother about correcting my American colleagues when they mispronounced my name.

I also got to know Professor Liu Zhongde, who had been Teacher Peng's teacher. In '75, Professor Liu brought a class of his students at Hunan Teachers' College from Changsha to Yueyang No. 1 Middle for practical training. One day Professor Liu gave a public lecture on translation, attended by all the English teachers in the city. I got wind of the lecture from Teacher Peng and as I had done at Teacher Shen's astronomy lecture a few years back, arrived early and sat in the front row. Sometime later Teacher Peng introduced me to Professor Liu, who said he remembered me from the lecture for the understanding expression on my face. Still later, Professor Liu headed a translation group at the new urea (a nitrogen fertilizer) plant being built north of Yueyang, where I visited him quite a few times.

One summer evening a middle-aged man who said his family name was Qi visited me. Mr. Qi said he had heard I was learning English and would like to hear me read a text. I read a paragraph on imperialism from one of my English books. Mr. Qi didn't say anything was wrong with my pronunciation but suggested my intonation was a bit stiff. Then he read a short paragraph and sounded better even to my untrained ear. Before he left, Mr. Qi said something about bringing me some reading materials later. After he left, I returned outside to enjoy the cool. I told our neighbor Grandma Mao about the mysterious visitor. Grandma Mao said the visitor might be an important person looking for talent and someday I might end up at the United Nations. I was flattered but thought she had blown the thing out of proportions. I was right. Mr. Qi never visited me again. Then one day I mentioned the incident to Laya. It turned out that Mr. Qi had also visited him. Laya had heard that Mr. Qi had been a translator in Beijing and been dismissed from his job for some wrongdoing. He had also visited Teacher Peng and a few other young people who were teaching themselves English. Our conclusion was that Mr. Qi was trying to make a name for himself in our small city, having been somebody before but was now nobody.

Grandma Mao, our neighbor, had three daughters the oldest of whom married a carpenter. Master Cui, an enterprising and talented craftsman, made wooden models. Once he asked me a math question I couldn't answer, so I took him to see my old math teacher, Teacher Zhang, who answered his question. Master Cui had a son who was about to enter middle school. He told me his son was smart but didn't like to study, and asked me to share my study methods with him. I said it was important to lay a good foundation for learning in middle school and the three most important subjects were Chinese, math, and English. This was because, I continued, one had to be good at math if one wanted to go into science or engineering, English would open the door to the outside world, and Chinese was the foundation for everything else. I don't know what became of Master Cui's son; Master Cui himself became director of a factory for the blind.

Since I was no longer in school, I helped with housework on a daily basis. I continued shopping for food and helping Grandma cook. Another chore was dumping and cleaning Grandma's chamber pot, the Chinese equivalent of an indoor toilet in those days. Every day I took the pot down to the cesspool in the vegetable garden behind the houses, even when I was substituting at Yueyang No. 1 Middle. Occasionally, a student of mine would see me on her way to school. I told Grandma about this and for years she teased me about students seeing their Teacher Liu emptying a chamber pot. I didn't feel the least embarrassed.

Another major chore was washing clothes and bed sheets. This was a girl's chore but I was both the boy and the girl help in the household. Hunan is a humid place. Every spring, housewives take out their moldy winter clothes to clean or just air out for a couple of days in the sun. We washed our bed sheets about once every two months. Then there was the long, hot summer, when we changed and washed our clothes daily. To make things easier, especially when washing bed sheets and heavy clothing, instead of using the washing board, I used my feet. I would soak the clothing in soapy water in the bathtub and walk all over it while holding a cigarette wrapper with English words on it and trying to memorize them. Fifteen to twenty minutes later I would announce to Grandma, "I must have covered dozens of li by now," for which she would tease me after I went to college.

A special task was cutting Grandma's toenails. Like her best friend, Grandma Estuary Street, Grandma had had her feet bound when she was young. The toenails on the bent third, fourth, and fifth toes would grow toward the sole instead of straight out. As Grandma got older, her eyesight, flexibility, and hand-eye coordination all deteriorated. Every once in a while, when her toenails bothered her, she would soak her small feet in hot water and then ask me to dig out and cut the toenails. When I gingerly trimmed Grandma's toenails, she would grin with relief.

In late spring '74 Grandpa had a stroke. Unlike Grandma, who had had three operations on her stomach, Grandpa had been blessed with good health all his life. Though Grandma liked to repeat the saying, "A healthy poor man is a very lucky man," she also used to warn Grandpa that when a healthy person got sick, it would be serious. Indeed, I had heard from quite a few old people that a healthy person tended to die quickly, whereas a weak or sickly one had more staying power. Regular checkups being nonexistent, there hadn't been any signs before the stroke. Then one day, he was lying in a hospital bed, his face flushed, his breathing heavy, and one side of his body paralyzed. Mom and Dad were still working in the country and could only take off a week to ten days. I became Grandpa's primary caretaker. In Chinese hospitals, patients' families rather than nurses take care of them; nurses are only responsible for giving shots and taking vital signs. I brought a reclining canvas chair and slept beside Grandpa's bed. During the daytime, while Grandma prepared Grandpa's burial clothes, I helped a carpenter in his sixties make Grandpa's coffin.

When the county's Propaganda Department learned of the news of Grandpa's hospitalization, its deputy director, Director Fang, came to the hospital to see Grandpa. He called a meeting of the best doctors of the hospital, telling them that Grandpa had once made a contribution to the revolution (referring to his mutiny), so they should try their utmost to save Grandpa's life, including combining the treatments of Chinese medicine and Western medicine and using the best drugs, however expensive. The hospital followed the director's instructions. When Grandpa was admitted into the hospital, we were told that his chances for survival were 2 to 3 percent. Forty some days later, Grandpa not only didn't die, he could walk quite well with a cane.

In this six-week period, except when my parents were there, I watched Grandpa closely and slept only a few hours a day. When Grandpa was sound asleep, I read a book on Chinese grammar, then one on rhetoric.

When I was having my growth spurt in '74 and '75, my personality and values were also taking shape. I became a bit less sweet, a bit more naughty. I began to think about a lot of things on my own, from contemporary politics to the rationality of Newton's invocation of a Prime Mover in explaining the source of motion in the universe to the philosophical issue of reflexivity. Integrity and consistency in my thought and action became matters for deliberation. But particularly idiosyncratic was the burgeoning of an outlook on life that may be characterized as "One could live simply" and "A simple lifestyle is better than one that is not." (I had no idea that I was echoing an ancient Greek saying, "A rich man is either a crook or a crook's heir.") A manifestation of this outlook was the shunning of durable goods my peers coveted. I still have this image in my mind, fresh as ever, of walking along Meixiqiao toward Yutoutian (two streets in Yueyang) while a thought occurred to me: "I won't get a watch, at least not until I am thirty years old." At the time, Shanghai watches, practically the only good brand available, were hard to come by and cost a hundred and twenty yuan (about a worker's three-and-a-half-months' pay). It was a peculiar vanity, as I felt I had no materialistic desires and, in that sense, I was better than my peers. Forty-seven years later I still live a plain life, the difference being that I am now more self-conscious about my "philosophy of life" and the occasional vain thoughts about it. This may be smart, but it would be better to be a certain kind of person without being too self-conscious about it. I am unable to transcend this self-consciousness.

5. Misbehaving Factory Worker

Built in 1966, Yueyang Prefecture Nitrogen Fertilizer Plant produced one fertilizer: ammonium bicarbonate (NH_4HCO_3). This was the main nitrogen fertilizer manufactured in China before thirteen urea plants were imported in the '70s. (In other words, technological modernization began *before* 1978.) Yueyang had two such plants, my plant and Yueyang County's plant.

Beginning in January '76 we new recruits had a three-month orientation. The orientation was so long because the plant was undergoing an overhaul of the equipment. It began with meetings at which we learned about the history of the plant, its technology, etc. The better part of the three-month period was spent helping revamp the plant.

Though most of the new recruits wanted to begin apprenticeship right away, I was not one of them. I thought, "We have a whole life in front of us; what's the rush to become an apprentice?" Indeed, in retrospect, the orientation was the most memorable and fun period of my stint at the plant.

We boys were put up, or rather we put ourselves up, in the plant's auditorium, whereas the girls were assigned to a dorm for women workers. In the auditorium a platform was set up all around against the walls as makeshift beds with the middle being occupied by clusters of real beds. At night some played cards; others, Chinese chess. Those not playing a game chatted, laughed, and horsed around. A few sang songs from the Cultural Revolution period and one played tunes from Tchaikovsky's *Swan Lake* on his violin. I shared a bed with a Changsha native, who had been a sent-down youth on a state farm in our prefecture. The auditorium was connected to the plant's kitchen through a hall, where workers lined up at meal times in front of the small windows in the wall dividing the hall and the kitchen. Every morning at 5:30, I would get up for the first batch of steamed buns and eat three big ones. The new life was exciting and the physical labor assured a ravenous appetite.

When we entered the plant, it was right in the middle of renovation: old equipment was being torn down and new, large machines were being installed. Five tasks were especially memorable.

Hauling a new steamer took a few days. It had been unloaded from a train a few hundred meters away from the plant. An uphill slope close to the plant followed a stretch of level road. Without a big enough moving vehicle we had to use a hoist engine to haul it on railroad tracks. The steel cable made a few turns along the road stretching between the steamer and the plant. Under the direction of older workers, a dozen of us new recruits moved and then replaced sections of railroad tracks as the steamer inched on.

Cutting winds needled our faces and penetrated the canvas gloves. While our bodies were warm from moving the railroad tracks, our toes were numb from standing around part of the time and slow movements the rest. Stamping our feet helped little, so a few of us lit up a fire with the lumber scraps lying around. The steel cable was so taut it seemed the hoist engine was exerting its utmost. When we finally reached the top of the hill, looking at the big pile of steel, I felt a sense of achievement.

A second task was transporting refractory bricks, which came in all shapes and sizes to fit the curvy reaction towers and pipes. One day, Li Enlong, a childhood pal in marble games, accidentally released some ammonia while playing with some equipment. The smell irked him so much he withdrew from the plant. As he was the only friend among the new recruits, I was sorry to see him go. The lesson was driven into us: be careful with the machines and don't play with something you don't know how to handle.

A third task was breaking up machine bases with a sledgehammer. The machines were bolted down to concrete bases for stability; now that the old machines had been removed, so also must their bases. It was awesome to see veteran workers swing sledgehammers weighing fifteen to eighteen jin. The more skilful ones could swing a sledgehammer full circle, which was a scary sight: "What if the hammer misses the spike?" After a few days, I also learned to swing the hammer that way but my movements weren't as smooth: I would halt the hammer momentarily when it came over my head so as to have a better aim. I was afraid of smashing the hand of the spike holder. As the hammer came down on the spike, pieces of the concrete base were chipped away. We needed no gym to pump iron; my muscles began to bulge after a few days of being sore.

We also moved parts of old machines from one place to another. Motors were particularly heavy. One piece of machine weighing over eight hundred jin was carried away by four strong new recruits. By now I was already strong for my tall but slim body, but most of my coworkers could carry heavier loads on their shoulders. Only once did I carry a piece of equipment weighing over six hundred jin with three other workers.

Later we shoveled sand on the waterfront. The sand had been unloaded from tugboats and piled up like hills by the lake. We used long shovels to throw the sand onto trucks, which hauled it to our plant. This task was a good muscle builder, too. I could feel my body tightening up as the shovel was dug into the sand and then thrown skyward with the sand. At the end of the day, the stomach eagerly greeted the plain dishes from the workers' canteen, and a shower cleansed the grime from the skin. A sense of relaxation and contentment would fill me. The monthly pay was eighteen yuan, enough for food and everyday expenses.

One amusing incident occurred during the orientation. Chen Yu came to work without his eyebrows one day: he had shaved them—maybe in the same adolescent exploratory spirit as that of my American students who dye their hair green or decorate their nose with rings. He looked scary without his eyebrows. This was still 1976 when bell-bottoms and long hair on boys would be frowned upon. He was criticized for the naughty stunt, but the misbehavior could not be corrected until the eyebrows grew out again.

The plant had four sections or workshops. The first workshop generated hemihydrate coal gas by mixing coal, steam, and air. The second synthesized hydrogen, oxygen, and nitrogen into ammonia after a copper solution, copper acetate ammonia liquid, had absorbed the useless and "poisonous" elements such as hydrogen sulfide, monoxide, and dioxide. The third section carbonized liquid ammonia with carbon dioxide to produce the crystalline ammonium bicarbonate. The fourth workshop was maintenance. The plant ran around the clock with the workers in the first three sections working four shifts. One worked two days of each of the three eight-hour shifts, a regular eight-to-five maintenance shift, and then had a day off.

Toward the end of the orientation, we were assigned to our posts in the four workshops. The best posts were those in the maintenance workshop. First, one worked regular day shifts. Second, most were not tied to a workstation, as were those in the other three sections involved in the production process. Of the jobs in the maintenance workshop, electrician was probably the best as one worked all over the plant and the skills would be useful elsewhere should one end up leaving the plant. A lathe or drilling machine operator was tied to the machine but the smell of carbon monoxide from the first workshop and that of ammonia from the other two were negligible. Then there were those maintenance workers assigned to the first three workshops. They went to a particular station if a problem developed in a machine there. Many of my fellow new recruits wanted to be assigned to the maintenance workshop, some of whom had their wish fulfilled. I didn't care one way or another. I had no idea how the assignments were made, nor did I even think much about the whole thing. I ended up being assigned to the copper-washing station in the second workshop. My mentor was Ouyang Zuoyu, one of the first-generation workers. He was a tall, strong man; he could carry a rock weighing over two hundred jin up a hill. He was also full of wisecracks and loved teasing his fellow workers. Like most of the workers in the plant, his wife and children (he had three or four) lived in the countryside due to the household registration system. Like a Scottish shepherd but unlike any other Chinese man I know, he knew how to knit.

When the new recruits were assigned to the workshops, we boys were also assigned to dorms. I shared a room with two skilled workers, Master Zhou of my station and Master Long of the Carbonization Workshop. The married men went home to visit their wives once in a while; their wives rarely came to see them. Whenever a fellow worker's wife came to visit, the other roommates would find another place to spend the night, which was easy because there was always a zero-o'clock shift.

My post had three pumps, a copper-washing tower, and a test station. The copper solution was pumped up to the top of the tower, while the source gas consisting of hydrogen, oxygen, and nitrogen, etc. was led into the tower at the bottom creating a countercurrent, so that the copper solution could have an optimum contact with the source gas and the best absorption of the poisonous gases. The cleansed gas was sent on to the next post to be synthesized into ammonia. The test station was run by a woman analyst, who performed a simple test to make sure the source gas had been cleansed of the "bad elements"; otherwise, these elements would poison the catalyst in the synthesis tower. Pressure, temperature, and the level of the copper solution in the copper-washing tower all needed to be watched closely and controlled within an acceptable range. A typical accident would occur if the temperature in the washing tower were not high enough causing the cleansing to be insufficient. When this happened, the source gas would have to be released through an exhaust, its high pressure creating a shrill that traveled far beyond the workshop. This accident was called "the red light is on."

During orientation we'd acquired some basic knowledge about the technology of the plant as a whole. Our initial months of apprenticeship were spent watching the skilled workers operate the machines and trying to understand the ins and outs of the particular posts to which we had been assigned. I watched my mentor and Master Zhou as they went about their business: one monitored the level of the copper solution in the washing tower, while the other adjusted the temperatures. The pumps that pumped the copper solution into the tower also needed occasional checking for pressure and leakage. I read a bit about the technology of my station and asked my mentor questions as I checked what was in the book against what I saw in operation.

After about three months I began assuming each of the two roles of copper washing under my mentor's supervision. It was easy to monitor the level of copper solution in the reaction tower. Monitoring the temperatures was trickier. If the temperatures were too high, the solution would evaporate too quickly; on the other hand, if the temperatures were not high enough, absorption of the poisonous gases would be incomplete and an accident would occur. Theoretically, there was of course an appropriate range for the temperatures, but actual operation did not always jibe with the theory. One of the sticky factors was it took some twenty minutes for the solution to go through the system. If the dipping of temperatures was spotted too late, an accident would last a while.

In my second year working at the plant, I had such an accident. It occurred between 4 and 5 a.m. when I wasn't at my most alert. I saw the temperatures go down to 45 degrees

Celsius but wasn't alarmed: they had been that low before without causing an accident. Soon it was too late: The amount—not the number—of poisonous gases in the hydrogen and nitrogen being sent to the synthesis tower exceeded the acceptable level, so we had to "turn on the red light." The ear-splitting shrill of the exhaust must have woken up workers from far and near. At least ten minutes had passed before the normal conditions were restored. For this accident I was told to write a self-criticism poster. I was embarrassed by the accident partly because the poster was pasted at the gate of the plant for everybody to see. As I passed by it, I heard one worker say, "Look, the calligraphy is pretty good. Too bad it's a self-criticism." Two days later I asked a friend of mine to tear it down in the middle of the night.

The three eight-hour shifts went from 8 to 4, 4 to midnight, and midnight to 8, respectively. The best shift was the one from 4 p.m. to midnight, because one was free until 4, or 3:30, to be exact. The worst shift was, of course, the midnight shift. We were told that we'd get used to the shift after a while. But soon we found out those who had worked there for ten years were still not used to it. Whereas many workers dozed now and then on the midnight shift, a few (including two of the founders) never did. When it was our turn to work the graveyard shift, we would go to sleep before 9 p.m. At about 11:35, Supervisor Tan Taiyu would come and knock on our doors to wake us up. We would quickly get up, brush our teeth and wash our face, and go to the open area in the front of the plant to hear a report on the last shift. At 1:30 a.m., we would be on our tiptoes for the food cart carrying our early breakfast. My favorite dish was chilies fried with fermented black beans at five cents per serving. It beats all of the dishes I've had at the Chinese restaurants in the United States. In fact, it beats most of the dishes at the restaurants I've been to in China!

The hours from 3 to 6 a.m. were hard to get through—the temptation to doze off was so strong. We could stave off our drowsiness by chatting, smoking, or finding small chores to keep ourselves busy with. It was on these midnight shifts that I learned how to enjoy a cigarette. Some workers smoked self-rolled tobacco, which was cheaper and more pungent than the cigarettes sold at stores. Having taken drags on such "horns," I found them an easy transition to regular cigarettes. I didn't smoke regularly, though. Outside of working the midnight shift, I usually smoked when I got together with friends.

Most of the time I was a good worker. Whenever we transported things—be they machine parts, coal, or dirt—I always exerted my utmost. On one maintenance shift, the dirt load I was carrying was so heavy the shoulder pole broke. This was because I thought one *should* work hard, but I worked hard also because I really enjoyed the sensation of physical exertion. I didn't work hard so that I could climb up politically such as being admitted into the Party. Still, I gained a reputation of being a naughty boy. In retrospect, my reputation was not baseless.

At work, though I rarely left my post to chat with others at another post, my occasional improper behavior must have left a bad impression. For example, the valve adjusting the level of copper solution had a small handle, which was normally turned by hand. Sometimes, propping up my feet on the valve, I would kick the handle one way or anoth-er. Not that I was the only one doing this, but it looked different if you were a new recruit. Another inappropriate thing I did was reading at work. One day, shortly after I began manning the valve, I took out a notebook to read, something I was not supposed to do. I was simply bored by the lack of activity at work. The notebook contained excerpts from Nehru's autobiography, which stood repeated reading. My mentor might have frowned upon my behavior, but he said nothing. Before the college entrance examinations in late '77, I also brought my review notes to work on several occasions. Only by then I was already notorious.

A main source of my notoriety was a visit paid by a prefectural deputy bureau chief in charge of fuel and chemical industries. The official came to inspect our plant, about which I was in the dark. Neither did I recognize him. It was only much later that my coworkers told me that I had been insolent during the official's visit. They said that when the official came, I simply sat there with my feet propped up and totally ignored him. But I didn't remember seeing any visitor, alone or flanked by the plant's officials. Older workers must have recognized the prefectural official and showed proper courtesy. If I had seen a visitor, an official or an ordinary worker, I would have stood up and offered to show the visitor around. I felt I'd been wronged but my reputation was fait accompli.

On the other hand, I was the main culprit in another incident that sealed my reputation of a bad boy. It was a snowy evening. Two of my friends and I took the back roads from the city to our plant. On the way we stopped by a cabbage plot and plucked a head of cabbage for the dumplings we were going to make the next day. Soon we reached the vegetable plots bordering our dorms. As I was carrying the cabbage, my two friends went into a plot to get some garlic. My eyes followed my pals into the plot with my back turned toward the village. Suddenly, my pals bolted and I could hear footsteps approaching. I might have gotten away if I'd started running right then; instead, a moment of gallows calm came over me: "It's no big deal; we're merely stealing some garlic," I thought. No sooner had the thought flashed through my mind than two pairs of hands grabbed my arms from behind me. My pals got away. It turned out that the village had been plagued by my fellow workers who had often stolen vegetables from its plots. Now the villagers finally caught someone. The group of thief catchers brought me to a hut and threatened to hang me up if I didn't give up the names of my pals. For a few seconds I was seized with fear, but calm followed immediately. "Big deal," I thought again. I told them the names of the two who'd got away. The villagers were talking about bringing the matter to the plant's leaders when my two pals and another good friend showed up posing as youth leaders at the plant. To their surprise, I betrayed them by pointing them out to the villagers. After a few minutes' confusion, the villagers released us. My pals teased me about my betrayal but bore no grudges.

A week or so later, a workers' meeting was held in the auditorium. Several minutes into the meeting, a deputy director of the plant shouted at the audience: "Those vegetable thieves, come out to the fore!" The three of us walked to the front and turned around to face the crowd. I turned to look at my pals: they bowed their heads in dejection. I then panned the crowd, calm as a still pond. The speaker at the podium said something about our act being unworthy of the working class, etc. Luckily, the denunciation was brief and the meeting went on to some other business.

I also remember the one time when I walked on top of the copper-washing tower like a daredevil. It was a maintenance day. Dai Dingchao, a repairman and a fellow new recruit, and I were climbing up the flight of stairs leading to the top of the reaction tower about four stories high. I walked up the stairs slowly and unsteadily. Dai Dingchao laughed at me: "You coward." Though it wasn't a malicious insult, I couldn't swallow it. We reached the top in no time. Beside the tower stood a cement frame with ledges of the width of one-and-a-half lengths of my foot. I challenged him: "Me a coward? Let's see who dare walk to the corner of the cement frame!" He looked at it and shook his head. I gingerly stepped onto a ledge and slowly walked to a corner of the frame. I looked around and felt fine: other reaction towers and the distant chimney were taller. I then looked down and felt dizzy: the people on the ground looked like midgets, while the straight vertical frame appeared crooked. The Party branch secretary of our workshop, Yang Shuyao, looked up and yelled at me, "Liu Xiuwu, get down *now*!" I looked down again, and then collected myself for the walk back. To everyone's relief, I didn't fall off the ledge. Dai Dingchao said, "You daredevil, are you crazy?" Nowadays I can only gloat over my past glory, as I not only get claustrophobic occasionally but also suffer from vertigo while riding in a cable car.

There was something else I did that must have made me look like the opposite of a docile lamb or should I say, a cog in the revolutionary machine. I continued reading all kinds of books some of which could be seen beside my pillow on my single bed. Having read more of Marx and Engels, I bought a used two-volume set of Lenin's selected works, which contained, among other pieces, *State and Revolution* and *Imperialism Is the Highest Stage of Capitalism*. When I could only keep a borrowed book for a short time, I stayed up late into the night. I finished reading the two-volume history of the French Revolution, borrowed a biography of the Soviet marshal Zhukov, enjoyed volume one of Churchill's memoirs of WWII, and perused a biography of the infamous hooligan of old Shanghai, Du Yuesheng.

I continued making friends who liked to study. Zhang Xinhua, a fellow new recruit and friend, introduced me to a friend of his, who lived near the train station. This friend had a big dictionary covering both domestic and international affairs. I borrowed the heavy book, read all the entries that looked informative to me, and took copious notes.

Of the more scholarly books I read and took notes on were Hume's *An Inquiry Concerning Human Understanding*, Dampier's *A History of Science and its Relations with Philosophy and Religion*, *A Concise History of European Philosophy* by Chinese philosophers, and volume two of the Chinese translation of Russell's *A History of Western Philosophy*. While reading chapter 3 of Hume's slim volume, I bought *The Philosophy of Western European Countries, 16th–18th Centuries*, one in a series of anthologies of Western philosophy edited by Peking University faculty members. Since the anthology included most of Hume's piece, I stopped taking notes on it; instead, I added the missing paragraphs in the margins of the anthology. With all the notes I took over the four years, when I had a comment on an excerpt, I jotted it down within parentheses with the words, *ji shi*, or my comment.

There was one difference from my previous two years' studies, however: I stopped learning English sometime in '75. There was no particular reason for this change, certainly not because I thought I had learned enough English. But then again, there was no reason for me to read at all. My work at the factory didn't require it, nor was I hoping I would get out of there by studying. Even though from time to time I had a vague sense that I wouldn't just spend the rest of my life that way, I was a happy worker and had no specific life goals.

The main source of joy in my life at the plant was my four friends: Zhang Yuejun, Huang Changchun, Yao Xiang and Tu Chunfen all of whom were from Yueyang. (Tu Chunfen was a girl; the rest were all boys.) We often got together to make *jiaozi* or dumplings. For fillings we used minced pork, cabbage, green onions, ginger, and garlic. We used half-a-jin bottles as rolling pins and always had a great time. We boys visited one another at home regularly and for a while Yuejun and I played Ping-Pong. I also visited Tu Chunfen in her home at the hospital several times. Once I invited her to a movie. I joked once or twice about her being my girlfriend but actually we were just good friends.

The older workers played card games. More often they played a game with cards that looked like dominoes. When they played in our room, I would watch. Unlike nowadays, no gambling was involved. In the summer the plant distributed watermelons from time to time. Before the Spring Festival we would get some fish from the plant as a bonus. Once we cooked some fish on a self-made stove, and three older coworkers and I downed three bottles of liquor. (China didn't and still doesn't have a drinking age; in this respect and many others such as control of medicine it is a freer country than the United States.) I wasn't much of a drinker but with my honor at stake I couldn't have chickened out. At first, only one bottle was on the table, but as the drinking got under way, another then a third bottle was brought out. The boasting and contending also got wilder. For the last bottle we had to draw lots to see who would go first with the agreement being that one would down two small cups in a row. When the last drop of liquor was gone, it was past 3 a.m. Staggering out of the room across the hallway where we had been drinking, I found myself unable to hold down the liquor anymore. After cleaning up my vomit I went to bed. When I got up around seven the next morning for the maintenance shift, the hangover was unmistakable but slight. Again, my youthful age made a difference.

My plant was one of the five factories north of the city, called collectively the "Five Factories at the North Gate." In order of the distance to the city lay the paper mill, the pharmaceutical factory, my plant, the phosphate fertilizer plant, and the flax mill. The factories showed movies in the open air and movie nights at the pharmaceutical factory and the flax mill were especially memorable. A couple of hours before the movie began, children would occupy the best spots in the big yard, usually the basketball court. The good thing about an open-air movie was one could sit on the backside of the screen when the front was full. The bad part about the free seating was once fellow moviegoers surrounded one, it was a big hassle to get out. Once, I really had to go to the bathroom but couldn't pluck up the courage to break through the packed audience. As the pressure became more and more difficult to bear, I started imagining peeing right there on the ground while everybody else was glued to the screen. When the movie was finally over, my bladder was so full it hurt. From then on, I didn't dare to sit in the middle of the crowd anymore.

In retrospect, of the movies we watched during this period one stood out. It was a Romanian movie about an underground anti-Fascist fighter who managed to steal or smuggle arms for guerillas. The captain of the ship transporting arms on the Danube had a voluptuous young bride. When he died toward the end of the movie fighting Fascist soldiers, he entrusted his wife to the hero. I said "In retrospect" because I was too postcocious to find the bride attractive at the time.

Like peasants, workers enjoyed telling obscene jokes. Unfortunately, I only remember one obscenity circulated among my fellow workers. It had to do with the gender imbalance at two neighboring factories. Whereas the phosphate fertilizer plant was full of male workers, female workers dominated the flax mill. Hence the saying, "Whereas the cocks at the Phosphate Fertilizer Plant cry with hunger, the pussies at the Flax Mill are so numerous they can cover a house." (The original saying rhymes.)

But if loose language was not frowned upon, loose morals were. Once two veteran workers were caught committing adultery. The woman was subjected to the humiliation of being paraded through the corridors of the dorms, a gong in one hand and a shoe in the other. She was made to bang the gong with the shoe as she walked disheveled and dejected in front of her fellow workers. (The shoe because "a loose woman" is called in China "a worn-out shoe.") The man's wife lived in another county, while the woman's husband was in a different province. The household registration system separated countless couples, who could only have "conjugal visits" once in a great while. At the time it was a mere spectacle to me; I didn't analyze the situation, let alone see the double standards — the woman, not the man, was made a spectacle. But given the situation, was it any wonder that the adultery had occurred?

This reminds me of a judgment pronouncement rally held at our plant. In those days, such rallies were often held at the East Wind Square, reputedly the second largest meeting ground in the province. Criminals were lined up in the front of the stage, their crimes briefly described, and sentences announced. They were then paraded through the streets on trucks and those receiving the death sentence taken to the execution grounds in a suburb. For some reason, this particular rally was held at our plant. We were gathered to listen to the judgments. Among the dozen or so criminals being sentenced to prison terms was a man in his forties. The woman reading the judgment described his crimes. She said he had committed burglary at private homes, which understandably was a punishable crime. Then she said something odd: the man had maltreated his wife, his crime being to have "sucked his wife's private parts." She said the man's wife had pleaded with him to stop but he wouldn't listen. I had heard a man could strengthen himself by taking a woman's "essence" in sexual intercourse. I thought, "Maybe by doing what he did to his wife, the man has weakened his wife's health, which seems to be what's implied to be wrong with his act." Did the woman hold this belief and report the "crime" to the authorities when her husband was apprehended for burglary? Did the man perform the act in order to strengthen his own body or merely get sexual pleasure? Whatever the case, the indictment says something about the unenlightened state of sexual practices of that time.

The basic pay for a new worker was eighteen yuan a month. In the second year it was raised to twenty. There was also a nutrition supplement of a few yuan, as coal gas and ammonia were harmful to our health. We got free work clothes and work shoes. Medical care was free; the plant had a clinic with one doctor who treated minor illnesses. Food was our main expense, about twelve yuan a month. The rent on our dorm space was either nothing or a negligible sum. The income was indeed low, but as that was the standard, I didn't feel we were underpaid. (However, when I went to college for free, I joked about having produced enough surplus value while working at the plant.) I still managed to buy books from time to time and went to Changsha and Wuhan, the latter being the capital of Hubei Province. Once, on my way to the plant, it occurred to me that my mentor had a large family to feed and could use some help. He declined it repeatedly before accepting my offer of twenty-five yuan. I didn't consider it a loan, though he did, because before I left for college, he insisted on not only returning that money but also giving me twenty yuan as a gift. I said I would accept the gift but the earlier sum had not been a loan and therefore shouldn't be paid back.

Toward the end of the second year, we took a written examination on the technology of our specific stations. Thus ended our apprenticeships. The monthly pay was raised to thirty yuan.

Though I lived at the plant, I went home frequently, both to enjoy Grandma's cooking and to help with chores, especially washing bed sheets and making honeycomb briquettes. At first, I went home about once a week. Later, I was able to buy a bike through Dad's connections at a country store in Matang, about fifteen kilometers from Yueyang.

With a bike I could go home more frequently. I got reckless a few times and once nearly broke my neck. From Yueyang No. 1 Middle on northward was a long downhill slope with minimal traffic. One day, not long after I got the bike, I was on my way to the plant. It was already dark out; the street was dimly lit. I put my left foot on the rack behind the seat (American bikes don't have the rack so Paul Newman's Butch Cassidy stood on the seat) and raised my right leg toward the sky. The bike accelerated on its own momentum. When I reached the water plant halfway down the slope, a boy learning how to ride his bike suddenly turned in front of me. It all happened in a second. Luckily, before I crashed into him, he turned farther right and missed me. That was the last time I tried the stunt on a slope.

Nineteen seventy-six was a turning point in Chinese politics. Zhou and Mao (and Zhu De) died and the "Gang of Four" was arrested. It was only a matter of time that revolutionary politics would give way to the drive for the "Four Modernizations." On January 9, Premier Zhou died. Then on September 9 or 10, a rumor was heard that Mao had passed away. I was home when a neighbor told us the rumor in a hushed voice. The next morning, the loudspeaker at the plant announced the news in a solemn voice. There followed a flurry of mourning activities. Every unit decorated a mourning hall lined with wreaths. Besides the mourning activities at the plant, we also went to the prefectural headquarters of the Party to pay our respects. Hundreds of workers from our plant and other prefectural plants waited outside the large mourning auditorium, then filed past Mao's portrait flanked by gigantic wreaths that extended to both sidewalls. Both at the plant and in the prefectural hall many people wept; some even sobbed. More people cried and cried louder at the prefectural hall, maybe because the atmosphere was more solemn. I heard that the daughter of a deputy director of my plant, a fellow new recruit, cried so hard she fainted. I, however, didn't cry. I was neither sad nor happy, being merely analytical about Mao's death and the mourning ritual. The unlikely successor Hua Guofeng had declared his loyalty to Mao's policies, but I sensed things were to change, though not how soon and in what specific ways.

I wasn't alone in being analytical about contemporary politics. I had made two friends with whom I was having frequent discussions of current affairs. Considering their penchant for secrecy, I won't use their real names here.

I met Pangpang in '75 while temping at the tax bureau, where he was also a temporary employee. Pangpang had a close friend, Zhongmou. Zhongmou was two years older than Pangpang, who in turn was two years my senior. Pangpang must have noticed that I was a bit different from the other temps and introduced me to Zhongmou. Zhongmou made a living pulling carts, one of the lowest occupations for a city resident. But he wasn't a typical cart-hauler. According to Pangpang, Zhongmou had only attended grade school. Wildly ambitious, he began educating himself by reading a small Chinese dictionary. He didn't have to go to the countryside as would an educated youth, and yet he volunteered on the grounds that Mao had based his revolution on a shrewd understanding of China's peasants. He went out of his way to find books to read and was Pangpang's bosom friend.

Pangpang paid me a visit and saw a full bookshelf. He said nothing at the time but later opined that it was unsafe to let visitors know I had so many books. That is, it was better to hide one's ambitions. I thought nothing of his circumspection, because I had no ambitions and saw no danger in letting people see my books. Meeting Pangpang and Zhongmou made me feel self-important because, of all my friends, they were the only ones who were politically acute. They acted as if they were engaged in some secret, important activities. I clued in right away, though in retrospect we were all wrapped up in a neurotic seriousness.

For a while they didn't let me into their circle. I had to pass a few tests. First, they wanted to see whether I had any political acumen or was I just a bookworm. One evening we were enjoying the cool under a streetlight. Zhongmou threw me a question casually, "Why do you think middle school graduates were sent down to the countryside?" I had not thought about this question before but sensed it was probably a test. In two seconds, an answer formed in my mind: "To solve China's employment problem, maybe." They neither agreed nor disagreed with me. And the conversation went on to other topics.

Having learned I had many more books stored in the attic, the two schemers gave me a more severe test. One evening in early '76, they accompanied me all the way to the gate of my plant. I had a zero-o'clock shift that night. On the way they told me they would like to see all my books and gave an ultimatum: If I wanted to be their friend, I must say yes before we reached the plant. My mind was in a turmoil: If I said no, I would lose the excitement of being associated with them, but if I said yes, they might know too much about me and my liaison with them might be dangerous. Prior to that evening Pangpang had asked me what I thought they were up to. I had said maybe they or their organization had some secret political activities. And I knew involvement in secret political activities was a grave crime, punishable to ten to fifteen years in prison. Heads of secret political organizations had even been executed. Right before we reached the plant, I buckled under the agony of indecision and said yes, they could have access to all my books. They turned around, while I went to the auditorium where the new recruits slept. It was about 9:30, two hours before I was to begin the night shift. I lay down in my bed but couldn't go to sleep. For two hours I drifted in and out of half-sleep, my head seeming to be about to explode. I have never before or since experienced that sensation: It was anxiety, fear, fatigue, and exhilaration all mixed up in a muddle.

On my next day off, Pangpang and Zhongmou came over to see my books. We climbed up the ladder to the attic, where I opened up my boxes of books to them. They picked fifty-six to borrow! As a friendly gesture, Zhongmou led me to his attic, where I saw a big wooden box full of books but borrowed nothing. He had no bookshelf downstairs for people to see.

As our books were limited, Pangpang and Zhongmou asked me if I knew any officials from whom we could borrow books. They of course knew about internal-distribution books not available to ordinary citizens. I said no. I did know one official at the county's Propaganda Department and another at the Taiwan affairs office of the prefectural Propaganda Department but didn't think they would let me borrow books from their offices. They said maybe we could try to make friends with somebody with such connections but we didn't know where to start. Zhongmou said he had heard one could buy Hegel's books in Shanghai, but Shanghai was too far off.

Zhongmou had a relative in Hankou, a city larger than Changsha and only a few hours away by train. We thought we must be able to find some books there. To save money we tried to get a free ride. Then an opportunity came. Laya told me he knew an engineer of a freight train that made regular trips to Wuhan (Wuhan being a tri-city metropolis made up of Hankou, Wuchang, and Hanyang). He said I could bring a friend with me to go to Wuhan with him. We were to ride on the locomotive. Around 10:30 p.m. on the day we were to leave, we met at the agreed-upon location near the train station.

Laya said his engineer acquaintance could only take him along, not us. Our hopes were dashed. Worse, we felt slighted. In the heat of anger Zhongmou and I decided to go to Wuhan on a passenger train that very night. We went home to get more money before meeting at the train station around midnight. We didn't have to wait long for the next train to Wuhan.

A few hours later the train pulled into Wuchang. I thought Zhongmou knew what he was doing but I was wrong. His relative lived at Hankou, the next stop, half an hour away. And yet he and I got off at Wuchang. It was not yet 4 a.m. We got out of the deserted station and headed for Hankou.

Before long we reached the magnificent bridge spanning the Yangzi River. The bridgeheads towered high above us, while the waters below shimmered in the lamplight. We walked across the kilometer-long bridge and then all the way to Hankou. Once in Hankou we followed one main street after another, making brief stops at bookstores. In half a day we had finished walking the main streets, so we headed for Hanyang. By the time we walked back to Hankou and found Zhongmou's relative, it was already 8:30 in the evening. The next day we went out again, this time taking our time to look around.

Zhongmou had heard that some people were so poor they sold their small children at street curbs. We kept our eyes peeled but didn't see such a scene. Neither did I buy any memorable books on this trip. I do remember, however, going into a foreign language bookstore, where the shelves extended all the way to the ceiling and a ladder was used to reach the higher shelves. The books were all science and engineering titles most of which were incomprehensible to me. I bought nothing. Zhongmou didn't even bother to look around, as he knew no English.

When Pangpang and I or the three of us got together, we talked about current affairs and books. I remember discussing Premier Zhou's death, even though we didn't know anything about the cliques at the top. Given China's long history of palace politics, we suspected there was something fishy about the fact that Zhou had died before Mao. I was also puzzled at the public's affection toward the deceased premier, not because I disliked him but because I was seeing the world, especially politics, with an analytical detachment. I did wonder, however, about how he'd managed to survive all those political campaigns, including the Cultural Revolution. He seemed to have been a political roly-poly (*budaoweng*).

Pangpang's neighbor was a county official, so we took precautions to prevent him from overhearing our discussions. When we took a stroll, we would watch our backs in case somebody was following us. In retrospect, all this secrecy seems a bit silly, because all we did was reading and talking. We formed no political organization, let alone have a program or platform. They, and I, knew better than that.

The scheming Zhongmou did talk me into a few intrigues. He had a theory that one could make friends with a complete stranger. He suggested that we try it on a doctor at the hospital close to the city center. Zhongmou had found out that this doctor knew somebody at my plant, and our goal was to persuade the doctor to use his connections to buy some fertilizer. His plan was he and I would pretend to be sick when the doctor was on duty. While being seen by the doctor, he would try to strike up a conversation with him and make his acquaintance. After a few visits, the doctor would become our friend. Excited by the scheme, I went along with the plan, acting as a witness and keeping him company. First, we paid the registration fee. Then I watched as a patient-in-waiting as he struck up a conversation with the doctor. (The patients waited in the same room in which the doctor saw them.) Their conversation didn't go beyond two minutes' casual chatting. We gave up the operation.

One day, Zhongmou proposed something shadier. Having heard Laya and I were friends and Laya also had many books, he proposed that we sneak into Laya's room to take a look. If we saw something good, we'd steal it. He asked me the kind of lock Laya used and said a key to the same kind of lock would open it. I felt uncomfortable with the idea but gave in after some hesitation. The three of us went to Laya's room on the second floor of an old building outside Yueyang No. 2 Middle. The door opened just as Zhongmou had predicted. Laya's books didn't interest Zhongmou that much—he was concentrating on mathematics and political economy, subjects too technical for Zhongmou. Uneasy about breaking into a friend's place and afraid Laya might come back and catch us in his room, I was relieved when we left in a few minutes without stealing anything. Laya and I remained good friends, but I was too ashamed to tell him of this unfriendly visit.

In the summer of '77 I heard a rumor that colleges were to reopen to general admission. For ten years the Cultural Revolution had wreaked havoc on China's higher education. In the first few years, colleges were busy making revolution. Then college students were chosen from the ranks of workers, peasants, and soldiers. In theory, the policy was to make higher education more egalitarian, while in practice probably a disproportionate number of those students were children of officials rather than of ordinary workers and peasants. Family background and conduct were the main entrance criteria, and because most of the students were underprepared for higher education, what was taught in colleges and universities was not up to standard. After Mao died and the "Gang of Four" was arrested in '76, the revolution in education lost its motor (and Chinese education the valuable criticisms of such old practices as setting tricky and odd questions in examinations and overemphasizing rote learning). According to the rumor, colleges and universities were to reopen to current middle school graduates and social youths, who would compete in entrance examinations for the limited spots in institutions of higher learning.

To confirm the rumor, I went to Changsha to see my old classmate Li Hongzhuan, whose father was Party Secretary of Hunan Teachers' College. Hongzhuan's father said, yes, both current middle school graduates and those with work experience were eligible for the entrance exams. I had been studying for nearly four years since graduation from middle school just for fun; now an opportunity to engage in full-time study was beaming at me. For the first time in four years, I was to study for a specific purpose: to pass the college entrance examinations.

With no favorite subject but numerous interests, I went to my old teachers for advice on what exams to take. I talked to Teacher Zhang, the teacher-in-charge of my senior middle class. I also stopped by to see Teacher Hu, an English teacher and Teacher Zhang's neighbor. Both said I should take the science exams on the grounds that I had done so well in math, physics, and chemistry in middle school. Teacher Hu, who was from Beijing, also hinted at the relative safety of studying science as compared to the humanities and social sciences. Indeed, we had a saying, "Once you become good at math, physics, and chemistry, you can make a living anywhere in the world" (*xue hao shu-li-hua, zou bian tianxia dou bupa*). "But I've forgotten most of what I learned in middle school," I explained. With the examinations approaching and not enough time to review the subjects, I decided to register for English. Though I didn't touch English books for nearly two years, I thought I needed the limited time to review math and to study history and geography.

For English I sought out Teacher Luo through a good friend of my cousin's. Teacher Luo reputedly was going to be on the county's Admissions Committee. She had majored in English in college. I showed her a few of my notebooks and she gave me a practice test. My performance was good but far from being stellar. To thank her and also to impress her even more, I invited her and her husband over for dinner. I brought down some books from the attic and piled them up on a stand by Grandma's bed. I showed her some more of the sewn notebooks from '74 and '75. The unadorned notebooks impressed her.

Meanwhile, the exam dates were rapidly approaching. Having heard that some units gave their employee candidates fifteen days of leave to prepare full time for the exams, I talked to the officials at my plant. The answer? "No." Not only was I denied a leave, a deputy director of the plant was furious at me for making the request. His eyes bulging and spittle flying, he pointed his index finger at me and cursed, "I'm determined not to grant you a leave. Even if you had the leave, you wouldn't be able to pass the exams!" Having done nothing to offend him personally, I couldn't put my finger on the source of his anger. Maybe he just didn't want a "naughty" employee to break free of his control? Pressed for time, I asked my dad to talk to the Party branch secretary of my workshop. As a result, I got three days off before the exams.

Shortly after the written exams I received a notice to take the oral English test. Upon entering the test room, I saw Teacher Luo and the examiner, a faculty member from Hunan Teachers' College. I sat down in front of the examiner and Teacher Luo said, "He's the most promising candidate I've seen." The test consisted of reading out loud the English alphabet, some sentences, a paragraph, and a short conversation in English with the examiner. I did well.

Even though the written exams were not difficult, my performance was only so-so. On the English exam, I misunderstood the sentence, "Is there room in the car?" as "Is there a room in the car?" in part because I vaguely recalled a piece in the journal *English Monthly* that said "car" also meant a carriage of a train and reasoned that that kind of car could have a sleeping room in it. A more experienced test taker would have known the question was meant to test the student's grasp of the distinction between countable and uncountable nouns, which doesn't exist in Chinese. My reading of *Reference News* carrying only foreign news a few years back helped in translating a piece of news except that I couldn't figure out what "detained" meant. I only knew it didn't mean "arrest." Unable to think of a verb to fit the context, I knowingly used the latter, wrong word. In my rustiness I even forgot the meaning of "keep."

I did much worse on the math exam, because I walked into the exam room without having reviewed the senior middle textbooks.

On the other hand, my application materials helped. Together with the application form I submitted the translation of the motor's manual I had done and the translation of the Japanese truck manuals I had copied a few years before. As a result, the county's Admissions Committee made me an "Outstanding Candidate" and put together a file on me.

On the application form we were given three choices. I put down Beijing Second Foreign Languages Institute as my first choice, Peking University (major in international politics) as my second choice, and Changsha's Hunan Teachers' College as the last choice. I didn't think I was good enough to compete for a spot at Beijing Foreign Languages Institute and thought my second choice might give the admissions officer a clue that I was knowledgeable about international affairs, which would certainly be a plus for a would-be student in English. I even secretly hoped that I just might get lucky and be picked up by Peking University. We had had to submit our preferences before the exams, so our choices couldn't have been based on our estimate of how we did on the exams. The admissions process had its own intricacy, and I was told later that picking the schools was almost as critical as one's test scores to getting into a school of one's choice. Without any guidance, I relied on my own reasoning, which was probably wrongheaded.

Although I knew I didn't do too well on the entrance exams, when the admission notice came in February '78, I wasn't at all caught by surprise. I felt I deserved to go to college. Of the sixteen workers from my plant who had taken the entrance exams, I was the only successful candidate.

The admission letter did contain a surprise: none of the three schools I had picked admitted me. Instead, I was admitted by Hunan University in Changsha. An engineering school, Hunan University had no English department. It turned out that its Basic Courses Department admitted several teacher-training classes, among which was our English class of thirty students.

I could have stopped working at the plant the day I received the admission notice. Instead, I stayed for the upcoming zero-o'clock shifts. Before leaving for Changsha, I went to say goodbye to Teacher Peng. I wanted to give him something as a token of my appreciation for the instruction and help he had given me over the years and being short of money I gave him my own set of Sima Qian's *Shiji* (Records of the Historian).

I also went to see Zhongmou. Knowing that he didn't intend to return my books (I was too thin-skinned to ask him to), I said I'd like to have back the three volumes of Shakespeare's plays. Also, to get even (hardly so since he still had over fifty of my books), I borrowed volume one of Russell's history of Western philosophy with no intention to return it. The book contained many of Zhongmou's notes in the margins. I was intrigued and looked at his notes once I got home. To my disappointment the notes merely repeated certain sentences in the book, and not particularly pithy ones at that. Zhongmou did not have, or put down, a single philosophical thought of his own in the margins.

When I returned to my hometown for the first vacation in summer '78, I went back to the plant to see my old friends. I even stayed for a zero-o'clock shift for old times' sake. From then on, nearly every time I went back to Yueyang, I would go back to the plant. In the following years, tragedy struck several of my former fellow workers. Dai Dingchao, the maintenance worker who had worked with me on top of the copper-washing tower, was burned to death in an explosion. Li Heng, who looked like a warrior out of *Three Kingdoms* or *Water Margin*, lost a leg in another accident. Master Tan was brutally murdered by his apprentice, who stole his money and expensive watch. My good friend Zhang Yuejun was killed in a car accident after having been promoted to vice-magistrate of a county. Of the rest of my old pals, Yao Xiang managed to transfer to the Prefecture Economic Commission, while Tu Chunfen married a graduate student and moved to Nanjing. Only Huang Changchun stayed at the plant, where he was vice-chairman of the Workers' Union (in '99, when I wrote the 1st draft of the 1st five chapters of this life story). When I went back to visit in later years, many of the workers didn't recognize me, not because I sported a suit and a tie (I didn't) but because they had been hired after I left the plant in '78. This reminds me of a famous Tang poem about an old man returning to his native place after having spent his life away from home. The smiling children ask the stranger, "Where d'you come from, Sir?"

6. Cavalier College Student

Hunan University is a park. Actually, it hugs the entrance of the Mount Yuelu Park, whose best attraction is Mount Yuelu with its famed Aiwan Pavilion, cool streams, tombs of revolutionary martyrs, midmountain temple, and numerous trails and hideouts. The late chairman frequented the pavilion in his student days in Changsha, and the mountain became a favorite haunt for Changshanese on weekends and holidays.

The mountain extends in both directions for a few kilometers. On the other side stood an institute (now of course a university) of mining and metallurgy, by bus less than ten minutes away to the southwest. Next to my school to the north lay Hunan Teachers' College (which also has upgraded its name to university). The Xiang River meanders between the city and the college district, a graceful bridge spanning the river that embraces the Orange Island. It was difficult to imagine a better locale for a school.

My class was assigned to dorm two. That is, we boys were; girls lived in a separate building in a different part of the campus, the forbidding dorm nine. Seven or eight of us boys shared a room, and each of us got a bunk bed, a desk, and a stool. Having grown up in confined quarters, I didn't even notice the crowdedness of the dorm room. Even though early birds picked their spots in the room, there was neither squabbling among those who arrived about the same time nor grumbling among the latecomers. The Cultural Revolution closed colleges and universities for over a decade for regular admission; maybe we were too happy to be able to go to college to be particular about dorm space. We stayed in this dorm for the next four years, even though our rooms did change a few times.

My class was part of the Basic Courses Department consisting also of classes of math, physics, and politics. Unlike in the United States, the same class of students lived together and attended the same classes—there were as yet no electives. The university was an engineering school, even though it was designated as one of the eighty plus "key" universities in the country.

Orientation. All the students in our department gathered in a terraced classroom by the main road threading through the campus and connecting the three schools. It was the first day of orientation and the first time I had ever been in a terraced classroom. The cadre in charge of students, a former army-man, spoke about the orientation and the university. No rousing semi-intellectual speeches, no parade of bespectacled scholars. Although the orientation was hardly inspiring, I was far too excited about college to mind the meetings.

To prevent students from overstudying themselves to ill health, the school turned the lights off at 11 p.m. (Or was it 10:30?) One night, I woke up around 3:30 and was too excited about being in college to go back to sleep. Tiptoeing out of the room with my stool and *After Nehru, Who?* I went to the dorm's latrine to continue reading where I had left off, neglecting the stench (after all, I had got used to the aroma of ammonia at the fertilizer plant) and the occasional visitor. But the dim light in the latrine did strain my eyes after a while. Lucky for my eyes and my health, I slept through the following night and the next and never resumed my toilet reading.

Classes soon began. The main course was an all-purpose English class drilling us in listening, speaking, reading, and translating. Instead of beginning at college level, we started with the alphabet, being told that our current pronunciation needed to be rectified. Our teacher was a recent graduate of the same school, a former worker-peasant-soldier student but one with excellent pronunciation and intonation.

Even though schoolwork was unchallenging, I was happy. Just a few months before, I had had to find time to read on weekends and in late nights but now I didn't have to do anything else but study. I had my own books, the library's reading room was full of journals and magazines I had never heard of, and the reading rooms of both the Teachers' College and the Institute of Mining and Metallurgy were a short distance away. I also went to the provincial library in the city one Sunday (I had read it was there that Mao had seen a world map for the first time) and read from a collection of Plato's dialogues.

At first, I didn't go beyond our English textbooks but continued my random reading in the humanities and social sciences, especially international politics and world literature. I remember vividly, on May 1, 1978, International Labor Day, several friends of mine and I went to the small but well-stocked bookstore between the Teachers' College and my school. We had heard that a spate of Western novels would be for sale that day, the first major release of such books after the Cultural Revolution. With my pal Yueshan pitching in I bought five novels including Tolstoy's *Anna Karenina* and Stendhal's *Red and Black*. These two novels turned out to be less than captivating for my unsophisticated taste, but I couldn't put down Balzac's *Father Goriot* and *Eugénie Grandet* or Hugo's *Les Misérables*. Again, I had no reading plan; one day I was poring over Lucretius; another day, Clausewitz; yet another day, *Scientific American*. I plunged right into journals in world trade, world literature, philosophy, economics, Chinese, linguistics, and literary criticism. Of course, there was much I didn't understand, but the more I read the more I understood.

The English our teachers spoke was neither purely British nor distinctively American. Luckily, each dorm room was provided with a large tape recorder that could play conversations and readings by native speakers, both British and American. Roommates with radios regularly tuned into the U.S. government's Voice of America with English news and language lessons. Indeed, in the beginning listening comprehension seemed our weakest point. Our inadequacy was made clear to me two-and-a-half months into the first semester when a delegation of Australian teachers and students came to visit us. When the leader of the delegation finished speaking, the ritualistic clapping didn't come until a few seconds had elapsed. Of the entire speech I only understood one word, education, pronounced of course the Australian way. Still, we didn't seem embarrassed by our inadequacy. After all, we were just beginning our studies and that was the first native English speaker we had ever heard face-to-face. When another Australian delegation came in June, we could carry on a simple conversation with them. I even led my class in a chorus of "Waltzing Matilda," which charmed our guests.

In October, an American teacher came to lecture at the neighboring Teachers' College. They had much more students so the big classroom was jammed. To gain a better view of the speaker, students in the back stood on stools and desks, struggling to peak through the throng in front. The lecture consisted of a series of stories. The speaker was immensely engaging, so the audience oohed and aahed with the twists and turns in her stories, and those of us in the back stood through the all-day affair with but a lunch break.

On November 17 we got our own foreign speaker, the wife of a foreign engineer helping to set up the urea factory in my hometown. There was nothing special about her speech but she gave us a big stack of glossy magazines full of seminude models! When the magazines went around the classroom, I was too coy to take a good look, thinking I could look at them closely once we were back in our dorm. Somehow the school authorities got wind of these eyepoppers and took them away. Did our guest not know what she was doing? Or was it meant as an act of subversion or "resistance"?

As time went on, more and more Western tourists came to see Mount Yuelu. Even though we enjoyed proximity to the Aiwan Pavilion, students from the Teachers' College were far more aggressive in seeking out foreign tourists to practice their English on. Some of them, all boys to my knowledge, would wait near the pavilion just in case they might get lucky. I was too shy to engage in this type of guerrilla learning.

Starting with our sophomore year, we had an American teacher, Mariana Fehd. She taught us oral English then literature then writing. It was in her class that I wrote my first English essay, a subtly satirical piece on "red" things in China, from the fluttering red flags to the throbbing red hearts of the young devoted to the Party. She and her husband, Ronnie, brought two little girls. They picked up Chinese in no time, especially the younger Amanda, who would be their parents' interpreter when the student interpreter wasn't with them.

Native speakers of English were not the only foreign "things" we were hungry for. There was a latent craving for foreign movies. Up till 1978, the few foreign movies we had been allowed to see had come from such ideologically correct countries as North Korea, Albania, Romania, and the early Soviet Union, so when some Japanese films were shown, they became hugely popular among students. There was the life story of a prostitute. When it was shown in a classroom, even the windowsills were taken, creating a mob scene more unruly than that at the foreign teacher's lecture at the Teachers' College. Several lines of another Japanese movie, one about pursuing bad guys in the business world, became quotable quotes and etched in my memory.

Beginning in the second semester, I frequented the science and technology reading room, which housed all the foreign language journals in science and engineering. Strangely, I also found copies of *The China Quarterly* on a shelf, the only foreign language journal in the social sciences and humanities I had seen there. I spent numerous mornings and afternoons in this reading room, which had few visitors. I didn't know much science or engineering, but as an English student in an engineering school I felt I should be able to read technical English.

Academics got more colorful in the second year. First, I won a waiver of class attendance for the main English class; second, I became an interpreter for a visiting American computer science professor.

For the main English class in the first semester of second year, our instructor was another former worker-peasant-soldier student, one who was not quite up to the task. Possibly, this teacher's Party membership mattered, as we had heard that on an earlier occasion the same teacher instead of someone else who spoke better English was chosen to accompany a visiting foreign delegation. At any rate, the teacher's incompetence was soon revealed: sometimes she couldn't understand a student who spoke correctly or was unable to answer a student's question.

I decided to petition for a waiver of class attendance on the grounds that I would be able to learn more on my own than in class. Considering that I wasn't the only one dissatisfied with the teacher and getting more petitioners would strengthen the case, I talked to two of my classmates: Fang Yuan and Tian Jin. I chose Fang Yuan because he had entered with the highest English score in my class and though a poor test taker, he was probably more advanced in English than me. As one of the eight classmates who had applied as science students, Tian Jin had been less advanced in the language to begin with. However, he was a fast learner and had shown great promise by the end of the first year. Fang Yuan agreed to my idea immediately but Tian Jin declined to join us, explaining his situation and insisting that his English wasn't good enough. That might be so, but I thought he was also being cautious.

Insolent though we were, we weren't totally inconsiderate. First, we went to see our instructor, telling her that we would like to request a waiver of class attendance so that we might be able to learn more on our own. She received us calmly. We then went to see the leaders of the teaching and research section, who were noncommittal about our request.

Seventeen days later, an examination was administered to the whole class. It turned out that the exam was a "competition" and our petition would hinge on its results. Most of the test resembled the TOEFL (Test of English as a Foreign Language), which foreign students have to pass to get into U.S. and Canadian colleges and universities. It was more difficult than any of the previous tests we had taken and as "champion" I only got 76 percent. The only other student who had passed, Li Wendan, scored under 70 percent. The oral part of the competition followed two weeks later. Then ten days after the oral exam, the waiver was granted! Only that Fang Yuan had bombed again. We were told that the two who had passed the test and two others, Qiu Xi and Zhang Xiaoheng, who had scored close to 60 percent, had the option not to attend the English class. We still had to take the midterm and the final, of course. From then on, we would go up Mount Yuelu once a week to compare our answers to the exercises in our textbook, but otherwise we had our daily class time to ourselves.

Instead of punishing me for my disobedience, the authorities rewarded me for my performance at the competition. It was the first English competition of the university, and I received my prize together with other winners in similar competitions in other subjects at a departmental meeting. The prize consisted of the four-volume set of *Essential English* (two of the volumes I happened to have hand-copied in 1974), a fountain pen, and a fancy notebook. (The last item I gave to my best friend, Yueshan.) Later, the university's youth league wrote a feature story on me, which was aired on the provincial radio, Hunan People's Broadcasting Station. On the day the piece was to be aired, we were told to listen to it in order to "learn from" this student. Come airtime, I was so embarrassed that I lowered my mosquito net and hid in my bed. Who would have thought that the loudspeakers at my mom's school in Yueyang blared out the same report? Even more surprising, in a remote region of the province where an ethnic minority lived, an aspiring student of English heard the piece and wrote me a letter expressing his admiration and asking for my advice on how to learn English. I mailed him *Essential English* and he thanked me with some produce from his region.

When next the whole university held its English competition, they asked me to prepare the questions and supervise the grading of test papers. My mug shot and the photos of those who had prepared other competitions were showcased across from the administration building by the motor road. I didn't gloat over this ill-deserved honor: In my one-line-a-day diary entries I only wrote "competition," "oral competition," and "absence from class formally approved" under the relevant dates; there was no mention of the prize or of any other honors.

As time went on, I spent more time reading journals. Finding it inconvenient to read the libraries' copies, I decided to have my own subscriptions so that I could underline important parts instead of copying them. By senior year I had taken out ten journals: four in foreign languages, four in Western social sciences and humanities, one in current world affairs, and one in recent developments in science and technology abroad.

How did I manage my budget, you may wonder. At that time, thanks to socialism we paid no tuition or fees; had free medical care, free textbooks, free newspapers, and free room; and being relatively poor I also received a second-grade grant of twelve yuan a month, enough to cover food. My grandparents gave me fifteen yuan a month, which covered everything else. (There was no such thing as students working part time for pay.) Most of the spending money went to buying books, subscribing to journals and going out with friends. The clothes and shoes from the fertilizer plant lasted me through college; I bought no wallet, no shirts made of Dacron (which was becoming popular), no handkerchief (I used my hand or sleeve to wipe my mouth), and no toilet soap. (I used the coarser soap for washing clothes to wash my face and body.) For breakfast, others sent down their steamed buns with a bowl of rice porridge and some preserved vegetables, but my appetite was so good and I so prized austerity that I ate my buns pure and simple.

Contrary to the proverb, "Good fortune doesn't come in pairs," my good luck doubled. In June an American computer science professor arrived to teach faculty and researchers from Changsha. As my school couldn't find an interpreter, they had to "borrow" an earlier graduate now working in another school. The university chose me as the foreign expert's interpreter for daily-life situations. I met Tom Sager on June 26, 1979. His arrival changed my life and his friendship and help would benefit me greatly in the future.

At first, he called me "George," but soon he started learning Chinese and could say my Chinese name effortlessly. We also became friends with Feng Jinwen, an engineering graduate working in one of the departments. Tom was a jogger, so we went jogging together.

Before long Tom's fiancée Suellen came to join him and on October 24 they were married in the administration building. Tom looked very handsome in his suit, with Suellen smiling from ear to ear in the picture taken in front of the building. Onlookers mobbed the large, decorated meeting room on the second floor and fought for the candy I threw up into the air. The celebration continued into the evening at Tom and Suellen's residence, which had housed Russian experts in the 1950s.

Weeks before Tom's arrival, the university had asked my classmate Zhang Xiaoheng and me to read about computers so that at some point we could translate Tom's lectures. We sat in on Tom's lectures on computer programming. On December 12, I tried to interpret Tom's lecture for the first time. He would say a few sentences in English and I would repeat them in Chinese. For about half an hour I felt confident. Then Tom used a technical term about which someone from the audience raised a question. Too nervous to comprehend Tom's explanation, I panicked. Seconds later I asked the official interpreter to take over. Luckily, when I resumed interpreting the following day, I didn't lose my compo-sure. Technical translation involves a limited vocabulary but accuracy is crucial. I would go over Tom's lecture notes beforehand, asking him questions about anything new I didn't understand.

At the end of the year, a delegation of four computer scientists came from Wisconsin for a three-week visit. With the help of two participants—they helped me go through the lecture notes the previous evening—I translated some lectures on data structures given by the head of the delegation, Larry Landweber. Although I didn't panic, I was more nervous than usual as the audience was twice as large as Tom's. I muddled through places (the audience might have mistaken my lack of clarity for the depth of the message!) and remember one error clearly. When Larry was explaining pointers, he used the expression "counting sheep." Instead of asking him what he meant as someone with greater composure would have done, I tried to guess its meaning and translated it as the programmer being confused by the pointers. As I gestured with my hands, the audience laughed. If the audience didn't detect the error, a fellow interpreter—a teacher from Shanghai who had published articles on technical English—muttered in Chinese, "No, it was 'counting sheep.'"

A small cross-cultural encounter occurred during the visit of Landweber's delegation. When he complimented me on my English, even though in the back of my mind I knew the proper American answer was to thank him, my Chinese self immediately reacted with a modest denial, leading him to say, "Fishing for compliments, huh?" Having lived in America since '86, I still find it hard to respond to a compliment with the expected American reply and usually either say nothing in response or offer a qualifying explanation. When around '87 I noticed in *My Darling Clementine*, the heroine didn't say "Thank you" to a compliment from the hero, I put it down in my notebook.

The following semester Tom lectured on operating systems, which Zhang Xiaoheng and I took turns interpreting. Although it looked like I understood everything I was interpreting, my understanding was superficial. I had no interest in the subject itself beyond the basics about computers, so I only tried to understand enough to do the interpreting. Zhang Xiaoheng, on the other hand, had the ambition to use this opportunity to eventually go into computer science and so studied the subject studiously. He did realize his dream later on.

Over the winter break I accompanied Tom and Suellen to Kunming, which boasts the longest couplet in the world as well as spring weather all year round. We climbed the cliff-hung plank road overlooking the vast mirror of Lake Dianchi, trekked far into the wilderness dotted with limestone, sauntered in the botanical garden full of tropical plants, and squeezed through the narrow passages in the Stone Forest. We were especially lucky to see the total solar eclipse on this trip. The clever Suellen asked me to call the observatory to say that an American computer *scientist* was in town and to ask if they could accommodate us in seeing the eclipse. The answer was that we could get our own sunglasses and watch it in a park, which we did.

One late afternoon we chatted with some American tourists, among whom was a seventeen-year-old boy with his girlfriend. They were handing over their room to another tourist, who offered to pay the boy half the cost for the night. I was impressed by the fact that such a young couple was traveling—and sleeping—together in a distant foreign country and inferred that when it comes to money Americans, as the Chinese would say, don't stand on ceremony.

Working for Tom had other benefits. Even though eight of us shared our dorm room, distraction was not a problem. For one thing, there was no TV. Still, I loved studying in Tom's office. It had more space, the books Tom and Suellen had bought in Hong Kong, and a small cassette player on which I could play songs. I listened to a tape of Leonard Cohen's so many times that I still remember the tunes of "Suzanne," "Sisters of Mercy," "So long, Marianne," and "Hey, That's No Way to Say Goodbye." Lines such as "tea and oranges / That come all the way from China," "Jesus was a sailor," and "she's touched your perfect body with her mind" drifted from the background to the foreground while I studied, but it was the melancholy music and Cohen's serene voice that filled the office with the perfect ambience in the middle of the night. The Taiwanese singer Deng Lijun (Teresa Teng) was a sensation, and my friend Ruijun and I would play her songs over and over. But above all I studied. For a few weeks I stayed up in the office all night through, only to return to my dorm room to sleep when my fellow students went to class. Besides reading, I translated some ninety pages of a psychological novel about an Eskimo boy. In the wee hours of the morning, I was transported from a muggy Chinese campus to the icy wilderness of Alaska, accompanied by Leonard Cohen's deep voice.

Tom returned to the States in August 1980; for three weeks I helped him and Suellen pack and then saw them off at Guangzhou. Before Tom left, he offered me a sum of twenty yuan a month for the time left of my college education. I had managed without his help for two-and-a-half years but after consideration accepted his kind help. He also left me the handy cassette player, which at the time was still a prized item. Back in the States he took out a subscription of *Time* magazine in my name.

Less than a year later Tom went to teach at Hefei's China University of Science and Technology. When he invited me to go to Huangshan (Mount Huang) with all expenses paid, I jumped with joy. I had just decided to take the entrance examinations for the Graduate School of the Chinese Academy of Social Sciences, but as eager to see him again as I was to visit Huangshan, I put the visit above my preparations for the exams.

The day we climbed up the mountain it was raining; the rain mixed with the usual mist and clouds adding to the overwhelming presence of the mountain and dampening not a bit our high spirits. How could it when men and women porters were scaling the heights with loads of supply or tourists' baggage on their backs? The well-known scenic spots didn't disappoint me the least. The otherworldly rock formation dubbed "Monkey Looking Out to the Sea," the magnificent Lotus Peak with its heavenly height and winding paths, the narrow ridge that drops down on both sides at ninety degrees for hundreds of meters: All this awesomeness is, to borrow an old Chinese cliché, beyond the power of my poor pen, and of my failing memory.

I read voraciously in college but study like a grind I did not, nor did I take schoolwork too seriously. Most of the time I did study for the exams; for a couple of semesters though, I didn't review the textbooks. Instead, I used the time to read other things and to visit friends. (I had a half-serious rationalization: If I miss something on a test, that means I haven't learned it, and one remembers one's misses better than one's hits.) As a result, I missed things here and there and my grades were in the eighties instead of nineties. I also always left the exams early, that is, as soon as I had finished the items and checked them once. At one of Mariana's exams, I left the classroom well before the allotted time was over and returned to the dorm. Mariana must have graded my exam at the lectern, because when my roommates came back, one of them told me I had scored ninety-eight. Feigning skepticism, I said, "Only ninety-eight, not one hundred?" It turned out he was pulling my leg: I had scored only eighty-eight.

The lights-out-at-11 policy meant that burning the midnight oil was possible only if you used a flashlight, which would be hard on the eyes, so students would get up early in the morning to read out loud, in part due to the widely held belief that early morning is good for memorizing new words. But instead of studying I took to jogging and would run up Mount Yuelu, half the way to the temple or straight to the top. The parklike campus already had fresh air, and yet the misty slopes and dewy greenery beckoned to many, among whom was a white-haired man at least in his late 60s; his steady steps always carried him to the top of the mountain. Before dinner I enjoyed kicking a soccer ball by myself, high jump, horizontal bar, and dumbbells.

Then there was Sunday, the only weekend day of the week. Students went into the city, washed their clothes, and called on friends. A few also studied. I spent most of my Sundays visiting friends. Although I got along with everybody else in my class, my close friends were from my hometown, none of whom majored in the humanities or social sciences.

First there was Ruijun, my middle school classmate, who lived in the dorm next to mine and majored in mechanical engineering. Several times a week we would either walk up the mountain or, more often, walk down to the bank of the Xiang River, talking about whatever came to mind. One summer evening we kept walking along the river, reached the bridge, crossed it, and continued until we came to a noodle shop. We each wolfed down a bowl of hot-and-sour noodles and strolled all the way to the south gate. Then without stopping we walked all the way back to the campus.

A few bus stops away was the Mining and Metallurgy Institute, where Ruidan (Ruijun's elder brother) and Yueshan were, Ruidan studying chemistry and Yueshan mathematics. Sometimes I would stay overnight; eating at their canteen we always went "mining," as we called searching for pieces of meat from beneath the vegetables. Once, walking through the nearby rice paddies and then around their large campus we started counting four-character idioms beginning with the word "one." Among the three of us we came up with some eighty idioms! Checking against a small dictionary I found out we had only missed a few.

Then there was Yajun, who was studying engineering at the Agricultural College on the other side of the city. Once in a while he would come over to our side; we also went over to his campus after he'd won a local People's Congress election. On a bright summer day, the five of us hiked up Mount Yuelu with a bottle of liquor. We took turns drinking from the bottle—no need to hide the bottle in a paper bag—and before long the spirit was gone. When we got together, we would get some cheap cigarettes, a famous brand being Red Orange, at thirteen cents a pack, nicknamed pumpkin brand. When a cigarette came around to me, I would take such a deep, long draw that it seemed as if the smoke would come out of my other end, provoking Ruidan to tease me about my lack of class—not for the draw but for not minding the cheap brand with its inferior taste, knowing all the while that was all we could afford.

Of these friends Yueshan became closest to me. His lack of artifice, generosity of spirit, keenness of intellect, and sense of humor immediately drew me to him once we started visiting each other in college. (As an example of his keen intellect, I watched with him on television in Guangzhou the ceremony returning Hong Kong to Chinese rule. Though hard to believe, the Chinese interpreter mispronounced a word and Yueshan detected the error instantly. My reaction was slower; I didn't recognize it until he'd blurted out his discovery.) He and Ruidan had both graduated from the same middle school as I, but being in two different grades—they being one grade higher—we had had no interaction. The first time I met Yueshan, I was studying for the college entrance exams. A mutual friend from my plant took me to see him. When he asked me about my intentions toward college, I feigned indecision; my association with Zhongmou and Pangpang was still affecting me. Who would have thought he would soon become my bosom friend? I remember, after spending one weekend together at his school he walked me back to my school. Not wanting to leave him I accompanied him back to his school, upon which he insisted on walking me back yet again.

Another friend from my hometown was a former middle school classmate. For the first year or so Guangwen was a stevedore on the other side of the Xiang River bridge and I saw him often. He asked me how I felt living away from home and I told him that a week after being in Changsha I felt completely at home, as if I had grown up there.

Most visitors came from Yueyang, some of whom more than once: my pals from the fertilizer plant; Zhongmou's junior co-conspirator Pangpang; my middle school classmates Shuiping and Jinjun; my childhood neighbor Wuhe, who was teaching himself English; my cousin the ex–Cultural Revolution rebel; my dad; and my brothers. Whenever I had a visitor, I would skip class and accompany him on a tour of Mount Yuelu and of downtown Changsha, or help him attend to the business of the trip.

As I mentioned in the previous chapter, Hongzhuan's father was the Teachers' College's Party Secretary. His mother was also an official, at the Chinese medicine research institute. Now that I was living in the next school, I went to see him from time to time. They would keep me for lunch or dinner and I got to observe more closely how an official lived. When Hongzhuan took the English exam for a junior college, his parents asked me to accompany him to the test site in the city. He did well enough to be admitted—notice that his father's position didn't give him the privilege to attend the Teachers' College, a four-year school, irrespective of his academic performance.

Also at the Teachers' College was Professor Liu Zhongde, whom I went to see much more often than Hongzhuan and his parents. I would walk over to his place after dinner on Saturday evening or sometime on Sunday, in which case he and his wife would keep me for lunch or dinner. Even though Professor Liu and his wife were older than my parents and he was a dignified scholar of deep learning, I felt completely at ease while visiting them.

At my own school I was on good terms with my teachers. Teacher Zhou (Peijun) invited me over for a meal at least once and I visited her quite a few times. I also visited Teacher Lin (Ruchang) a few times, who never taught us but who spoke English most fluently among the teachers. Teacher Xie (Zuojie), the only associate professor of English at the time, was very kind to me. In the summer of 1980 Teacher Xie gave me the opportunity to help him with an English textbook for engineering students. The engineering faculty had prepared answers to the translation exercises and Teacher Xie wanted me to check their accuracy. He also taught us a course in translation. One day, to help us start thinking about our graduation thesis, he read a paper of his in class. Sensing something was not quite right, I asked to see his paper after class. I read over it at lunch break and wrote a page of criticism including pointing out a straightforward error in translation. Then I paid him a visit in his home and gave him the sheet. He read over it and accepted my comments graciously. Later on, when I went back to visit from Beijing, he and his wife invited my wife and me over for dinner.

One of the two Chinese teachers we had was Liang Zai, who remains the most passionate teacher I have known. A Communist guerrilla fighter before 1949, she had been as deft with guns as with the pen. She told us she had read *Dream of the Red Chamber* seventeen times. Once, having heard that I was the best-read student in the class, she sent word that she'd like to see me at her home. Though I admired her, I was not always mentally present in class. When writing an assigned essay, I struck the fancy of doing it Ruijun's way, that is, writing directly into the exercise book without drafting. As I lacked Ruijun's talent, the essay was not a serious effort, as Teacher Liang pointed out in her end-of-the-term evaluation. In this three-page handwritten assessment of my work, she said that in class I had the ability to do more than one thing at a time. As for my writing, I didn't tackle complex issues, and my earlier work *even* contained inappropriate diction. In addition, she said that one must have beliefs to lead a meaningful life, implying that I lacked them (see app. 10). Her subtle but well-intentioned sarcasm was refreshing, her assessment of my weaknesses made me think, and her dedication to students touched me.

Politics only played a minor role in my life in those years but a few things need to be reported. First, although I was a two-bit academic star, the only student cadre position I held was being in charge of physical labor or periodic spring cleaning. Second, I never strove to join the Communist Party. A few classmates came in as members, maybe as a result of being good sent-down youths before matriculation. Several became members in the course of four years. One day in my junior year, a Party member had a talk with me while we walked around the sports field. She said that since I was a good student and was always willing to help fellow students with their questions, I should draw close to the Organization (*xiang zuzhi kaolong*, which meant, besides behaving oneself, writing thought reports to the Party regularly, and applying for membership). But five years before I had "grown up" politically and started looking at politics and society with an analytical eye and was now ideologically as well as temperamentally unable to be the Party's "good son." Not wanting to antagonize the Organization, I wrote not a lengthy heart-to-heart to the Party but a one-page application, in which I tried to walk the fine line between uttering the expected platitudes and maintaining my integrity, something I had to repeat nineteen years later when writing the tenure statement at an American university. (In both cases I had to engage in subtle and not-so-subtle self-promotion, and in both cases I had to appear to be correct: in the former, ideologically; in the latter, professionally. One difference is that whereas the former is optional, the latter is mandatory, that is, if you want to keep your rice bowl.) Lucky for me that the Organization never tried to foster (*peiyang*) me again, and I carried on in my merry old ways.

There was much political agitation in the late '70s and early '80s: the famous Xidan Democracy Wall in Beijing, dissident Wei Jingsheng's arrest and trial, and the participation of self-nominated candidates in local People's Congress elections, to name a few headlines. Closer to home, more than once I saw a young man on a bike distributing a mimeographed newsletter on campus, which carried news of political crime cases, crimes committed by children of high-ranking officials, political jokes, etc. There was the election incident at the Teachers' College, of which Liang Heng (of *Son of the Revolution* fame) was one of the instigators. The story went that the college authorities had illegitimately removed the properly elected student representative to the local People's Congress and replaced him with a student cadre of the official student union. Protest speeches were followed by a hunger strike. During the hunger strike carried out in front of the provincial Party headquarters, students from my school and others lent their support. On the afternoon of October 15, 1980, I walked all the way to the strike location and back, just to see what it was like. That same evening, we had gone to bed when suddenly shouts of slogans came in from the street. We went out and it was a protest march from the Mining and Metallurgy Institute. Roused by the excitement students at my school spontaneously formed into a procession and followed the one from the institute. Student cadres led shouts of slogans, of which I only remember one: "Down with bureaucracy!" We must have also shouted about democracy, etc. Feeling a bit comical about shouting slogans in the streets in the middle of the night, I nonetheless walked with the procession all the way to the strike again. The place was as crowded as in the afternoon, with the strikers sitting or lying listlessly under the streetlights. A rumor had it that some strikers couldn't stand the hunger anymore and were secretly drinking milk from their military water flasks, which had been extremely popular during the Cultural Revolution. It was also said that some famous old writer had donated one hundred yuan on the spot, etc, etc. Since it was really late by now, I didn't hang around for long and walked back to campus.

At my department but not in my class, some students formed groups to help student candidates to run for the local People's Congress. Big-character posters were plastered all over the place announcing their views, the scene resembling that of the Cultural Revolution. I read some of the posters with a mixture of amusement and curiosity, and that was the extent of my nonparticipation.

Noon, November 4, 1979: A telegram came from home that my grandpa was critically ill. He had suffered another stroke and could die at any moment. I hurried home. He showed no sign that he recognized me. My parents and, in particular, my dad, had been caring for him. Old people have their idiosyncrasies and sick old people even more so. My grandpa, for example, several times a day asked my dad to remake his bed, saying that something was wrong with it, my dad's reassurances to the contrary to no avail. I gazed at Grandpa, my heart filled with sadness, remembering my prescient regret that I would no longer be able to ask him any questions about his life and the past.

On the morning of the 11th, seeing that Grandpa was in a stable condition, I went to mail a letter in which I asked a roommate to renew one of my journals, which I had forgotten to do. When I came home, I found Grandpa had died at 8:35 in my absence.

The city government was notified, a mourning hall was set up inside my parents' school, and Grandpa's old colleagues and friends were sent the grievous news. An obituary was composed in the name of the funeral committee, of which I made half a dozen copies with a writing brush and late in the evening biked around the city with my old friend Jixin pasting it at various crossroads. The vigil lasted two days and two nights. On the evening of the 12th, the coffin was to be closed. I stood beside it, looking at Grandpa's sunken face and thinking I would never ever see him again. Tears welled up and quietly ran down my face.

The next morning was the burial. At the head of the cortege, two rows of silver-haired men on canes tottered out of the gate of the school and slowed the traffic in the streets. As we turned onto Dongting Avenue, I glanced at the slightly weathered obituary on the wall, wondering what my life would be like without Grandpa. After the procession disbanded, my family and a few close friends rode the hearse to Grandpa's native village in Xitang. He was buried in the plot that had been chosen long before, on a hilltop by the road, overlooking an expanse of rice paddies and his village.

Grandma was relieved that she didn't have to deal with Grandpa's increasing petulance anymore; besides, her own health was also failing. Days were long, and so were the evenings. Mom told me that as soon as it became dark out, Grandma would ask her to turn on the TV, a black-and-white set that belonged to the school, even though at that time, there were hardly any entertaining programs. If only there had been half of today's channels!

Less than a year later, on September 29, 1980, another telegram came. I had told Grandma that I now had a girlfriend, and that usually meant we'd get married. Since Grandma had wanted to see the girl so that she could die with peace of mind, Ningnan and I took the 9:50 p.m. train and arrived home past midnight. We came up to her bedside and told her the girl standing in front of her was the one she had wished to see. She showed no sign that she was aware of her surroundings. The following day Grandma died around 4:40 a.m., with me dozing off and missing her last breaths. Vigil, then burial beside Grandpa. This time I didn't cry. On the way back from the funeral I curled up in the hay in the back of the truck, tossed around by the bumpy country road, the untimely autumnal wind hissing in my ears: I was enveloped in the darkness of the night, sad, exhausted, and chilled to the bone.

I met Ningnan, the first girl I was to date in my life, on June 2, 1980. (I withhold her last name here for her privacy's sake.) Ironically, if it hadn't been for another girl who was trying to court me with me totally in the dark by asking me questions on schoolwork, I would never have met Ningnan. This other girl had asked me to help her with her spoken English in the language lab, where she introduced me to Ningnan, who was a physics lab assistant studying for the entrance exam for the English course of TV University. Inexplicably, I thought—or, following Lichtenberg, it thought—"this girl isn't pretty enough to be my girlfriend." Inexplicable because I wasn't looking for a girlfriend at all, even though I had had a few suitors.

I agreed to help Ningnan prepare for her exam, so she came to Tom's office where I spent my evenings. One evening, in part due to the relatively late hour, I offered to walk her home. For the first time in my life, I talked strangely; I sounded to myself like a first-time lover. Her response sounded the same to me. Indeed, we started going out, about once a week, not more frequently, because I didn't want to be too distracted from my studies.

On the evening of June 14, we took a walk down to the bank of the Xiang River. It was balmy. Sitting at the edge of the bank, we were too absorbed in each other to relish the stars twinkling above or the waters shimmering below. With nobody else around I took her hand and guided it toward my fly. When she touched me, the sensation was indescribably wonderful. She was a bit shy, her fingers tentative, but she stayed there for a minute or two. Neither of us even knew about stroking, but being touched like that was heaven for me. I didn't dare to touch her.

A week later we spent a whole day together, visiting a friend in Changsha, the Martyrs' Park, and then the Orange Island in the middle of the Xiang River. Dusk came. We sat down on the grass and this time I made her feel wonderful with my fingers. And we forgot time. Around 1:30 a.m. we walked onto the bridge and sat down on one of the winding staircases. Half an hour later a young man walked toward us from the city's direction. "What if he harbors bad intentions toward us?" I thought to myself. In no time he started descending the staircase. I got an idea. When he came close to us, I raised my head and stared at him grimly with my big eyes. He didn't look at us straight in the face but my eyes kept fixed on him until he reached the bottom of the staircase. Soon he disappeared out of sight. Though he was probably just a guy returning home late, under the circumstances I congratulated myself for my quick thinking. We stayed there a couple of hours before walking back. It was about 4:30 a.m. when we came to our side of the river and we still didn't want to go home, so we lay down on a pile of construction rocks by the road, watching quietly the first rays of dawn slowly brightening the sky. Before long, early morning traffic started moving and we kissed one more time before heading home. It was past six when I returned to my dorm, just about when everybody else was getting up.

From then on, I visited her in her dorm room, we took walks up Mount Yuelu and down to the Xiang River, and later on her parents regularly invited me over for a meal. (Her father taught in the Department of Electrical Engineering, her mother at the grade school attached to the university.) I don't remember when or where we "did it" for the first time (except that it wasn't within three-and-a-half months of our first date) but we did quickly fall in love without saying so much to each other.

Two months later, my close friends in Changsha plus Yajun's elder brother Yafei and I gathered at the Mining and Metallurgy Institute. We went for a walk and it turned out their mission was to persuade me to break off with Ningnan. They argued that she showed a lack of self-cultivation in her interaction with others and that I should find someone better educated. Believing that this is a matter of the heart, or, in his words, "it's OK if it feels OK," Yueshan was the only one who didn't object to my relationship with Ningnan. Being for the first time in love, I turned a deaf ear to my friends. After they realized I wasn't going to listen to them, they accepted Ningnan as my girlfriend and we got together quite often. That wasn't the first time I'd received such advice. During the previous summer vacation, my cousin the ex–Cultural Revolution rebel had counseled me to use marriage as an opportunity to gain political capital. Priding myself on being above worldly considerations (*ziming qinggao*), I brushed off his advice.

Senior year quickly rolled around. For the graduation thesis, I decided to use the opportunity to read more literature instead of putting together some of the notes on sundry aspects of English I had collected over the years. Having noticed that English uses "twenty" to mean "many" (e.g., Beatrice in *Much Ado About Nothing*: "There's not one wise man among twenty that will praise himself.") and "*san*" (three) in Chinese doesn't always mean two plus one, I thought of the idea of comparing the figurative uses of English and Chinese numerals. Going through various sources, especially American short stories and classical Chinese poems and Chinese dictionaries, I collected hundreds of examples. As a result, I wrote a purely descriptive—that is, superficial—paper, without delving into the whys. Still, the examiner, Teacher Xie, was impressed, more by the collection of Chinese examples than by the English ones. Since it was handwritten, I handed in the only copy I had.

Now what would I do after graduation? I had a good chance of being kept by my school as an English instructor; after all, we had been admitted as a teacher-training class four years before. But I hadn't had enough school. So, what graduate program should I apply to? True, I'd been an English major, but I had spent most of my own time reading in the humanities and social sciences. I looked through the admissions catalogs and Wuhan University's sociology program seemed right for me, so I dug out the various books I had read and should read to prepare for the entrance examinations, including some sent by Tom, who had kindly sent me two boxes of books. This was mid-June 1981. About a week later, walking by the administration building I had the urge to go in and look at the admissions catalogs again. And lo I struck gold. The Institute of American Studies of the Chinese Academy of Social Sciences was admitting four graduate students. I thought American studies would enable me to make better use of my knowledge of English than would sociology, but at the time it had not occurred to me that my intellectual interests were too wide-ranging for me to go into a traditional discipline. To put it in terms I didn't learn till much later in the U.S., I would have to enter an *interdisciplinary* program.

The institute wanted to admit one student in each of the following areas: American foreign policy, American politics, American economy, and contemporary American society. I decided to go for the last, which looked more colorful and wide-ranging than the other three. The exam subjects were the same for the four areas: politics (i.e., Marxism, Leninism, and current Party policies), English, world history (modern), American history, American politics, and American economy, each exam lasting three hours. I quickly weighed my strengths and weaknesses: Politics and English I didn't need to study but all the other subjects I did. On the one hand, I hadn't taken a single course in the four substantive fields (my college transcript lists "American History," but that was a case of creative accounting: I was interpreting computer classes for Tom and the university let me skip the history class—actually taught by Tom's wife Suellen—as well as the regular English class; my grade for the former had nothing to do with American history but was based on my performance as an interpreter); on the other hand, I had read extensively, though unsystematically, in them, so what I had to do was to organize what I had read, read more with the exams in mind, take notes, and cram as much into my head in the next two-and-a-half months as possible.

What made the prospect of going to the institute doubly exciting for me was that the advisor of the future graduate student in American society would be Dong Leshan, a famous translator. Among other things, he had translated Snow's *Red Star Over China*, was the lead translator of William Shirer's *The Rise and Fall of the Third Reich*, and was one of the three scholars who had checked the accuracy of the translation of William Manchester's *The Glory and the Dream: A Narrative History of America, 1932–1972*, the Chinese version of the latter two works each running up to four volumes and close to 2,000 pages. Later, I would discover he'd also translated George Orwell's *1984* but that book was for internal circulation only (though enterprising readers could find the original).

Meanwhile, my deep admiration for Dong's translation skills didn't blind me to the problems in an article of his, published in the fifth issue of 1980 of *Fanyi tongxun* (Translators' Notes), which I subscribed to. Titled "Translation and Knowledge," the piece was a compilation of mistranslations he'd found in his wide-ranging reading. I learned specific pieces of information but nothing beyond that. His point was that to be a competent translator one has to be knowledgeable about the target society and culture, but the examples he gave concerned items some of which, as he acknowledged, even someone with his background and privilege had found puzzling. So, the question is, what is an ordinary poor translator to do to become more knowledgeable about, in this case, the U.S.? I especially objected to an example he gave at the end of the article. He said, "function" has a specific meaning in mathematics vis-à-vis its everyday meaning of "a characteristic activity" or "use," and if a translator hasn't studied math taught in English or hasn't even studied advanced math, then an error in translation will occur, and in mistranslating it in a piece on foreign relations, the error becomes a political one! I saw three problems: 1) he might have studied math taught in English but that was before 1949 in a missionary school, a condition unmet in the 1970s; 2) one doesn't have to study "higher mathematics" to learn about "function" in math—my generation, one that didn't grow up in the best of times in terms of formal education, for example, studied a lot about "functions" in lower math in middle school; 3) the "hat" or *maozi* of "political error" smacks of the type of Cultural Revolution rhetoric called *shanggang shangxian* or criticizing something from the higher plane of Party principle and two-line struggle. "Function" in math might have been the root meaning of its current use in foreign affairs talk, but it has come to refer to a situation in which one thing changes according to another or depends on another; a Chinese translator doesn't have to study math at all, let alone math taught in English, to grasp this meaning. This taught me that, what's the saying, even Homer nods.

I estimated my potential competitors. Students of English didn't worry me, nor did students in traditional disciplines such as history: the former would not be that strong in the subject areas, whereas the latter's English would compare unfavorably with mine. I was only afraid of students of international politics at such institutions as Peking University and Fudan University. I thought they would be strong in both English and the substantive areas. The fact that these were much more prestigious schools and were located in China's metropolitan centers whereas I hailed from a provincial backwater didn't even register in my mind.

To show the Institute of American Studies that I wasn't a typical English student, in my application I included a statement of what I'd been studying on my own. For maximum effect I broke it down to two parts. In part one I organized what I'd studied into six "courses": Marxism and Leninism, Philosophy, World History, American History, American Politics and Institutions, and American Economy. Under each I listed some of the books I'd read and briefly described the extent of my knowledge. This part couldn't include the dozens of books on international affairs and related subjects I'd read, so in part two I listed those under "Other Books on the United States," "Biographies of Foreign Leaders and Theorists," and "Other Books in Philosophy and the Social Sciences." The titles in the two parts added up to ninety-three. I ended with four of the ten journals I'd subscribed to during my college years.

The intense preparation didn't begin until I had returned from the trip to Huangshan. On July 24, I returned to Yueyang and set myself up in a room between two classrooms away from my family. Sleeping about four hours a day, for four weeks I was possessed (though I didn't forget to visit my friends at the fertilizer plant). Running short on time, I enlisted the help of my sister Xiaoling and my brother Huiwen: I asked them to copy the passages I had picked out of books and journal articles onto index card–sized pieces of paper for me to review.

The exams took place on September 12, 13, and 14 in a large classroom at the Teachers' College. The first exam was in English. A glance at the questions showed they were meant for non-English majors and hence a breeze. That afternoon's subject was politics, and I ran aground. Right after receiving the test paper, I felt dizzy and had to put my head down on the table and close my eyes. Scary thoughts raced through my mind: "It's over for me like *this*?! How hard I've worked for this day! Institute of American Studies. . . ." The guy sitting in front of me had a water flask, so I raised my hand for permission to ask the guy for a drink of water. I remained on the verge of breakdown for an eternal half hour before I finally collected myself. But then something else went awry. Answering one of the early questions I forgot a basic strategy of test taking: Don't spend too much time on one question! Remembering an involved journal article on the topic I got carried away and wrote way too long an answer, thus leaving even less of my already shortened time for the remainder of the test, which I had to hurry through.

Despite my scare the previous day, I got up at 5:30 the following day to do a bit of last-minute studying for the exams in American politics and American economy that day. Ditto for the final day of exams in world history and American history. For the exam in American history, when the time came to enter the exam room, I still hadn't finished reading the relevant part of the world history volume of the *China Great Encyclopedia*. So I decided to defer my entrance into the exam room for half an hour. Left alone in the classroom opposite the exam room, I tried to be calm while going through the remaining entries of the *Encyclopedia*. Taking my seat just before the allowed time ran out, I quickly glanced at the questions: Lo and behold, one of the short questions was on something I had just read, so I answered it first. After the ordeal was over, I took two days off—I needed to par-tee, par-tee!

You may wonder what were on those exams. The four subject tests had the same structure: several small questions of five points each followed by big ones of twenty points each. The test in American politics had a question on lobbyists and one on how Ford became the president, the one in American economy had questions on the Tokyo Round and the causes of the stagflation, "World History" had one on the early Soviet period, and "American History" asked about the WASP and the Civil War, among other things. My preparations were still insufficient, but in the perceptive words of Peter Ustinov, I had "injustice working in my favor": Since these were the first entrance exams of the institute, I had thought, there must be some questions on the obviously important topics in each area, and it was uncanny that I had guessed so many of the questions.

On September 20, I received a letter from the University of Alabama at Birmingham admitting me to its MBA program. Tom had managed to get me admitted with an assistantship. The letter said that even though I had not submitted any test scores (TOEFL and GMAT), it was a special opportunity to have a student from the People's Republic of China (China and the United States had only established diplomatic relations in 1979 after three decades of hostility), and I could make up the GMAT in the States. Business was far from my cup of tea, but one doesn't pass up an opportunity to study in the United States, then or now, and nobody could guess the results of the exams for the Institute of American Studies, so I set about getting permission from my school to go to the States. Having had pretty good relations with the university authorities, I paid the president and several other administrators a visit. They all seemed supportive, although in the process I heard the president had a small grudge: when I served as his interpreter at the farewell meeting of the Wisconsin delegation, I made him turn back a page so that I could translate a long sentence accurately. (I had in fact translated his speech beforehand, but not knowing I could simply have read from my prepared translation, I looked at the president's text at the meeting.) I then remembered that when I interpreted for the president at the reception of a delegation from Northeastern University, I had worn my denim work clothes—though freshly washed—from the fertilizer plant, which also might have irked him. Ningnan's mother being very good at using connections to get things done accompanied me on all these visits. Meanwhile, life went on and I had my thesis to write, which took about a month.

On November 26, the day after I handed in my thesis, which was also the day our American teacher Mariana taught her last class, the secretary of the section sent word that a lady from the Institute of American Studies was here to see me! I was told to go to the hotel in the city where the lady was staying to take yet another test.

Hardly able to contain my excitement, I found the hotel in midafternoon. The lady from Beijing (I imagine a movie title as I write this) told me I could call her Teacher Tian. (She was actually in charge of personnel at the institute, not a research fellow or advisor.) The institute had decided to select two students from Beijing and two from the rest of the country. She had arrived from Sichuan where she had seen the first candidate from the provinces (if Beijing be Paris) and was going on to Shandong and Shanghai to see the other two. In other words, I had a fifty-fifty chance of being selected. She asked me how I thought I'd done on the six tests. I said that I'd done poorly on the politics test, in part because I'd felt dizzy during the test, and that I hadn't done well in world history, either. After the interview, it was time for the final written test, an essay in English on why I chose to pursue American studies. She left me in the room, while she retired into another. Before she left, she said the director of the institute liked concise essays; "Just my style," I thought.

Teacher Tian wanted to see my school and to talk to my department about my conduct. The next day, I brought my girlfriend when I went to meet her at the bus stop (not a smart move, I was to find out later). Teacher Tian needed to leave the next day but at this time Changsha was the site of some national conference and no train tickets were available. She asked me for help, which—without my knowing it—was a godsend. Through Ningnan's mom, I sought out a cadre with connections to the Railway Bureau. This cadre worked in a department of the provincial government but lived in the same "village" as Ningnan's parents did. I went to this cadre's office and obtained a seatless ticket. Teacher Tian was favorably impressed: This kid not only knows his books but also can get things done. I went to the train station to see her off. The train was so crowded that there was hardly any standing room. At least Teacher Tian traveled light. Before we parted, she gave me her umbrella, saying that I could bring it when I came to Beijing. "Does this mean she has chosen me as one of the two successful candidates from the provinces? Why else would she leave me the umbrella, though, sure, the train was a jam?" I couldn't help but wonder on my way home from the train station.

Since I had just completed my thesis, I had told Teacher Tian about it the previous day and she had suggested that I send a copy to Beijing. I obliged by borrowing my thesis from Teacher Xie and copying it with a pen.

Almost four weeks passed with no word from Beijing. Meanwhile, graduation was fast approaching. I decided to call to find out. Imagine my excitement when I was told that I had been admitted! Four days later, my school received a telegram from Beijing that I'd been admitted to the Graduate School of the Chinese Academy of Social Sciences, mine being the very last notice of graduate admissions received by my university.

I returned to Yueyang to tell my family about my plan to get married before I left for Beijing as well as the news about graduate school. My parents—my mom especially—were against the former. They said that I shouldn't get married when I was about to start graduate school, that I should concentrate on my studies. Plus, there was the problem of living in two places (*liangdi fenju*). I argued that if I were to marry some famous actress, they would certainly not oppose it; and that yes, we would be living in two places, but eventually the leaders in Beijing would have to solve her residence-status problem. Two days later I returned to Changsha to go through graduation orientation. On January 12, 1982, Ningnan and I got our marriage license. On the 18th we went back to Yueyang. My parents had prepared a room for the newlyweds with the customary "double happiness" sign on both the front door and the door to the new room. I joked that this was *dongfang huazhu ye* (the nuptial chamber illumined with painted candles on wedding night) combined with *jinbang timing shi* (success in the civil service examination at the highest level in imperial China).

At sunset I went with my brother Huiwen to the school's well to take a shower in the open air despite the subzero temperature. Mom tried to stop me, and I said, "I'm getting married today; how can I not wash myself clean!" "You are being silly." Mom liked to say I'd never grow up.

As if she needed proof. The next day Ningnan and I went to visit some friends. Suddenly I remembered that I had left my used condom from the previous night hanging over the headboard. We hurried home but the damage had been done. My parents were entertaining two guests in our room, colleagues from their school, one of whom being a vice-principal and a sister of one of my classmates at college. Ningnan went in, grabbed the thing, and came right out, without saying so much as a hello, and we went out again immediately. As for the wedding banquet, we had a small one at home, with three guests. Ningnan being very capable and diligent did the cooking herself. There were no rings, no wedding ceremony, and no pictures taken.

7. Self-Taught America Hand

After receiving the admission letter from Beijing, I wrote to Tom that I would go to Beijing instead of America. The city, the unit, and the subject matter I was going to study: I couldn't imagine a better future. My heart would race at the thought of receiving instruction from some of the best scholars in the country and of being in constant intellectual excitement as an America watcher. I assumed that a research fellow at the Institute of American Studies (IAS) would have plenty of opportunities to visit the United States. Indeed, Teacher Tian had told me that at any time half of IAS's fellows were doing research in America.

The Graduate School of the Chinese Academy of Social Sciences (CASS) turned out to be inside a middle school in a western suburb, not far from the Yuquan Avenue bus or subway stop. The Graduate School had two two-story buildings: one primarily administrative, the other mostly residential. I found my room on the second floor of the first building with six sets of furniture: a bed, a desk with a chair, and a large metal bookshelf. The room was spacious with a large window facing the door. Fan Tining, a Beijing native and fellow student of IAS, was the only roommate in, and he immediately offered to help me with my baggage left at a hotel the previous evening. On the bus both of us were full of anticipation about the institute and our studies, and we also talked briefly about our backgrounds. Lao (Old) Fan, as we would call him, was ten years older than me. He had spent a decade at the Great Northern Wilderness as a sent-down youth. Despite the long years in the countryside, he got into Peking University (Beida, for short) as a history student when universities reopened for regular admissions in 1977. When he registered to take the entrance examinations for IAS in '81, he barely fell within the age limit of thirty-five. But there he was, at thirty-five, ready to plunge into another three years of studying at a cold window (*hanchuang*), as an old Chinese phrase describes the life of hardworking students.

This being the first time I'd set foot in the capital, I went to see the heart of the city the next day, a Sunday: Tiananmen Square, the Forbidden City, and Wangfujing, the busiest shopping street in Beijing. Everything was big—the Square, the Palace, and the department stores on Wangfujing. The immenseness of the square made even the large weekend crowd small pockets, absent the thronging streams of weekday bicycles flowing unceasingly on Chang'an Boulevard. The February air was crisp, the sandy spring winds yet to come. Wangfujing being much narrower than Chang'an Boulevard was the most crowded street I'd seen, with tired tourist shoppers sitting in front of stores and squatting along the curbs. I soon discovered that Beijing cuisine was too bland for my Hunan palate; besides, there was only one leafy vegetable in winter, napa cabbage.

Monday morning we formed classes according to our fields of study. My class had eleven students, all studying some international subject: four in American studies, two in Japanese studies, and five in international economics. We were six boys plus five girls, who lived downstairs. The third IAS student was Ren Yue from Shandong, also an English major in college. The fourth was Zhao Yujiang, the second IAS student from Beijing; she too had studied English in college and had been an interpreter at some central government office. Zhao Yujiang chose American economy as her specialization, while Lao Fan and Ren Yue both ended up with American politics; the advisor for American foreign policy somehow didn't work out.

My other roommates all came from Beijing. Ji Tingxu was admitted to the Institute of Japanese Studies, studying Japanese politics; both Mao Xiaowei and Liu Zhaobin were students of the Institute of World Economy and Politics. (The political tail was usually dropped, similar to the case of London School of Economics.) Both Zhaobin and Xiao (Little or Young) Ji (though he was a few years older than me) had been language students, clearly showing the importance of a foreign language as a gateway to other fields.

Monday through Thursday of the orientation week were filled with meetings, including the opening convocation at the auditorium of the Museum of History, at which a vice-president of CASS gave a nonmemorable speech. What I do remember from these four days is an incident involving a student in Russian and Soviet literature. This guy was already an assistant research fellow—equivalent to lecturer at a Chinese university and assistant professor in the States—at his institute. He became a grad student presumably for the degree rather than the education and in fact got the highest total score of all the candidates for his institute. He was twice late for the orientation meetings, at which administrators seemed to treat the new students a bit like grade school kids. The rumor was that he'd been told to clean up his act or else, and he decided that he didn't have to put up with this nonsense. He withdrew from the Graduate School and returned to his institute.

We were scheduled to have our institute orientation on Friday. Since the Graduate School exercise was hardly stirring, I couldn't wait to go to my institute to meet with the fellows, above all, my advisor the first-rate translator I'd known through his publications. Just as the Graduate School was at a temporary location, so was IAS homeless. At this time the institute was housed in a posh military hotel that I was told cost ninety yuan a room a day, which of course only the government could afford. The institute occupied one wing of one floor of the hotel.

The four of us were taken into a cozy, small room at the end of the hallway. A few of the fellows who were there that day (most of the time they worked at home) including my advisor came in to meet us and then left the room. My advisor, Dong Leshan, was not tall, of median build, and wore glasses. His smile and movements seemed typical of a genteel scholar. The director, Li Shenzhi, on the other hand, looked more distinguished. Tall with a receding hairline and an occasional hearty laugh, he exuded presence and a sense of self-importance: you could tell he was the boss. He told us a bit about himself. He used to work in journalism and like numberless others had suffered during the tumultuous years of political campaigns. When denied access to the internally distributed publications about the world outside China available only to the political elite, he developed a knack for reading between the lines of regular news sources and filled a desk drawer with index cards full of revealed information as a result of his code-breaking. This reminded me of the similar intellectual-cum-political acrobatics described in Solzhenitsyn's *Cancer Ward* I had just read two months before. He said he was giving us the small-stove treatment (*kai xiaozao*, or special mess, a treatment in the military only high-ranking officers could enjoy). The director said that the foreign policy section of the Party Secretary General Hu Yaobang's report at the recent Party Congress had been penned "by your director" (instead of "by me"). He also mentioned that the actual power hierarchy at the top was not what seemed to the public, with Chen Yun (the old economic planner) being No. 2 and Hu Qiaomu (the Party's theory authority) being No. 4. The director had been present when top American delegates went to Beijing and had talks with Chinese leaders. As for his tips on how to become a good America watcher, he said that Chinese is the foundation of other skills; a good scholar must be good at Chinese. Which didn't sound strange to me at all, because back in '74 I had offered the same piece of advice to my neighbor's grandson.

Then we briefly introduced ourselves. When it was my turn, still feeling high under the influence of the director's ebullient though measured talk, I said that I had gotten married before going to Beijing, which should enable me to concentrate on my studies even better. Unbeknown to me, I'd dropped a bomb.

My advisor's office was a few rooms away, across the hallway. During our short conversation, Teacher Dong said that working as a researcher meant a willingness to sit on a cold bench (echoing the old cold-window metaphor) for years on end. I said that that wouldn't be a problem for me. Then without a word he disappeared, leaving me alone in the room. Minutes passed. I waited but he still didn't come back. After a while I decided to leave the room to find out what had happened. (I didn't have the presence of mind then to wonder whether *that* meant a test of my ability to sit on a cold bench.) I found out, to my crushing disappointment, that my advisor had taken a shower (at that time no hot showers were available at people's homes) and then gone home. Without a word to me, his student who was still waiting in his office?

Strangely, the following week Teacher Tian had a short talk with me at the institute, asking me whether I had any interest in studying American foreign policy, adding that the field required great mental agility. Its sexiness made me faintly dizzy but I regained my bearings moments later. I said to Teacher Tian that foreign policy is too much guesswork; who knows what's really going on behind doors, whereas society is much more tangible. (I should have known that in society, too, there is a great deal of difference between what appears to be going on and what's really happening: What is really happening in an organization or in society at large is rarely talked or written about.) While I was saying this to her, my mind flew to the never seen United States and imagined myself immersed in its variegated forms of life, especially its seedier ways. Teacher Tian didn't say a word to sway me one way or the other but simply acknowledged my sense of the matter. Forty-one years later, I suddenly realized the only explanation of Teacher Tian's offer is Teacher Dong wanted to wash his hands of me.

Later on, my roommate Liu Zhaobin, who had graduated from Beijing Second Foreign Languages Institute, told me he had been in a class about journalism and translation taught by Dong Leshan. At the first class the classroom was bursting with students: like me they'd also been attracted to him by his fame and achievements as a translator. To the students' disappointment, Teacher Dong put his feet high up on the lectern, leaned back in his chair, and spoke from behind a newspaper without so much as looking at the students. By the second class the classroom was no longer full. The rumor was, as reliable as rumors go, that he was disgruntled at the school for not promoting him to full professorship. (The bio written by his son in lieu of the preface to his collected writings edited by Li Hui after his death seems to confirm the rumor.) At any rate, exhilarated at being able to study there I quickly recovered from the shock of the meeting. Still, every time I thought about it or talked to friends about it, I felt upset. At other times I thought that no matter what, I should be grateful to him for insisting on admitting students from outside Beijing; otherwise, I would not be there at all.

Before long it became clear that my offense was to have gotten married, which, due to my wife's residence problem, must have greatly disappointed the institute. I was told that some of IAS's fellows and the director had wanted to admit all four students from Beijing, their rationale being an unfair though understandable one. They figured that the entering class of '77 were older, some even much older, than the usual cohort that go directly from middle school to college. Being older meant that they would likely have family, which meant living at two places, which in turn meant problems for the future fellow and the institute. (In other words, the institute had no power to help its fellows' spouses get Beijing residency.) Other fellows—especially my advisor—argued that they should admit the best candidates, no matter where they came from. The compromise was two from Beijing and two from the provinces.

Teacher Tian told me that, after seeing me with my girlfriend in Changsha, she thought (and apparently shared her thoughts with the institute) that I was a smart young man and wouldn't marry right before I was to leave for the capital and that with time I'd forget my girlfriend. She added that it wasn't as much of a problem in Ren Yue's case. He also had a girlfriend, but Mu Aili was a graduate student in English and so it would be far easier to change her residence from Jinan to Beijing. (Indeed, Aili was assigned to Foreign Affairs College upon graduation.)

In my subsequent meetings with Teacher Dong, which after the first semester occurred about once a semester or less frequently, I said nothing about my marriage or the strange meeting between us on that Friday. Neither did he.

Besides housing and feeding us, the Graduate School offered common courses in Marxism, foreign languages, and mathematics. The first category was probably the most thorough of all the graduate curricula in the country, with us being under the leadership of CASS, which served as the central leadership's think tank and the country's ideological tone-setter. It had three components: Marxist philosophy, Marxist political economy, and scientific socialism. The main text for the first course was Engels's *Anti-Dühring*, whose main doctrines had been regurgitated several times in our previous politics classes but which contained elements hard to follow; for example, to get a grip on the discussion on time, I even consulted analytical philosophy, and told the class that I didn't quite understand it. For political economy, we were assigned volume one of Marx's *Capital*. I spent fifteen days poring over the text then three days on an exegetical work, as *Capital* was one of the main texts of Marx I hadn't studied. Come exam time, a group of students met outside by the sports field pooling their wisdom for the closed-book final, a sign that the course wasn't taken seriously. When we got to scientific socialism, even the school was lackadaisical about it: there was no serious content but some materials on current Party policies.

As for foreign languages, we were supposed to study two. After a few class periods the school gave us a test; as a result, former English majors were exempted from the English course. Since I had taken three semesters' Russian in college, I picked Russian again for my second foreign language. But as in college, I never got really interested in the language, despite Soviet Union's geopolitical importance, which had prompted me to study Russian in the first place. I merely went through the motions for two semesters.

Math was only required of students of economics. But with so few classes to attend, I thought, "Why not study a little math?" I lacked the motivation to devote the time necessary to learning the material but I greatly enjoyed watching others do math, so I audited two math classes: Linear Algebra, and Probability and Statistics. Over the summer, I studied a bit of calculus, first on my own, then tutored by one of Ningnan's colleagues in physics.

My advisor didn't teach me a single class or tutorial. As far as I knew, this wasn't unusual at CASS, because fellows were all busy with their own research and we were expected to teach ourselves with all that time on our hands. Since my concentration was contemporary American society, it seemed to me I ought to study a bit of sociology beyond the haphazard way I had read in it and various other social science disciplines. When I mentioned this to Teacher Dong at our second meeting on March 24, he became flustered and muttered that he couldn't offer any tutorials in sociology. But I wasn't suggesting that he teach me the subject, knowing well that he was a topnotch translator and had a lot of what he called *zaxue* (miscellaneous learning) but not a social scientist. I merely wanted to tell him that I would like to study the subject myself. On June 14 I reported to Teacher Dong on what I'd been studying the first semester and my future plans. I said that I'd like to get some instruction in inferring connections among material conditions, attitudes or values, and behavior. I gave the example of the first half of an old Chinese saying, "*yizhou-yifan, dang si laichu buyi*" (in taking a mouthful of porridge or rice you should bear in mind that its production is not easy), and how shortage of food in the old days must have given rise to this saying and the behavior of picking up dropped rice from the table. I then contrasted it with the contemporary American attitude that food served people and one would dump the leftovers without qualms as long as one had enough to eat. (I was ignorant of the use of the doggy bag.) I had in the back of my mind my Grandpa's grumble to my Grandma that she always insisted that we finish what was in the bowl, calling her attitude, "*ningke wang ren, buke sheng fan*" (rather stuff yourself to death than waste rice). And I said the American attitude toward food had to do with its abundance. Teacher Dong said nothing.

What might be unusual was Teacher Dong gave me very little guidance of any kind, the only concrete help he offered being, after a year-long visit to the States (his visit might have been longer) during my first and second years of residence, giving me a copy of C. Wright Mills's *The Power Elite*, suggesting that I read as many of his writings as possible. Teacher Tian must have been aware of the situation. For the first semester, she suggested that I attend the lecture class on American government and one on American foreign policy given by a visiting Chinese-American professor at Beida. So twice a week Lao Fan and I went to Beida. The second semester Teacher Tian suggested that I audit Beida's sociology and anthropology classes, which I also did. The sociology course was a dud, but the anthropology class was more engaging, consisting of lectures by a series of teachers, beginning with the old physical anthropologist Professor Lin Yaohua, who had been trained in the West before 1949. One teacher even told us things that needed to be hushed up, having to do with how the government had dealt with an ethnic minority. Since there was so much free time, I also audited the two-semester course, History of World Economic Thought, at my own school, hearing quite a few leading scholars on their own specialty.

During the commute between Beida and my own school, I had the only literary urge during those years. One day, at a bus stop, a woman asked me for directions to a place. Unfortunately, I didn't know the answer. Minutes later I got on the bus. Then I remembered how to get to the place the woman had asked me about. Without getting off the bus and turning back to inform the woman, I nonetheless fantasized about doing so, imagining when I returned to the earlier stop, the woman had gone. I thought, "This could be the beginning of a short story," and remembered "A & P" by John Updike. In Updike's story, three girls went into a supermarket in bathing suits and were told off by the manager. The narrator, a nineteen-year-old checker in the store who found one of the girls very attractive, was upset about the manager's attitude toward them and quit his job right then and there. When he went out to catch up with the girls, they had disappeared.

At the Graduate School, IAS did provide lecture classes such as History of Sino-U.S. Relations and American Economy. No reading was required, nor were there any exams, at least not for me, who was not specializing in either area. The only class that required a paper at the end was American History, a seminar given by Yang Shengmao, who was a professor at Nankai University in Tianjin and affiliated with IAS.

Most of my time was spent reading on my own, from American textbooks—some sent by Tom—on world history, American history, sociology, cultural anthropology, social problems, and sociological theory to Chinese books on the United States and a host of other subjects to American, Chinese, and European novels to Western philosophy. Much time was also spent in the reading room on our floor, where both foreign language journals and the highly informative *Reference Material* (*Cankao ziliao*) were housed with other restricted Chinese journals. The big brother of the more easily available *Reference News* (*Cankao xiaoxi*), *Reference Material* was a compendium of translations of selected pieces from newspapers and magazines published all over the world. It came out every day, sometimes twice a day, ranging from sixty to ninety pages. Thinking like a self-appointed intelligence officer, for much of the three years I perused that publication and occasionally its subject counterparts such as *Reference Material on World Economy* and took hundreds of pages of densely packed notes and made bundles of note cards.

The Graduate School also provided several newspapers for each room: *People's Daily*, *Chinese Youth*, *Guangming Daily*, and *Reference News*. Of these, *Guangming Daily* regularly carried lengthy theoretical articles in economics, philosophy, and so on. I read most of these, thinking that a good America watcher should also be an informed China watcher. In fact, I was intensely interested in how foreign commentators—academic or otherwise—saw contemporary China, and took copious notes on my readings. Newspaper clippings—some had been from my college years—were stuffed into large manila paper bags by subject: American politics, American economy, China, etc. (Tom also sent me clippings from the States.) On August 1, 1983, I began a daily log of important news and analyses, which ended on December 12 and page 136 of my notebook, when it became tiresome for me.

One benefit of studying in the nation's capital was the many opportunities to attend lectures by foreign scholars. Some spoke at IAS, others elsewhere. The big names from the States included Seweryn Bialer of Columbia, Robert Dahl of Yale, and Gabriel Almond of Stanford. However, I don't remember any *ideas* from their lectures. One idea or provocative observation I do remember did not come from a visiting American academic heavyweight but from an ethnology conference at another CASS institute. There a CASS fellow spoke about his recent visit to America, during which he had found racism to be very strong among Chinese Americans. For example, there was little interracial marriage between Chinese-Americans and blacks and the former commonly harbored racial prejudices against the latter. In China, official pronouncements always pointed to racism as one of America's major social problems.

Among the prominent Chinese scholars who lectured to us were philosophers Li Zehou, who talked about cultural psychology with respect to China's national characteristics, and Xing Bensi, whose speech touched on the Frankfurt School among other things. A theater scholar spoke of semiotics. Out of curiosity I also went to a class in history of Western philosophy when the Hegel scholar Zhang Shiying was to teach that day.

The school's credit system, a result of mimicking American higher education practices, was more nominal than real in that the duration of all the master's programs was three years. In my peculiar case, when the final year rolled around, I only had the credits from the common courses plus American history. Teacher Tian again was helpful. She asked me to make a list of the courses I had studied on my own and present some written work to Teacher Dong for evaluation, so I put down Sociology, Cultural Anthropology, Western Sociological Theory, Survey of American Society and Culture, and Studies in Social Problems in the U.S. as my courses. I gave Teacher Dong a detailed report on what I'd been studying, including a list of the books I'd read and the subjects my notes and newspaper clippings had covered. The latter included China—politics, foreign affairs, economy, foreign analyses, history, philosophy, literature, and society; the U.S. — politics, economy, foreign affairs, literature, and society; European economy; Japan — economy and politics; the Middle East; the U.S.S.R. — politics, economy, foreign affairs, and foreign analyses; Eastern Europe — economy, foreign affairs, and foreign analyses; world economy; sociology; anthropology; and recent developments in science and technology. As for papers, one piece was "Chance Gleanings of Mistranslations" (Wu yi ou shi), collected from mostly literary translations, such as Saul Bellow's *Humboldt's Gift*, Herman Wouk's *War and Remembrance*, the screenplay of *It Happened One Night*, and a volume of American songs. The second piece was a paper on China's population problems, based on my reading of various journal articles on the topic. The third paper analyzed the concept of deviance, and the final piece sketched out my thoughts on the etiology of drug abuse in the U.S., as an exercise for the thesis. Besides, I translated excerpts from American textbooks in sociology, cultural anthropology, and sociological theory. I got the credits. This was the second help Teacher Dong gave me.

In contrast to college, at CASS my studies became more academic and slightly more systematic. But I remained an innocent student in that I didn't think about producing scholarship, nor did I harbor any scholarly, let alone political, ambitions. Just more reading, more note-taking. Meanwhile, unlike some other students, such as my next-door neighbors Li Anshan (now a professor at Beida) and Wu Enyuan (now a fellow at CASS), who studied well past midnight, I went to bed at around 11 (and at times annoyed my roommates with my radio English: there were as yet no earplugs). On Sundays all the Beijing natives went home. I went into the city from time to time, mostly to bookstores, but sometimes I pined for entertainment. Having enjoyed Chaplin's movies, I wandered from one movie theater to another looking for his movies, just so I could see them again. Speaking of movies, there was some foreign cinema available to privileged Beijingers. The Graduate School being a unit with some cachet, we occasionally enjoyed this privilege. Once, we went to the Film Institute to watch the 007 flick, *From Russia, with Love*. Another time we were shown two Russian movies with breathtaking country vistas at the Beijing Foreign Languages Institute. Yet another time videos of *Mandingo* and *Apocalypse Now* were shown at a Navy auditorium. The TV drama, *The Winds of War*, was shown at Foreign Affairs College. Most memorable were the film retrospectives that featured, for one, good old British films such as *The Bridge on the River Kwai*, and for another, Italian films such as *The Bicycle Thief*. I liked them so much that I saved the booklets from these festivals. Alas, we were only given one to two tickets to these retrospectives; what I wouldn't have given to be able to watch them all! While in college, when new Chinese movies were shown in the sports field, I often stayed in the dorm listening to the songs from the Indian movie,

The Wanderer's Song. Now in Beijing, I found myself reading screenplays of foreign movies and biographies of Western movie stars such as Ingrid Bergman and Vivian Leigh. And I wasn't the only one who was into Western movies. My next-door neighbor Wang Chaoguang, though a student of Republican China, was a Hollywood movie buff and talked about Clark Gable and Cary Grant as if enumerating family heirlooms. We also went to the People's Art Theater to see Arthur Miller's *The Death of a Salesman* and Lao She's *The Teahouse*.

Another change from college was I could no longer hang out with my old friends on a weekly basis. Ruijun returned to Yueyang after graduation, working as an engineer in a lathe factory; his brother Ruidan went on to grad school at his own institute in Changsha; Yueshan was assigned to a new university outside Nanchang. Yajun did go north, to Nankai University as a grad student in economics, so we could only visit each other once in a while. Fortunately, Laya, my friend from Yueyang and our precollege days, came to the Institute of Economics. For lack of space some of his class had to stay in a hotel not far from the school. We saw each other often and took long walks along Chang'an Boulevard and in nearby parks.

Yueshan came to see me a few times, and on his first visit he brought an anthology of Shen Congwen's stories. Shen came from western Hunan and his stories depicted in raw and vivid strokes the brutalities of old mores, the exotic customs of love and courtship of lads and lasses, and the simple joys and hardships of the rural folk in his native land. I immediately fell in love with the author, whose innocence and compassion endeared him to me more than did Qian Zhongshu's wit, wisdom, and erudition. I gave Yueshan my copy of Milovan Djilas's *The Unperfect Society*.

At the Graduate School, as the only out-of-towners in our room Ren Yue and I got to hang out together on weekends. He not only made me realize I'd mispronounced Herbert von Karajan's name when reading a *Time* magazine piece out loud, but would go out of his way to help me more than once. In summer '83, both Aili and Ningnan came to visit; the four of us climbed the Great Wall, even eating our home-cooked lunch right there on the Wall. Xiao Ji, Lao Fan, and Zhaobin all invited the rest of us to their home for a meal in the final year of our studies. Next door there was Lao Li, who like me came from Hunan but was studying African history. His gentleness and humor made it always a pleasure to be with him. Once, we took the same train home. At the train station, I left my heavy baggage with him, while I went back out to get some of Beijing's famous preserved fruits. I was so unhurried that when I returned to the station, the train was about to leave. I ran in and had to jump on when the train started moving. I threaded my way through to our car, where he greeted me with his disarming smile, without a word of complaint.

On the same floor at the Graduate School lived Zhu Yuelin, also a Hunanese. He had studied physics in college and was now studying philosophy of science. He had conducted his college's orchestra and occasionally wrote poetry as well as music. I didn't find out all this about him until one evening he and I were standing on the terrace and started talking. Later Hu Yafei joined us. A fellow IAS student in American literature, like Yuelin she had entered the Graduate School in fall '82. She was a friend of Yuelin's, apparently drawn to him by his intensity. The three of us sat there: Yuelin talked about his years in Changsha working at a foundry, I about my years growing up in the country. Having grown up in Beijing, Yafei must have found our tales exotic; she sat through the night with us till dawn, hardly saying a word.

Fellow students had various ways to break the monotony of full-time study. Some had badminton matches. One evening, a few students ran out into the sports field in a thunderstorm, getting soaked from head to toe. Another time, there was a bet to see who dared to run naked from their own room to the washroom down the hallway. And of course, they cooked.

On our floor, four to five students had kerosene stoves outside their door, on which they cooked an occasional dish whether there was a guest or not. The cooks were from Hunan except Lao Wu, who was from Sichuan. Given our spartan conditions, we couldn't be fancy. In my case, I only cooked stir-fried potatoes and omelets.

We even had a food uprising. For reasons that now escape me, the food at our mess hall got quite bad. What did the students do? Being good with the pen, in this case, the writing brush, and having grown up during the Cultural Revolution, they put up big-character posters protesting to the school authorities about the food, demanding improvement. As a result, the mess hall added evening snacks, including dumplings boiled and pan-fried, different types of noodles, and other treats. Around 8 or 9, we would treat ourselves to a delicious snack.

Now you may wonder about our financial situation. Thanks to the socialist state, our stipend was 90 percent of a college graduate's salary. At the time, a college graduate made fifty yuan, so we got forty-five yuan, which was a handsome income. Plus free tuition and fees, free health care, free room, and free newspapers.

Of course, our life had its vicissitudes. A classmate was criticized for having spent a night with her Hong Kong boyfriend in Guangzhou, making one wonder about the degree of such surveillance at the time. I sympathized with her and expressed my annoyance at the authorities' attitude toward the matter; why, it wasn't their business. Another student was caught stealing books at a bookstore; yet another, stealing glances at women breast-feeding their babies at a hospital. The sex problem for single students was something nobody talked about. Technically some of us weren't single, and yet our separation from our spouses meant we lived like monks and nuns—I didn't hear of any hanky-panky between schoolmates. As for me, I missed my wife dearly, and we wrote each other regularly. In my letters I expressed my longing for her in mildly erotic language and varied the salutations. When once I thought about going for an outing with a fellow female student, I tried to justify it in my own mind. Luckily, I had by then learned how to comfort myself, under the blanket, when lights were out or when I was alone. The bad part was there were no visual aids; three years of using my imagination hardly expanded it.

Both my wife and I were at a school, so we could or could only meet during summer and winter breaks. I went back to see her and my parents and siblings, and she also came to Beijing, first briefly in the summer of '82 then in the summers of '83 and '84. A month or so before her first visit, out of the romantic devotion of a newlywed, I began saving rice coupons for her. Back then food was still on rations and Beijing residents had more flour coupons than rice coupons. To save up more rice coupons for her visit I refrained from eating rice and ate only flour several weeks in a row, a sacrifice for a southerner like me. When I told her what I'd done, she said I was silly.

The third time Ningnan went to Beijing she became so sick that she had to stay in the hospital for three weeks. Inconsiderate and careless, I got her pregnant. As she had taken too many drugs, the pregnancy had to be terminated. But the doctors were unwilling to perform the procedure due to the potential risks involved. We were at our wits' end when she thought of the idea of seeking help at No. 301 Hospital, a military hospital nearby that reputedly treated high-ranking officials as well as the rank and file. The hospital only treated patients in the military and civilians on contract. "If I plead with them, maybe they'll help me," Ningnan hoped. When she emerged from the hospital with the good news, I felt a great burden had been removed from my shoulders, deeply grateful to the doctors at No. 301 Hospital and very impressed with Ningnan's ability to get things done. The procedure was done a week later with no complications.

Since I could only see Ningnan twice a year, every visit was full of anticipation. Every time when the overnight train was a few hours away from Changsha, I would imagine seeing her again, how I would kiss her and caress her, and my body would react. Once, I went home without warning to surprise her. Unfortunately, she stayed at her parents' place that night and was startled to find a man in her bed early next morning.

Of the three years of study the final year was allotted to writing a thesis. In reading about social problems in America, I became interested in drug abuse. Specifically, I wanted to sort out the various causal explanations for drug abuse, because scholars typically presented their own idea either as *the* explanation or as a better explanation than existing ones, whereas I thought different explanations addressed different aspects of the issue.

This was the formal beginning of my attention to both the conceptual or methodological questions and substantive ones concerning an issue. In this case, to figure out the whys of drug abuse, the researcher must not only look into drug abuse itself but also think carefully about the concept of cause. While reading philosophical and sociological analyses of causation, I searched for the literature on drug abuse. I wrote to my old friend Tom in the States, who most helpfully sent me a box of books borrowed from libraries. Meanwhile, I went to the main libraries in Beijing, including Beida Library and Beijing Library.

Then we learned that we could take one research trip funded by the school. So Lao Fan, Ren Yue, and I decided to travel together to some of the main institutions and libraries in the country. From mid-April through mid-May 1984, we went south then east. Lao Fan returned early to Beijing but Ren Yue and I continued the journey. We visited Zhongshan University in Guangzhou, which had one of the few sociology departments (with its own library) in the country; Nanjing University, including its Department of History, Foreign Languages Institute, and the new Nanjing-Hopkins Center; Fudan University in Shanghai, where we stayed for five days and visited Fudan's law and international politics libraries, Shanghai University's sociology department, the Party School, Shanghai Foreign Languages Institute, Shanghai Academy of Social Sciences, and Shanghai Library; Shandong University, Ren Yue's undergraduate school, which had both a literature institute and an American literature institute. From there I traveled to Nankai University in Tianjin where Yajun was and where there was a sociology department with its own reference room as well as a good university library. I took notes, made photocopies, and looked through lots of material; usually, a relevant book had never been checked out before. Along the way, we did some sightseeing, including a side trip to Mount Lu, accompanied by none other than Yueshan, whose university was a few hours away by train.

In reading through the books and articles, I arrived at a scheme for sorting out the various causes of drug abuse. In brief, at the microlevel abuse of different types of drugs may not have the same reason or cause (*yuanyin* for both in Chinese), people of different socioeconomic backgrounds may have different reasons for abusing a certain drug, and different stages of drug abuse may have different causes. At the macrolevel I raised two questions: 1) why did drug abuse become such a prominent problem in the 1960s and 1970s, and 2) why did the U.S. have such a big drug problem? The draft was revised several times after Teacher Dong read it and after a fellow IAS student in American economy made some suggestions. It was concise: the typescript (typed and bound by the Graduate School) was only thirty-two pages of text and forty-seven pages with notes and references.

The oral defense of the thesis took place on December 22, 1984. Teacher Dong had just injured his leg, so he couldn't make it. Present at the defense were Wei Zhangling, a fellow of the Social Science Intelligence Institute, specializing in following and reporting on developments in sociology in the West, especially the U.S. (I had read her articles back in college); Teacher Li, a colleague of Teacher Dong's in the Society and Culture Section of IAS (whom I had only run into at IAS a few times and who didn't seem to have published much); one or two other examiners whom I don't remember; Teacher Tian; and someone who operated the tape recorder. I began my defense, as I did the thesis, by explaining the inadequacy of the Chinese term for "drug abuse" (*xidu*, "inhaling drugs") and the ambiguity of the English phrase. I then gave a synopsis of my thesis, followed by Q and A. A question was raised about my definition of drug abuse, under which I included abuse of both legal and illegal drugs. I said since abuse of legal drugs was considered drug abuse in some of the literature I'd studied, I used the more inclusive definition. Still, most of the thesis was on illegal drug (ab)use. Teacher Tian said the thesis wasn't guided by Marxism and Leninism, even though she wasn't a fellow and shouldn't have expressed her opinion at the defense.

The examiners soon finished asking their questions. I was told to leave the room while they deliberated. Standing in front of the wall-to-wall window, I looked down at the miniature people thirteen floors below and then into the distance, my heart racing just a little. Minutes later I was called inside and the verdicts were announced: They voted unanimously for my graduation but also unanimously against granting me the degree. The reason? My definition of drug abuse was unclear. What they meant was that my definition was *wrong*. This could be inferred from the fact that in the very first note on the opening phrase of the thesis I had explained the point often made in the literature that "drug abuse" is a problematic phrase and how so, not to mention I had also explained my definition at the beginning of my defense right there. (The "drug" in "drug abuse" includes legal drugs, illegal drugs, and other abused substances such as paint thinner and banana peel. Whereas the first and third are "abused," the second is "used.") In fact, entitled *Meiguoren xidu yuanyin lun* (literally, the etiology of Americans' drug abuse), the thesis was an analysis of the elements making up the title: 1) Americans (who, i.e., demographic features); 2) drug abuse (what and when, i.e., what drugs and at what stages of abuse) and 3) why (microanalysis, i.e., 1) above and 2) macroanalysis, i.e., why reaching a crest in the 1960s and 1970s and why in the United States). They did give me another chance: I could revise the thesis and defend it again within a year, but then and there I was too dumbfounded to rejoice at this ray of hope.

The subway ride back to the school is a blur to me now. That evening I went to see Teacher Dong at his residence, an even longer ride from the school. After I told Teacher

Dong the negative verdict without knowing whether Teacher Tian had already informed him, he flew into a rage, accusing me of having been arrogant all along, and so on and so forth. Afraid he might have a stroke, I tried to calm him down, saying, "Please don't get too upset, I'm concerned about your health" repeatedly. Then I went to the next room to get his wife to come over to calm him down, saying, "Teacher Dong got very upset, please calm him down, I'm concerned about his health." He did calm down and we talked a bit more. He said I should get Teacher Wei's advice on how to revise the thesis but nothing about my definition of drug abuse.

The next few days I discussed the issue with Teacher Tian, Yuelin, Laya, Lao Li, and my roommates. I went to IAS to borrow the recording of the defense, saying that I needed it to help me revise the thesis while fantasizing about using it as evidence to somehow show the committee was in the wrong. But of course, the committee is always right. I was thinking of just forgetting about the damned degree when Aili came to see Ren Yue. She said being without the degree would cause a lot of inconvenience in the future such as having to explain why I failed to get my degree. I started to come around and thought I should swallow my pride and do the revision, which technically would be no sweat at all. I paid Teacher Dong one more visit at his home before going to the Intelligence Institute to make an appointment with Teacher Wei. Lastly, I talked to Teacher Wei herself at her home. As a result of my notoriety, nine fellow students or their friends wanted a copy of my thesis. Of those who expressed sympathy and moral support was Zhou Xing—a taciturn student in ethnology who had never spoken to me before—who said to me, "You can stay at my place when you come back to defend it again." I was touched. Paperwork for graduation and packing were done. In three days, I was to quit the capital where I had longed to be three-and-a-half years before, graduating with the distinction of being the only one of my cohort of two hundred plus students who had failed the defense.

Despite my disillusion at IAS after the meeting with my advisor within the first week of arrival in Beijing, I didn't rule out working in the capital after graduation. To crack the tough nut of the residence problem, Ningnan and I resorted to the exchange mechanism suggested by friends and made promising by a friend's friend's colleague who wanted to leave Beijing to return to Changsha. This woman was working in a Beijing factory, while her husband was a cadre at the Party School in Changsha. According to the residence policy, one couldn't just move to the capital but one could exchange residency with someone else. We visited the intermediary many times and the woman's husband once without making much progress. In early '84, our final year of study, the Graduate School began the process of assigning students to their post-graduation units as had been the practice, though by this time one could also find one's own unit. Most graduates would become researchers either at their home institutes (of which CASS had over thirty) or at other research institutes in Beijing. Others would take up teaching positions at such distinguished institutions as Beida. Those with residence problems faced the prospect of returning to their provinces of origin, not a step up.

On March 10, the Graduate School's personnel office told me that IAS was not going to keep me, asking me to look elsewhere. (This was forty-one days before I submitted my work to Teacher Dong for credits, which means the personnel decision couldn't have been based on the quality of my work.) The news wasn't a blow; I had seen it coming. One morning a few days later, I was standing on the roof terrace when a car drove up and out came two uniformed men, who went to the personnel office. Curious, I came downstairs and walked over some five minutes later. Passing by the personnel office with its window ajar, I overheard the woman personnel officer talking about me. Unable to resist the temptation to eavesdrop, I stayed just long enough to hear her say that this student had an agile mind productive of new ideas.

Afraid of being caught eavesdropping in the corridor of the administration building, I walked away feeling elated at the unexpected encomium. I then pondered about how the personnel officer had arrived at her evaluation of me, given that I had only said hello to her a few times in all the time I was there and given IAS's attitude toward me. I searched for clues but found next to nothing. The only talk I had given was a short, informal one at my class when the class monitor, fellow IAS student Zhao Yujiang, had asked me to. Using America's debt, Democrats vs. Republicans in American politics, Kant's philosophy and pre-Qin philosophical schools as examples, I talked about the importance of looking at multiple perspectives on, or aspects of, an issue to avoid undue biases, which was hardly a new idea.

The next thing I knew, I was told to go to the Academy of Military Sciences, the military counterpart of CASS, to discuss the possibility of being a researcher there. It so happened that they also wanted to see Ren Yue, my roommate studying American politics, and Lao Wu, a student in Russian and Soviet history. On March 17, the three of us went to the academy, intrigued. We had to go through one or two guarded entrances before meeting a fellow at the rank of a division commander in the army. The fellow talked about the difference between CASS and his academy; there the chances of going abroad were slim. On the home front, they couldn't promise to solve my wife's residence problem soon. (Lao Wu had the same problem; his wife was still in Sichuan.) None of us was enthusiastic about going there to work, though for some brief moments I toyed with the idea of going there, not being seduced by a sense of self-importance but rather imagining immersing myself in the nitty-gritty details of research, sitting on the cold bench for the rest of my life. (Indeed, soon after arriving in Beijing, disillusion helped me outgrow my limited sense of grandeur, and by the second year I found myself imagining not the least bit excited at being made a full professor right then and there: I would still be the same person, with no change inside whatsoever.) That evening Yuelin and I discussed the matter while walking around the sports field. He said, "Why serve the government?" He had a project for me: building China's own sociology. But I had neither the interest nor the ambition, let alone the ability.

Prior to this I had started thinking about going south, to Shenzhen, which was renewing its face daily. Shenzhen University (Shenda, for short) had just been established and was recruiting faculty and staff, so I'd contacted Shenda and on March 25 received the recruitment forms. On April 2, a professor at Beida interviewed me in English, asking about my background and how it would fit a teaching position at Shenda, where I would be teaching English. The personnel officer from Shenda was present. After the interview, the Beida professor and the personnel officer conferred while I waited in another room. A few minutes later I was told the answer was yes, they wanted me. Knowing my separation from my wife, the personnel guy said, "It won't be a problem," meaning they could transfer my wife's residency from Changsha to Shenzhen. Given that Shenda needed to do a lot of hiring and that my wife had been working at Hunan University's physics lab for a number of years, I thought there should be no problem getting her transferred to Shenda. It never occurred to me that I should get a promissory note from the guy about transferring my wife to Shenda once I report to work. Hence, the seed of a future headache (to mix metaphors) was planted.

On May 25, the Graduate School's personnel office said that the Central Committee of the Communist Youth League needed someone for their foreign affairs office and asked me whether I'd like to go there. The Youth League is a training base for Communist Party members and leaders. For someone with political ambition, it might be a very good ladder to climb up as had been for some top Party leaders (Hu Yaobang was the most prominent), but how could I function in such an organization? Apparently, the personnel office didn't know me well after all (thank goodness). I told the personnel officer that Shenda had already hired me. I was eager to go to the free land, not of laissez-faire capitalism but of relaxed political atmosphere and of Western movies: I wanted to watch a movie a day! (I had heard that Hong Kong channels showed one every evening.)

Not that the last year was dreary. While doing research for the thesis, I continued my "leisure reading," including reading more Shen Congwen. The Graduate School organized ballroom dancing lessons, and the film retrospectives mentioned above also occurred in this period: A more open society was emerging but I could hardly wait.

On January 3, 1985, eight days before I left Beijing, Teacher Dong wrote an evaluation of me:

> This graduate student's English is quite good, [he] can independently read original materials and translate excerpts, [his] mind is rather agile and lively, but [he] lacks rigorous training in doing basic scholarly research, [and] for a while won't be able to produce relatively mature research results; from a short-term point of view, am afraid teaching is relatively more appropriate [for him] than research.

I was going to Shenda to teach English, so he put in a word for me! Seriously, his evaluation would have fit me at my graduation from college. As for teaching, from November 6 through December 29—thanks to Zhaobin—Ren Yue, Zhaobin himself, and I each taught an English class at the Ministry of Aerospace Engineering, where a group of engineers were getting ready to go abroad. At the end of the short term, they threw a big party at which they lavished praise on us.

The Graduate School required each student to write a self-evaluation upon graduation. Mine was dated December 30, 1984:

> Have a large pair of eyes with 1.5 [i.e., 20/20] vision; partial to track-and-field sports and sports requiring physical strength; admire a strong physique; approaching twenty-eight but feel only twenty-five; knowledge not systematic enough, poor in thought; have an amateur intelligence agent's eye, a bad poet's imagination, and a philosophy dabbler's ability to think abstractly.

On January 10, Ren Yue, my cellmate for three years, gave me a photo album as a parting gift; the inscription inside, a thirty-two-character couplet, summed up the hapless past and prognosticated a rosy future:

> *Ruoda gudu shijunzhe liaoliao jin keyi yixiao-liaozhi*
> *Danwan xinbu yongerchu haohao dang keyi xiaoshi-shenshou*
> (In such a big, old capital, few are those who can appreciate you—just laugh it off.
> In the tiny, new port city, many are places that can use you—should be able to display a small part of your talents.)

On the same day I shipped my baggage containing everyday items, leaving tons of books behind to bother Ren Yue. Two old classmates from college came to say goodbye. That evening Yuelin put his excellent cooking skills to good use and whipped out a farewell dinner, an age-old tradition of Chinese men of letters, which has left behind countless poems. We conversed till 3 a.m., moving to the washroom in the wee hours. Later in the morning I boarded the No. 1 train headed south. When friends waved goodbye, I could see on their faces complex emotions, emotions that matched my own.

Shenzhen, here I come!

8. Semiwild Instructor

My wife and I arrived in Shenzhen on January 26, 1985. The former fishing village was being transformed into a glittering and glitzy bridgehead of commercial capitalism, whose breakneck development needed trained employees. Shenda was founded in '83 to meet that need; its location in the country's first Special Economic Zone and close to Hong Kong combined with the boldness of the school's leaders made certain unorthodox practices possible. For example, Shenda was the only university in China at the time that had abolished ideological indoctrination meetings. In tune with the entrepreneurial spirit of the place, Shenda students copied their American counterparts in working part time for pay: dining halls had student helpers, guesthouses were staffed by student workers, and a variety of cleaning and other jobs were done by students, too. I liked what I'd heard about these and other innovations of the school, and upon arrival didn't mind the sight of half-finished buildings or overgrown tracts.

The university put us up at a guesthouse on campus. Shenzhen's "open city" status had been attracting tens of thousands of applicants from all over the country, from discontented academics in their fifties to young Turks like me. The school was in a building frenzy but still couldn't house all the new hires coming in in droves. On February 2, we moved into an apartment in Haiqing Hall. The two-bedroom apartment already had a family living there, Teacher Zhou and his wife, from Shanghai. An ambitious artist, Teacher Zhou was experimenting with some new styles and motifs. His calligraphy also showed mastery, an art form I could appreciate better than paintings, especially those of avant-garde pretensions. For a short period, a driver stayed with us in the living room. Li Xiaolong was a handsome Guangdong youth whose driving was the smoothest one could imagine: when he came to a stop, the passenger felt no jolt whatsoever. In May another Shanghainese moved in. Jiang Yigang brought his mother, the old lady probably also curious about this new place. They stayed in the living room in the middle, while the three families shared the kitchen and the bathroom. We lived harmoniously together: no quarrels, no conflicts. Jiang Yigang, or Ah Gang, became a close friend, and we would spend much time together with a few other friends. He had majored in Chinese in college, but searching for greater certainty in knowledge, he went on to graduate school to study logic and ended up writing his thesis on Peirce's logic of relations.

My department didn't ask me to teach the first semester. Rather, in March the chair sent me to Guangzhou Foreign Languages Institute to learn to use some computer software for two weeks. The rest of the semester was rather idle; between exploring Shenzhen, Shekou (the bay area across from Hong Kong), and the surrounding area and hanging with friends, I spent much time in the reading room housing books published in Hong Kong and Taiwan, including translations of Western authors.

Shenda's other amenities included a grand administration-cum-classroom building modeled after one at The Chinese University of Hong Kong, which had wall-to-wall windows with tinted glass, air conditioning, and bathrooms with huge mirrors and spotless washbasins. The shiny ground floor alone cost a hundred thousand yuan, I was told. "Wasteful," I thought, "but it looks good," I admitted. At the dining hall, where both single—really or circumstantially—teachers and students ate, chilled carbonated drinks accompanied a meal or simply helped them cool off. The temporarily crowded apartments were fitted with water heaters providing hot showers, a luxury in China at the time. Midway between the work area and the faculty-and-staff residential area was another guesthouse with a spacious restaurant-like facility offering dozens of dazzling plates and steamers of dim sum on weekends. Even with the higher prices in Shenzhen, Shenda teachers were still much better off financially than their inland colleagues. (My monthly salary was close to two hundred yuan, over twice as much as my peers' in Beijing.) Besides two Cantonese TV channels from Hong Kong, two English channels broadcast news and Hollywood TV serials and movies with Chinese subtitles. It was funny that shortly after we arrived at Shenda, my wife and I sat in front of the television with some other new arrivals all night through, hoping to catch a glimpse of the "naked butts" (i.e., soft porn) rumored to beam out only late at night. All we got was one old Taiwan flick after another, including a paean of a KMT agent working heroically in a Japanese-occupied area, giving us a sense of déjà vu: he was the mirror image of his Communist brother whose patriotic heroism had been repeatedly pounded into our heads before the late 1970s. Admirable, but not exactly what we wanted to see then and there.

Since I planned to defend my thesis again before the spring semester was over, I revised it in mid-April. The revision consisted in narrowing the definition of drug abuse down to the (ab)use of illegal drugs and making corresponding changes in the rest of the paper. Just as I had expected, it required little thought. In May my wife returned to Changsha with no hope of transfer in the near future.

Shortly after arriving at Shenda, we paid a visit to the personnel officer who had recruited me at Beida. To our dismay, the officer told us my wife would have to wait at least a year before a transfer could be considered and *that* was university policy. You might wonder, as we did then, if that was university policy, then how come I hadn't been informed of it at the job interview, especially considering the fact that the recruiter had known well my wife's residence had been a major reason I had applied for the job in the first place? Sorry, can't help you there. Running into a wall at the personnel office, Ningnan tried to find a solution by pleading with the head of physics who happened to have come from Changsha. She only got equivocations. Then she tried the library, thinking the new library to be built would need lots of librarians and maybe she could learn the trade. No luck there, either. The situation wasn't improved by the discovery that she became pregnant. In the meantime, her leave couldn't be extended indefinitely, so she went back to work.

I returned to Beijing on July 4 and defended the revised thesis two days later without argument. Teacher Tian said the committee knew I'd taken the trouble to come all the way from Shenzhen, seemingly implying it was a charitable pass. Maybe it was; but suppose the committee didn't want to be charitable and instead held up standards: On what *grounds* would they shoot down the thesis that now accommodated their earlier objecttion? There was a follow-up to the story, though. One day during the second half of '85 or the first half of '86, I was browsing in my department's small library and came across *Reference Materials for Research on the United States*, published by IAS. I was of course familiar with that journal but was so surprised to see it at my department that I cried out, "Look, *Meiguo yanjiu cankao ziliao*" (the journal's Chinese name). I asked the librarian, Teacher Zhao, a rare German-Chinese, how come we had that journal. He said, well, he'd started subscribing to it sometime before. I looked through the table of contents of the various issues and guess what I spotted? A piece by your humble author! I quickly looked through it: it was my revised thesis. Since the theses of my fellow IAS graduates had also been published in the journal, I assumed IAS had simply decided to publish these papers by its own students. And since the papers were written as graduation theses, the institute must have thought it owned them. That might be why I hadn't been informed of its publication. Thinking it was no big deal, I didn't make a copy of it, nor did I jot down the bibliographic information so that I could list it in my vita. (In fact, I didn't even have one. At the time, whatever its other faults, Shenda at least didn't have the anti-intellectual policy of requiring its faculty to publish, and unlike my more ambitious colleagues in other departments, nor did I have a research agenda.) Years later when I had to put together a curriculum vita, I remembered this publication but couldn't recall when it was printed. At first, I thought it was '85, so I put down '85. But then I thought maybe it was '86 and not knowing for sure it would be better to err by post- than predating it. (It was Sept. '85.)

Yuelin and Yafei were about to graduate. On the evening of July 12, they made me a tape, using a simple tape recorder with only a built-in mike. Yuelin played the guitar and sang, and then the two sang duets. They sang both songs Yuelin had written himself and Chinese, Soviet, and American favorites. The one I liked best was a sentimental song about two boys riding an old ox in the singer's (and the listener's) native countryside:

A winding hill-path,
An ox lurches along.
Two young lads are riding,
Their bare backs a-glistening.

Limpid flows the river,
Therein swims the ox.
Two young lads are singing,
Enlivening the waters.

How many hills?
How many river-bends?
My oxherd pal has gone far away.
Do you still remember our birthplace's hills?
Do you still remember our birthplace's river-bends?

Winding hill-paths, twisty river-bends.
Winding hill-paths, twisty river-bends.
Only the old ox's calling,
Only the old ox's calling.

Later in the evening, I started singing some old folk songs and revolutionary tunes popular in Mao's era. Students living in the neighboring rooms came over and joined me in a chorus of several tunes.

In fall I began teaching in the foreign languages department, including night classes enrolling both workers and managers. The main assignment was a second-year all-purpose English class for majors, while the night class was introductory English. With eighteen hours a week, from Monday through Thursday the schedule was 7-2-7-2. (The hours seem too many but that's what my diary recorded.) Night classes carried extra pay, and I enjoyed teaching the older students as much as the younger ones. I became friends with a few night-school students but only visited the day students at their dorm once. Several students came to my apartment to converse and borrow books from my overflowing shelves. Once, asked by a student to record an English text, I read from Studs Terkel's *Working*, complete with sound effects such as barking. Still with time to kill, from late September through early January I sat in on a calculus class.

In mid-September I moved into my own apartment in Yun'ou Hall, No. 510. Being "single," I only got a studio, but it had a narrow veranda that could serve as a kitchen, plus a bathroom with a flush toilet, a small tub with a shower, and a water heater. Standing or sitting on the veranda, I could see the bay in the distance, a view only partially blocked by another building to the right front.

Maybe the new atmosphere was invigorating. In mid-September Ah Gang, who had also moved to Yun'ou Hall, and I started talking about setting up a young people's academic club. The club would organize lectures, evening gatherings with students, and meetings of young faculty interested in sharing their thoughts on scholarship or life at Shenda. Later in the month I became instant friends with another young hire from Shanghai. Unlike the typical Shanghainese, Chen Anding had a romantic streak beneath his gentleness. The next day I got to know Liu Xiang, who had achieved the rare feat of becoming a scholar of, by first teaching himself then studying with Professor Rong Geng, pre-Qin Chinese writing such as inscriptions found on bronze objects. After a-month-and-a-half's consultation and deliberation, we decided to launch the club with a university-wide lecture series. On November 2, 1985, a poster for the lecture series was pasted round the campus. There would be thirteen lectures with two a week, with me opening the series and Ah Gang closing it. We thought rhetorically before hearing about "the rhetorical turn": I would speak on drug abuse in the U.S. and Ah Gang on logical proofs of God's existence, both topics likely to draw large crowds. Nearly all speakers were young faculty in their twenties and thirties.

The first lecture took place on November 5. The large classroom was filled to capacity, with more listeners craning outside the two doors. I presented a popularized version of my thesis on drug abuse, dropping a literary reference here and there, and managed to make the audience burst into laughter once or twice. Three days later, the second lecture, then the third, the fourth. I also gave one of the middle lectures, a hodgepodge of observations on modernization ranging from the relationship between a society's material abundance and its abundance of cultural resources such as museums and libraries to the coexistence of religiosity and secularization. (Later, a correspondent for a Shenzhen newspaper asked through an intermediary if I'd like to write a piece on modernization for the paper. Since I didn't feel I had anything of substance to say, I didn't follow up.) On December 17, Ah Gang performed at the grand finale. The lecture took place in another jam-packed classroom. I ended up opening six of the lectures by saying a few words about the topic and introducing the speaker, while Ah Gang hosted most of the rest. In our organizational meetings, Ah Gang mentioned that such clubs were usually short-lived, all hinging on the founders' enthusiasm, which eventually wanes. Still, a formal meeting was called, chaired by Ah Gang and attended by university leaders.

Another activity we had envisioned was having student-faculty get-togethers at which open-ended discussions of mutual interest would occur. The first and only such gathering took place on the evening of December 27, ten days after the lecture series had ended. A few dozen students came to the large gathering hall in the central building and chatted with one another and with faculty members.

By the next semester we'd lost steam, and various personal matters consumed all our energies. Although the club was a fleeting adventure, it was something while it lasted. Besides, something tangible resulted: a collection of papers was edited in the name of the club and published as a supplement to *Shenzhen University Journal*.

The fall semester of '85 turned out to be a wild one for me, beyond the activities for the club. In spring, Shenda had started having dance parties on Saturday evenings at the central building. Disco alternated with waltz and tango. I wasn't a good ballroom dancer, having had but two short lessons back at the Graduate School, but I let it all hang out with the beat of disco. Peasant construction workers and younger village boys and girls would look on, curious and amused at the city slickers kicking up a frenzy. Sometime during this period, Ah Gang got to know Da Han and he introduced her to Anding and me. Both Da Han and her sister worked at Shenda and we would go dancing together with a few students. On November 30, a Saturday, we brought a tape recorder to the beach behind our halls and danced under the moon, forgetting the world around us. We didn't come out till past midnight so now it was really late. Two border patrollers came over and questioned us. We told them who we were and offered them cigarettes. The guards didn't give us any trouble, merely reminding us of the late hour.

Flashback: On the day Ah Gang and I went to put up posters for the lecture series, we ran into Meng Wen, an accounting student Ah Gang had met when he helped unload the baggage of new students two months earlier. Meng Wen was a petite girl with sparkling eyes. Since my lecture on drug abuse was listed first, she said, "*Who's* this Liu Xiuwu?" I answered, "Seemingly far away, actually right here under your nose" (*yuan zai tianbian, jin zai yanqian*). She looked at me, "So *you* are Liu Xiuwu." She came to every lecture and would hang around afterward. Four or five of us would go for a snack or soft drink. After Meng Wen became friends with all of us, Ah Gang described her as having an inspired intelligence (*you lingxing*), and I concurred.

One day in mid-December, I asked Meng Wen to come and hang out at my apartment. At the appointed time, she didn't show up. For some reason I began feeling uneasy and went outside a few times to see if she was coming. During my anxious wait, I felt as if a girl I was dating had stood me up. In the back of my mind, I did sense something improper, not that she was a student and I a teacher—she wasn't my student, nor that she was so young and I much older—she'd just turned seventeen, while I was going on twenty-nine. The faint feeling of impropriety was "I'm seeing a girl; this is cheating on my wife." But the anticipation was intoxicating and eclipsed the inhibition. When she showed up in her bubbliness half an hour later, I felt like a lad having his first date. She looked at my books and around the small apartment; my walls were bare, so was my desk.

We chatted casually and yet intimately. I talked about my wife, as if to tell her I wasn't hiding anything from her. Meng Wen was her innocent self and wasn't put out by my clumsy hypocrisy.

Five days later, a Saturday. At noon I suddenly had the urge of taking Meng Wen out. Her face lit up when I told her. With her sitting on the back rack of my bike, we rode on the highway to Shekou. She put one arm around my waist to secure her position; I felt closer to her. We rode for maybe half an hour, didn't stop at the tourist sites or shops but went all the way to the end of the road, till we came to the seaside, by a hill with huge boulders lying jaggedly around the foot and up. We sat down, not a soul in sight. The sea was calm with an occasional cargo ship snailing by in the distance. The warm December sun shone brightly, a breeze caressing the cheeks. I felt as if we'd been transported to a place far, far away from the world we were living in. We sat there, for a while wordless, immersed in the milieu. At first, we sat on different boulders, both facing the bay instead of each other. Maybe an hour passed, maybe longer. I then moved to sit beside her, and we talked quietly about the place: the boulders, the sea, and the hill where it looked like something was being built at the top. Tentatively I drew closer to her, eventually helping her sit in my lap. At some point I looked back up the hill and saw a young couple looking out to the sea. I didn't budge. Our faces touched and I couldn't help kissing her on the cheek, her shiny dark hair tickling my forehead. I thought of kissing her on the lips but restrained myself, partly because of not knowing how she'd react and partly inhibited by a distant sense of my being bad. Later, we got up and walked down to the water's edge, where wavelets gently beat the boulders. We jumped gingerly from one boulder to another and squatted to scoop a wave and splash it on the stones. Five hours passed quickly; the sun felt less warm, the breeze a bit chilly. We decided to head back. Just like when we came out in the early afternoon, we biked back with her arm around my middle, only a bit more tightly and naturally.

The next day I read, prepared my lessons for the following week, and marked students' homework. Monday, Meng Wen came to see me. For the first time I kissed her. Tuesday, Ah Gang gave the final lecture; Meng Wen again came. From that day on, she came to see me almost every day. On a walk along the beach, I showed her a letter I'd just received from my wife, continuing to deceive myself that I was being honest with Meng Wen and faithful to my wife; I thought I was also warning her not to get too involved. One evening, she came and didn't return to her dorm. We curled up in my single bed and snuggled all night, though we didn't undress, nor did we go beyond kissing. Another evening, we again took our now almost daily walk. When we reached the bottom floor of my hall on the way back, I suddenly swept her off her feet and carried her quickly up the flights of stairs, passing a neighbor on the fourth floor. I ignored him and kept going;

Meng Wen didn't struggle, nor did she make a sound. Reaching my door and entering the apartment, we both laughed mischievously. The next morning, I walked her over to the work area, where student dorms were also located. Not far from the central building, we ran into my chair, a professor "on loan" from Beida. I said hello to him as on any other day. But our walks had roused people's attention; when we strolled along the perimeter road by the bay, I seemed to feel the gaze and hear the gossip of students standing on the top floor of a hall a few hundred meters away. And yet we continued our walks. I even visited her in her dorm several times. George Peter Murdock calls sex the "imperious drive," echoing the Chinese expression, *sedan-baotian* (sexual desire drives one reckless).

Before long, Meng Wen came under some pressure, from where I don't remember. Ostensibly her schoolwork had suffered lately. But she continued to see me daily, while I asked her to pay more attention to her classes. Faculty also had eyes, especially that we weren't exactly discreet. Sometimes, she ate with Ah Gang and me at the new faculty-and-staff dining hall, where other diners could of course see her. Anding told me that his boss, a woman, was saying that if two people of the opposite sex spent this much time together, there *had to* be some hanky-panky going on. Having full trust in me, Anding disagreed. As close as Anding and I were, I didn't tell him anything about what went on between Meng Wen and me when we were alone. The truth is that we did get more intimate, although physically I didn't treat her as a lover in the full sense of the term due to a combination of my cowardice, my concern for her well-being, and my self-delusion that if I didn't make love to her, then I was still faithful to my wife. Her shyness and inexperience in affairs of the flesh deterred her from being her spunky self.

Otherwise, we consorted as a pair of lovebirds. Waltzing in the large dance hall in the central building, more than once she looked up at me and said she was going to faint; seeing that she liked the melancholy "Green Sleeves," I adapted the lyrics to dedicate the song to her. I made a tape for her, pouring out one love song after another, while her volumes of diary read like a love story written by a gifted writer.

Alas, all banquets come to an end. At the end of January, school was over. We decided to take the boat from Shekou to Guangzhou instead of the usual train from Shenzhen to the City of Rams. Ah Gang and Anding joined us. The four of us went to the wharf slightly before midnight. Our boat bobbed almost imperceptibly at the quay. The crisp, faintly saline air sent a chill down my neck. The cabin full of passengers restored the needed warmth and coziness. Our hands clasped tightly together, Meng Wen and I sat side by side, ignoring our two friends. The hour and the mode of transport made the trip feel romantic, but the imminent separation weighed us down with a gnawing sadness.

All three of them came to see me off at the train station. Just before I boarded, Meng Wen gave me a letter, asking me to read it later. After the train pulled out of the station, I opened her letter: It was, of course, a love letter. For the first time she told me she loved me. Memories of our time spent together carried me back to the campus by the sea. Then a jerk of the train shook me out of my reverie, reminding me I was on my way to my wife. And my son, too, who'd come into the world a few months before.

In mid-October I'd had a two-week leave to see Ningnan shortly before her labor. On the evening of October 21 her contractions became frequent. Her mother and I took her to No. 4 Hospital not far from the university. Around 9 she was wheeled into the delivery room. In China the husband couldn't be in the delivery room while the wife was giving birth, so I waited in the hallway, pacing back and forth. Two hours later Qiyu arrived, both mom and child in good shape. Presently a nurse brought him to the maternity ward, where I was chatting with my wife. I held him in my arms: his head was slanted front to back, maybe as a result of being squeezed on the way out. Strangely, instead of feeling "*I* have a son!" I felt he belonged to himself, not to his parents, let alone to the Party or to the motherland.

In early February the three of us went to Yueyang for the Spring Festival. On the evening of arrival Ningnan was mending something on my coat when she felt a bulge along the hem. The love letter from Meng Wen was totally unexpected and devastating, but the first thing she did wasn't yelling at or hitting me but showing it to my parents, who became visibly upset and criticized me. Ningnan was inconsolable; she cried and yelled: How could I have done such a thing, and at such a time, too. I didn't know what to say except when we went into our room, I tried to reassure her that I still loved her, that my love for her didn't diminish no matter what had happened at Shenda. Ningnan cried and cried, reminding me that my love was her only emotional support and that she had lacked undiluted parental love growing up. I could only repeat that I still loved her while trying to console her by holding her in my arms. We made love before falling asleep.

The next few days we went to see our old friends, Yueshan and his wife Su Jun and Ruidan and his wife Yitao. Ningnan poured out her anger and bitterness in front of them; they tried to comfort her while cursing me in a half-jocular tone. We only stayed in Yueyang for a week. On February 18 Ningnan and I left Changsha with Qiyu for Shenda. She had taken another leave from her school.

For the spring semester I was assigned eighteen hours of class a week again, but the load was reduced by four hours in the fifth week. Otherwise, work was uneventful.

Although my wife told me never to see Meng Wen again, I couldn't break it off with her just like that. We continued to meet, though a lot less frequently than before, sometimes outside the campus, sometimes at Anding's apartment, which was half a floor below mine by the landing. One day, Meng Wen came to Anding's place and I came downstairs. Ningnan must have suspected something, because she soon appeared, and to her outrage she found Meng Wen there. She yelled at Meng Wen while Anding tried to calm her down. After Meng Wen left, we went back to our own apartment, where she continued her scolding. It was then that I realized I had to both restrain myself and make Meng Wen realize that we couldn't carry on like that anymore. In late March and early April, I talked to Meng Wen several times—behind my wife's back of course—about breaking up for now. I was worried that she might not be able to take it, so I asked her to study well, be healthy, and wait patiently. For what I didn't say, nor did I know. Several months before we had started the whole thing innocently enough; during the intense two months I never worried about the consequences of what we were doing except that it might affect her adversely. But now I found myself saying such strange things as "we can't elope," and "nobody can escape the nets above and snares below (*tianluo-diwang*) of the proletarian dictatorship." Meng Wen was crestfallen, so was I. But at least she wasn't saying the kind of stupid things and making insincere promises as I was. In the meantime, Ningnan continued to chide me. One day I just couldn't take it anymore, so I hit her on the arm pretty hard while she was holding Qiyu. She hit me back a few times before I left the room.

Life dragged on like this. Ah Gang would tease me for what he saw as my vacant stares when I was standing on the balcony and looking ahead, with Qiyu in my arms. Meng Wen would tell me she was jealous of my son, who got to spend so much time with me, while she couldn't see me as often as she wanted.

Then a new development. On April 11, I received the documents to go to the United States as a visiting scholar. Chinese students had been going abroad since the late 1970s, both sent by the government and through private channels, the latter either through foreign scholarships or through a relative abroad providing the necessary financial help, whether real or only on paper. But being not particularly entrepreneurial in this regard and having a grand time—that is, until lately—at Shenda, I hadn't taken the initiative to apply to grad schools in the States. Instead, I'd asked Tom and Suellen for help. Tom invited me as a visiting scholar, which was easier than getting me into a school with financial aid. When I got the invitation, the first thing I did was to tell Meng Wen about it, not realizing that she might not be so happy about the news, which she received nonchalantly. I then found myself pretending not to realize that my going abroad would extricate me from the triangle, leaving her nursing her wound by herself.

Ningnan, however, received the news with good spirits. In time she would worry I might abandon her; she would also endure more hardships in caring for Qiyu. But for now, she stopped telling me off.

I spent the next few months trying to get the permissions to go to the States. The policy for studying abroad had changed a few times to stem the brain drain, probably with little success. At this time, those with a master's degree had to be *gongpai* (sent by the state) even if the money came from a foreign source. This was because a *gongpai* student or scholar bound for America (where most Chinese students going abroad went) would get a J-visa instead of an F-visa, and upon finishing their programs of study most wouldn't be able to apply for permanent residency in the States before returning to China and serving their own country for at least two years. In my case, I had to apply for a passport as a self-paying, publicly sent (*zifei gongpai*) student/scholar. Tom and Suellen had donated $5,000 to the university to fund my visit, hence "self-paying." From submitting my application to my department chair on April 12 to getting my passport at the provincial foreign affairs office on June 26, the whole process was taxing but not unbearable. The only hair-pulling frustration occurred when I had to fill out and submit the form for the provincial science-and-technology cadre bureau twice because it refused to accept the photocopied form provided by the local office; I had to *buy* their original form. It meant another trip to Guangzhou and more practice with my handwriting. Mercifully, the university authorities were helpful; they stamped all the forms after a brief interview with me and even let me borrow $1,000 as the policy stipulated. Tom had sent me a plane ticket, so I left Ningnan $800 to cover Qiyu's expenses and only brought $200 with me as an emergency fund.

The visa interview went smoothly. My invitation document said that my research topic would be computers' impact on society but the consul assumed I was going to study how to apply computers to teaching (good gracious, no) or some such topic. The consul asked me why I was working on computers, since my master's was in American studies. But I had also worked with computers, both in college and at Shenda, I replied, and maybe we'd set up our own system when I came back. I was good to go. Computer science was of course on the skills list that required two-year home-country service before one could apply for a green card. If the consul had seen my project as one in American studies, which was too new to be on the skills list, I wouldn't have been subjected to the two-year requirement. Walking away from the consul's window and answering inquiries from some of those still waiting in the room, I smiled. The whole thing seemed a comedy of errors, but then so is much of life (plus tragedy through the law of unintended consequences).

Even though I was relieved that my bosses at Shenda let me go, I remained resentful that the personnel officer had misled me into believing that my wife would be transferred there after I reported to work from Beijing. This despite the fact that my marriage was in trouble, so when I got the visa and started packing, I vowed not to return. Into the two bags I was allowed to check I packed all my notes from college and graduate school but left behind those from before college, most of which had been left in Changsha when I went to Beijing and would be lost forever. I also packed the newspaper clippings, four compact language dictionaries, two computer dictionaries, a Polish scholar's study of the societal impact of microelectronics, Douglas Greenwald's *Dictionary of Modern Economics* (in Chinese translation) and a dozen small books on China plus Feng Youlan's autobiography and Raymond Aron's *In Defense of Decadent Europe* (in abridged Chinese translation). Before I'd spent more time reading about America and the rest of the West than about China, now about to go to America I was thinking of studying China. A case of the "distance enhances the attraction" syndrome?

I left Shenzhen with Ningnan, Qiyu, and my mother-in-law on July 15 and spent two days in Yueyang. On July 24 I left Changsha for Shenzhen, from where I would be crossing the border into Hong Kong and then flying to San Francisco. *Meiguo*, the Beautiful Country, was beckoning me.

9. Visiting Scholar-cum-Handyman

The last eight days at Shenda were exhausting: fetching the passport with the visa stamp from the provincial foreign affairs office in Guangzhou, picking out the things to pack, getting the foreign-currency loan, loaning my natural-gas bottle to a colleague and dealing with other matters of the household, and of course, spending time with Meng Wen. According to her diary, which she sent me later, on the eve of my departure, I fell asleep in my reclining chair right in front of her. She sat beside me, gazing at my gaunt face, then kissed me without my awareness.

August 2: Ah Gang and Meng Wen went to see me off at the Luohu checkpoint between Hong Kong and Shenzhen. We came to the outer entrance, where the guard stopped her, saying only travelers beyond that point. That was unexpected; I was hoping, and she must have hoped too, that she could walk me all the way to the Customs. Somehow Ah Gang was let through, so Meng Wen had to stand there alone, watching me disappear into the customs house. I couldn't imagine a scene more heartbreaking. But I walked on.

The walk between the Customs and the train station was interminable. I had two large bags filled mostly with paper and two small carry-ons. Since the large bags were too heavy, I resorted to relay: I would leave one bag behind but in sight and then come back for it. By the time I reached the train station, the small wheels on the bottom of one of the bags were already damaged.

Standing outside the train station I waited for a taxicab to drive by. The scene was a familiar one from Hong Kong television: colorful cars speeding along the narrow streets overshadowed by passages for pedestrians and high rises. In a minute or two I flagged down a taxi for the first time in my life and gave the driver the address of an acquaintance. It was a short drive. The driver must have recognized my mainland country-bumpkin origin: when I asked him "*Gei men*?" (Cantonese for "how many dollars") in my best accent, he said, "*Ba men*" (eight dollars), while a glance at the meter would have revealed "five dollars." But being the country bumpkin I was, I paid him eight and then proceeded to take my baggage out of the trunk. Unfortunately, too weak from the long walk through the Customs earlier and from the draining activities in the prior week, I threw my back lifting one of the large bags out of the trunk. "This is not a good beginning," I thought as I struggled with the bags up the hill where Doctor Qu lived. Her son taught math at Shenda, while she herself practiced traditional Chinese medicine in Hong Kong. Her residence was a tiny shack with barely enough room to lie down. But her hospitality was heartwarming and her medical skills put me back on my feet. The next morning, she accompanied me on a tour of some of the streets and of the mountaintop with a bird's-eye view of the islands. Having seen the Hong Kong skyline on television, I was impressed more by the superabundance of fresh fruits and other foods than by the skyscrapers.

Tom and Suellen met me at the airport in San Francisco. I said, "I made it!" and we hugged, American style. They and their two adopted children, Bert and Lily, were staying with Tom's parents at their retirement home in Oakland. We would stay in the Bay area for a week before driving back to Rolla, Missouri, where Tom was teaching and where they had a house in the country. But first Tom and Suellen drove me to the Fisherman's Wharf to give me a welcome dinner, or, as the Chinese would say in the old days, to wash off the dust of travel.

I had met Tom's parents in Changsha when they visited China. Tom's father had wanted to be a classics scholar when he was young but ended up a physician. He kept his interest in literature and had a huge Shakespeare library. The food at the retirement home was sumptuous, the trays loaded with meats and fruits, but one staple was missing: Rice! I filled myself up with chicken and other tasty things but yearned for a less rich meal after a few days. Suellen called Tom's parents by their first names instead of "Mom" or "Dad" as Chinese daughters-in-law would. "Interesting," I thought. (In the old days, Americans did so, too. I don't like formalities but I don't think this particular change is progress.) Also intriguing, though in a different way, was that one day Suellen pointed out an old couple in the dining hall to me that they were in their eighties and had just gotten married.

Despite all the hospitality, my thoughts drifted back to my friends in China. Lying on the bed listening to the tape Yuelin and Yafei had made for me in Beijing a year before, I started singing along without realizing I was disturbing Suellen in the next room till she came over and closed the door between us.

In the week we stayed in the Bay area Tom and Suellen took me to the Muir Woods, UC Berkeley, and several museums. One evening, I ventured out by myself. I wandered around a bit before taking the Bart to San Francisco. The neon sign of an X-rated movie theater got my attention; I paid $6 to gain entrance to a double feature one of which was called, none too subtly, *Climax*. The experience of seeing a porno film for the first time is hard to describe, not excitement mixed with a sense of novelty as a young man feels upon seeing a naked young woman for the first time but mostly the latter sensation. The scene in which a girl spread her legs while touching herself was as eye-opening as reading Descartes's "I am thinking, therefore I exist."

Coming out of the movie theater I walked along the streets. Then I saw a strip club and walked in. Run by an Asian woman, the large theater had only three patrons, all sitting in the back rows. I walked up the terraced theater and sat two-thirds the way from the stage. As I ascended the steps, I glanced at the other customers, who were slumped in their seats seeming to show no interest in what was going on on the stage. A crimson, velvety curtain drooped along the back wall, which depressed rather than enlivened the atmosphere of the place. Only two or three dancers were working that evening and the routines were soon over. The attitude of the dancers matched that of the audience, lackadaisical and merely going through the motions. Their looks were as plain as their performances. As I was the only new customer, one of the dancers came over and sat by me, her bare arms and legs inches away. The Asian woman immediately came to ask me to buy the dancer a drink, which I obliged like a gentleman. The dancer and I engaged in some small talk with me wondering whether I could touch her or not. Two minutes later, the drink was gone. The manager said it was $25. "But I only have some twenty-four left in my pocket, and I need to take the train home," I said. She grabbed what I had, just leaving me enough to take the Bart home.

Making stops along the way, we spent seven days on the road. The day we arrived at Rolla I volunteered to cook dinner—I was starved for some home-cooked food. Having grown up in Hunan, I love spicy food. I asked Tom if there were any chili peppers and Tom showed me jalapeños, whose appearance was by no means impressive. (Chinese hot peppers have pointed tips.) I put seven in a stir-fried chicken dish. Tom saw everything but said nothing. The dinner was soon ready, and the first bite of a piece of jalapeño nearly choked me: I had hardly expected the plain-looking chili to be so spicy, to Tom's merriment. From then on, I'd only use three or four jalapeños. Jalapeños are not just spicy; they have a special flavor I love. Even though they are more Mexican than American, to me they are one of the main reasons that the U.S. is a great place to be. (I didn't find out till 2003 that hot peppers were native to South America and weren't introduced to China till the Ming Dynasty.)

Tom and Suellen's house stood on a farm some nine miles from Tom's school, the University of Missouri at Rolla. Rolla is a small college town and Tom's farm was even more secluded. On weekends, Tom went to Columbia where Suellen was attending law school, leaving me alone on the farm. I would take a walk to the main dirt road after dinner, thinking I could run around naked with no danger of being seen.

Social life wasn't totally absent on the farm. Tom's neighbor, a real farmer, came over once; Tom asked him to grab a beer from the frig, impressing me with American casualness as compared to the formality of Chinese customs. We also went over to the farmer's house once. Another time, a friend of Tom's came over in the evening; Tom heated up the Jacuzzi in front of the house, where we sat conversing under the moon. For Thanksgiving, an economics professor at Rolla invited us all over for turkey and the works. One weekend, two male relatives of Bert and Lily came to visit. I had previously expressed the wish to get to know America's workers and farmers, but when an opportunity presented itself, I was too shy to engage the two guests in conversation. Instead, I sat away from them, which upset Suellen. She mentioned to Tom how many social graces his first interpreter at Hunan University had.

That was far from my only faux pas. On the drive from Oakland to Rolla, one night we stayed at a motel bordering a graveyard. Taking a walk in the dark in my shorts I found myself exploring the tombstones, trying to capitalize on an opportunity to discover something intriguing about American society. Tom found me wandering around like a ghost and said my behavior would look suspicious to the locals. The first time I did the dishes when we got to Rolla, I only used hot water, not dish detergent; I also spat into the sink. Suellen corrected me. When I got my first haircut at a barbershop, I failed to give the barber a tip. (I only knew about tipping at restaurants and so on.) Those of you who've been to China or have heard Chinese talk among themselves must have noticed that Chinese are loud. One day, Suellen said to Tom and me that we men were too loud, which I thought was her polite way of telling me that *I* was too loud. In mid-November I went to Columbia to take the TOEFL. The day before the test, I was trying to do a bit of last-minute studying, so when dinner was over, I neglected to help clean up the table but immediately picked up the study book, which made Suellen quite upset. "A minor cross-cultural misunderstanding," I thought. In China, between such good friends, the host wouldn't have minded. But I wasn't in China. Even Tom must have felt uncomfortable with my obtuseness, because before we left Columbia, Tom reminded me to thank Suellen for her hospitality just in case I didn't know. This was but the first instance of what I would learn more about, relationships between friends and even spouses: Chinese tend to take a lot more for granted than Americans; in fact, the very idea of "don't take it for granted" I picked up only after I'd lived here for a while. In China, a more traditional code of conduct prevailed: no "thank you" between family members or good friends, no "I love you" between parents and children, rarely even between lovers or spouses, though things are changing due to Western influence.

On weekdays I audited classes and studied in the library. The class I enjoyed most was Data Structures; the professor made data structures sound as captivating as history, anthropology, or mathematics. Another class was on artificial intelligence taught by a philosophy professor. Both classes had fewer than twenty students, making for an intimate environment for both lecturing and discussion. The third class was Social Psychology, which I only attended for a while; this class was larger, but the teacher was also engaging.

I read and browsed in the library. One day, I read a couple of chapters from a strange book by Evelyn Fox Keller, *Reflections on Gender and Science*. It claims that natural science is gendered, which seemed to be a *non sequitur*. The history and politics of scientific inquiry are gendered, yes, but how could the *content* of science be gendered?

Her case studies of Plato and Bacon were historical, which to me didn't show that science itself is gendered. Puzzled, I photocopied the introduction and showed it to Tom, who had gotten an M.S. in mathematics before going into computer science and who also liked history and social studies. The next morning, Tom said Keller didn't know what she was talking about, "but she used to be a professor of some marine science at Yale," I said. We left for work, end of the conversation.

Since my goal was to continue my schooling, I needed to choose programs and schools to apply to. I thought of getting an M.A. in Asian studies first but then decided to go for the Ph.D. in American studies with a minor in Asian studies. Then I ran into a seemingly insurmountable obstacle: the foreign student advisor told me that a visiting scholar couldn't change his or her status to being a student, again having to do with making sure that scholars return to their home country after completing their studies in America. What now? I looked far and wide in the library: Canada was attractively close, whereas Australia and New Zealand appeared exotically alluring. It was already too late to apply to Australian schools, especially for financial aid, but I fancied the Asian studies program at Griffith University in Brisbane and sent in my application materials anyway. The envelope was sent to Down Under like a stone thrown into the sea.

Exchanging letters with friends let me in on a well-known secret: Visiting scholars had been going to another country and then reentering the States as a student. Many went through Canada, others England, and some even Africa. "So maybe I could attend school here in the States after all." Not to put all the eggs in one basket, I still looked at Canadian universities, including Simon Fraser and Manitoba, and ended up applying to the latter's anthropology program plus the University of Iowa's American studies program.

All the busyness couldn't completely dispel my loneliness. On weekends, I was all alone on the farm, with only books and two copies of a girlie magazine keeping me company. My wife and I wrote to each other regularly, her letters full of descriptions of hardship related to raising Qiyu without my help and of bitterness at my betrayal. I wrote to Meng Wen shortly after I arrived at Rolla, asking her to get on with her life. She sent me the last book of her diary covering the period right before I left Shenda as a goodbye souvenir and soon fell in love with a math instructor at Shenda.

After taking the GRE on December 13, I decided it was time to leave Rolla to strike it out on my own. Despite the visa complication, I remained optimistic about getting into some school somewhere, and despite the sarcastic and bitter complaints in my wife's letters, I planned to reunite with her and my son once I managed to get into a school. Which meant I needed to find a job and make some money. On the other hand, should I fail to get into a school for the fall, I would have to go back to China, and I didn't want to leave without having seen more of the country. I remembered what my former American teacher Mariana had said about learning about another country, that you have to make a living in that country in order to know it well. To fix me up for the road, Tom got me a pair of boots and gave me a traveling bag plus $500. Three days later I hopped on Trailways, a competitor of Greyhound at the time, and headed East where I had quite a few friends studying at different universities.

I made brief stops at St. Louis, Auburn, Atlanta, Chapel Hill, and D.C. before reaching New York City. Having checked in with Qiu Xi, a former roommate from college now living in Flushing, I came right back out. The crowded and dirty streets in Flushing gave me the impression that Chinese and other immigrants take their bad habits wherever they go. I took the train back to Manhattan, eager to see the heart of New York. I walked aimlessly, hither and thither, watching the multicolored crowds and buildings.

When the evening lights came on, I found myself near the notorious 42nd Street. Not far from Times Square was a strip club below street level. The large theater was almost completely full, with at least a dozen dancers and mostly middle-aged men. Some five minutes later a dancer drifted over and whispered to me: "Would you like a blowjob? $36." This was my second time inside such a club, so I wasn't as green as in San Francisco. I replied casually, "I just got here, maybe later." Intimidated by the surroundings and wishing to be left alone, I got up and left in less than ten minutes. Still curious about the variety of venues on offer along the street, I spent the next several hours going in and out of clubs, movie theaters, and video stores.

Leaving 42nd Street around midnight, I decided to walk as many of the Manhattan streets as possible. I wandered around for hours, at one point going through an area with lots of abandoned buildings. I wasn't the least afraid. Sometimes I saw a human figure, and I'd assume what I imagined to be the gait of a vagabond or homeless person. I thought, "Maybe the other guy's afraid of me!" By early morning I had come to the area of Wall Street. With no more energy to go on, I entered a church and lay down on a pew. Unfortunately, only about half an hour later an old man woke me up and told me that was no place to sleep. "What, even a church won't take in the poor and the weak, on this of all days, Christmas Day?" Feeling slightly refreshed but still groggy I got some breakfast to refuel my body. Then it was on to Wall Street, the Twin Towers, and Chinatown. In the afternoon, I stopped at a secondhand bookstore and picked out a dozen books, thinking maybe I'd have to go back to China in seven or eight months. That was how I spent my Christmas Eve and Christmas Day in 1986.

On January 2, 1987 I finally arrived at Boston, where I was hoping to find a job. I had two acquaintances there: Xiong Xiaoge from college and Huang Yi from Beijing, who'd been Yuelin's roommate. Huang Yi let me share a room with him in the basement, strictly speaking part of Boston University's student housing. Cooking was done in the hallway, on a stove shared by many more moles of the basement, one of whom was a former conductor of Beijing's Youth Orchestra. At that time, BU had many topnotch Chinese musicians studying there, so the evening show for the Chinese New Year was outstanding. But I'm getting ahead of the story.

I spent the first six days resting, looking at the city, visiting the Harvard-Yenching Library, and browsing in bookstores. On January 9, Xiaoge took me to BU's student employment office where want ads were posted. He was helping me, though he himself also wanted to find something. One ad said handyman needed for helping remodel a house in Cambridge; qualifications: good with tools. Xiaoge had been an electrician before college so he was pretty handy with tools; I had less experience but I did work in a fertilizer plant for over two years. Xiaoge called the number, the employer said he was interested, then Xiaoge said there was someone else here who could work, and bingo! Both of us were to report to work the next day. "No wonder they call America the Land of Opportunity."

The house was about a twenty-five-minute walk from Cambridge Square. When we got there, our employer Ken said the first two days he'd pay us $7 an hour, and then, if we were any good, $8 from the third day on. The pay was good in my eyes, though the work was hardly enjoyable. The old shingles had just been replaced and bits and pieces were lying behind and between the shrubs, some buried under the snow, so the first job was to pick up these and other kinds of debris from around and inside the house. It was cold and wet in the garden, and unlike when I worked at the fertilizer plant hauling a steamer, I couldn't light a fire. This work took a while. Xiaoge was both a faster and a pickier worker than me; a few days later he quit.

For the next seven months I performed every imaginable task around the house. Often, merely looking at the big mess upstairs and downstairs and thinking I would have to perform *every* task to put the place back in order disheartened me. The situation was both eased and aggravated by the weekly cleanup Ken asked me to do. But I stuck it out, from late May through late July only taking one day off.

During the seven months, I had four coworkers for short periods of time (not counting Xiaoge or the contractors doing carpentry or drywall). First, a BU engineering student worked with me for a while. One day we played a vocabulary game after he asked me about the GRE: we took turns quizzing each other on words and came out about even. When told of his birthday, I bought him one of the books by Douglas Hofstadter, which surprised him. I was yearning for friendship. Once, I even asked him to introduce me to a girl to go out with; his Burmese girlfriend who brought him lunch mocked me, "What are you, a dirty old man?"

The second coworker was a boy of Korean descent. He only worked with me on one weekend. The first day he drove an Audi; the second, a new jeep. With a rich dad he was just making some spending money. On the second day, I rode with him to his apartment, where he had a personal gym. He treated me to dinner and told me his father had given him some pills to take so that he wouldn't get VD sleeping around. That pill was news to me (I still don't know what it might have been) but I was too shy to ask him about it.

The third coworker was a former college classmate of mine, who was finishing up his education degree at Oklahoma State University. He wanted to make some money but quit after two days scrubbing a stove, feeling the work was beneath him. The fourth coworker also only worked a short period, and nothing memorable occurred.

Of the carpenters who worked periodically on the house, Paul stood out, because one day he said in regard to a Sino-American-relations issue in the news, "If John King Fairbank doesn't know what's going on, then not many people do." I was duly impressed that a carpenter in Cambridge knew about Fairbank.

Ken was a meticulous but good employer. He'd graduated from MIT and had his own small architectural firm in Cambridge. Ken wrote out detailed instructions for each day's work; the job list looked like a computer flowchart. He was never rude to me and from time to time asked about my wife and son still in China. I thought he worked too hard—he never ate a meal without reading something.

My time in the Boston area wasn't all work and no play. Taiwanese students organized an evening party during the Chinese Spring Festival, and as I mentioned above, top Chinese musicians in the greater Boston areas put on an excellent show for the same occasion. For the first four-and-a-half months when I only worked five days a week, I roamed the streets of Boston and Cambridge on weekends, spending most of the time browsing in the dozens of new- and used-book stores in those two cities. One Sunday, I went to BU's Marsh Chapel to listen to the sermon entitled "Are You Free to Choose?" Occasionally I went to the movies. But many a lonely and restless night was spent on the porn row in Chinatown, sometimes increasing the loneliness rather than alleviating it.

My wife's letters continued in the understandable depressing tone until I got news of admission to graduate school. One evening not long after I went to Boston, I felt so despondent that I went to a bar with Meng Wen's diary and read it from beginning to end. Aili stopped by once, so I entrusted the diary with her, not wanting my wife to see it when she got here.

In April, I received an admission letter from Iowa but no financial aid. I wrote back saying I wouldn't be able to attend without aid. The chair of American studies, Richard

Horwitz, was kind enough to find $1,700. Manitoba only admitted me as a pre-M.A. student in anthropology, of course with no aid; given my background in American studies, it was a reasonable decision. In fact, later when I saw Chinese students with no degrees in education being admitted directly into doctoral programs in education at Iowa and elsewhere in the States, I thought Canadian schools had more rigorous standards.

I still had my visa problem: I'd come on a visiting scholar's visa; now I needed a student visa. A trip to Toronto did the trick: I went as a tourist and came back in as a student. By then Yuelin had come to Cambridge to attend Harvard. On August 14, we went to Walden Pond. Thoreau's cabin fittingly stood alone on the hill overlooking the pond, whose serenity was disturbed by the sunbathing crowds. Disliking the latter, we hiked along the trails threading through the surrounding woods. The next day I flew to Cedar Rapids. My wish to continue my education finally came true. Deeply felt in my being was a sense of liberation. Lonely, yes, but in important ways, *free*.

10. Recovering Student, "Single" Father

Having worked so hard to get into a school so that I could continue my education, now I would throw myself into my studies. Or so you might imagine. On the contrary, barely a month into the fall semester, I dropped two of my three classes and nearly had a nervous breakdown. What happened?

The circumstances of my life in Iowa City were, if anything, more livable than before. When I landed in Cedar Rapids, a fellow student sent by the Chinese Student Association met me and drove me to the campus. I immediately found a place to stay; to save money three other students from China and I shared a large studio at the back of a building, a semi-basement space. Despite a couple of petty misunderstandings, we got along well.

I also found a friend in Li Xiaoying within the first week of arrival. Lao Li not only had more interests but also seemed to know more about everything than me except English and philosophy. He might be an even better cook than Yuelin and treated me to a delicious meal in his room above mine, where we listened to a tape of Russian vocal music that was absolutely enchanting. We talked about China's history during the Republican era: I related my grandpa's experiences, while he knew a former commander of the fort barbette in Nanjing. He was knowledgeable about art, architecture, and music, not to mention the natural sciences—he had a master's degree in chemistry from China. Moreover, several years older than me, he was also a man of the world, a shrewd observer of politics and society. As I was yet to immerse myself in academics, we had frequent, long conversations. Besides chats with Lao Li, there were outings and group shopping trips.

Unfortunately, friendship or social gatherings could allay loneliness only temporarily, which became unbearable for me. In late August, Iowa City was showing *No Way Out*. I saw it. It was an average thriller. The next day I felt so restless I didn't know what to do. Mentally with no way out myself, I went to watch the movie again. With hindsight, the loneliness and restlessness in part had to do with becoming a full-time student again after a two-and-a-half-year hiatus. My condition might also have to do with the transition between the blind working frenzy after I'd heard from Iowa and the reality of finally being able to continue my schooling. But the main cause might have been that I'd been living a single life for too long, if one year could be too long under the circumstances. This last condition was compounded by what I *was* acutely aware of at the time—the hurdles my wife would have to clear to reunite with me: She would have to get permission from both her own school and mine. "What if Shenda insists that I return instead of letting me pursue my Ph.D.?" Without its permission, my wife wouldn't be able to get her passport. My mother-in-law had written me in April that China's study-abroad policy was tightening up, that the chair of mathematics at my wife's school had told her Beida was asking its faculty going abroad to pursue degrees to resign from their positions first, and that two young faculty members in mathematics at Hunan University had failed to get permission to come to the States. I became distraught thinking if my wife and son couldn't join me, I couldn't go on with my schooling in the States, because I couldn't contemplate another five or more years of separation needed to finish my degree; that is, assuming I could somehow find the money to support myself in the meantime.

By mid-September I became mentally unable to continue as a full-time student, something that I had never imagined would happen when I was working nearly nonstop in Cambridge trying to make as much money as possible so that I could bring my family over. On the evening of September 24, Lao Li and I went to see *Betty Blue*. Afterward, we went to the area in downtown Iowa City close to the public library where eateries, tables with benches, a children's playground, and a small water fountain provided an intimate environment. We talked till dawn. It was during that night that I decided to deal with my anguish by dropping two of the three classes I was taking.

The three classes were a methods course taught by Rich Horwitz, a course on American childhood taught by Al Stone, and a course on the black woman taught by Mae Henderson. I read the assignments carefully and was learning much from all three courses. Reluctantly I decided to keep only the methods course so that I could maintain my sanity. I didn't talk to my advisor, Wayne Franklin, right away, though. Three days later, my state of mind didn't improve, as can be seen from the fact that I went to watch *Betty Blue* again, just as I had done with *No Way Out* four weeks earlier, with the French movie being depressing rather than thrilling and my torment becoming more acute. The next day, September 28, I finally went in to see my advisor. Wayne (we were told to call our teachers in the department by their first names) was very understanding, so were Al, Mae, and our chair, Rich Horwitz. The deadline for refunding the tuition for the dropped courses had passed, but Rich was so kind that he wrote a letter on my behalf requesting a refund, which the university granted.

Having dropped two courses and thinking that I was returning to China soon, I wanted to make the best use of my time here. I didn't want, nor did I have the concentration, to read as many books as I could before I'd have to leave; one could find Western books in China, either in English or in Chinese translation. It wasn't hard to find a mission for the imagined limited time left. Before then, instead of falling in love with computer science, I'd been in love with Western movies, so I decided to watch as many movies as possible. In the previous month, I had watched the French film *Thérèse*, the Swedish films *Miss Julie* and *Fanny and Alexander*, the Italian film *L'Avventura*, and the American movies *Exorcist* and *Liquid Sky* at the university's movie theater. In the meantime, I had discovered that the university library had a large collection of movies with viewing rooms. For the next ten days I redirected my passion for books to movies and watched a whole bunch of them in the library.

A week or so into my movie-watching marathon, I began to feel that spending this much time watching movies was too decadent, that I should find a job, which would not only improve my finances but also serve as a diversion. On October 9, I found a job washing dishes in the kitchen of the university's hospital, twenty hours a week. The job wasn't exactly washing dishes; it consisted of such chores as sorting out tableware, scrubbing pots and pans, loading all the items onto or taking them off the Hobart dishwashing machines, and delivering loaded carts to another area. Monotonous as all this may sound, I enjoyed the mindless repetition.

The reunion with my family looked rather distant if not hopeless. In two of her letters my mother-in-law wrote that if Shenda refused to sign the documents to "release" my wife, she'd try transferring me from Shenda to Huda (i.e., Hunan University), my college alma mater, where I'd left a good reputation and where she could pull some strings. By November, however, there was progress. I immediately shared the good news with my chair, Rich Horwitz, because he'd been so kind to me: that my wife had gotten her passport. As a result, my mental condition improved and I resumed my reading in philosophy while continuing my movie viewing at the library and my patronage of the university's Bijou screenings of Hollywood as well as European fare.

Then a setback in my wife's quest for a visa. Though I'd saved up $8,500 during the seven months in Boston, it was far from the amount required to show that I had adequate funds to support my family during their visit. In the case of Chinese, it's hard to say whether they are thrifty or stingy; a little money goes a long way. But rules are rules, so the stipulated figure had to be met. (The rules are correct: in my second year at Iowa money problems forced me to take one class per semester fewer than the unenforced regulations required.) It was no secret that most financial guarantees were only nominal, not real. You get a rich-enough friend to provide a statement, and the requirement was met. I had again asked my old friend Tom for help. But when my wife went to apply for a visa, she was rejected for having insufficient documentation. She wrote me right away and I sprang to action. Thank God, the second time she was successful.

I had been thrifty while waiting for my wife's paperwork to go through. When grocery shopping, I'd look at a relatively pricey item and think to myself: "Wait till she gets here." I'd balk at fish or meat that was $3 or more a pound (actually only $2.98) and always went for something cheaper. When I added up my receipts for food for one month, they came to eighty some dollars. On the other hand, I wasn't as scrimpy as my roommates or other Chinese students. One roommate, a visiting scholar, bought lots of pork and beans instead of fresh meat and vegetables; Chinese students typically ate instant noodles for lunch or even dinner. Not me. I refused to eat instant noodles and insisted on fresh foods, although I shopped at discount outlets as well as at regular grocery stores. Knowing she was coming in December, I bought a '72 Pontiac for $450 when a fellow student offered it to me. I didn't get a TV set till the day after she and my son arrived in Iowa City.

There was a misadventure in our meeting at L.A. Her flight was due in on December 30 and I thought of getting there two days in advance to find a hotel, etc. To save money and to give her an opportunity to see the country, I got one-way Greyhound tickets for her and two-way tickets for myself. Planning to leave Saturday afternoon but ignorant of the fact that the bank closed at noon Saturday, I didn't go to the bank till after noon and when I got there the bank had just closed. I waved to a clerk inside but she waved back indicating they were closed. Thus, I couldn't leave till Monday morning, the bus schedule telling me I was cutting it really close but if all went well, I'd still be able to get there in time.

The bus was on schedule till Denver, where a big snowstorm stranded us for six hours. Once in L.A., I rushed to the airport knowing that her flight had already arrived two hours before. I looked all over the airport including checking the airline ticket counter but my wife and son were nowhere to be found. (Why is it that when you *need* a plane to be late it's on time?) I paced up and down the entrance hall and then the street curb, at a loss as to what to do. Then a minivan pulled up and there they were! It turned out despairing of seeing me at the airport my wife had checked into a hotel with a Mexican-looking guy offering his services. My relief and joy at seeing them are hard to describe. Climbing into the van I saw my son for the first time in seventeen months: he looked meek and sweet. "It's my boy," I thought. My wife said to him, "Call him '*Baba*,'" and my son said meekly, "*Baba*." My wife proceeded to tell me her ordeal at the airport. Shortly the van pulled up in front of the hotel; happy and grateful I gave the driver a $10 tip.

The next day we looked for a hotel in downtown L.A. Walking around all I could find were large, gloomy, redbrick buildings that looked like boardinghouses; indeed, these places had weekly rates for those who couldn't afford better housing. We stayed in L.A. for five days, visiting the usual tourist sites.

My reunion with Ningnan and Qiyu returned me to my old self: I was no longer anxious or lonely. I registered for three classes for the spring semester: the second installment of the methods course taught by my chair, that of American Intellectual History taught by Kenneth Cmiel, and Philosophy of History taught by Allan Megill. I continued watching movies and working at the hospital's kitchen, except now I could also concentrate on my schoolwork.

All three professors were sharp and learned, but Horwitz and Cmiel had a down-to-earth demeanor, whereas Megill was more intense. Cmiel gave us an extended bibliography on the period of American intellectual history covered in the course. A student must have been impressed by the number of books on the list, because he asked, "Have you read *all* these books?" Cmiel answered with a twinkle in his eyes, "Three times." Horwitz asked us not to end a paper with a cosmic question and not to use the word "interesting" in our papers (in other words, "interesting" is not interesting—oops, how easy it is to slip; I meant "vacuous"), so in one of my papers I used "intriguing," adding in parentheses "I didn't use 'interesting,'" and he wrote in the margin, "thanks." He said that there is a thin line between "why" and "how" and illustrated his point with the example of explaining why or showing how the light comes on when the switch is flipped. "Why did the light come on?" "Because I flipped the light switch," or "When I flip the light switch, the current goes through." (It's only recently—in 2022—that I learned that it's the electromagnetic field *around* the wire that carries the energy down the wire. See the YouTube video, "The Big Misconception About Electricity," or the post by Craig Tullis on Quora.) Megill's course was on historiography more than on philosophy of history. He asked us to collect certain samples of historical writing. Reading a biography of Picasso, I saw a reference to a philosopher Professor Megill had talked about. I copied the relevant page and sent it to him. Another time I spotted the piece on the why question by Paul Edwards in his eight-volume *Encyclopedia of Philosophy*, which I'd bought at a used-book store in Iowa City. Since we'd read about explanations in historical narratives, I told him about my find. He wrote a page of commentary on my term paper that analyzed the narrative strategies of William Cronon's *Changes in the Land*, advising me to write more, meaning I was too terse.

Ningnan seemed to like it here. We moved into a one-bedroom apartment upstairs. We could drive to the grocery store, and we got a TV and a VCR. With a history of tensions between her parents and her she was never homesick. Qiyu was also doing well. We had a neighbor, Lao Tang, whose wife was still in Guangzhou, so he was lonely, as I'd been before. He would come over and chat with Ningnan; knowing he yearned for company, especially female company, I didn't mind his visits. One early afternoon in mid-March, I had the sudden urge to go visit Tom in Missouri. Unsure about the reliability of the old Catalina, I asked Lao Tang to come along with us in case we had car trouble, as he knew a thing or two about cars. Thirty minutes later, the four of us were on our way to Missouri. By then Tom and Suellen had separated and they'd sold their farm. Still, history is history, so Ningnan and I drove to Suellen's place to see her and to give her the presents Ningnan had brought from China. Suellen's large waterbed mattress was laid on the ornate, old-style Chinese bed she'd shipped from China back in 1980; with a tester to match, it was quite a sight.

We became friends with a Taiwanese grad student in computer science, who lived upstairs with a Malaysian girlfriend. When he went home to Taichung for summer break, I asked him to deliver a letter to my uncle (my mom's elder brother) who had fled with his school to Taiwan in 1949 and whom my mom had gotten in touch with only recently. Since my mom couldn't go to Taiwan to visit him, she asked me to when I got a chance. I wasn't able to make the trip till '99.

The honeymoon period was soon over. In early April, worried about our finances, Ningnan insisted on finding a job. I disagreed, asking her to relax, not to worry too much about money. Summer would soon be here, when we could all go to Boston where jobs would be more plentiful and the pay better. Ningnan wouldn't listen and right away found a job at a Chinese restaurant. Qiyu was sent to a daycare center.

Summer came soon enough. On June 8, we left Iowa City for Boston, my old revolutionary base, as we would put it in Mao's time. It was of course Greyhound again. In Boston Ningnan again became a waitress, we put Qiyu in a kindergarten, and I continued the work on Ken's house, repeating what I'd done the previous year: In two months I only took one day off. If I was incapable of taking care of my family, at least I wasn't lazy.

It was school time again. Making good tips Ningnan didn't want to return to Iowa City. I tried to change her mind, saying that although there was less money to be made back in Iowa, we'd be together. She was determined to better our financial situation by making the sacrifice. Now that I'd regained my stoic equanimity, sweetened by my son's company, I didn't insist. Ningnan came to the bus depot to see us off. When the bus pulled away, Qiyu didn't even blink, let alone cry like a baby. The not-yet-three-year-old Qiyu was no trouble on the bus, behaving better than a typical adult, making me proud and happy. Back in Iowa City, the university's student family housing had an apartment for us. Qiyu and I moved to No. 266 at Hawkeye Court.

There followed a happy period of my life. When I was at school or working, Qiyu was in daycare. Around 3:30 p.m., I'd pick him up on the way home, and then we'd play in the big yard outside. The laundry room was at another complex a few minutes' drive away, where we'd play in the sandbox while waiting for the laundry. At night, we watched David Letterman in bed together, with him laughing with me at times. On weekends, Qiyu went everywhere with me, including to the library, sometimes staying for a few hours. When I attended the conference on Plato's *Gorgias*, Qiyu played quietly in the hallway.

Only once did he make me fly off my handle. I asked him to get ready for his bath but he refused to take off his clothes after I told him to several times. I put him in the tub and slapped him hard on the butt a few times, yelling at him all the while. The next day and long afterward, I felt bad whenever I remembered the incident. I didn't hit him again.

Ningnan called from time to time, mostly telling me about the conflicts she was having or had had with her coworkers. She had moved to New Hampshire and then to Cambridge, working at Chinese restaurants. Unable to be there to comfort her or to help her in any concrete way, I could only tell her to take it easy and to exercise some self-restraint.

One day in December, feeling an acute pain in my throat I drove to the university hospital. When I got there, I was breathing with difficulty; even swallowing my saliva hurt. The nurse taking my vital signs told me to calm down, insinuating that I was being histrionic. Surprised I'd driven myself to the hospital, the doctor put me in an inpatient ward. I struggled against the pain to call a friend to pick up Qiyu at the daycare and look after him while I was bedridden. I was in the hospital for two nights before the acute laryngitis went away, racking up a bill of over four grand. Luckily, my insurance covered it; no wonder the university insisted that foreign students get health insurance.

Schoolwork was as exciting as ever. The only downside was my bank account only allowed me to take two classes instead of the full-time course load (three classes) required by the (unenforced) regulations. I wanted to take the first installment of the two-course sequence in American intellectual history, so I signed up with Cmiel again. Only beginning to become au courant with the academic scene, I was unsure whether to take Sartre or Wittgenstein for my second course. I went to see my advisor, who said Wittgenstein was influential in many disciplines. So analytical genius trumped existential guru. The professor, David Stern, was a young British philosopher who'd been drawn to the field (as he told us) by the austere beauty of the *Tractatus*. His thoroughness was shown in our reading list, which included a nearly six hundred–page Course-Pak (mostly as reference) plus the two main texts and *The Blue and Brown Books*.

My fascination with Wittgenstein's character exceeded my ability to fully appreciate his philosophy, despite my dedicated attempts to find illumination in the un-Wittgensteinian fast-growing secondary literature on his work. I looked through the entire section of books on him and his work in the library and for the final paper on Wittgenstein as a critic of civilization I read everything I could find on the topic, including part of the brand-new biography of the young Ludwig by Brian McGuinness the library didn't yet have. (Professor Stern loaned his copy to me with the words, "Take good care of it.") Though based on thorough research, the paper lacked an argumentative focus. There was too much exposition of others' views and not enough of my own, which had to do with both the specific views examined all of which made sense to me in some way and my tendency to see various theories on any issue that way. As Professor Stern put it, "In other words, it's good as far as it goes, but I'd have liked to see it go further."

To be in more classes than I could pay for, I asked for permission to audit two: Formal Logic taught by Phyllis Rooney, in which I learned that De Morgan's doctoral dissertation consisted of a one-page proof, and Origins of Contemporary Thought taught by Allan Megill, which dealt with such big names as Freud, Nietzsche, Heidegger, Foucault, and Derrida. Professor Megill would walk into the classroom with a stack of books to be referenced in his lecture, some visibly well-thumbed including one whose cover was barely attached. In one lecture, he said that *The Social Construction of Reality* was more often cited than read. The book indeed turned out to be tedious after a while. I enjoyed Megill's class so much that I asked him for a complete set of his syllabi.

It was in Iowa City that I discovered one of my favorite American places: the public library. While studying there, I would take a break by browsing its shelves, which was how I discovered Richard Armour's spoofs of history, literature, and academe. His spirit stayed with me when I went to Minnesota and beyond, and to show my gratitude I put a few of his satires in the bibliography of my dissertation. (Apparently irrelevant, but one of the skills acquired in academic training is to make what's irrelevant seem relevant, although in this case I only needed to justify it to myself—no dissertation committee member would, or did, ask me about the relevance of these items.) The only imperfection of Armour's books was that the author bio on the dust jacket said that before he started writing funny books, he'd been an author of serious tomes, which left a bad taste in my mouth. I only excused him by thinking the bio had come from the inferior pen of the publisher.

Toward the end of my first year, I'd begun looking for another school. Not that Iowa wasn't a good school. My main difficulty was financial. With its four faculty (two of whom also served in the English department) and several dozen graduate students, Iowa's American studies department had too many monks and not enough gruel (*zhoushao-sengduo*). Besides, even though the chair was interested in American studies abroad, my interests became increasingly cross-cultural and theoretical. I wanted to find a program with better financial aid and a more international and more theoretical orientation. After a few unpromising probes and some research, I applied to Berkeley's rhetoric program, Santa Cruz's history of consciousness program, Minnesota's comparative studies in discourse and society (CSDS) program, and as a last resort, Boston's American studies program. I also considered Chicago's Committee on Social Thought, but Professor Megill said Allan Bloom had a group of disciples, which turned me off.

The spring semester I signed up for Modern China taught by R. David Arkush and a seminar on the rhetoric of inquiry cotaught by John Lyne and Donald McCloskey (now Deirdre McCloskey), thus continuing my simultaneous engagement with substantive and theoretical or methodological questions. The social epistemologist Steve Fuller was visiting with Iowa's Project on Rhetoric of Inquiry, so he was invited to chat with the class. Introducing him John Lyne said, "Steve may be said to have a lot of knowledge," an unusual characterization of a colleague. But it was no exaggeration, because Fuller knew as many fields as Nicholas Rescher had written books. My term paper for Professor Arkush's course scrutinized Western explanations of the Cultural Revolution, making a passing shot at Wittgenstein's anti-explanatory stance in his *Remarks on Frazer's "Golden Bough."*

In early February I received an admission letter from Minnesota. The good news was I was in but the bad news was there was no money. However, I was encouraged to apply to the composition program for a teaching position. The program required two writing samples, a non-scholarly piece as well as a scholarly paper. I didn't know what to do about the non-scholarly piece. Then I got an idea (with Armour being my muse?): I wrote three jokes based on actual events to send in together with one of my term papers. Two shorter jokes ran as follows:

> I spent my last summer in the good old city of Boston. As a believer in a frugal life, I took the bus back to my school in Iowa. At the Greyhound bus depot in Boston, I inquired about the price before asking for a ticket. The young man behind the counter took out a book of tickets, asking, "Iowa City, Iowa?" "Yes," I answered. A second later, he raised his head with a puzzling expression on his face: "Iowa? How do you spell it?"

> We were sitting in the classroom waiting for the professor. This was a small class of nine new students and we would chat a few minutes before class began. This time we were talking about schizophrenics and the institutions in the United States. One Chinese student said that she had seen some crazy people on the street in some big city and asked the Americans how come they weren't in a madhouse. One American student gave some explanations, one of which being that there were too many lunatics nowadays. Then he said he had read that there were no or few institutions in China. "Do you have many schizophrenics in China? What d'you do about them?" asked my American classmate. To which I promptly answered, "They come to the United States."

After a face-to-face interview and an oral English test, I was hired. Thanks to Minnesota's CSDS program and its composition program, I was finally able to put myself through school and to feed my family, too.

Conflicts with her coworkers and sometimes with her boss made Ningnan's life increasingly unpleasant, so in early April she returned to Iowa City. I was glad that the family was living together again, but her news that while in Cambridge she'd slept with a man who was helping her gave me a strange feeling. I felt lousy every time the image of my wife sleeping with that man appeared in my head, though at the same time I didn't say a word of blame to her, thinking that she'd been in a difficult situation and that I'd betrayed her first. As time went on, the image appeared less and less frequently and eventually stopped bothering me.

Soon it was summer again. My old boss Ken still wanted me back, this time to work in Medford, on the house of his mother-in-law, who had moved into a nursing home. This time around I wasn't desperate, so I took the weekends off. In that summer the most memorable job was smashing up an old piano. After an appraisal proved the instrument's lack of monetary value while its size prevented its being picked up by the garbage man, Ken asked me to swing a sledgehammer against it, thirteen years after I'd swung one at the fertilizer plant and three years after I'd helped Tom knock down a section of a wall in his house on the farm. The large metal plate inside couldn't be smashed, so Ken told me to bury it in the woods behind the house, providing a potential, rich archeological find for the fortieth century.

11. Comp TA, Lonely Divorcé

Our 8-cylinder Catalina made moving easy. When I moved with my son to Iowa's student family housing, I put the quilts and other finery in the back seat and furniture on the top, parading through town like a circus. For the move to Minnesota, we traveled lighter. All the furniture was given away, the only big piece strapped onto the top of our sedan being the mattress. Four backbreaking boxes of books I'd acquired mostly from combing Cambridge's used-book stores over the summers had been shipped to my department. It was a joyful move: I got a job, the family was together again, and I was about to embark on the final leg of my graduate career.

Ningnan's church friends had introduced us to a Taiwanese couple living in St. Paul, whose husband half was an engineer by profession and a Christian community leader in his spare time. They kindly put us up in their basement for a week while we looked for an apartment, which we found at 814 8th Street SE, not far from the Minneapolis campus. Since we'd given our furniture away, we needed to pick some up at the dumpsters or on the roadside around Dinkytown, stuff that'd been thrown away by students leaving town. Driving around with our eyes peeled and stopping to look into dumpsters we failed to find any treasure, only to be fined for leaving the car running unattended for two minutes while hurrying to and from a dumpster, with Ningnan ignoring my plea to stay in the car. Well, sometimes in life you win nothing and lose something. In mid-November, we moved into St. Paul's student family housing, a two-bedroom, two-level apartment with a huge yard in the back shared by the surrounding houses. Life seemed to settle into a normal rhythm in this nice environment.

School began in mid-September with foreign-student orientation followed by a weeklong training for composition instructors, at the end of which we all had our draft syllabus. In the comp program, one section counted for 40 percent employment. We got two sections for one of the three quarters, sometimes two. For summers we got appointments every other year, unless special circumstances opened up more sections. Tuition waiver amounted to twice the appointment time; when CSDS folks got one section for a quarter, our own program picked up the 20 percent difference, so we ended up paying no tuition as long as we taught in the comp program. For the five years with the program, I got paid some $11,000 a year. CSDS also gave me a $500 fellowship for the first year and, due to the hard times, $200 thereafter.

My own coursework proceeded much like it had in Iowa. CSDS required a three-quarter basic research seminar taught by the core faculty, with John Mowitt, Richard Leppert, and Bruce Lincoln teaching my cohort. In these courses I became familiar with the theories in cultural studies. I chose my other regular classes from anthropology, political science, and speech communication. Meaning to pursue a supporting field of study in modern China and to work on some sort of Chinese-Western cross-cultural studies for my dissertation, I sought out Edward Farmer, Ann Waltner, and C. C. Lee for tutorials. For theoretical issues in cross-cultural studies, besides writing my term paper on the subject for Lincoln's seminar, I wrote four papers for Lisette Josephides, my advisor. I chose Lisette as my advisor because as an anthropologist she seemed to me both theoretically informed and empirically grounded. She'd just come from England and had done her fieldwork at the classic site of Papua New Guinea.

To supplement my formal coursework, I audited as many classes as I could: four each in anthropology, philosophy, and history and one each in political science and semiotics.

Of the seventeen teachers I had in Minnesota Daniel Kelliher was the most engaging and most irreverent. When I signed up for his course in Chinese politics and government, he asked me, "Why are *you* in this class?" implying it'd be a waste of time for someone like me who'd grown up in China. I said I was interested in Western studies of China. In the opening lecture in the big classroom, he said he'd graduated from Oberlin and then Yale, but please don't hold the latter against him. He asked students to call him by his first name, because "Dr. or Professor Kelliher gives me the willies, and Mr. Kelliher reminds me of my father." He told us that at the time of his hiring when the dean assured him he'd got the best salary deal, he was tempted to post the figure on his office door. In another lecture he said, "Economists are bad lovers." I knew he meant male economists (how many female economists are there?) but I wondered, "How does he know?" (The things students remember about their teachers' lectures! Theorists of pedagogy, beware.) I enjoyed the class so much that I asked to audit his course in peasant politics, which examined cases in France, India, and South America in medieval and modern times.

The comp program at Minnesota served a large number of students. The university required undergrads to take two writing classes: a freshman comp class and an upper-division writing class in one's major area of study. The program had four professors, eighteen adjuncts, and a hundred and eight TAs, who came from English and eleven other departments.

As a new instructor, I was assigned to teach freshman comp the first year. From the first summer on, I got mostly upper-division assignments and ended up teaching Intermediate Expository Writing, Writing in the Humanities, Writing for the Social Sciences, Writing about Science, Pre-professional Writing for Business, and Technical Writing for Engineers in the following four years.

The program also had a writing lab, where we both critiqued (to use a college buzzword) students' papers on a first-come, first-served basis and, on a weekly basis, tutored honors students writing their graduation theses. During the five years I tutored students writing theses on sports psychology, the policies of HUD, Japanese national character, Polish politics and the Holy See, the Maastricht Treaty, water in the Middle East, and Chinese politics.

Writing is hard, even harder to teach. Although I wouldn't go so far as to parrot Oscar Wilde who famously quipped, "Nothing that is worth knowing can be taught" (or I'd be either obviously inconsistent or arguing myself out of my livelihood), I did, and do, think there's little a teacher can do to help students write better. No, let me rephrase this: what I mean is, though there are rules of thumb about writing that a teacher can impart to students, and, of course, though a teacher can point out the problems in a student's writing, what's crucial is that the student *cares* about writing. If not, the rules of thumb would be forgotten or applied mechanically instead of according to the circumstances, or a teacher's comments would be ignored and only the grade would garner the student's attention.

In my five years of teaching composition and then over a decade of teaching undergraduate interdisciplinary courses in the humanities and social sciences with an emphasis on writing, I've seen too many students make the same mistake after it's been pointed out to them. The care element applies to learning other things, but because writing well requires rethinking and revising what one has drafted, it demands greater dedication and alertness than does typical content intake and digestion.

For my first comp course I chose argumentation as the mode of writing for students to work on and called it Reading, Thinking and Writing, which crystallized my conception of writing: Good writing is based on careful reading and clear thinking. For stimulation and models, I picked the following topics from a book series: "Debating Educational Issues," "Debating Social Issues," and "Debating World Politics." The class went well in part because students were given plenty of room for choosing topics for their papers. The second time I taught the course, in the winter quarter, I reordered the readings according to both students' suggestions and my own sense: "Debating Social Issues" became the first segment, followed by "Debating Educational Issues" and "Debating World Politics." I also reordered the readings within the now first topic. The first year soon went by, with only one obviously prejudiced comment in the course evaluations. The student said that she (I happened to have recognized her handwriting) couldn't understand 95 percent of what I said in class, and she didn't like foreign TAs in the first place.

As a writing instructor, I did have high expectations for my students. All good writing is done with care, but writing about science, engineering, and business requires greater accuracy than writing in other fields. For the business writing class, I told students that if a piece contained more than three (or some such number) simple errors, then it wouldn't receive an A, no matter how brilliant it was otherwise. I said to them, "Would you want to hire someone whose cover letter contained several simple errors?" One straight-A student decided to change his registration from A-F to S-N (Satisfactory-Not Satisfactory), afraid he wouldn't be able to maintain his perfect grade point average. Most of the classes gave me mediocre ratings, and I knew how I could have improved a class or what my idiosyncrasies were. For example, some students suggested, and I concurred, that for Technical Writing for Engineers and Writing About Science, it would be helpful to invite some engineers and scientists from private companies to talk to students about the role of writing in their work. But I lacked the entrepreneurial spirit to initiate such contacts. Instead, I asked students to interview science and engineering faculty on campus. In one section of Writing for the Social Sciences, a student said that I was way too analytical, even much more so than a friend who was a philosophy major. Another student said I taught Writing About Science as if it were a philosophy course, making mountains out of molehills (not his words) in explicating our thin text. He said I should be teaching philosophy not writing. When I got the assignment to teach Writing in the Humanities, I did seize the opportunity to sneak in a bit of philosophy, using a text on philosophical rhetoric, but I was by no means inconsiderate of students' needs. I also chose an anthropology text that addressed issues of culture and value, thus balancing the unfamiliar with the familiar, the abstract with the concrete.

Out of the hundreds of students I had during those five years, three seniors took the trouble to cowrite a one-and-a-half-page letter of complaint, not about anything egregious I'd done, but about their dissatisfaction with the way I taught the class. The faculty member in charge of upper-division comp courses, Donald Ross, called me into his office and showed me the letter, adding that it was rare for students to write a letter like that. After I read the letter, Don said, "*You* can do this," his tone suggesting that I should have been able to avoid this kind of problem. He didn't say anything harsh or even critical, just asked me about my class. I was grateful that he didn't take any action against me because of that letter. The only other time a student complained was when I missed my office hour. I had always kept my office hours, even though it was a rare student who came in to ask me to look at a draft. (I did have some class time devoted to looking at drafts while students revised theirs.) But on that day, I went to a dentist appointment. A student showed up and I wasn't there. The student then went to Betsy, the executive secretary, to lodge a complaint. The next day Betsy talked to me; she was upset. I tried to explain instead of apologizing. She said, "But you were still not in your office." I never repeated the delinquency.

For reasons I couldn't fathom, one class liked me much better than all the others. I did the same things in this class as in others: trying to be demanding while helpful, rigorous while good-humored. But when I saw the evaluations, I was surprised that several students had rated me as among the "Top 10%" of all the teachers they'd had. This was Technical Writing for Engineers in summer '90, when I'd taught in the program for only three quarters and that particularly course for the first time. Some of the positive comments provided clues:

> He enjoyed what he was doing and that helped me enjoy myself.
>
> I learned to be more careful when I'm writing and acquired a better technical style of writing.
>
> The teacher was very open-minded to new ideas. . . . I feel prepared for the job market after taking this class.
>
> Learned: Inc., flower is not flour [the student had written a set of instructions for making a pizza and had used "flower" as the basic ingredient].
>
> I learned that using pompous words (which I always used to use) are [*sic*] wrong and make the reading much more slower and difficult [*sic*].

When I taught the same course again, using the same textbook and similar assignments, the same head and face, the reception was nonmemorable.

I fulfilled the credit requirement for my degree by the end of the second year. To prepare for the comprehensive exams and to lay a better foundation for my dissertation research, I spent the third year continuing reading intensively and extensively in the theoretical literature on cross-cultural studies. For books, I did comprehensive bibliographic searches in Minnesota's main library and then read important texts on such topics as realism, relativism, constructivism, rationality, representation, philosophy of criticism, and methods in Chinese studies. I took two credits with my advisor for the work, which resulted in a fifty-page, single-spaced bibliography of two-dozen themes. For periodicals, I sat in front of the shelves in the library for hours on end, looking through and reading pertinent articles; made photocopies; and checked out current and bound issues.

I took my comprehensives in the winter quarter. As was the procedure, I chose the committee members before presenting them with topical areas each with a book list for examination. The five examiners wrote their questions; I had a week to answer them.

Richard Leppert asked me to discuss the procedural apparatus of Adorno's *Minima Moralia*, and to identify its strengths and weaknesses as they bear on my project. (His alternative question was on cultural studies in Great Britain.) Bruce Lincoln wrote three questions. The first question asked me to identify three examples within Chinese popular culture on the U.S. and examine how aspects of American culture, history or social practice have been represented, the processes producing such representations, their effect on the audiences, and the interests they serve. His second question told me to do the same with three examples of American popular representations of China. The final question asked me to compare and contrast the processes I had explored in the previous two answers and account for the similarities and divergences. My advisor posed the following question: Mudimbe's *The Invention of Africa* describes how Western definitions of Africanism together with Western style scholarly discourse bring about a crisis of identity. Do I see the same thing happen in China, and if not, why not and how would I describe the impact of such representations? Edward Farmer's multipart question asked me to weigh the pros and cons of an area studies approach to the understanding of China or the U.S., whether this approach is more appropriate when applied within or from the outside of the target culture, what does Edward Said find fault with in his critique of Orientalism, and whether there is a parallel problem in American Studies. Ann Waltner asked me to select three recent works by Americans on China, show how these are theoretically informed, ways the authors are or are not aware of their theoretical underpinnings, and in as much detail as I could, suggest ways more or different awareness might have changed the accounts. (I have borrowed the wording of the questions almost verbatim without adding quotation marks.)

I answered these questions in seven essays, mostly by drawing on my memory of the relevant literature. Only one new idea (new to me anyway) emerged in the process of writing the essays. In answering Professor Farmer's question, it occurred to me that Chinese views of America might be characterized as Occidentalism and reverse Occidentalism: the former treats the U.S. as a negative other, whereas the latter sees her as a model to emulate.

The response was mixed. Professor Farmer liked my essays best. When I called him about my exam, he said it was "very erudite and very articulate." I was elated until he said, "but I have a stinging criticism"; for a split second I was at a loss as to what my fatal flaw might be. It turned out my dot-matrix printer had made the script difficult to read. "You shouldn't hide your thoughts behind the ink," he said. I could sense a smile on his face. Richard's brief note ended with "I vote to pass." Ann said my discussion of the first two books was detailed but my analysis of the last book was too sketchy, adding maybe I was pressed for time. She let me pass. I had actually had a question about my advisor's question and thought of ringing her for clarification. Instead, I went ahead and wrote my answer based on my misinterpretation of part of her question. But she also let me pass. Bruce didn't like my answers at all but let me pass nonetheless.

In the oral part of the comprehensives, besides answering questions about the written part, the student must also delineate a plan for the dissertation. About the latter, I mentioned a title brewing in my mind at the time, "Representing the (Un)Representable: A Model for Cross-Cultural Studies with an Examination of Western Representations of (Aspects of) Modern China." I said half-jokingly that the title was postmodernist but the subtitle sounded like something out of the seventeenth century. The oral exam took place on March 11, 1992. (Just for fun: the longest book title I've seen is Thomas Campanella's discourse on the Spanish Monarchy published in London in 1660 – *Thomas Campanella, an Italian friar and second Machiavel. His advice to the King of Spain for attaining the universal monarchy of the world. Particularly concerning England, Scotland and Ireland, how to raise division between king and Parliament, to alter the government from a kingdome to a commonwealth. Thereby embroiling England in civil war to divert the English from disturbing the Spaniard in bringing the Indian treasure into Spain. Also for reducing Holland by procuring war betwixt England, Holland, and other sea-faring countries, affirming as most certain, that if the King of Spain become master of England and the Low Countries, he will quickly be sole monarch of all Europe, and the greatest part of the new world.*)

On March 20, CSDS students received a memo from the director of graduate studies John Mowitt that the program could nominate two students for a dissertation fellowship, whose winner or winners would be able to devote full time to research and writing the next year. The university would award approximately forty such fellowships. Since I'd just passed the comprehensives and I seemed to have a pretty good idea of how to go about my dissertation research, I prepared my application materials. Even though I gathered Mowitt might not have been impressed with my work (I'd gotten a C in his class), he signed the form. But because my advisor wasn't a full member of the graduate faculty, I had earlier picked Bruce as my co-advisor with the understanding that all actual advising would be done by Lisette. Bruce refused to sign the form, saying that he didn't think I was ready for my dissertation. Worse still, in his letter he wrote that my background (meaning I'd grown up in China) might have led to a lack of ability to think critically. Since Bruce sent a copy of the letter to my advisor, Lisette phoned me and we agreed to have a chat. She assured me that she disagreed with Bruce. Then it was revealed to me by chance that I wasn't the only student who'd been written off by Bruce. At a party, another student, who was white and had been educated in the U.S., told me that Bruce was unable to understand him. (He transferred to another school soon afterward.) Thankfully, I had the comp program's position to support me through the research and writing of my dissertation.

Next, I worked on my dissertation proposal a bit more. Still in the grip of theoretical issues, I sketched out a proposal that was way too theoretical, revolving as it did around such philosophy-of-science concepts as theory-ladenness and commensurability or incommensurability and how they play out in empirical cross-cultural studies. My advisor said I needed to be more empirical. Thinking that she didn't fully appreciate my fascination with theory, in my revised proposal I wrote that when the project got under way, it would be "excruciatingly" empirical. That didn't go unnoticed. She commented, "Why 'excruciatingly'?" Later on, I realized her advice worked for my benefit. If I had followed through on my original proposal (assuming she let me have my way), the project would have taken much longer to finish, and I am not sure it would have been a better project. And given the state of the relevant scholarship, the project might even be a dead end.

So far, I've concentrated on my studies and teaching, but during the same period a lot more—both institutional and personal—happened. I'll be brief about the former and give the highlights of the latter.

For financial and other reasons, in the early 1990s Minnesota decided to close its humanities and linguistics departments. Petitions were signed, articles were published in the papers, and hearings were held. Scholars in linguistics from all over the world wrote to support the continuation of the linguistics department, both on the grounds of the importance of the subject and of the quality of the Minnesota department. CSDS was housed in the Humanities Department, which served majors and offered general-education courses. Our program also received letters of support, including letters from such academic stars as Stanley Fish. All to no avail. In the midst of this, some faculty members understandably began looking for greener pastures, while students became anxious about their future. Amitava Kumar, a fellow student, even circulated a pungent memo of complaint. Still in the heat of battle with constructivism and various other isms, I didn't get worked up about the crisis. When CSDS was merged with Comparative Literature to form a new department, the crisis was officially over. At home, however, a crisis had been broiling for a while.

Ever since my wife and I got married right before I went to Beijing, we had been separated much of the time. In the first three years, when we got together during summer or winter breaks, it was like a honeymoon. Because we never lived together for long, the differences between our personalities and attitudes toward life didn't loom large. When I had the affair in Shenzhen, it broke her heart. Slowly but eventually, she recovered from the blow. When I got into Iowa in spring '87, I became more optimistic about our reunion, so in a letter I asked her whether she still loved me, whether she wanted to reunite with me in the States. In her response she emphatically stated that that was the only thing she wanted, even suggesting my question showed a lack of understanding of her feelings for me.

After I got the job at Minnesota, which fundamentally improved our financial situation, I thought our troubles were over. But once we moved there and lived together for a while, we started having arguments, nothing major, just everyday things. For example, she didn't like my going to a mechanic for an oil change, insisting that I learn to do it myself to save money, so I did. After we moved to St. Paul, the quarrels became more frequent. She complained that I wasted too much money renting movies, that I bought too many books. In general, she thought I was inept at providing for the family: I paled in comparison with other Chinese students most of whom being in science and engineering got higher stipends. My mind and heart were not in how to make small improvements in the material conditions of our life. When a graduating student family threw away some furniture, she wanted to pick it up so that our slightly inferior furniture could be replaced. I would very reluctantly go along, complaining about the hassle. Gradually, quarreling became a way of life. Realizing my feelings for her were getting more and more tenuous, I pleaded with her more than once: "Please stop when I still have feelings for you; once those feelings are gone, then it'll be too late." Her nagging continued. But if something else hadn't happened, maybe I wouldn't have taken the decisive step.

Ningnan's sister had graduated from college and wanted to come to the States for graduate study. Both she and her mother asked us to help her. This is typical of Chinese families, and I suspect, of families from many other countries. Shortly after we moved to Minnesota, Ningnan started working at a Chinese restaurant so that she could save enough money to help her sister, which I fully supported. Meanwhile, the only way to bring her sister here for her expected matriculation was to get a friend to be her nominal sponsor, with the hope that once her sister got here, it'd be easier to get financial aid.

To find a sponsor for her sister, Ningnan started to befriend a businessman, Don, who frequented the restaurant where she was working as a waitress. Not surprisingly, as he told me later, Don got the impression that our marriage was over. One day, Ningnan asked Don to come over to our home before going out with her and Qiyu. Feeling a lump in my chest, I went outside to the big yard when the time Don was to show up drew near. That was their first "date."

A business broker, Don made commissions on his deals. His income was enough to support himself but he was far from being well off, so the financial guarantee he signed wasn't good enough. Ningnan eventually asked the CEO of a company, who was a member of the church she attended, to be her sister's sponsor, which solved the problem like a sharp knife cutting tofu: one stroke and it went through.

The next thing we knew, her sister was flying into San Francisco on December 8, 1990. Ningnan decided to continue working, while Qiyu and I took Greyhound to California to meet her sister. When we returned to Minnesota on December 17, Ningnan told me she'd overworked during the time I was away with Qiyu. One evening she was so weak that she fainted in Don's bathtub, and Don had to carry her out of the tub and put her to bed. Why was she taking a bath at Don's place? She felt no need to explain, and I didn't seem to have cared to ask. On January 12, I told her I wanted a divorce. She was ambivalent but didn't object to it strongly.

The three of them continued going out. Don liked Qiyu a lot and would take him golfing; he had a set of golf clubs made to Qiyu's size. Qiyu also liked him. Even I became Don's friend. When Don and Ningnan had fights, he would come to me to vent. He took me to bars and strip clubs.

We agreed Qiyu would stay with her, with me paying child support and sharing legal custody. Because the divorce was an amicable one, we needed no attorney; a paralegal was sufficient. I filed the papers with Ramsey County family court on April 5, 1991, and on July 3 the divorce was granted.

Although a sense of liberation accompanied my decision to get divorced, most of the time restlessness and depression were mixed with longing, for love and for the cutaneous pleasures given by a lover. In their absence, books consumed me. I drove my still chugging Catalina to all the used-book stores I could find in the Twin Cities, all the Borders, all the Barnes and Nobles in the suburbs, and all the used-book sales in large warehouses I saw advertised in the paper. I read through book catalogs such as the thick Oxford University Press philosophy catalog and ordered books from out-of-town used-book sellers who sent out their catalogs regularly. At a bookstore I'd sit on the ground and go from one end of the shelf to the other. With a dwindling bank account, I kept buying books.

I could write a short piece about my trips to bookstores. I remember exactly where I saw Stanislav Andreski's *Social Sciences as Sorcery* in a used-book store in St. Paul—Tom had sent me a copy while I was still in college—and where I leafed through the dusty *Scientific Explanation* by R. B. Braithwaite in a Minneapolis suburb—the old seller had a Ph.D. in philosophy. I remember how I bought a hardback copy of David Stove's *The Plato Cult and Other Philosophical Follies*—when a well-stocked bookstore in Minneapolis that was going out of business put all its books on a 50 percent discount, and how seeing Edward Said's *Beginnings* in an old-book store in St. Paul reminded me of an idea I'd had for some time, that the result of an inquiry or even an argument hinges, in a nontrivial sense, on where one ends or stops.

When books couldn't dispel my loneliness, I patronized strip clubs and massage parlors, horny and expectant on the way there but often sad, empty, and unsatisfied afterward, similar to what Yu Dafu had experienced when he studied in Japan in the early

20th century. To supplement my income in summer, I worked in a warehouse, delivered phonebooks, bussed tables, and painted houses.

I went out with fellow female students, including taking a tall girl from Europe to a movie on a white evening, but we never went beyond talking. Then one day in the spring quarter of '91, a fellow student in a class I was auditing and I started talking in the elevator, and we decided I'd go over to her place on Saturday afternoon. Louise (I use her middle name to provide a small measure of privacy) gave me her phone number and address in uptown Minneapolis. I left my home in St. Paul half an hour early but in my excitement forgot to bring her address with me. Driving through the West Bank, I ran through a red light. When I found her number in the phonebook, called her, and got to her place, I was half an hour late. It was a beautiful afternoon, so we went for a walk around Lake Calhoun, all the while talking about our backgrounds and our studies. Louise had just been divorced but, I could tell, emotionally she was in a much better shape than me; she also had fewer bones to pick with academe. When I left in the evening, she came downstairs to see me off. Before I knew it, she kissed me on my right cheek, just a peck, and I didn't know how to react. Walking toward my car I felt her eyes hot on my back. The next day, at lunch in Stadium Village, I asked her what she thought about after I left the previous night. She said, "A lot."

We had some more dates, going to parties and cooking a dinner at her place. Then one weekend she told me she'd left me a letter in my mailbox at CSDS. I asked her what it was about; she said I'd find out when I saw it. I had to wait till Monday while imagining ways to break into the office. When I saw the letter Monday morning, I became dejected. She said the reason she wrote a letter was she could express herself better through writing than through talking, and she and I could only be friends for the following reasons: that by my own admission I'd been seriously lonely for the past year; that it was important that I see it wasn't she that made me feel better, it was only what she'd done, and all she'd done was to talk to me and listen to me and by doing that she reminded me life shouldn't be so terrible; that she couldn't make my life wonderful, only I could do that. I asked her to meet me at the student center to talk things over. I bookishly quoted Santayana and some other author, trying to convince her that a person on the rebound doesn't have to be a liability. She was unperturbed by my clumsy rationalizations. Given what I'd said and done, it isn't surprising to me now that she said we could only be friends; i.e., we should stop seeing each other. When I cooked a dinner at her place, I'd said half-jokingly that if she could make enough money, I wouldn't mind staying at home doing the cooking. I had also given her a two-page poem I'd handwritten expressing my desire to be with her. She'd been upset, saying, "How can you say you love me when you don't even know me?"

After that, I had a dream in which she let me kiss her. How did Shelley sing: "What is all this sweet work worth / If thou kiss not me?" While on the phone telling her about the dream, I sensed she was annoyed, so I called her no more.

Desperately lonely, I called a former student a couple of times at the instigation of a friend. We agreed to meet at the student center, but at the appointed time she didn't show up. Too dense to realize this was her way of telling me not to bother her, I called her again. When her roommate answered the phone, I realized my blunder and discontinued my silly behavior.

Then I looked at personals and responded to several ads. One person wrote back that she'd just found someone, which I thought could be true or was just a polite rejection. Another woman, a librarian living in a distant suburb, agreed to drive up to meet me. We had lunch and that was it. One day, I spotted an ad in a personals booklet. A middle-aged woman was looking for a man, especially a Chinese man. I thought, "Well, I certainly qualify." I wrote her, and she wrote back enclosing a photo of her standing on a beach, adding it wasn't the most flattering of her pictures. She lived in Duluth, quite a drive from St. Paul. But a man starved for intimacy will jump at any opportunity. One weekend I drove up to Duluth. Before going to her place, I stopped by a flower shop in Duluth. When she saw me, she said, "Ah, roses." The first sight of her made me realize what "middle-aged" means in this country. Still, I cooked the noodles I brought and just when she thought I was going to leave (as she told me later), I said, "Let's go upstairs." I stayed the night. Two pathetic souls struck a fleeting connection—between a male and a female, between two generations, and between the Orient and the Occident. Jobless, the lady wrote poetry and liked reading novels about the Orient. She described how a novel of John Hersey's had roused her erotic fantasies. And now, from nowhere, a lean Oriental boy floated in and helped her live out her fantasy.

A month later, I went up to Duluth again. The lady had told me one of her poems had been published in a collection but she didn't have the money to buy a copy of the clothbound book, so I brought my checkbook with me and wrote her a check for forty some dollars. While we were in bed, her daughter called. She said with a grin, "My boyfriend is here." When I was leaving, she came out to the porch and kissed me, saying that she wanted her neighbors to see her with me.

Having failed to find someone by responding to ads, I thought maybe I could do better by placing my own ad. Two ads got me four responses. I saw a nurse twice, an artist twice, and a math professor once. Nothing happened with any of them. I suspected that they probably thought I was just trying to get a green card. At least the nurse and the artist did: one through her questions, the other a reference to it. The funny thing is, the artist answered both of my ads placed some time apart! What are the odds of that? Later, when I told her over the phone I had gotten hitched, she said, "Now you can stay in the United States." Being an expert in cross-cultural misunderstanding, I didn't feel the least offended. For my date with the young math professor, we went to Dinkytown's Café Royale, a place where serious-looking grad students, self-important artsy types, and lost souls hung out. On the short walk there, I said if I'd known we were going there, I'd have brought my cigarettes, knowing well smoking was a vice to most academics. (I'd started smoking again after filing for divorce and quit a hundred times.) We chatted for less than an hour, and when we parted, she expressed no intention to see me again.

Years later, I realized that I'd misremembered my height and put in the ads 5′6″ instead of 5′9″, which was far from the only incidence of my absentmindedness: I finished the fifty-page bibliography on my birthday without realizing it until I saw the date on the document again a year or two later and remembered I'd worked nonstop that day to finish the thing.

Between 1990 and spring 1992, I rarely wrote my parents—I was in such a lousy state of mind that I didn't want to write. My mom was so upset about my failure to tell them how we were that in one of her letters she said something equivalent to disowning me. I wrote back to explain that "no news is good news," asking her not to worry. Eventually, she stopped being angry with me, and surprisingly, in one letter she said she regretted having treated me too harshly when I was living with her in the country, referring to her frequent beating of me. But, as I said back in chapter 2, when I reflected on my years living in the countryside, I held no grudges against my mom and honestly thought that though beating was bad, spoiling would have been worse. Plus, I knew she had suffered too much during those difficult years. I wished I could help her financially, the only thing I could do from a distance, but I was eking out a living myself. It wasn't until years later that I was able to help her pay her medical bills and buy an apartment (the latter with only a check for three grand).

Ningnan's relationship with Don stagnated. Feeling guilty about "abandoning" her, I didn't ask her to move out. I put a mattress in Qiyu's room and shared household expenses with her. On May 1, 1992, I moved out of student family housing and into Dinkytown, leaving Ningnan and Qiyu there because of the safe environment for my son and the low rent for Ningnan. This was, of course, against the rules, as the apartment was rented under my name and student family housing was meant for students. The co-op eventually discovered who were living there and asked me to surrender the apartment.

In the same month I moved out of student family housing, I met Madeleine Raffel, and we began a whirlwind romance.

12. A Cross-Cultural Marriage, an Interdisciplinary Dissertation

On the evening of May 23, 1992, a Saturday, the Indian students put on a show of song and dance at the auditorium on the St. Paul campus. There was a large audience. During the intermission, I stood against a wall in the atrium, watching the bustling crowd. A few feet away stood another lone figure, a girl, also looking on. I decided to strike up a conversation. She said she came from the University of Chicago, here on a research trip trying to get data from the U of MN for a big study of suicide among college students that her boss was conducting. Hearing that she was a student in the Committee on Social Thought, I said I had almost applied to her program three years before, and our conversation became livelier. She told me about her first encounter with Saul Bellow. When her class was first introduced to the faculty, Saul Bellow walked up to her and asked her name. She said her name was Madeleine Raffel and then asked Bellow, "Who are *you*?" The intermission was soon over; going back in we decided to sit together. Even though we'd just met, during the second half of the show we exchanged a few comments in hushed tones and I felt as if we'd come to the show together as friends in the first place.

Coming out of the auditorium I asked her whether she'd like to go get a drink. She smiled and said yes. Walking up to the car I saw a flat tire on one of the back wheels. "Oh, no!" Immediately I decided to drive the car to the gas station nearby, where a mechanic could be found. I asked Madeleine whether she would come with me. When she smiled and said yes again, I was relieved. We got into the car and drove slowly toward the gas station. When we got there a few minutes later, the mechanic was just about to leave for the day. But he was kind and agreed to help us. We stood around talking while the mechanic found a used tire and replaced the flat. "Would you still like to go and get the drink?" Madeleine smiled again.

Off we go and in less than five minutes we come to a bar on University Avenue connecting the Twin Cities. We walk in and sit in a booth. Each of us orders a beer. Our conversation turns to academic subjects and becomes more animated when suddenly a young man comes over and says hi to me and asks, "How's your wife?" I recognize him as our neighbor in the next building when we first moved to Minneapolis. I walk over to the counter and say hi to his wife and tell them I've been divorced since last year. Coming back to my seat I anticipate a question from Madeleine about "my wife." Madeleine is her previous self and asks me the question with a smile. I tell her and that's that. We talk a little longer till the beer is gone; neither she nor I drink so one beer is enough. I take her back to her guesthouse on the St. Paul campus, next to the auditorium where we met.

At the guesthouse she invites me in. We go in and I stay for a short while. Since it's getting late now, I must leave. I lean against the foot of the bed, while she stands against the wall facing me. I stand up and draw her close to me and kiss her on the mouth; she kisses me back. We kiss a bit more with my arms around her tightening slightly. She says, "I have to go back, you know." "I know," I reply and kiss her more. "I have to go back to Chicago, you know," as if to tell me (and herself?) not to get too worked up. We kiss some more and then I leave. We agree to go to the lakes tomorrow, a Sunday.

I drive home in a reverie. I go back to my Dinkytown hovel (as Madeleine later called it) and lie in bed, a single mattress on the floor. Too excited to sleep, I twist and turn, turn and twist. There isn't really that much to think about but I just can't go to sleep. I remain in this mental priapism till around 4 a.m. when fatigue finally gets to me. But some forty minutes later I wake up again, my head now in an achy buzz. I can no longer go back to sleep.

In midmorning I drive over to the guesthouse. We head to the lakes. The May sun is smiling, a perfect day for a stroll. The circular path around the lake is already dotted with joggers, walkers, skateboarders, young and old, male and female. We perambulate a full circle with more conversation, both academic and personal. She tells me about the suicide study she's helping collect the data for and how the data are corrupted with nobody in charge paying any attention and how she's found ways to rectify the problems. She tells me about her academic history, that she went to St. John's College at Santa Fe as an undergrad, what her first visit to the college was like, what the seminars there were like, and what some of the faculty were like. She tells me that she got a scholarship to go to Chicago. She tells me about her friends. She tells me her main academic interests are poetry and history of science, the latter especially of the seventeenth and eighteenth centuries. She tells me her advisor is Mr. A. K. Ramanujan, the noted translator of Indian literature. She tells me about Allan Bloom, that he has a Chinese butler and leers at handsome, young, male students when he lectures. I tell her about my background and my friends. Back to the parking lot, we get into the car. I kiss her. The rest of the day is a blur. I seem to remember we went to the other two lakes, too. By the time we got back to the guesthouse at night, I'd become exhausted. I crashed in the bed by the window, while Madeleine slept in the other bed in the middle of the room.

The next morning, she needed to go to work, maybe so did I. That night she stayed at my hovel. The small room steamed up with the May heat and our passion.

Madeleine had to return to Chicago; we agreed to keep in touch.

She left, but strangely I had zero anxiety that we'd never see each other again, that it was just a one-night stand with me being thrown back into the abyss of loneliness. No. She called me when she got to Chicago and then I called her and she called me and I called her. We talked from half an hour to an hour and a half. At first almost daily. I worked on my dissertation proposal for several days and on June 2 finished it. Then I flew to Chicago—I had to see Madeleine again, and I had a week.

Madeleine met me at the airport. She and a housemate lived in an old building with high ceilings and a spacious dining room and a large kitchen near the university. In the following days, she takes me to see a friend at work and orders a famous Chicago pizza with spinach. She takes me to the university library and her department. We go to an industrial museum not far from Lake Michigan. We walk along the lake and ask somebody to take our picture with us holding each other sideways. We look at the vast expanse of the lake. She drops me off at the Seminary Co-Op, the best-stocked bookstore I've ever seen, where I spend a whole afternoon—it's the only bookstore that has Max Black's tome on the *Tractatus* on the shelf. We go to Powell's—the best used-book store I've seen, beating the dozens I visited in Boston and Cambridge—where I see several volumes of *The Cambridge History of China*. We go to another used-book store, where I buy a large book on Chinese architecture as an informal birthday present for her. We visit the Art Institute of Chicago to look at the engravings of William Blake, one of her favorite poets. We sit in the arched entrance of her building, where I tell her about the stories of Shen Congwen, scenes of life from a border town in Western Hunan. The second morning, she makes the most scrumptious breakfast I've seen, with half a dozen fresh fruits to go with something hot I no longer remember. I think to myself: "Is this a typical breakfast for her? I can certainly live with this!" She introduces me to Ben & Jerry's ice cream, which ranks with jalapeños in making America a great country. She shows me a short paper and I make some inane comments as a composition instructor. We go to a movie; we rent a movie. Taking a shower together I suggest that at some point we check out an orgy somewhere, not necessarily participating, you know, just to see what's going on, in the spirit of Dan Greenburg's *True Adventures*. She frowns at my naughtiness as a knee-jerk reaction but coyly agrees. (I don't mean to disappoint you, but it was soon forgotten because it was out of the question.)

A few days into my visit we seemed to have reached a tacit agreement that we were headed toward the M-state. Sitting in bed one early afternoon, I asked her whether she wanted me to formally pop the question. We both seemed to think, "Is that formality necessary?" She wrote a letter to her father, a multitalented and internationally known hydraulic engineer, about us, saying, "he definitely is the man for me."

The honey-week in Chicago had only one unpleasant moment. Before we went out the second or third day I was there, she freshened up and put on a pretty blouse. Shortly after we left her building, she asked me how I'd introduce her to my family. Guileless to the point of stupidity, I began, "Well, I've met an average-looking girl" when she cut me off, her expression changing from gay to angry. "An average-looking girl? Why, I took all that trouble before coming out; it was a waste of time!" I immediately said I was sorry, that I didn't mean she wasn't attractive. I apologized again and again, trying to repair the damage. A few minutes later, her anger subsided.

Whereas I had been pining for love, Madeleine had been considering taking a leave from her studies when we met. She'd been at Chicago for six years but still needed to finish her incompletes before she could take her comprehensive exams. She was thinking of moving to the West Coast. Now that we were madly in love, it was either moving to the West Coast, which would spell an end to our romance, or moving to Minneapolis. She was hoping, which I didn't know at the time, to get some psychological support from me so that she could continue her studies.

In mid-July, she moved in with me, her boxes of books—mostly classics from her college's Great Books curriculum—piled up in the middle of the tiny room in Dinkytown. We decided to marry on July 23, exactly two months after our first meeting, which happened to be her father's birthday.

Preparations were simple. We didn't think of changing her family name to mine, nor did we have the imagination to consider changing my family name to hers. But we wanted to mark our union. In one of my few creative moments, I came up with an idea of making her part of me and me part of her; that is, I take her family name as an added middle name and she changes her middle name to my family name. We got two unadorned gold bands and had the following engraved on the inside: on hers, "XRL+MLR" facing "23 May 1992" and on mine, "MLR+XRL" facing "23 May 1992." My friend Dubem would be my witness at the ceremony, and her friend Astrida hers.

We had a small crisis on one of our daily evening walks around Dinkytown. In my happy, uninhibited mood, I told her that I'd dated this nurse between our first meeting and my trip to Chicago. Madeleine went ballistic and wanted to call off the wedding. I was seized with panic, as if standing on the edge of a precipice. I explained that the reason I'd gone out with the nurse, twice, was that when I met Madeleine, I had just received a few responses from my second personals ad, and having had little dating experience in my life I went out with the nurse out of curiosity. Pressed by her questioning, I told her about the artist but not the math professor. By this time, I was so scared of a breakup that I couldn't be completely truthful. I frantically explained again and again that it was merely out of curiosity that I'd gone on the dates. Half an hour later, she finally calmed down. I told myself not to be stupid again.

The brief ceremony took place in a judge's office in downtown Minneapolis. Our faces gleamed with happiness. Madeleine was twenty-eight, and this was her first marriage.

We moved to a one-bedroom apartment. Madeleine soon found a job as a secretary in the Dental School and took an evening Chinese class in the fall. She made such rapid progress that a few months later she was able to write a short letter in Chinese to my parents, which thrilled them. I did the cooking most of the time. I joked that the main reason we got married was she liked Chinese food and chilies. When I was cooking dinner one day, she took down her Shakespeare from the bookshelf and read to me in front of the stove. We watched the Chinese TV dramatization of the epic *Journey to the West*. One day, she brought home Amy Tan's *The Joy Luck Club*. I read twenty odd pages and couldn't go on. Neither could she. For a while, we read from a book aloud in bed before going to sleep: *The Brothers Karamazov*, *Mao Tse-tung and I Were Beggars*, and *Against Deconstruction*. I'd be drifting off to sleep, she'd kiss and caress me, and I'd be wide-awake. I was happy. When I met Madeleine, I was still smoking. Before we got married, she said I could continue, as long as I did it outside. But as if to show the power of love, I quit two days before our wedding and didn't feel the craving to smoke again! At school, my advisor said I looked like a new person, and my fellow student Negar said I radiated joy. At work, Madeleine was extremely efficient, soon finishing the pile of work left over by her predecessor. Her boss appreciated her. One day, her sister Beth called from Florida, saying she'd heard Madeleine was deliriously happy, which, unfortunately, was an exaggeration.

We had a few problem areas. When we got married, I was unaware of her expectation that I give her lots of encouragement to finish her studies. She registered as a continuing student and mentioned many times that she'd call her advisor to set up a date for the comprehensive exams, but she never made the call or wrote. When I urged her to call, she'd say she'd call from work, and when I asked her in the evening whether she'd called, she'd say not yet. After a while, I said, "Well, if you're not preparing for the exams, then why waste money registering for the continuing-student status," which, unbeknown to me, she took as a sign that I was unwilling to spend money on her education. Later when she told me so, I felt I'd been misunderstood, even wronged. Underlying the problem was the distance between her academic abilities and her confidence. As she told me later on, she had wanted me to give her a lot more encouragement, my earlier assurances to her that of course she could do it, that all she needed to do was to buckle down and finish the job, having been woefully inadequate. I'd been so impressed with her academic ability as to find her unwillingness to get on with her work puzzling and frustrating. In my self-blaming moments, I thought I should have been more supportive. Later on, she told me she had many incompletes, how many she wasn't even sure. On reflection, I came to the conclusion that our mutual misunderstandings were both interpersonal and cross-cultural, and given that there was so much more work she still had to do to finish her degree, even if I had understood her better and been more supportive, she probably wouldn't have had the perseverance to go the rest of the distance, which meant several more years of dedicated work. As I liked to say, the Ph.D. takes more perseverance than intelligence to get.

The problems of self-confidence and perseverance were minimal to unheard of among Chinese college and graduate students when I was a student in China. In part, the intense competition to get into college or grad school made sure that only those with brains *and* perseverance could get into higher education. Culturally, students were not pampered or pandered to; it was *assumed* that they would act like adults with a great sense of responsibility, not be pleased as consumers. (In fact, the very idea of "consumers" hardly existed in society at large, let alone in schools.) Incompletes didn't exist. It was a rare student who couldn't handle the pressure and had to withdraw from school. In Madeleine's case, the problem wasn't being pampered as a child, or a lack of brains; according to her, it was her confidence having been undermined by a harsh father when she was growing up. (China, and I suspect, traditional societies in general, didn't lack harsh fathers, but somehow a lack of self-confidence didn't exist there as a *cultural* phenomenon. Intertwined with the causal chain connecting political democracy and economic opportunity to greater educational access to the success myth of you-can-be-anything-if-you-just-put-your-mind-to-it, there may be a series of causal links connecting capitalism to consumer society to narcissism to the variety of psychological and psychosomatic ills—afflictions of the self—in American society today, which may develop in places like China in hot pursuit of modernization.)

Another source of tension was my ex-wife Ningnan. After Madeleine and I got married, we gave Ningnan $2,300 over the stipulated amount of child support, besides paying several of Qiyu's expenses. I helped Ningnan do paperwork as regards her worker's compensation case and served as her interpreter at the deposition. All this goodwill did nothing to allay Ningnan's resentment.

Ningnan called Madeleine at work to tell her that being married to me she would suffer and to slander me, saying that I'd married her only to get a green card and that I'd forced her to sleep with me after we were divorced. She would call me at home asking for more money and we'd get into an argument, repeating our old pattern. Madeleine would be upset and tell me to hang up. The next time Ningnan called, we'd start arguing again.

Madeleine would say what a bad person Ningnan was, and out of a sense of fairness I would defend Ningnan, because I thought despite her faults, she wasn't without good points. Then Madeleine and I would get into an argument, with her telling me to go back to my old wife. One day, Madeleine saw the old pictures of Ningnan and me and demanded that I destroy them. I thought, "You can't erase history; why let some pictures bother you." Not wanting to deal with the problem anymore, I tore up all the offending pictures. At one point, Madeleine said the only area where we didn't have a problem was our sex life.

We got married in July '92 but didn't go to the Immigration and Naturalization Office in a suburb of Minneapolis to apply for my green card until three months later. By then Congress had passed a bill making all Chinese citizens who'd been in America before April 1990 eligible to apply for a green card. This was the result of intense lobbying on the part of some Chinese students and scholars in the wake of the suppression of the Tiananmen protests of '89. Their main argument was that if we returned to China, we'd be facing the danger of political persecution. True, the Chinese government had used surveillance equipment to monitor protesters and there'd been rumors of student spies collecting information about activists in the U.S. But I thought the danger of persecution was exaggerated and the lobbyists ran around more out of their desire to stay in this country than a genuine fear of retribution by the Chinese government. At any rate, I had the luxury of being able to choose between basing my green-card application on the special act and on my marriage to Madeleine. If I chose the former, I'd get my permanent green card right away, but if I chose the latter, there'd be a two-year temporary green card before the permanent card would be granted. The latter stipulation is meant to guard against fraudulent marriages for the sole purpose of getting a green card. You should have guessed the choice I made. Still, I did benefit from the special act, thus becoming a free-rider not by intention but by result, for even though I'd married an American citizen, the two-year home-country residence requirement was applicable to me as to others. Without the act, I would have had to go back to China and stay there for two years before I could apply for a green card here. Most likely, Madeleine would have gone with me and found a position teaching English there. Our subsequent life would have changed drastically. With the act, history smiled on the Chinese students and scholars here, resulting in one of the largest brain drains in world history.

As the summer of '93 approached, we made preparations to go to China to visit my family. I hadn't been back since I left the country in '86, seven years before. But before I tell you about our China trip, let me say a few words about my dissertation.

When I wrote the dissertation proposal a year before, I'd chosen as my object of analysis Western studies of prominent aspects of modern China such as the May Fourth movement, the Communist land reform, and the late chairman. Then I realized the empirical data lacked focus. One weekend in September or October '92, I hit upon the idea of using Western studies of Chinese education as my raw data. An extensive bibliographic search followed, which yielded a manageable number of studies to work with if the literature was narrowed down to studies of contemporary higher education. In the midst of this, I got some friendly advice that a good strategy would be to do an easy dissertation to get the degree instead of attempting a serious intellectual task. The latter could come later when the degree was in hand. I thought, "I've spent so much time wrestling with thorny issues, how can I not do the best job I can, to tackle the difficult issues? If I spend two years writing this thing, I'd like it to be publishable." Although I couldn't boast that I'd always acted as Schlegel counseled, "One should drill the hole where the board is thickest," for the dissertation I certainly didn't want to drill it where the board is thinnest. By this time, I'd made some eight hundred note cards on theoretical and methodological points, so the rest of the school year was spent reading studies of Chinese higher education and related literature. By June '93, I was almost ready to start writing. But first I wanted to take Madeleine to see my family in China. I also wanted to return for a visit myself.

The stopover in Hong Kong was pleasant: we looked around with no tourist destinations in mind, and Madeleine looked lovely beaming at the camera. Once we got to Shenzhen, though, travel became a headache. Tickets for northbound trains were sold out for the next three days. I found out tickets were available at the windows for Hong Kong residents and overseas Chinese with foreign currency, so I got two, only to Guangzhou, not to Changsha or Yueyang. "Well, better than getting stuck in Shenzhen," I thought. The new Shenzhen train station was palatial, with more brand-new buildings and storefronts down the streets. The attitude of the merchants, however, didn't match the modern-looking environment. When I asked a woman behind a temporary counter for directions, she turned her head away as if she didn't see me. I was told later that no business, no service. The scene at Guangzhou's train station was unreal: hundreds of migrant workers and other travelers jostled in several seamless queues snaking far beyond the ticket hall with the rest of the square being occupied by travelers standing, sitting or lying on the ground. At a loss as to what to do, we got a room in the hotel above the baggage hall. Checking our baggage on the ground floor I recognized the accent of the young man taking our bags. He came from Hunan, more specifically, from Pingjiang, one of the six counties of Yueyang Prefecture and the home county of my mentor at the fertilizer plant. I struck up a conversation with him, making a connection by being his *laoxiang* or fellow townsman. I told him my situation and asked him for help. He said he'd try. I then called my dad from the hotel, who was working at the small factory of his middle school. When my dad heard my voice, the first time in seven years, his voice quivered a little, which made me do the same.

In the late afternoon, the young man from downstairs came with two hard-seat tickets for a slow train to Yueyang. He wanted to exchange a hundred yuan in foreign-currency certificates; I of course obliged.

When we got on the train, a teenage girl had taken the window seat on the two-seat side. My seat was right beside hers, which left Madeleine sitting across the aisle. I asked the girl to switch seats with Madeleine but she refused. At first, Madeleine and I could still talk across the aisle. But when more passengers got on the train at the following stops and thronged in the aisle, we couldn't even see each other, let alone converse. This made her very uncomfortable, so she asked me to inquire about a vacancy in the sleeper, saying that she was feeling sick because of the sweltering heat (no air conditioning on the train) and crowdedness. I squeezed my way through to the conductor's cubicle and explained the situation; with a long face she said everything was full. Back in my seat, I felt impotent.

After a while, worried about Madeleine I stood up in the packed aisle so that I could at least see her. A middle-aged man standing next to me who looked like a cadre struck up a conversation with me about society. He assumed I was Madeleine's interpreter. Unwilling to rouse unnecessary attention, I didn't correct him. The train ride being a grueling seventeen hours, Madeleine became more and more uncomfortable. At last, reaching the end of her patience she yelled at me for leaving her sitting alone while feeling sick. Embarrassed by her getting angry in front of all those passengers staring at us and by my inability to alleviate her plight, I sat down beside her squeezing four people onto a bench for three. The other two passengers didn't protest. Failing to calm her down, I yelled back at her, with those around us probably wondering how an interpreter could be so rude to a foreign guest. Slowly we both calmed down; I sat with her for the rest of the journey. At one point I joked, "Now this is experiencing Chinese life as an ordinary Chinese lives it"; she didn't find it amusing.

Yueyang's old train station looked dingy and decrepit, right out of a 1930s Chinese movie set. My dad, my sister Xiaoling, and my brother Huibin were waiting at the exit. Not knowing how to greet Madeleine, my dad made a praying gesture and bowed to her slightly. When we were walking up the alley toward my parents' building, my mom smiled at us from the distance. Later she told me that the moment she saw Madeleine she was relieved that the sweater she'd knitted her wasn't too small. My parents had a two-bedroom apartment but had made up their own bed for Madeleine and me to sleep in, while they would sleep on the living-room floor, where the concrete ground was cool.

A few days later, my middle school classmate Jixin invited a dozen old classmates to his new restaurant for a celebration dinner. Jixin was a manager at a public company, but at this time cadres with an entrepreneurial spirit were starting up their own sideline businesses. We had a dozen-course banquet, as was typical of such occasions. My classmates couldn't speak English, so they laughed and joked among themselves, sometimes teasing me or asking Madeleine a question through me. Madeleine seemed to have had a good time. The next day, though, she became sick, her throat covered with huge canker sores. My parents and I thought it was partly the heat and partly the chilies she'd had; in terms of Chinese medicine, she had too much *huo* or fire in her. We took her to a nearby clinic, where the doctor wrote a prescription for her. My parents decocted the herbs and Madeleine drank the bitter liquid bravely.

Then another middle school classmate, Guangwen, invited all the old classmates he could find to his birthday dinner and sent two hostesses to my parents' place to fetch Madeleine and me. Madeleine was too sick to go, so I went alone. In the evening, Madeleine felt increasingly miserable, with her painful throat, her fever, the heat, and my absence being compounded by her inability to communicate with my parents. She must have gotten upset, because my parents sent someone to look for me at the restaurant where the dinner party was held. By then, the party had moved to a nightclub for dancing so I couldn't be found. When I came home later in the evening, Madeleine was still upset, saying I should have kept her company.

We had planned to go to Nanchang to see Yueshan and his wife Su Jun. To welcome us, they even redid their kitchen and bought new furniture. Yueshan had put aside 5,000 yuan for us to go on a tour in China. Since Madeleine became ill, we couldn't go. Yueshan then came from Nanchang to see us and talked to Madeleine in his broken English by her bed. Seeing the debilitating heat was making it hard for Madeleine to recover, Yueshan bought an air conditioner with the money he'd saved for us. After Madeleine recovered, we went to the fertilizer plant to see my old pals, where I showed her around and my old friends treated us to a banquet.

Parts of my hometown had changed beyond recognition. Streets and new buildings replaced the valley of the huge vegetable garden. Entirely new neighborhoods had sprung up in the eastern part of the city. The old city center now looked rundown, even though some new department stores and restaurants had opened up there. What remained bustling, and much more so than before, was the vegetable and meat market.

Another change was people seemed to have a lot more money than before. When my grandparents were still alive, a hundred yuan was a big sum: they had put aside only a few hundred for their own funerals. But now I saw people brandishing stacks of hundred-yuan bills. Part of it was inflation but real income had also increased greatly. My feelings were mixed about all this change brought about by capitalism with Chinese characteristics. On the one hand, material abundance meant people ate better, clothed better, and had more spacious living quarters. They also enjoyed greater personal freedom in important areas of life such as jobs and entertainment. On the other hand, the craze for money led to overly selfish pursuit of one's own interest at the expense of the interest and well-being of others, which would worsen in the coming years with counterfeit merchandise flooding the markets and rampant corruption becoming the norm instead of the exception. Even new, spacious apartment buildings had negative consequences: in the old days, neighbors had interacted much more frequently, even though that had also meant less privacy and more friction, but by the 1990s neighbors often were strangers and children were rarely seen playing in the yards or streets.

Though the ordeal of the trip from Guangzhou to Yueyang was now history, something I told Madeleine continued to bother her. I told her that those around us on the train thought I was her interpreter and that unwilling to attract any unnecessary attention I played along. Madeleine took it as a sign that I was reluctant to acknowledge her as my wife. I said, "Didn't I take you to my classmates' gathering the other day? These people matter, whereas strangers on the train don't." She wouldn't listen. I thought her insecurity was making her paranoid.

With open-return tickets we needed to book our return flight. Summer being a busy tourist season the only seats we could find were in a week or so, which meant we would be able to stay in China only for three weeks. Otherwise, we'd have to wait over a month. With me anxious to get back to my dissertation, we decided to take the next available flight back to the States.

The problem of getting train tickets presented itself again; at least this time we weren't away from home. Through a friend's friend we got two hard-sleepers on an air-conditioned train from Changsha to Guangzhou. On the day of our departure, my family and a few friends came to see us off at the bus depot. Right before we boarded the bus, I suddenly hugged my mom and dad for the first and only time in my life, subconsciously because Madeleine was there. Madeleine then hugged them. Onlookers murmured as the solemn goodbye occurred, and I heard someone say, "Don't know when you'll see them again." After we got on the bus, I saw my mom in tears. My sister Xiaoling and her husband Huiqin accompanied us to Changsha.

As soon as we were back, I plunged into the last readings for the dissertation. Soon, with all the preparatory reading completed I turned on my easy PC to start drafting my magnum opus. For four years I'd typed my course papers on a typewriter bought at the Goodwill in Iowa City for $12, which had the question mark and a few other keys stuck.

Now, armed with a magical machine plus a headful of advanced philosophy and the new idiom of cultural critique, I was eager to begin. I opened the dissertation tendentiously:

> In this essay I aim to show how we may deploy our subaltern positionality strategically to resist the hegemony of global capitalism; to mobilize the inscrutability of reference and indeterminacy of intra- and interlanguage translation to undermine the neocolonial and postcolonial discourses; to deconstruct the social construction of the nonnatural as natural; to reveal the embodied and metaphoric nature of human thought, and hence the unreason of reason and the irrationality of rationality; and to unmask the rhetorical and ideological historicity of sundry discursive formations and metanarratives—all in an attempt to promote better cross-cultural understandings in our increasingly interconnected world.

No, I didn't have the imagination of Malcolm Bradbury or Raymond Tallis. Even if I had, writing a dissertation this way might have led to degree suicide (or pass with distinction). No, the very first sentence I put down was this: "Any errors that remain in this thesis are the fault of my advisor, my other teachers, or the authors whose books I've studied." No kidding.

As a matter of fact, I was drawn to the view that has the construction, "X is socially constructed." The "X" refers to both an aspect of society and a study of it, the latter being my main concern. In cross-cultural studies in particular, errors and distortions are nearly impossible to avoid, no matter how sharp the student, how prolonged the time of study (which in real life is often quite limited). Moreover, epistemologically it seems naïve to see a truthful representation as the truth pure and simple, free of the modes through which the truth is presented. On the other hand, I was deeply dissatisfied with the "X is socially constructed" approach, especially if a project ends at the metalevel, with showing how or, less frequently, why so. My main complaint was that as students of another society—or of one's own, for that matter—and as people with practical needs, we have to, and do, try to understand whatever aspects of the target society we are studying or dealing with. So critical projects that end at the metalevel don't go nearly far enough.

My second problem with ideological unmasking or cultural critique was the constructivism underlying it. First, another society would exist even if no study of it had ever been done; it and the things making it up have the properties they do independently of the studies. In contrast, constructivism gone awry conflates a representation and its object. Second, for a lot of projects of social research such as those based on existing texts, the study doesn't change the data being collected. Third, if the act of study affects the data being collected such as in an interview, then the effects need to be taken into account, though probably never perfectly.

Meanwhile, whatever is correctly identified as features of some reality, they would be *partial*. But due to the limited vision of researchers and the interested nature of a particular inquiry, there is always the danger that that partial nature is forgotten. More important, if the point that numerous factors inform a cross-cultural representation is an obvious one, *how* a specific representation is informed, is not. Even less obvious is how to do better. Hence, moderate constructivism or moderate realism—the need to pay close attention to both the inquiry-independent reality and the way an inquiry is done and written up.

In brief, I felt the pull of both the realist and constructivist dimensions of cross-cultural writing, so much so that I ended up calling my model "realist constructivism."

But at first, reversing my earlier preoccupation with theory, I decided to let the data drive the theory by doing the empirical analyses first and then summarizing the theoretical and methodological points at the end. I wrote a chapter on translation and one on selective representation and showed them to my advisor and Richard Leppert. Richard said what I'd written read like a giant book report, and I needed to be explicit about what *my* views were. My advisor also had her reservations. As a result, I changed the structure of the work and sketched out a model for cross-cultural writing in the first chapter. In the next five chapters, by examining five modes of writing—assuming, selecting, translating, viewing, and evaluating—and by scrutinizing Western studies of Chinese higher education in light of these modes, I tried to show how realist constructivism applies both as a descriptive model (how cross-cultural studies are written) and as a normative one (how cross-cultural studies should be written). The final chapter acknowledges the model's weaknesses. My head was so full of theoretical references that I didn't even touch the eight hundred note cards I'd made over the years. When Madeleine read my drafts, she thought I was too terse, so she fleshed things out, expanding on nearly every other sentence. Her thorough revision of my writing improved it so much that I joked that the dissertation should carry her name, too, but she said the ideas were mine and I also felt she was a bit heavy-handed in her editing.

Writing the dissertation damaged the only area that Madeleine said was fine, our sex life. Once I started writing, all my energies and attention went to the dissertation, leaving Madeleine feeling neglected. I had a pad and a pen by my side of the bed and would jot down anything that occurred to me in the middle of the night. A worry lurked in the back of my mind that there might be a fatal flaw in my model I failed to see, and the whole thing would collapse at the oral defense. For weeks at a time, I didn't touch her—I didn't feel horny at all; unlike when we'd been just married, she didn't take the initiative either. Of course, I didn't stop loving her, despite our quarrels. But she took my inattention badly. She complained about my not asking her more questions about her background, and I told her that Yueshan and I were the closest friends and yet I'd never asked him about his past. Her catching me staring at other girls worsened her sense of insecurity. She was convinced that I liked thin girls, even though I protested that I found plump girls sexier than thin ones. I said I was fascinated by the eye colors of American girls. (No amount of critical reading unmasking the male gaze could reduce the attraction of exotic eyes to me.) I said looking at them didn't mean I'd run away with someone, again, to no avail.

We continued to quarrel. Every time she'd get upset first, followed by my bad reaction, followed by her making up with me. She noticed this pattern and resented me. Once, I was so fed up with her carping that I took our kitchen knife and pounded it on the counter, not that I was going to kill her or that I wanted to scare her; I was merely venting my anger and frustration. I must have looked ferocious, and she must have been scared for a few seconds.

My absentmindedness was another source of irritation to her. After the old Catalina was impounded following a snowstorm and we decided not to reclaim it, Ningnan's boyfriend Don found us a decrepit Dodge for $250. This piece of junk not only had difficulty starting in the Minnesota winter but would run out of gas when the gauge didn't quite reach "E." I should have learned the lesson; instead, I let it run out in the dead winter twice. I was almost as bad as La Bruyère's Menalchas.

On the sunny side, Madeleine and Qiyu got along famously. She insisted on getting new sheets and new pillows for Qiyu after we moved again, decorating a corner of the living room for him. Even my friend Ruidan and his wife Yitao, who stopped by on their drive to the West Coast, were impressed by how nice Madeleine was to my son. (This is another area where American society is superior to Chinese society. In China, the stepmother is a stock evil character both in folklore and, if to a lesser extent, in real life.) Whenever Qiyu's Monday classes were canceled, he'd stay an extra day with us. By this time, Ningnan was living with her new boyfriend in a suburb of Minneapolis, where we picked up Qiyu every weekend. When Madeleine introduced Qiyu to books, movies, and games, I also got a dose of pop culture: I loved the stories of Winnie the Pooh; enjoyed such movies as *Mary Poppins*, *The Princess Bride*, and *Willie Wonka and the Chocolate Factory*; and even though I didn't care for the values embodied in the game, played Monopoly with them from time to time.

If time spent with Qiyu was always a joy, meals were a mixed blessing. Even though I did most of the cooking, Madeleine liked eating out. As long as there was money, I went along to Greek, Lebanese, Thai, French, Mexican, and American restaurants. The best of the lot was the Sri Lankan Curry House. Their chilies were so hot that we could only enjoy "moderate." When we tried "hot" (there was still "very hot"), we had to drink cold water between bites. They also offered royal portions; we could never finish our plates. To top it off, they had a dessert called "mango delight," which featured Häagen-Dazs ice cream with perfect consistency surrounded by fresh mango slices. Nothing beats mango delight, nothing. OK, maybe comparable is the ice cream at another Uptown eatery, Sebastian Joe's. Its ice cream had a flavor I'd never tasted anywhere else, far surpassing Ohio's Graeter's ice cream, I'd discover later on. Eating out might be romantic and fun, but our purse was getting thinner and thinner. Once, we were so broke that we had to borrow $20 from my eight-year-old son to tide us over. Here's another cultural difference: Americans, young ones anyway, enjoy themselves first, worry about money later; racking up credit-card debt is no problem. The Chinese are as a whole thriftier though younger ones are turning into eager consumers. In my case, I was a cheapskate in some areas, such as buying clothes and furniture, but a spendthrift in others, such as buying books and going out with friends and with my American wife.

I continued visiting secondhand-book stores. Unlike Ningnan, Madeleine never asked me not to buy more books. One day, browsing in a bookstore on the West Bank, I spotted Montaigne's autobiography, which was based on his essays edited by someone else. The Minneapolis Public Library had an ongoing canceled-book sale that sometimes held treasures: it was there that I got a set of the 1968 edition of *International Encyclopedia of the Social Sciences*. This was only an extension of my earlier love of English dictionaries. I bought my first dictionary in America at Iowa, *The Harper Dictionary of Modern Thought*. Since then, I've acquired fifteen dictionaries and encyclopedias in philosophy alone. Madeleine said of my habit, "It's a thing with the Chinese; they like dictionaries and encyclopedias." I wasn't going to stickle over that.

Another activity I first enjoyed as a familyless man and then with Madeleine was to watch the films at U of MN's Rivertown International Film Festival, many of which we wouldn't have heard of otherwise. I still have the program for the eighth annual, which featured sixty-seven films from thirty-six foreign countries and twenty-three from the United States. One thing I noticed was that I saw very few Chinese students—Chinese students and scholars at the U of MN at the time numbered over eight hundred from the mainland alone—at the film festivals, which to me indicated a lack of cultural interests among them.

Since I was making steady progress in my dissertation, I began looking for a job. I'd gone for the Ph.D. with no career in mind, though given my training and temperament, I would probably be good for nothing but being an academic. However, at the beginning of my job search I didn't want to become an academic: I didn't like the publishing requirement at institutions of higher learning, even though I wouldn't mind doing research for the federal government or at a think tank. I thought research units within the government and think tanks in general are meant for research that deals with practical issues or exigencies, whereas at institutions of higher learning, where research is more basic than applied, faculty should publish only if they are convinced that they have something significant to say, which means there shouldn't be a publishing requirement.

Having been a student of the Institute of American Studies, a Chinese think tank, I looked into think tanks here. After reading a few books on them, I discovered I didn't qualify. American think tanks have few full-time fellows, who are established experts or famous scholars. I thought about working for the United Nations but found out that they required a lot of experience in a field; seven years minimum was the figure I saw. Then I thought of working for the federal government. But when I called a government office, I was told I'd have to be a U.S. citizen to work for the federal government. State governments would hire permanent residents, but I was not an economist or someone trained in a practical field, so a state government was unlikely to hire me. I didn't even bother to look for vacancies. Madeleine and I also talked about, but didn't seriously consider, teaching English around the world. We then went to the career planning office to look at some job-hunting literature for someone like me, a jack of many trades and master of none. We considered the publishing industry. "Maybe I could be an acquisitions editor or something, scouting out new talents." A look at the qualifications made me give up: I couldn't type. Now running out of choices, I sought help at the student counseling office. The director had a Ph.D., so he ought to know. I took a test and he told me teaching at a small liberal arts college, where the pressure of publishing is smaller, would fit me. Instead of using my critical skills to unmask the epistemological and ideological underpinnings of the test, I took it at face value.

As I did enjoy teaching and teaching seemed the only job for me, I looked for jobs in interdisciplinary programs, which were very scarce. In several months I found a dozen ads, including one for a resident director of a study abroad program in Beijing. I got a follow-up from Shimer College, a tiny college in Illinois that has a Great Books curriculum, and a conference interview at Boston for a position in Chinese culture at Stony Brook.

While at Boston, we received the sad news that Madeleine's dad had died. We immediately flew to El Paso, where I met her siblings and their families. I'd met Madeleine's dad twice, so he hadn't been a total stranger to me. At the funeral, when the rabbi performed the ceremony, I couldn't hold back my tears.

When we were in El Paso, I received a phone call from Bill Green at Miami University, who amazingly tracked me down there. He said Miami's School of Interdisciplinary Studies would like me to come to Oxford for a campus interview. I was thrilled. "What is my training if not interdisciplinary?" I was my animated self at the interview and was sold on the idyllic campus.

I had two short chapters of the dissertation yet to finish, so I took care of that. Two weeks after my interview, the call came. It was after 5 p.m. on a Friday afternoon. I'd been hoping the call would come, so I delayed my trip to Madeleine's workplace to pick her up after work. When I told Madeleine I got the job, she smiled but didn't look thrilled.

The oral defense of the dissertation took place in the conference room of my department. I was waiting outside the entrance when I saw Professor Waltner and Professor Farmer walk in one after the other. With my dissertation in his hand, Professor Farmer said to Professor Waltner: "This puts our students to shame." Professor Waltner said nothing in response. I didn't let this unexpected praise go to my head. In my opening statement I said that the dissertation had four strengths and four weaknesses, that I should be ashamed that I knew Western philosophy better than I did Chinese philosophy, and that if we took it for granted that multiple representations are the norm, then the emphasis should be on trying to arrive at more accurate representations, not on showing their multiplicity. The questions were all friendly, partly because the committee members were glad that I'd gotten a job in a tight market. They were not going to kill "the guy with a job," a nickname I got for my fleeting moment of glory. Bruce, whose famous (to me anyway) claim was that "nothing is natural," raised a point or two along that line, questioning the independent existence of social reality, and I answered according to the main drift of the dissertation, that cross-cultural representations are constructed, but I wanted to emphasize ontological realism or the independent existence of another society with its complexity, because insufficient attention to that reality would result in distortions, while at the same time arguing that an acute awareness of the factors affecting the construction of a representation would lead to its improvement. I suspected that my approach was not critical enough for his taste, but he didn't raise any objections. My calling as a lifetime student was far from being over but my career as a grad student finally came to an end. It was during my Minnesota years that I matured intellectually; to borrow the pithy words of Pope, by the time I graduated from CSDS, I was no longer "bewilder'd in the Maze of Schools." I owe much of this maturity to my teachers—as well as to the comp program, which fed me—and I am grateful for the opportunity and freedom to study, think, and write there for five years.

My mom had asked for a photo of me wearing the academic gown for the Ph.D. When Madeleine and I went to the bookstore on the West Bank to rent it, the clerk didn't ask me to show any documentation that I'd passed my oral defense, which led me to remark, "If I'd known this, then I wouldn't have bothered with all that work. Just rent a gown and have a degree photo taken!" I donned the smock and posed for Madeleine to snap pictures of me in front of the auditorium, sticking my tongue out in one of the shots. After receiving my diploma months later, I framed it crookedly before putting it away in the closet of my office.

Before we left Minneapolis, Madeleine and I had a meeting with Ningnan in an attempt to agree on the monthly child support for Qiyu. We said $400 for starters, but Ningnan had heard from someone that she could get $1,000 out of me probably without asking what the man's salary was. She set her mind on that sum and we couldn't come to an agreement. She warned that she'd hit us with a court case that would make us dirt poor. Which would turn out to be only one of the exciting events in the years to come.

13. Halfhearted Academic

All but one of the core courses, which made up most of a student's coursework in the first two years, were semi-team taught at the School of Interdisciplinary Studies, or, as the locals called it, Western. (The one exception was fully team-taught for a while.) The basic structure of a core course was one lecture and two seminars a week. The team picked a topic, designed the syllabus, and took turns lecturing, but individual faculty members led seminars. When I arrived on campus in early August 1994, my team teachers had already written the syllabus for the course I was assigned to teach, Individualism and Success in America. As I would soon discover, Western students were creative, many wrote well, some were truly outstanding. The school had a palpable ethos of social concern, mixed with a bloated sense of entitlement and self-righteousness. Its main weakness as a place for learning showed up not far into the semester: few students did the reading, or did it thoughtfully enough to participate meaningfully in seminars. To rectify the situation, I suggested to my two team members to assign short questions on the reading. As a result, more people did the reading, but there were complaints about the questions being a nuisance, which in a sense they were.

In response to local practices and student reactions, I adjusted my teaching. I valued subtlety and flexibility in thinking and writing, among other things. But my approach was often seen as unclear: students in general preferred crystal clear explanations and instructions telling them exactly why we were reading a particular piece or what I wanted in a paper. I made the change from being "unclear" to being "clear" reluctantly, because I thought it would push students to think harder if everything were not spelled out for them and because strictly speaking, *I* didn't want anything. As time went on, teaching became a matter of managing the classes, in terms of meeting students' expectations and cooperating with team teachers.

Other changes included incorporating multimedia and finding ways to make my lectures more engaging. Since I loved movies, incorporating feature films and documentaries into a course, as was the school's tradition, was easy for me. To enliven my lectures without sacrificing their rigor, I resorted to humor, generally to good effect.

Another way to engage students I came up with was to find less academic but still solid readings for my classes. In the face of student resistance to tackling difficult theoretical material, I reluctantly opted for less theoretical readings, reluctantly because then students would lose an opportunity to learn how to tackle difficult abstract material. For example, for a course in social change, my colleague Mark Pedelty and I chose two biographies to address issues of social change in two societies in the first half of the twentieth century: of Mexico's Frida Kahlo and China's Liang Shuming. In spring '98, I chose Steven Lukes's *The Curious Enlightenment of Professor Caritat* for a course in utopias.

In addition, I advocated reducing the amount of reading while increasing its depth, the former to respond to the complaint that there had been too much reading and the latter so that the courses wouldn't be watered down too much. Curious about how much time students spent studying per week, I surveyed my three sections of a first-year class in fall '96, which showed that students studied between eight and nine hours a week, making a travesty of the credit hour, which means one hour in-class study plus two or three hours' study outside class. Students typically take fifteen credit hours a semester, so the actual study time is only a fraction of what's expected. But there was nothing unusual about the finding, as it was barely above the national norm. In his 2001 "State of the University Address," the then president said that half of Miami's students studied fewer than ten hours a week and 92 percent studied less than twenty hours a week. In contrast, according to *The Fiske Guide to Colleges 1999*, students at Caltech typically studied over fifty hours a week. Just about meeting the expectations were Harvard undergraduates, who, according to *Making the Most of College*, studied about thirty hours a week.

All of the above methods worked to some extent but none with great success, either measured by student conduct or by their satisfaction with the classes as shown in course evaluations.

I used the content-flexible curriculum to teach new classes on China, cross-cultural understanding, and philosophy, in part to generate student interest in the content itself so that they would invest more in their studies. What with changes in teaching teams and in my own reading, by 2004 I'd taught twenty-five new courses (by 2022 over forty), learning a great deal in the process. This is the best part of my job: it not only brings constant intellectual excitement to my life but broadens the horizons of students, many of whom appreciate the new material. As a result, most of my research and writing has been done in winter and summer breaks.

My nonstop schedule may give the impression that all was well at home, whereas in fact all hell broke loose. Fortunately, I didn't let my familial problems get in the way of my work. As I wrote in the report for my third-year review: All work and no play makes me a productive boy.

The main source of trouble was my ex-wife Ningnan. As I mentioned at the end of the last chapter, she was dead set on getting $1,000 a month from us while we were still in debt due to our trip to China the year before and, I must confess, to our frequent eating out, which we continued in the not-so-metropolitan Oxford. First Ningnan retained an attorney, who asked Madeleine to disclose her personal information such as her social security number and her income. (Madeleine's superb editing skills quickly landed her a job as a technical editor with an environmental firm in a suburb of Cincinnati.) Already burdened with a tense relationship with me, Madeleine refused to provide the information, thinking it absurd that she should work to maintain my ex-wife. Regardless, Ningnan filed a court case that she thought would bring us to our knees. With neither of us having any experience with the court system, Madeleine found an attorney with a major law firm in Minneapolis. The retainer was $3,500, which I had to borrow from banks at exorbitant interest rates. The first bank we went to let me borrow $1,000 at the rate of 27 percent! The loan officer was extremely friendly, offering us coffee more than once. A few banks turned me down, even though now I had a stable income as a professor at a respectable university. One loan officer asked me, "Do you have any collateral?" "I have lots of books." "Sorry, can't help you." Eventually, I borrowed $6,500, some of which from my old friends Zhaobin and Yajun, without an IOU. Miami let me take out the $1,000, interest-free emergency relocation loan.

The first time the case was heard I had to teach. It was just as well I didn't go: the referee sent the case back for insufficient documentation. More paperwork meant more attorney fees. Soon the retainer was exceeded by a few grand, but the case had just begun. I had to fire my attorney and take on the defense myself. When the case was heard again in February '95, the judgment was against me. The referee not only ordered me to pay $493 a month for child support, but also stipulated a monthly spousal maintenance of $300 for six years. The problem was, as the referee's order stated, if I paid as ordered, I'd be in the red for several hundred dollars a month. Where would I get the money to stop the gap? Because of this case, Madeleine and I had separated in January. So the calculations were based on my income alone. I had no choice but file an appeal.

The main reason that the referee ordered me to pay spousal maintenance was Ningnan had lied about her education, claiming that she'd quit college to support me. But anyone somewhat knowledgeable about Chinese higher education in the late '70s and early '80s would know that college was free. To inform the judge who would review the case, I wrote a statement, and then asked Ruidan and Yajun each for an affidavit; both had known Ningnan at the time and both had attended college at the same time I did. When the case was still in progress, I had to leave for China to do fieldwork. Madeleine was kind enough to write some of the correspondence when I was in China. (I guess she also didn't want Ningnan to get away with her cheating.) When the judge reviewed the case, she only upheld the child-support ruling, which I hadn't contested in the first place, and threw out the maintenance order. Ningnan was only thirty-seven, certainly capable of supporting herself.

At first, Madeleine had only separated from me. Then one evening she told me she'd made up her mind about our marriage: she wanted a divorce. We'd been having problems before Ningnan had riled things up; now it looked to her the trouble would be endless. Qiyu was only ten; who could tell how much more trouble Ningnan was going to create for me and hence for her? With our lease expiring in May, we agreed to move into our own apartments after that.

Another source of stress for Madeleine was her dad's death. Even though they'd rarely talked on the phone when he was alive, Madeleine felt her dad had been the only person she could talk to, and losing him was a big blow to her. In addition, she found Oxford devoid of opportunities. She excelled at her editing job, but the job was intellectually unsatisfying.

Maybe because Madeleine was in a lousy mood, she sometimes said things that hurt my feelings. Once she called me a "jerk." That word stung me: "How can my wife, the woman I love, I've been so intimate with, use that word on me." Her "*Je t'adore*" on a later occasion did little to palliate the earlier sting. To be fair, once I was standing in the dining room in a momentary daze. She came up to me and kissed me on the cheek but I stood there like a wooden statue.

In the final months in which we shared the house, I slept on the bare floor of the small room beyond the bathroom. One evening, the wind howled, and the windows shook. She said I could come to bed, but only to sleep. A minute later, she said I'd better stay on the floor. What added to my sadness was she took all her pictures she could find out of the envelopes where we kept our photos, so now I can only visualize her winsome smiles in the pictures we took when we visited Hong Kong in 1993. (I do have some of her older pictures, including one from her childhood.)

Although dedicated to my work, I found many aspects of the academic life in general and of that at my school unsatisfying. I've mentioned some of the problems in an earlier section, but there are more. One of these is basing the evaluation of teaching almost exclusively on student reactions. This reflects the increasingly business-like mentality of institutions of higher learning: Colleges and universities need students' tuition to survive, especially in these hard times, while students see themselves as consumers buying a commodity, skills and a degree. Customers had better be satisfied, and one way to do this is to let students decide which teachers are good and which ones suck. But how reliable are the reactions of students? You'd think in a place called an institution of higher learning, people would talk about it, weigh its strengths and weaknesses, for example. But this is an established, though relatively recent, practice; who wants to rock the boat. Wait a minute: limitations of student evaluations of teaching have been recognized. Not only that, the faculty senate of my university even passed a resolution to that effect:

> Teaching is a complex and multi-faceted process, requiring multiple approaches to measurement which extend beyond student evaluations of teaching. Much of the richness of information is not necessarily quantifiable, but relies instead on qualitative information.

The resolution has become part of the faculty handbook, a compendium of university policies regarding faculty rights and responsibilities. But going beyond student evaluations would require too much work, so at my school we only talked about peer evaluation and its pitfalls; nobody wanted to do it. Most of the faculty members were tenured; why would they take on this thankless task. In fairness, I should say that I wouldn't want to do it myself. The crux of the matter is that monitoring teaching by regular evaluations is a bad idea. How so? First, faculty normally do a decent job of teaching classes. Second, relying on students as judges of teaching tempts—indeed, impels—a teacher to degrade himself by teaching to the evaluations; as a result, to an unknowable extent, the quality of teaching actually goes down as the ratings go up. Third, even more so than scholarship, the quality of teaching is reduced to its perception; indeed, as long as your ratings are OK, it's not an issue.

Although the administration doesn't require student evaluations of teaching in order to improve its quality, let me digress by making the point that though small adjustments may be profitably made in one's teaching, a teacher's abilities cannot be improved that much. This is because how good a teacher is depends on factors whose great improvement is unlikely to be achieved by evaluation. For example, if a teacher is not an eloquent speaker, can evaluation of his lecturing improve his speaking ability? Can attending seminars on teaching achieve that goal? Can reading about how to be more eloquent help him become a much better speaker? The answer to these questions has to be "No."

For another example, other things being comparable, enthusiasm makes for a better teacher. But enthusiasm has to do with how a teacher feels about her job, the course in question, and her personality, none of which is likely to improve with evaluations. Other aspects of the talent for teaching, such as a knack for presenting dry material in engaging ways, are also unlikely to improve much through evaluations.

What about preparation? Good teaching may not need a lot of preparation if, for example, the course is a repeat, and preparation alone without the accompaniment of other factors will have little effect on how "effective" (another unexamined criterion) the delivery is. Moreover, preparation like so many other things related to job performance is a matter of conscientiousness. How does the administration police conscientiousness? If an instructor is not conscientious, evaluation can hardly rectify the problem.

I could go on but to conclude, some people are born teachers, most teachers are OK or good enough, and a few really suck. (This is more clearly so as regards any one ability, rather than the ensemble of abilities.) Such slogans as "Excellence is our tradition" are what Kenneth Hudson calls "diseased English," Mario Pei "weasel words," Arthur Herzog "the Fake Factor," and Paul Fussell "BAD." The problem goes beyond the wording and has to do with having a slogan at all: What else could it say? "Mediocrity is our tradition"?

Back to my university's reliance on student evaluations. The president was quite aware of the problem and called on the university community (sorry about the chummy cliché) to confront it in his 2001 "State of the University Address" (things have gotten worse: in recent years, before the new school year begins, the university places a sign around the campus saying "Welcome to the Miami Family!"):

> And finally, let's get serious about student evaluations. We've been talking for five years about how they're misused, about how they intimidate junior faculty. Let's do something about them. If we truly believe they give a misleading and distorted picture, that they've become a popularity vote aimed at generating high grades, then let's stop over-analyzing them and relying on them. Let's come up with better ways of measuring teaching performance and let's do it now.

I've said above that evaluations of teaching have little use. But suppose we have to evaluate. Are there better ways? Only with a great deal of work. Syllabi can be evaluated, an instructor's feedback to students' papers can be evaluated, the quality of lectures can be evaluated, and seminars can be evaluated. But are the faculty prepared to do the work? Unlikely. Furthermore, even if the faculty were willing to do the work, that is, up to a point, there would be numerous complications. Concerning classroom instruction alone, as the Solomon brothers pointed out in their upbeat *Up the University*, merely visiting a class a few times is insufficient. How would the faculty deal with the qualification and neutrality of evaluators? What if the senior faculty member is a less capable teacher than the junior faculty member being evaluated? Teaching is different from scholarship, even though the same problem may appear in peer review of scholarship, too. About quality in the areas I'm familiar with, the humanities and social sciences, how would the faculty judge a teacher who sounds eloquent but whose ideas are facile, or one whose speech is halting but whose ideas are profound? What about one whose ideas only seem profound but upon examination turn out to be tumid, obfuscatory platitudes, or one whose sanctimonious criticisms of society are only surpassed by his clangor for money, status, and power? (Malcolm Muggeridge calls the latter "the great moral fallacy of our time—that collective virtue may be pursued without reference to personal behaviour.") What about a lukewarm scholar or a passionate ideologue? And what about short-term versus longer-term effects? All in all, not worth the trouble.

As for publishing, scholars much more accomplished than I have expressed the view that good ideas are scarce. To mention but a few, Jon Elster has written somewhere that one is lucky to have a few good ideas in one's entire life (even though he himself is a prolific author), and Susan Haack is only slightly more optimistic in *Manifesto of a Passionate Moderate*: "Few if any of us will have a truly original idea every few years, let alone every few months." Such being the case, arbitrarily raising the bar concerning publishing is bound to produce much feuilletonistic, repetitive busywork instead of significant, long-tempered scholarship. Just as silly, if less obviously so, is the situation that even a lot of the significant scholarship is so much sound and fury, signifying little. Indeed, in what Europeans call the human sciences the apparent significance of a work is usually proportional to how flawed it is.

At my own school, an undergraduate unit, the pressure of publishing was minimal, with articles on teaching counted as scholarship. But having aimed to write the dissertation in a publishable form and needing to publish *something* to keep my rice bowl, I set about revising it for a press in my first year of employment. Then the story Yueshan told me in '93 of the trials and tribulations he and his coadventurers had gone through to found a private electronics company was so captivating that I decided to record it for the annals of history. As for this autobiography, the idea was first suggested to me by my senior advisees in '96. After Madeleine and I separated, my loneliness frequently transported me to my childhood years. Added to the personal reasons was my dissatisfaction with the intentionally or unintentionally crowd-pleasing narrative focus of the memoirs of recent Chinese immigrants: so many focus on the excesses of the Communist revolution, especially of the Cultural Revolution. I wanted to show that there was more to Chinese life than had been written about in the published memoirs. And I wanted to show people as fully human—warts and all, as the saying goes—instead of as mere windows onto their society. When I wavered over including my life in America, my former teacher Edward Farmer persuaded me to proceed.

I've written no journal articles and have only given one conference presentation—while I was still at Minnesota. I disliked the entrepreneurial spirit that goes with the conference scene; reading David Lodge reinforced my attitude even further. In *Changing Places*, he so characterizes a hip radio call-in show, "To Philip it seemed obvious that beneath all the culture and the eccentricity and the human concern there beat a heart of pure show-business." In the prologue to its sequel, *Small World*, he writes, "The modern conference resembles the pilgrimage of medieval Christendom in that it allows the participants to indulge themselves in all the pleasures and diversions of travel while appearing to be austerely bent on self-improvement." More than self-improvement, in fact: it is, first of all, self-promotion.

About the third duty a faculty member is supposed to perform, service, I didn't mind serving on committees, not because I wanted to show how well-behaved I was, but because, besides a sense of fairness that committee work should be shared, I had an anthropological interest in how committees work, in clues about what makes the microsociety tick or creak. But even though every time I received notices I volunteered, as a new faculty member I was rarely appointed to a university committee.

A new assistant professor is usually assigned a mentor who knows how to play the academic game. I wasn't, although one of the senior colleagues talked to me from time to time, or as he described it, acted as an informal mentor to me. Another senior colleague, whose writing I regard highly, gave me much encouragement, especially concerning the writing of this autobiography. Although I recognized the utility of receiving pointers on how to beat the ticking tenure clock, I was also uncomfortable with the conforming pressures on the neophyte.

Needing ways to vent, besides participating earnestly in the college's discussions of its curriculum, I looked for humorous nonfiction books on higher education and found Norman Runnion's dusty *Up the Ivy Ladder*, Harold Benjamin's irreverent *The Saber-Tooth Curriculum*, Wayne Booth's short but smart *The Art of Deliberalizing*, Pierre Van den Berghe's understated *Academic Gamesmanship*, Joel Gold's harmless *The Wayward Professor*, and the colorful anthology edited by Mark C. Ebersole, *Hail to Thee, Okoboji U!*. I needed the humor to help me breathe in the somewhat stifling atmosphere.

The third-year review came soon enough. By this time, my ratings had improved from the first semester's dismal numbers but were still below the very high divisional norms, my first book had come out, and I'd finished drafting my second book. I'd participated in numerous student-organized activities, partly because students invited me and partly because I had an anthropological interest in them. The school's Promotion and Tenure Committee, or P & T Committee as is known in the business, wrote its obligatory review. The assessment of my scholarship was quite positive:

> The committee is highly impressed with your productivity since you arrived here. The committee notes that your first book is innovative, imaginative, and much more than a rewrite of your dissertation. [Actually, having written the dissertation like a book, e.g., without a literature review, I only added a short summary chapter as suggested by the referee; the revision of the rest of the dissertation was merely stylistic, such as cutting out some one hundred footnotes and general fine-tuning.] We are amazed that

> you have completed another book manuscript in such a short time. . . . You are doing remarkably well in this area.

As for service, my divisional service was deemed good, but the committee urged me to "serve on a major university committee in the near future."

The problem area was teaching. While recognizing my contribution to various aspects of teaching at the college, the committee noted the following:

> As part of your pedagogy, you apparently place the basic obligation for learning on students. This seems to be very effective with motivated students, yet much less effective with unmotivated students. Course and instructor evaluations suggest there are problems with the implementation of your teaching philosophy in your seminars. . . .
>
> Clearly, you are concerned about students' performance. The committee was impressed with your efforts to interview each student in your recent classes to discuss their performance and course concerns. The committee also recognizes that you haven't taught the same course twice! However, in the area of teaching, a successful tenure review in your sixth year will require evidence of continuing the improvement you have demonstrated thus far. Suggestions from the committee include using varied approaches to seminar activities to engage students, and making sure that students understand why you are taking the approaches you employ.

The provost's handwritten notes on the review packet only mentioned teaching and scholarship, not service:

> I agree with the Western faculty & Dean that you need to continue to improve the quality of your teaching. I strongly urge you to identify a teacher mentor & work closely with that person. . . .
>
> You appear to be quite active in research. I urge you to seek higher or more prestigious outlets in terms of publishers. And to also seek publication in refereed academic journals of substantial repute.
>
> Overall, you [are] doing reasonably well. . . .

I noticed that in the provost's remarks on my scholarship, no mention was made of its quality or lack thereof, though she couldn't be expected to read it. What mattered was the outlet's prestige. I had this immediate reaction: Suppose the faculty member in question doesn't have the ability to produce the high-level scholarship required to be published in more prestigious outlets. Even if the poor fellow aims for that goal, his chances of success will be slim. Now suppose the poor fellow does have the ability, but is too dumb to realize that getting published by a more prestigious press will do much good to his career . . . but wait, this scenario is not realistic, because in all likelihood the fellow ought to know *that*. Then there's the possibility that the fellow did try prestigious presses but was just unlucky, in which case the advice would make him try even harder next time, though that may set him up for disappointment again. My final thought was that if the quality of scholarship is high, then it shouldn't really matter to the administration whether or not the press is a prestigious one. True, if more faculty publish with prestigious presses, then the university's prestige will increase. But jockeying for prestige looked to me like high school kids competing for popularity among their peers, not exactly worthy of an institution of higher learning. For a few days in '96 I'd thought about applying for tenure and promotion a year ahead of schedule if I could get my second book published soon enough. My informal mentor said I should continue strengthening my record. How wrong I'd been.

The dean did find me a teacher mentor from another division, who happened to be a good teacher doing research on teaching. He attended two of my seminars and noticed both my strengths and the areas needing improvement. Even though his mentoring didn't help me improve my ratings, he would help me greatly in my tenure battle.

My scholarly interest in higher education as an aspect of American society coupled with my practical interest in finding out more about it prompted me to read more about teaching, student evaluations, faculty culture, etc. While such books as *College Thinking, The Elements of Teaching, The Elements of Learning*, and *Professors Are from Mars, Students Are from Snickers* provided practical advice, others exposed the distressing condition that in teaching style trumps substance.

Peter Sacks published a book in '96, *Generation X Goes to College: An Eye-Opening Account of Teaching in Postmodern America*. Some of his experiences resembled mine:

> Students working in groups was useful, because it used up time, and kept them busy. Indeed, as I dove deeper into the ways of The College, I would conclude that excellent classroom teaching was measured almost exclusively in terms of what "worked" to keep students' attention, rather than the actual content of the learning. Nearly everything we did and talked about as college instructors seemed to revolve around what "worked" on such terms.

Linda A. Jackson and Michael Murray analyzed teaching evaluation forms in their '97 book, *What Students Really Think of Professors: An Analysis of Classroom Evaluation Forms at an American University*:

> Student comments tell us some of the ways that a professor, even in a large lecture class, can establish a relationship with students. All revolve around the communication of "caring"—caring about whether students learn, about students as individuals, and about the subject matter itself.

An advice column in the *Chronicle of Higher Education* suggested that doing a midterm course evaluation gives students the impression that the instructor cares. Another piece provided the enlightenment that the key to getting good evaluations is to present a likable persona even if your real feelings about the class are different.

To use a different idiom I heard at the workplace, students need a lot of stroking. But I thought this type of "caring" would be harmful to students in the short term but especially in the long run: the former because rigor usually suffers when stroking becomes a condition for learning, and the latter because we are not helping our students to mature into responsible adults. To give one example of showing caring or doing everything to protect students' self-esteem: some composition experts urge their colleagues to use a pencil instead of a pen, especially a red pen, to mark students' papers in order to show that the instructor respects the students' work and to protect their self-esteem. I saw this advice as infantilizing students and thought students coming out of this kind of conditioning would be too soft. Instead, I showed my care by reading their papers closely and writing no-nonsense comments. (Going through my old files, I saw a copy of a student paper I'd saved from my Minnesota years on which I'd marked a dangler.)

At the end of my fourth year, the provost scribbled the following comments on my progress toward tenure:

> [A sentence about continuing to work with my mentor on my teaching.]
>
> It is now time to co[n]vert your work in progress to publications. You have one year + to tenure review. You might try publishing parts of your book ms. as articles if you cannot get the book published. Also I noted your comment about its lack of theory—this is not a good strategy in any field.
>
> Your service seems adequate.

The provost did read my report. But my second book *couldn't* be published as articles—it is a story, not a typical academic book that can be broken up into self-contained pieces. More disconcerting, the provost had different expectations for scholarship than my college did. Before I published my first book, a senior colleague (my informal mentor) had said to me that my scholarship would be "right up there" if I could get it published, meaning sufficient to meet the scholarship expectations for tenure. (His dissertation had been published as a dissertation in a series, not as a regular monograph. Indeed, in his long career, he wouldn't write a single published book.) When I completed the draft for the second book, the same colleague had said I could now "stop being a scholar and start being a dad." (Since we were on friendly terms, I snapped at him, "But how? By having five kids?" My son was living with his mom in Minnesota, and since I didn't have a woman in my life at the time, even having one child all by myself would be more than a miracle.) Lastly, the provost spoke of my second book's lack of theory in terms of a "strategy." But it wasn't a strategy to me at all, that is, not a strategy for pursuing tenure. I'd mentioned in my report that after writing my first book about theory, I was sick of it for a while. The introduction to the second book also hinted at a *theoretical* reason for eliding theory: I'd seen too much talk of civil society, public space, etc. in Western books on contemporary Chinese society that seemed to be motivated more by Western concerns than by an interest in Chinese reality. The unstated question seemed to be, "Is China like the West yet?" So, I intentionally eschewed theory talk. In fairness, the provost couldn't have known this consideration, but the comment still showed the conventional view of a top administrator.

The annual report for '98 was my last before the tenure review. I ended the final section, "Self-Evaluation: Prose Summary," with the following remarks:

> The P&T process has begun. With my anthropological eye I would be utterly amused by this ritual of Nacirema academe if not for the tedious paper work involved. On the other hand, the process provides an official occasion for me to take stock of my life and work past, present and future. Ironically, the format of the review is probably ill-suited for genuine reflection. Still, I'm sure I'll learn a thing or two.

I ended up learning a lot, or rather, writing a lot. What with my experiences described above and what with the tenure ordeal, I couldn't decide on an apt title for the chapter that would cover both what is now in this chapter and in the next. My first title was "A Half-Hearted Academic." Then I thought of "Do in Rome as the Greeks Did," then "The Tenure Farce," then "'I'm Not Worthy! I'm Not Worthy!,'" then "Academia, Schmacademia," then "Ah, Academe." None seemed to capture my complex feelings toward my years of being a full-time academic.

I'm not the only nonnative academic who's had P & T trouble. In spring '95, I heard the shocking news from a former teacher that my advisor at Minnesota had been denied tenure there. She was a very good teacher, a supportive advisor, and she'd published a book and several articles. I didn't know the ostensible grounds for the denial. She'd come to Minnesota with a book, so maybe she was expected to publish another one on top of a busy teaching and advising schedule. (At one point she sat on eight dissertation committees!) I thought, someone who'd published a first book plus articles *after* being hired would most likely be considered tenure-worthy. Shouldn't scholarship per se be more important that the timing? While at Minnesota I'd heard from her about the inappropriate comments some students had made in their course evaluations, which amounted to disrespect and ignorance. She came from England, so of course her ways were not exactly American, which should have been seen as an asset; instead, in an anthropology department whose main mission is to understand other cultures she was mistreated. I felt sure petty academic politics was involved; God knows whose sore toes she'd unknowingly stepped on. From four years of interaction with her and her family, I knew her to be a gentle person, not at all a teeth-gnashing go-getter. Since highly successful academics are typically aggressive careerists, she was disadvantaged by her gentleness.

Four-and-a-half years later, I ran into tenure trouble; my friend Dubem from Nigeria also got shortchanged at his institution. Countless foreign-born academics have had better treatments in this country, so one might blame the isolated cases of failure or difficulty on the individuals themselves. And yet the three cases I happen to know seem to indicate the crushing pressure of conformity in academe: most foreign-born academics probably make doubly sure they do the right things and since they are usually very capable people, they get to pass muster in the eyes of the committees. But if you diverged from the beaten path a bit much, then you would end up in a career dead alley. I'm far from being a fanatic about multiculturalism and find identity politics narrow-minded and self-serving. And yet my direct and indirect experiences show that while the United States may be more open than a lot of other societies, its institutions of higher learning harbor no small amount of hypocritical bigotry and sophisticated stupidity.

Madeleine left Ohio in '96. She was the one who'd initiated the breakup, but being the procrastinator she was, she didn't file for divorce; I had to do it in '98. (She changed her last name when she married again, which should provide some privacy for her concerning this book.) Rightly she'd refused to share the debt incurred in the court case started by Ningnan, but eventually she asked me to pay off all our debts, saying her job as a freelance editor wasn't as well paying as mine, to which I agreed. I lived as simply as ever, and paid off the $12,000 debt.

Alone and lonely again, I buried myself in my work. One Friday evening, I was reading upstairs in the library and didn't notice the warning about closing. When I came downstairs, the library's doors had been locked. At least I could leave the building. One day, a student came to my office to chat. He asked me how I was and I said all work and no play. He said, "How come, you look like a swinging kind of guy." Hearing a double entendre, I was shocked. Like Jimmy Carter, I am only a swinger at heart.

In '97, I spent seven months studying leisure activities in my hometown. My friends introduced me to girls as young as nineteen, but I found today's young people too practical, too materialistic, too self-centered. Even though I was with my family and had lots of old friends to socialize with, my loneliness became so intense that one evening I nearly had a nervous breakdown. Hovering on the brink of going bananas, I was terrified of the consequences and fought feebly against the slide for some thirty minutes. Unable to stem the slide, I went to my younger sister's place. Luckily, the slide stopped.

Then I met Haiyan, the head of a kindergarten, who'd been unhappy in her marriage for years and who had an agreement with her husband that they'd wait till the first anniversary of her father's death to divorce, five months away. We started seeing each other and soon became inseparable. For the first time in my life, I met someone whose spirit is freer than mine. Even though we were both in it for a fling, we couldn't help falling for each other. When I had to leave, she came to Beijing to see me off. We said goodbye at the airport, both thinking it was for good. But after I returned to Oxford, I missed her so much that I started our exchange of letters. (Later on, she told me her love letters had been drafted by her younger friends while she was busy playing mahjong!) Before long, I began thinking of bringing her over. Haiyan's mom was worried that I might sell her in the States. Haiyan reasoned with her mom, saying that if I'd been a human trafficker, then I would have tried to trick twenty-year-olds, not someone twice as old. Still, her mom's pressure made her break off with me, which took the pressure off me to decide whether to take the risky step to bring her here, risky because she spoke no English and I feared she'd be in a prison living in Oxford. My friend Dubem comforted me by saying maybe it wasn't meant to be.

In Oxford, the Uptown scene looked desolate to me. The violence in *Boogie Nights* sent me running out of the theater, and I declined to team-teach a course on violence.

I had to see Haiyan again, so in summer '98 I went back to China, this time staying with Yueshan in a suburb of Guangzhou while preparing a course on *Three Kingdoms*. Haiyan would take the grueling train rides to visit me on weekends. Once, seeing her off at the train station I felt dizzy, on the verge of breakdown again, even though she'd be back in five days. Back at Yueshan's residence I couldn't even stay on the balcony to cool off—I felt it was going to tumble over. I went inside to Yueshan's room, farthest from the balcony, and sat down on the cement floor. When I told him how I was feeling, he teased me about my Sister Lin–like frailty. (Sister Lin or Lin Meimei is the star-crossed heroine in *Dream of the Red Chamber*.)

Eventually, we decided to take the plunge. But not before I became a U.S. citizen so that we wouldn't have to wait several years for an immigrant visa. Our wedding ceremony took place in the front hallway of my office building in summer '99. I got the mayor of Oxford, a colleague at Miami, to preside over the two-minute ceremony. No dressing up, no wedding rings, no photographer. (A student grabbed a camera and took a Polaroid of us—see app. 11.) We've been happier than ever before, even though for a while Haiyan missed her family and friends in China.

When I met Haiyan, she was blissfully ignorant of the world outside her own unit. But her intuition combined with her duties as a lowly administrator gave her penetrating insights into society and people. I was particularly struck by her keen awareness of affectation, hypocrisy, and self-importance, especially of officials and intellectuals. Indeed, she'd repeatedly declined to be introduced to me, then a chance encounter led to a few dates and she was won over by my fun side that she said more than made up for my undesirable side of being an academic. She is not against education, though. In fact, she used to read like the child Rousseau and Herzen—staying up all night till the book was finished and reading every Western novel she could lay her hands on. Later she'd look up every new word in a dictionary and write it down in a notebook.

Haiyan has her faults—she has heavy hands, is superstitious, can hold a grudge, and is rarely willing to give offense—but to say that she is a rare gem is no exaggeration or fawning on my part. Growing up on Hainan Island she was—and still is—a gamine. She regularly ate bugs, drank snake blood (fed by her soldier dad), and did all kinds of naughty things the wildest boy wouldn't do. Her misbehavior led to frequent beatings, and when her dad asked her what she'd like to do when she grew up, she said she'd kill him first and then she'd go far away. But when she did grow up, she became a most filial daughter. As a child, she had a very weak what Graham Wallas calls "property instinct"; at forty, she had no idea how much money her husband had and it didn't occur to her to ask about it at their divorce. Indeed, she's incorruptible with regard to money. In Oxford, she didn't mind walking to Kroger and carrying the groceries back in a backpack before we had a car. She used to spend money like water, and her generosity borders on profligacy. I wrote the 1st draft of the 1st five chapters of this autobiography in summer '99. When I orally translated what I'd written to her, she fell asleep almost every time. While I teased her about her inability to appreciate its simplicity, she dismissed it as lacking color. She rarely dreams in her sleep, thus approaching Zhuangzi's "true man."

Haiyan doesn't know insecurity or jealousy. In 2000, we went to Shanghai to see my old flame Meng Wen. Haiyan tried to persuade Meng Wen to be intimate with me and gave us opportunities to make up for what we'd missed in '86, without success. She said she was disappointed at this country because before she came here, she (and some of her colleagues) had thought being a freer country the United States allowed a man to have more than one wife; to her larger families were more fun because more people could play together. (She might have felt at home among the Kaingáng, who practiced every known form of marriage. On the other hand, there is no evidence in the anthropological literature that group marriage has ever existed as the dominant form of marital union anywhere.) We went on a trip to Hainan Island shortly after we hooked up. At the hotel where we were staying one night, the phone rang. Haiyan answered it; it was a prostitute. She said promptly: "You are too late; he's already got someone." Later she joked that she should have added, "Unless you want to join us!"

Being a tomboy is only one side of Haiyan; she is also a selfless worker and a fast learner in many things. For almost two decades, she held the honor of "model worker" almost every year, yielding the title to a colleague in two years. And yet she never joined the Communist Party. When I met her, she ate no lean meat, only fat; she couldn't cook, either. But now she can stomach lean meat and has blossomed into a fine cook. She loves to fish while I love to eat fish. Can you imagine a better union? My mom once said to me that I'd worked hard all my life, suffered all my life, and been poor all my life (*zuo yishi, ku yishi, qiong yishi*). I thought that characterization fitted her much better than it did me. She also said with regard to my finding a wife that I didn't know how comfortable it'd feel to have a really good wife. Now I do. Because, as she said to me after meeting Haiyan a few times, "You two stink alike" (*chouwei-xiangtou*).

14. The Tenure Farce

In April 1999, six months before my promotion and tenure statement was due, I wrote the twenty-page document and put together an appendix of nine pages of student praises of my teaching and service. Feeling uncomfortable about the way we were supposed to blow our own horn, I thought of a way both to maintain my integrity and present the strongest case for my candidacy for promotion and tenure. I emailed a copy of the statement to my friend Aili, who was teaching at Vassar at the time. At first, she was concerned about the tone of the statement, but after reading the entire document she was convinced that the humor was just about right and that nobody who read through the whole thing could doubt my seriousness or the quality of my work. The statement's highlights follow. (Distracting errors in the original have been quietly corrected.)

Xiuwu R. Liu
School of Interdisciplinary Studies
Promotion and Tenure (PT) Statement
October 21, 1999

"[I]ndeed what is more befitting than that Folly should be the trumpet of her own praise, and dance after her own pipe? for who can set me forth better than myself? or who can pretend to be so well acquainted with my condition?"

Erasmus, *In Praise of Folly*

"Quantities are competitive, qualities are complementary."

Dietrich Bonhoeffer, *Letters and Papers from Prison*

Preamble

A century ago, in *The Real Chinaman* (Dodd, Mead, and Co. 1895), Chester Holcombe, an interpreter and Acting Minister for the United States in China, described a typical encounter between two Chinese meeting for the first time:

> What is your honorable cognomen?
> The trifling name of your little brother is Wang.
> What is your exalted longevity?
> Very small. Only a miserable seventy years.
> Where is your noble mansion?
> The mud hovel in which I hide is in such or such a place.
> How many precious parcels (sons) have you?
> Only so many stupid little pigs.

As one scholar of Sino-American communication points out, "the words may be dated but the spirit persists." And I was raised in that spirit (by my grandparents who had been born at the turn of the century). Therefore, you can imagine the imagination and courage required of me to pen the following self-exalting statement.

Top Ten Reasons I Deserve PT and Then Some

Since this will be an unavoidably long and tedious statement, it might be helpful to highlight the more important reasons I deserve PT before I get into the details:

10. I have made a significant contribution to the curriculum of the School of Interdisciplinary Studies and by extension, of Miami University. This includes designing (five) and codesigning (three) eight new courses that introduced students to such subjects as the Igbo of Nigeria; the Brazilian poor; French-American cultural misunderstandings; Mexican artists; urban cultures in various parts of the world; Chinese history, philosophy, politics and society; and the philosophy of social science. I also infused new blood into three old courses on social movements and strategies for change, utopian communities in the United States, and the rise of national socialism in Weimar Germany. The courses range from ancient history to contemporary society and from empirical studies to philosophy. In my teaching I emphasize methodology and comparative perspectives, and I place a premium on quality over quantity. In the past five years, I didn't repeat a single course, which means I have worked very hard to enrich our curriculum and I have been a good sport team-teaching with my colleagues. In addition, I have done research on several new courses in anticipation of the restructuring of our curriculum in the not-too-distant future: Time: What Is It Good For?, Progress and Its Discontents, and The Political Economy of the Social Construction of Humor as Cultural Critique.

9. Speaking of working hard, I have spent all five summer breaks and three winter breaks doing and writing up research or preparing new courses (without getting paid for the summers, I might add). I work or read seven days a week and go to the library at least once a week. During holidays I am often the sole biped pedaling a bike on the deserted Spring Street (the man's got to go eat) or the lone votary sublimating in the office building.

8. I am a good teacher, or to be more accurate, I am not a mediocre teacher. This in part can be seen in the fact that many students think I am superb, whereas a few give me the lowest rating across the board. In a form of life where quality is measured by averages, my ratings have improved a great deal since I came to Western [should have been "since my second year here"]. Now my averages for "overall instructor" move between 3 and 4 on a five-point scale. I am always open to good suggestions and responsive to students' needs.

7. My courses often play the indispensable role of fulfilling the Historical Perspectives, World Cultures and Non-Dominant Perspectives requirements of the Miami Plan for the School of Interdisciplinary Studies.

6. I have published one book, have a second forthcoming, and have written half of a third. All three books have to do with China, but they are on very different topics and are different kinds of books. This productivity is good enough even for a research institution.

5. I have been most active in community learning, participating in all kinds of student activities. [A footnote quoting three student praises.]

4. I have been a conscientious colleague, including doing committee work, sometimes going beyond the call of duty.

3. I can sing revolutionary Beijing opera, do Chinese calligraphy with a brush, cook a better Chinese meal than does Phan Shin [a local Chinese restaurant], am good at transplanting rice seedlings, and can eat a lot of bacon and ice cream. In a word, I am a versatile worker.

2. I have no house, no car, no furniture (except one table and four chairs), no computer of my own, no copy of my own book, no title after my name in the university directory and no piercing, facial or otherwise. How can this singular harmless exotic animal in the Western-Zoo not be treasured?

And the #1 reason I deserve PT is . . . (drum roll) I am cheap—I have been the lowest or one of the lowest paid faculty members at Miami for the good work I do. [A footnote: "However, I hope this will not deter the administration from bringing my salary up to the level commensurate with—as they say in advertising—my contribution to this institution."]

The foregoing list *tells* some of the reasons I deserve PT, but it may be just as important to *show* how sharp, learned, cool, entertaining and dedicated this fella is. [A footnote quoting student praises.] The following story I told as part of a lecture should serve this purpose well:

My adventure as an aspiring opera singer
(as part of the lecture, "The Chinese Communist Revolution as a Utopian Venture")

In the spirit of *The Curious Enlightenment of Professor Caritat*, let me tell you a story.

The year was 1972, when the model revolutionary operas were a rage in China. I was a junior in high school and had taught myself most of the arias of three popular operas. One day I went to audition for a local opera troupe.

"So, what do you want to play?" asked the director of the opera troupe.

"I want to be a concubine," I said.

He looked at me and frowned, "I don't think you can be a concubine."

"Why not?" I asked.

"Look at your eyebrows," he said, grinning.

"I can see the tip of my nose, but not my eyebrows."

"Have you ever thought of being a comic instead of an opera singer?"

"But I really *want* to be an opera singer!"

"Well," the director said, "Your eyebrows are too thick and you look ferocious."

I was undaunted. "But Sir, though I may look like a boy, I'm by nature a girl." (How many of you have seen *Farewell My Concubine*?)

He chuckled but said nothing. I pleaded, "OK, if I can't be a concubine, can I be a female revolutionary fighter? Let me sing an aria from *The Red Lantern*."

He nodded and I proceeded to sing. (Explain *The Red Lantern* and the libretto. Then sing falsetto.)

When I finished, he looked at me again and said, "Not bad. But I still think your eyebrows are too thick."

I was desperate. If it were today, I would have cried out loud, "This is eyebrowism!" meaning discrimination on the basis of the shape of one's eyebrows. I said, "Then can I try a male revolutionary hero, PLEASE?"

He exchanged a few words with the other two panelists and said OK. Then I sang the following aria from *The Red Lantern*. (Explain the libretto and sing.)

When I was done, the director looked me up and down and said, "Your singing is good, but I don't think you are tall enough to be the revolutionary hero."

But this is heightism! Right then and there I decided to give up my hopes of becoming an opera singer and to come to the U.S. to study philosophy. As a result, China lost a bright opera star, and the U.S. gained a mediocre philosopher.

In brief, the details below will show (that is, if the Top Ten list above hasn't done so already) that I have been an outstanding faculty member in all three areas evaluated in PT: teaching (except in student ratings but certainly in the quality and quantity of the subjects I have offered and of the work I have put into my courses), scholarship (both in quality and quantity, more so if divisional definition of scholarship—research for courses included—is taken into account), and service (especially divisional service).

Summary of Education and Professional Experience
[The details have been told in previous chapters.]

Teaching and Academic Advising
[A statement of my teaching philosophy is followed by eight pages of detailed description of my teaching and advising, and then two pages on my research and publishing, including a description of this autobiography with the following footnote:]
I don't want to count my chickens before they are hatched but I have made many an observation about the insanity of modernity (for example, (read the following with a British accent) Michael Jordan doing commercials for MCI—How much bloody money does the bloke want?), so at some point, I would like to write a book à la George Carlin's *Brain Droppings* or one that might be called *Xiuliver's Travels in Modernity*.

[Half a page on professional development, including the following paragraph:]
I have been a member of the Association for Asian Studies since 1993. I decided to join the American Philosophical Association and the International Society for Humor Studies in late 1998 and was admitted to both organizations in early 1999. I joined the former organization because it would look good on my vitae (of course I'm kidding) and I joined the latter because I need humor to keep my sanity (I'm not kidding) (even though scholarly studies of humor are rarely humorous).

[Four pages on service to the profession, the university, and my school; contribution to student learning outside the classroom; and service to the community.]

[One paragraph on the relationship of my teaching, research, and service activities.]

Coda
"I speak the truth, not quite my fill of it, but as much as I dare, and I dare a little more as I grow older."
—Montaigne

Appendix: Selected student praises of my teaching, advising and involvement in community learning
"But is it not a great impudence to bring our imperfections and weaknesses where we desire to please and leave a good opinion and recommendation of ourselves?"
—Montaigne (In the original document and the 1st edition of this book, I had misidentified the author of this quote as Horace; otherwise, I wouldn't have chosen two quotes in a row by the same author.)

[Six-and-a-half pages of student praises of my teaching, advising, and involvement in community learning, and two-and-a-half pages of praises of my role as faculty-in-residence.]

The preamble was a repeat of that for my third-year review. I decided not to use the version I'd written for the tenure statement that showed my true feelings toward the rigmarole:

I understand that I'm supposed to present evidence in this statement that I deserve promotion and tenure (hereafter, PT). If I were allowed to take my low-profile approach to things, I'd say, "Well, I've got the terminal degree, I'm a good teacher, a decent scholar, a smiling colleague. And I'll have been here six years. Therefore, I deserve PT." (Indeed, the case may be made even more simply: The man's got to eat, for crying out loud.) But apparently this wouldn't do. So let me begin at the beginning and

> show you how brilliant, learned, cool, entertaining, dedicated (these adjectives come from student evaluation forms) and therefore, worthy, I am.

As requested by the P & T Committee, I provided a list of potential external reviewers of my scholarship for the committee to choose from. To show my integrity, I indicated whether I knew the person or not and so on. The committee had a hard time finding senior scholars willing to read my work. Eventually, the chair found two readers from elsewhere (Columbia and Carleton College) and two from other units of Miami. The committee met to discuss my file and prepared a preliminary assessment letter dated November 2, 1999.

The preliminary letter is meant both to render an initial evaluation and to ask the candidate questions about areas the committee finds problematic or even not. Under teaching, the first paragraph noted my contributions to the curriculum and my other strengths as a teacher. The rest of the section went like this:

> Yet there are also substantial concerns which appear throughout your file regarding your seminar instruction. . . . For example, one student expresses concern about your ability to "facilitate conversation." Another student reports "he does not seem to ask a lot of the 'right' questions." A third student says, "Xiuwu did not deal with the problem that students did not do the reading and the course became quite painful to attend." These comments are reflected in the overall instructor and course averages in your student teaching evaluation over the last years. While there has been consistent improvement of about .25 points per year in the student ratings, your averages remain consistently well below the norm for this division. In fact, you have been above the norm only once. The committee takes teaching very seriously and is quite concerned about this issue.
>
> As you prepare your written and oral responses to this letter, the committee asks that you consider the following questions.
> • Can you be more specific about the particular steps you have taken to increase your teaching effectiveness?
> • Why do you believe your teaching evaluations are consistently below the WCP norm? Do you believe that they reflect the quality of your teaching? If not, why?
> • Explain what you mean when you characterize your teaching as "thinking oriented" rather than "activity oriented."
> • What is the pedagogical strategy that leads you to choose to focus a course around one major text? [This refers to *Three Kingdoms*, an epic of 1,096 pages in large dimensions and small print.]
> • When students do not find intrinsic motivation in course materials, what is the responsibility of the faculty member to motivate them?

The section on scholarship was more positive as was that on service, but the committee also had a few concerns and questions about my scholarship, mainly that I seemed to have undertaken my work without peer support.

The section on collegiality was the most positive of all:

> One colleague who has taught with you [this was Andy Garrison with whom I'd team-taught for three semesters by then, including the course on Weimar Germany] refers to you as a colleague with "great

> intellectual stature and integrity, widely and deeply read, with lived experience of two very different cultures . . . with an encyclopedic array of conceptual frameworks from both the social sciences and philosophy." Other colleagues report that they don't know you as well as they wish they did. What do you see as your contributions in providing guidance and help to colleagues?

The letter ended with requests for my annual reports, third-year review, student evaluation forms for all the courses I'd taught, and reviews of my book, to be submitted to the committee by November 8 at 9 a.m.

My response to the preliminary letter addressed the committee's questions and concerns in seven pages.

On November 12, the committee conducted its interview with me. The committee consisted of the entire tenured faculty, eight or nine present, and two students (a Western tradition of having student views represented, one of whom was not allowed to vote later for having missed a meeting). In my opening statement, I talked about my days as an avid book copier and notetaker in the mid-'70s in China and showed the committee volume one of *A Comprehensive Guide to Good English* I'd copied and my notes on Hume, Russell, and Dampier. I also gave an example of how I provide students with insights into the U.S. I gain from my cross-cultural eye.

Questions followed on my responses to the committee's preliminary letter. One interviewer said that my answer of waiting till I'm rich and famous to serve the profession was "a bit farcical." To which I wanted to reply that the whole affair is a bit farcical but I merely smiled. The same person said with regard to my second book that there are ways to present a long narrative in a twenty-minute conference appearance, about which I had to plead ignorance instead of saying I didn't really try. One of the students asked about my plans for writing articles besides books, and I said that my interests in higher education and in issues of modernity just might lead to articles in the future, even though what I wanted to say was "Why do I have to write articles? What's wrong with books?" Then a person said my teaching evaluations had numerous criticisms in them and proceeded to read the negative comments on the Weimar course I'd team-taught with my colleague Andy Garrison (who, like Madeleine, had graduated from St. John's College). The questioner said he'd counted twelve evaluations with negative comments, how would I explain that. I was for once stumped, and instead of saying, "Well, there were over thirty students in the two sections, which means there were also a few positive ones," I said, "they were a bit too harsh."

On the afternoon of November 24, I opened the committee's letter of decision in the hallway of the college's main building. I copy the letter below and ask your forgiveness for any repetition you may find.

Dear Professor Liu:

The Western College Promotion and Tenure Committee has met and discussed your candidacy for promotion and tenure. I regret to inform you ["A rejection!" But I read on.] that the committee did not recommend you for tenure or promotion. The following is our assessment of your candidacy. According to the Miami University Promotion and Tenure Policy, the order of importance given to the following criteria is, in descending order of significance, "teaching and academic advising," "research, scholarly and/or creative achievement," "professional activities," and "collegiality." [By this time, I'd come to my office, so I read the rest of the death sentence sitting in my ergonomic chair.]

Teaching:
Although you have contributed in many important ways to the curriculum of the college, student comments and numeric evaluations of your teaching show that your instruction has been consistently and substantially below the college norm. A key factor in this evaluation has been your inability to effectively lead seminar discussions. We value your many contributions to our pedagogical mission – your contribution to the international and cross[-]cultural dimension of our curriculum, your well designed lectures, the knowledge you bring to the topics you teach, and especially your significant personal relationship with individual students. ["Sounds too personal," I thought.] Yet teaching, and especially seminar instruction, is the central mission of the college. "Continuing achievement in high quality teaching" is a basic requirement of promotion and tenure, and your teaching record has not met this standard.

As you yourself have pointed out, often your "discussions can be a bit lacking." Many students addressed this issue in their written comments. For example, in the spring of 1999 one student wrote, "Xiuwu was very passive in leading most class discussions." In another section of the same course [the Weimar course that'd been picked on during the interview], a student said, "I feel fairly cheated about this course. From the reading that I did do, I could tell that this was actually a decent course. However, Xiuwu gave the class zero motivation in seminar. Discussion was nil, or slightly above nil – at best. There were next to no debatable topics brought up in seminar, and no probing or leading questions by Xiuwu to aid discussion." In your conversation with the committee you were concerned, as we all are, with the fact that discussion classes can suffer because students sometimes don't read course materials or come to class prepared to participate. Yet we also found little evidence that you have been willing to commit yourself to developing new strategies, or pedagogical techniques, to reach and motivate students. As a student in another section of one of your courses noted, "Xiuwu did not deal with the problem that students did not do the reading and the course became quite painful to attend."

While students use descriptions like "sense of humor," "fun," and "zany" to describe your approach to seminars, these same students also often express real concern about your effectiveness leading seminar discussions. Indeed, in your recent class evaluations it was often students who expressed affection for you who also noted substantial problems in your seminar teaching [how often?]. For example, one student said "I have a hard time being critical of Xiuwu because I like his personality, but as a teacher he was unsuccessful in this course." Another student reports "he does not seem to ask a lot of the 'right' questions." A third student relates, "our discussions are agony." These comments are reflected in the overall instructor and course averages in your student teaching evaluation over the last years. While there has been consistent improvement of about .25 points per year in the student ratings, your averages remain consistently well below the norm for this division [note that it didn't specify how much below]. In fact, you have been above the norm only once in 27 courses.

> We realize that, in the last years, you have followed the suggestions of this committee, and the dean, to take steps to improve your teaching. Yet from your teaching record we must regretfully draw the conclusion that this work has not resulted in sufficient change. We must conclude that your teaching is not of the quality that can recommend you for tenure or promotion.
>
> Research and Scholarly Activity:
> Your colleagues appreciate what an achievement it is to have finished two monographs and have a third underway since you have come to Miami. External reviewers to whom your work was sent were uniformly favorable regarding your scholarly output. N.T. Wang, of Columbia University, judges both completed books to be "well researched and convincingly articulated. They demonstrated the candidate's scholarly ability and achievements in both theoretical and empirical endeavors. In particular, the breadth and depth of theoretical discussions are uncommon even among well-established gurus." [see app. 12; this passage merely repeated the section's first paragraph of the preliminary letter.]
>
> Service:
> The committee was impressed with your contributions to the community life of the Western College. One faculty colleague noted that you are "among the most active participants in community life in the history of the Western Program." Students have remarked that you are a visible presence in the community and are often available to talk with them informally. However, it appears to the committee that you have made relatively modest service contributions outside the division. You have served on some university committees and as a reader for various scholarship programs.
>
> Collegiality:
> In general, we find that you have always been willing to perform the work necessary to the operation of the college, although you have seldom taken a leadership role in these activities.
>
> To conclude, we find you a collegial colleague, and we believe that your research and service are adequate. Yet we believe that your record of teaching is not of the quality that would recommend you for tenure or promotion.

I sat in my chair sad and angry, thinking what a battle I'd have to fight. I remembered my advisor, who'd written me three years before that she'd "had a watertight case" and yet had failed to win her appeal. I remembered the time when I'd failed the oral defense of my master's thesis in Beijing, although I'd felt a greater shock back then. Somehow, knowing "life isn't fair" didn't make me feel better. At this point, a student who'd taken a few classes with me came to see me, so I showed her the letter from the committee. Looking sullen, she said she couldn't believe it and added that students could start a letter-writing campaign to support me. Given the history of active student involvement in the college's affairs, her response was not unexpected. I printed out a copy of my P & T statement minus the appendix and gave it to her.

While dreading the uphill battle looming ominously in front of me, I wasn't hopeless. "Maybe the dean will support me, and then the case would go forward to the All-University P & T Committee and so on." (My school was a department-sized division, so we had a dean but no chair.) And I wasn't baseless in my hopes. The new dean had been rather positive about my teaching in his latest evaluation of me. To quote his summary evaluation of my teaching dated May 20, 1999:

> I applaud your work in course redesign and development, particularly with regard to the "Three Kingdoms" course. I am also pleased at your increased effectiveness in the classroom. Although I think there is still room for improvement here, I am confident that you are doing the right things to assure your success.

In addition, he had used superlatives to describe the manuscript of my second book after he'd read it. Indeed, the new provost had sent the message that my case would hinge on whether I could get a contract on the manuscript and the dean had twice contacted the publisher reviewing the manuscript for a verdict. Through a friend of his he even tracked down a senior scholar of Chinese economic history who was on leave that year, to see if he could help place my manuscript. The dean and I were also team-teaching a course on *Three Kingdoms* and *The Decline and Fall of the Roman Empire*, so over the weekend I wrote an informal response to the committee's judgment for the dean's sake, i.e., to try to persuade him to disagree with the committee.

I emailed a draft of this response to my friend Aili, who made extensive comments; I revised it accordingly. Ten-and-a-half of the eleven-and-a-half pages of this titleless rebuttal was devoted to my teaching. I pointed out, again, that the university has a policy that evaluation of teaching should go beyond student evaluations; that the committee had made no effort to conduct peer evaluations of my seminars, the crux of the matter; and lastly, the only peer evaluation of my seminars, that of my teacher mentor's, was generally positive. I briefly discussed other qualitative criteria for teaching and provided testimonials to the high quality of my teaching. I added another page on some fine points of evaluation before copying five pages of student praises selected from eleven letters supporting my candidacy. To excerpt the most relevant comments (with some ellipsis points omitted):

> Being a third year, I can say I've probably been in as many of Xiuwu's classes as possible – all of which I thoroughly enjoyed. For teaching style, Xiuwu is unique. . . . Honestly what I enjoyed the most was his straightforwardness. He understood that @ this level we should come to class with the questions & the will to learn and was able to overlook some of the formalities that are not appropriate for college teaching. He was always a passionate teacher & lecturer – something that is rare – unless the teacher is teaching *their* focus.

> The most notable traits of Xiuwu's conduct of seminar class would have to be his intense spontaneity and joy. He always came to class full of enthusiasm and passion for communication.

> Xiuwu's seminars involve discussion of the particular assigned reading, and he is always careful to remind his students to seek support for their views within the text. Sometimes, Western classes tend to

> become forums for people to air their feelings and opinions. Though feelings and opinions may be valuable in establishing a certain direction, the individual must also engage in and with scholarly works in order to grow. Xiuwu once pointed out that if we cannot be interested in and stimulated by classic works, we are not looking hard enough, digging deeply enough, for it is impossible to be bored once we find that core of resonance. This, I believe, is another valuable lesson Xiuwu is trying to impress upon his students, both within and without the classroom.
>
> Xiuwu is an asset to the Western Community. He adds spice to this rather homogeneous place. He is always the same person. He never puts on a mask to please us in the classroom setting. He is consistent and real. When I speak to him, I know that I can immediately cut through the B.S. and talk to him about whatever is on my mind.
>
> I have had Xiuwu for three consecutive semesters. He is uncompromising in his beliefs on teaching. He has never had an attendance policy, noting that such policies are often counterproductive, as they quickly become the only reason for class attendance. People have to want to learn in order to learn. Absent from his seminars are many of the inane "teaching activities" employed by some professors to force students to participate.
>
> His devotion to the subject matter he teaches is unparalleled. Unlike many other Western professors, Xiuwu extends this devotion to subjects that lie outside his area of expertise. He is diligent in his pursuit of knowledge and committed to sharing that knowledge with others. In my eyes this is the model of what a good professor should strive for.

I ended my rebuttal with the following reflections:

> I am writing a memoir about my life in China and the United States [which would become an autobiography] and cannot help but reflect on my PT case in broader cultural and philosophical terms. I see glaring ironies. One, as someone who grew up in a culture not known for its trumpet of individuality, I am crucified for using a "unique" pedagogy in a society that presumably celebrates it. Two, as someone who practices student-centered teaching and learning, I find that I have been uniformly appreciated by the two-dozen main-campus students I've had, but not so in a program proud of its nonmainstream values and experimental origins. And finally, ever since I came to Western, I've been trying to get students to read carefully and thoughtfully and yet at the end of my "probation," I find that many of my students are more careful and perceptive, not to mention caring, readers than some of my colleagues.

On December 3, I received the dean's decision, which concurred with the committee's. He said I had thirty days to submit a request for reconsideration, adding that I should "make it clear to the Committee what facts it failed to consider or what it otherwise failed to do in arriving at its decision. Merely to restate what it already knows would probably serve little purpose." The dean's five-page letter said that my "record of scholarship more than meets the threshold of expectations for a candidate being considered for tenure" and that I met "normal expectations" in service and collegiality. However, in three pages of detailed commentary he presented the case against my tenuring, expectedly citing student comments about "his inability and/or unwillingness to facilitate class discussion" and emphasizing that my ratings "**remain[ed]** among the division's lowest."

Now I must decide what to do. I remembered joking to a visiting colleague in the mailroom a few years before about suing the school for six million bucks if I were denied tenure; now faced with the prospect of a legal battle I wondered where the attorney fees would come from and whether I wanted to be involved in a protracted, emotionally draining struggle. I soon decided to appeal, putting aside whether to go to court or not for now. I contacted the university office that handles discrimination cases (EOE), talked to my teacher mentor about the crisis and asked him to write a letter for me, talked to my former dean who'd hired me in '94, emailed two of my former teachers at Minnesota for advice, contacted three senior colleagues elsewhere two of whom I'd never met but all of whom had read my scholarship, and told two academic friends the bad news and got their moral support. Epictetus and Haiyan provided consolation of philosophy.

The meetings with the EOE officers gave me some hope. A former attorney, the main officer said the dean's letter was vulnerable to a lawsuit. He suggested that I look up the ratings of my tenured colleagues. The dean's letter had stated that my "evaluations **remain[ed]** among the division's lowest," but since most of the college's faculty were tenured, it meant that some of the tenured faculty must also have ratings that were lower than the norms. I looked through the ratings records of all the courses taught since the fall of '94 when I joined the school, and guess what, four of the nine faculty members of the P & T Committee who'd voted on my candidacy had ratings similar to mine.

I then wrote a thirty-four-page request for reconsideration, put together ten exhibits, and sanitized the P & T statement, deleting most of the levity, the preamble, and other potentially offending elements. The top-ten countdown became a nine-item count-up. In other words, I bowed for less than five pecks of rice, though, really, as a student of humor I should have been commended for practicing what I study. The appeal opened with seven points I requested the committee to reconsider, followed by thirty pages of detailed argument amplifying the seven points, and ended with a summary of my qualifications for tenure and promotion.

I emailed a draft to two former teachers, one of whom provided detailed comments, while the other said my tone was just right and I didn't sound defensive. Two colleagues elsewhere expressed sympathy but gave no specific feedback. I also showed it to the EOE officers.

Besides critiquing my appeal, my teacher mentor Richard Quantz wrote a six-page, what-the-dean-called "eloquent" letter to the P & T Committee and to the dean, patiently arguing that "there is reason to think that Xiuwu's mean score on student evaluations is suppressed as a result of his cultural difference and the resistance and confusion on the part of *some* students to those differences" (see app. 13). I was of course deeply grateful to him for writing such a lengthy, thoughtful letter. Meanwhile, my senior colleague and friend Bill Green sent a strongly supportive letter from another institution where he was teaching at the time.

Before the school's P & T Committee met to reconsider my case, students in support of my bid took action. In the course of one day, they took turns dropping letters in the faculty's mailboxes for maximum effect. On that day, six letters were delivered and one was emailed to the assistant dean; an eighth was late by one day. The heartfelt testimonials brought tears to my eyes. (Some ellipsis points have been omitted.)

> The reasons for denial of Xiuwu's tenure remain unclear, though they likely reflect a certain disdain for Xiuwu's nontraditional approach to Western seminars. . . . Xiuwu constantly forces students to think about their often impulsive reactions and criticisms, rather than integrate such uninformed commentary into the seminar—as many Western professors do. His vehement disdain for thoughtless criticism serves as perhaps the most effective tool in developing intelligent and refined critical thought, which remains to this day a point of pride among Western students. To remove such a positive intellectual influence from this hotbed of potential talent would not only rob the community of a brilliant, gifted man, but would also serve to expedite the downfall of reason and accountability in Western classrooms.
>
> As a teacher and a friend, Xiuwu has the unique ability to reach students in an unparalleled way and to deny students this vital "living and learning" community member contradicts what I believe to be the essence of Western.
>
> Xiuwu represents what may be the ideal Western faculty member.
>
> His conception and preparation of the classes he teaches are of the highest quality. His commitment of time is unparalleled in the faculty. He consistently causes the students to challenge themselves by assigning some of the most complex reading on Western, and encouraging students to grapple with the new information. His ability to illuminate a student to the material he is presenting is tremendous and he is always academically well-backed and prepared. He is open and knowledgeable, and easy to approach. He supplements his classes in an interdisciplinary fashion, showing movies outside of class time which involve class material and consistently maintaining a supply of books to lend to interested readers. Xiuwu is open and honest with students and is willing to help with any phase of any problem, both academically and interpersonally. As a professor, he is indispensable to the academic and intellectual growth of the program.
>
> His ability to approach a subject in an interdisciplinary manner, to talk about a subject in a number of different ways and consider it from all angles makes him one of the best orators at the university. . . . Xiuwu has come to live in another country, gone from being a literal peasant to a collegial instructor, and affected for the better the lives of hundreds of people through his creative teaching and personal charisma.
>
> To ask this man to leave the program, to deny him tenure, is perhaps the most foolish thing that the faculty and administrative staff could do. . . . And it would deprive us of one of the most excellent people we know.
>
> It was a heavy blow to the student body to find out that he would not be granted tenure.
>
> Xiuwu has been a vital and integral part of my Western experience and he has touched the hearts and minds of many students.

> He has done more for this community than I can even write about . . . how are you truly able to express in words the energy or the feeling someone radiates that envelops and leaves a distinctive mark on you?
>
> His teaching abilities are ones that promote the individual's ability to have an active part in his or her education. . . . He's able to offer a unique perspective at Western, having had intensive schooling in both Chinese and Western thought. He is well versed in philosophy and has a sense of humor and air of lightness that can really put our lives as students here to learn, in a clear perspective.
>
> If he is denied tenure I feel that the sinking of my stomach and the ache in my heart will point accurately to the direction this program is heading . . . let us not forget our roots which are embodied in the dynamic and dedicated Xiuwu Liu.

> In his seminars, he provokes his students to really think about the material and participate in the discussions. Education is not based solely on the efforts of the instructor but of the students as well. Xiuwu always emphasized this point and refused to force us to read or participate in class. At this level in our academic careers, we, as students, are responsible for our education and will get out of it what we put in. Those students willing to dedicate time to Xiuwu's courses have an opportunity to learn so much.

> Xiuwu is singularly the most valuable asset to the Western community and experience. He has not only set high standards in the classroom but also the highest standards in thinking. While living in McKee and eating in Alexander Dining Hall he has opened himself up completely to me and the rest of the community. Unofficially he has taught me that I must constructively think before I discredit an argument. By no means have I mastered this skill and I wish to work on it further with Xiuwu.

> If the promotion and tenure committee is so dependent on shallow numerical evaluations in rating an instructor's skill, shouldn't you attempt to qualify student opinions first? . . . There is a disease raging among Western students and I'm sure you've noticed (Xiuwu certainly has, and rightly so). The disease is something more than apathy and lack of motivation; we feel compelled to blame the professor for an unsatisfactory learning environment instead of trying to better ourselves as students.
>
> I am saying all of this because I fear that Western is about to lose its greatest asset. Xiuwu has contributed more to the Western community (including both the academic and social community) than any other faculty member, tenured or otherwise. . . . When God created Western—or whoever did—it seems to me that a teacher of Xiuwu's brilliance and compassion was included in the divine plan.
>
> Xiuwu is involved in teaching students how to be better students, which is where education begins, if you ask me.
>
> In my opinion, Xiuwu Liu is the very embodiment of the Western College Program and should be looked to as an icon for any student with an interest in keeping Western alive and vital.

> [Before leaving Oxford, a student who'd been on my tenure committee but wasn't one of the above eight letter writers left me this handwritten note: "Xiuwu - Thanks for remaining an idealist in a hypocritical world - Good Luck in dealing with your 'colleagues[.]'"]

On January 21, 2000, I received the P & T Committee's reconsideration letter. The committee voted for tenure but not for promotion. The letter explained why the committee now recommended tenure:

> While it is true that your instructor ratings are the lowest in the College, the comparisons you offered with four tenured colleagues are instructive. A perspective that was influential is that your instructor's

> scores are roughly comparable to certain senior colleagues['] and that your lower scores may be due in part to your unique cultural background and seminar style.

The letter added: "The School of Interdisciplinary Studies wishes to be a leader concerning issues of pedagogical and cultural diversity." But due to "the areas of continued concern in the realm of teaching, especially seminar instruction," the committee reaffirmed its negative decision on promotion.

At last, a ray of hope. In my limited joy I couldn't fail to see that the "influential" perspective the committee said I'd supplied was nothing new to the committee, or at least to most of its members. I wished I'd had a bug in the conference room. Of course, they needed a rationale for changing part of their verdict without admitting they'd been wrong or unfair. Three of the four tenured colleagues were full professors—including the chair of the P & T Committee—and one was an associate professor, but I alone was not good enough for promotion. (The dean told me that I'd gotten only one positive vote and I'm quite sure—don't ask me how—it wasn't cast by one of those four.)

Three days later, the dean's letter came: he upheld his earlier negative decisions on both tenure and promotion. But due to the committee's changed verdict on tenure, now my case could move forward to the All-University Committee. I communicated with the university's attorney again, this time about my right to respond to the dean's second decision letter. The attorney affirmed my right.

Whereas the divisional committee accepted the comparison of my ratings and those of four senior colleagues, the dean insisted that such comparison was irrelevant, citing university policy that "each candidate for tenure is judged individually not relative to other candidates," and added a footnote asserting that "what **is** relevant are the mean scores for courses taught by you and by other faculty." Rendering his letter even more problematic, he went on to compare my record with the records of candidates from other divisions he'd seen over the two years he'd been on the university committee, thereby not only contradicting himself but setting up an unfair framework for debate because, unlike he, I was not privy to the P & T cases from other divisions and hence had no evidence with which to challenge his claims.

After a bit of research on the literature on how to use student ratings, I wrote a five-page response to the dean's second letter, selecting six exhibits including an article by William E. Cashin, "Student Ratings of Teaching: Uses and Misuses," anthologized in *Changing Practices in Evaluating Teaching*. Then I sought feedback from my teacher mentor, the EOE officer, two former teachers, and two colleagues elsewhere. One former teacher commented on my draft and said the language was too strong, so I toned it down. Another former teacher wrote: "I am stunned by the cogency of the documents you have written." The feedback included two other pieces of advice: 1) write an executive summary of the five-page response to the dean's letter, because my first appeal was thirty-four pages long and another five-page statement might just be the last straw that breaks the camel's back; attach the full statement in case someone on the committee wanted to see the whole thing; and 2) there was no way the university committee would grant me both tenure and promotion by overturning both the divisional committee's and the dean's decisions, so I should not appeal the decision on promotion, only the one on tenure. That way, I'd have the divisional committee on my side. I took the second piece of advice reluctantly.

My friend Bill Green once again helped me by sending a letter to the university committee headed by the provost. Meanwhile, students who wanted to help me win the battle rose to the challenge again. First, representatives went to a university administrator's office, where they got some advice on what they could do to help. They wrote a statement to the university committee, then collected and copied the IDs of sixty-eight students and had them sign the copy. On the day all the materials were due, right before the university secretary's office was about to close, they submitted the statement with the signed photocopies of their IDs.

The University P & T Committee voted to grant me tenure, and the trustees rubber-stamped the verdict.

My experience of both being the judged and a judge in P & T cases—all the tenured faculty were members of the division's P & T committee—shows that the whole thing is embarrassing. (In one promotion case at Western, the candidate for full professor—the one who had asked me to explain why there had been a dozen criticisms of my teaching of the Weimar course a few years before—presented no ratings of individual courses he had taught for the committee to review, nor did the committee ask to see the evaluation forms containing student comments—I of course didn't propose that the committee should.) First, the criteria are inane. The main areas of evaluation are teaching, research, and service. The candidate has to be "very strong" for promotion to associate professor and be "excellent" for full in two of the three areas, though service is actually less important than teaching or research. How can all the faculty members who get tenure or promotion—who are the overwhelming majority at my school where most faculty are full professors and at my university where almost all tenure applicants get tenure—be "very strong" or "excellent"? (There are a few casualties along the way, but it's a moot point whether those are not as "strong" as the survivors. The whole thing seems to be an exercise in a variation on the "narcissism of small differences.") We indeed live at Lake Wobegon, "where all the women are strong, all the men are good-looking, and all the children are above average." Or 94 percent are: A 1970s study of "a fairly typical university faculty" found that 94 percent rated themselves as above-average teachers. No wonder we get double-speak, double consciousness, maneuvering, and just plain nonsense.

A related problem is my university's rule of treating each candidate on an individual basis, not comparatively. That is, the committee or the dean is not supposed to compare a candidate with any other candidate or tenured person. Putting aside the improbable psychology involved, how does one evaluate a candidate without comparison when the criteria are fuzzy? I thought of discrimination lawsuits. If no comparison should be made, how can a charge of discrimination be made at all? The presumption seems to be that the committee is fair unless the recipient of a negative decision challenges the presumption, which hides the arbitrariness of the deliberations in the context of fuzzy criteria and is belied by the typical pettiness of academic gamesmanship. On the other hand, comparative judging is tricky. How does one compare two articles, for example, of different lengths, subject matter, places of appearance, and so on? Even more so, how does one compare the quality and potential impact of teaching of one teacher and those of another? The whole thing is a big muddle.

A third problem is that tenure and promotion expectations have risen considerably over the recent past. As some of my senior colleagues jokingly admitted at meetings that screened candidates for jobs, some of those would-be assistant professors had more publications than they themselves when they'd been tenured a while back. As a result, when a tenure case comes up, we see the folly, not to mention the unfairness, of less accomplished senior faculty members judging whether a junior faculty member has the right to eat.

Yet another problem is the secrecy of the whole thing. When the August Committee meets to deliberate about people's livelihoods or titles that mean status and money, it's serious business. But shouldn't such deliberations be open to both parties so that they can argue and fight it out? The sage advisor of the *Chronicle of Higher Education* has this to say:

> Ms. Mentor, in her infinite wisdom, would abolish the charade of confidentiality. She believes that smart adults should be able to discuss hiring, job performance, and money face-to-face. Millions of people do it every day, and hardly anyone goes postal.

Given the stakes, the vested interests, and the egos, however, such open deliberations may turn into nasty name-calling if not bloody fist fights. But at least the fight would be an open one.

In spring 2000 when my case was concluded, a student offered "a list of things that I think are always funny, lead to something funny, or I have found to be exceptionally funny sometime recently" in the Western student publication *The Open Forum*, which boasted "tantalizing debacles of joy and indigestion." The list included such items as people falling down (for any reason), Mr. T, Pat Buchanan and his supporters, hairy backs and slightly exposed butt cracks, and ended with promotion and tenure.

I prefer St. John's system where every faculty member is a tutor. Those who publish could get intrinsic satisfaction or fame or both, but basing rank and pay raises on publications leads to the production of the smallest publishable units and planned redundancy (e.g., a dissertation is divided into articles and then combined into a book). As for teaching, methods are overrated. All the conferences, workshops, articles, and books on teaching exist and are being constantly generated because one, the pressure of productivity is getting greater, and two, the anti-intellectual culture has nurtured anti-intellectual students, and faculty members think that only by coming up with "new teaching methods" can they "reach" today's students. More often than not, quality suffers, expectations are lowered, and the whole system stinks: In the words of George Carlin, parents are full of shit, and teachers are full of shit. Since he's pointing to the seemingly unlikely sources of bull, something is missing from his litany. With such teachers and parents, not to mention television, the Internet, alcohol, and now social media, what kind of students do we get? Students full of shit. Or, following the curmudgeon Patrick Scrivenor, we find education to be "the thrilling process of casting false pearls before real swine." I'm, of course, being hyperbolic. I've had some very good students at my own school. By "very good students" I don't mean those who get good grades, but students who care about learning more than grades. (I tell my students that in my son's entire student career, not once did I ask him about his grades.) They are curious about the world and take the initiative to learn things, whether in a class or, more indicative of such curiosity, by going to the library. The national mean of weekly study time of under nine hours is not indicative of such curiosity. (For comparison: When Lao She taught at the University of London in the 1920s, he found those from middle-class backgrounds to be the worst students.) Pressuring teachers to get good ratings is wrongheaded, counterproductive, and high folly.

Conventional wisdom has it that the United States is an individualistic society. Politically and legally, it is individualistic in that the individual enjoys certain basic rights; psychologically and socially it is individualistic in that the individual is egoist. But the society is not individualistic in the sense that its members typically show independence of thought and action. In fact, in any *society*, most of the time people act in a certain way because others do so, which is conformity by intention or habit and leads to considerable uniformity as a consequence. In a profession such as academia, conformity may be even more important to success than in the larger society. For if, like one of Ms. Mentor's correspondents, you fancy yourself "a high-minded, independent thinker," you'll "come across as an arrogant know-it-all," and only "deliberately sabotage" yourself. Richard

Armour's observations on teenagers' choice of clothing capture the spirit of academic conformity perfectly: "The ideal of the teenager, with regard to clothes, is to be neither conspicuous, in the sense of being different, nor inconspicuous, in the sense of being unimaginatively like everyone else and therefore not noticed."

Before graduating from Minnesota, I first looked for jobs outside academia because I disliked its publishing requirement, and yet one of the jobs I considered was an acquisitions editor at a publishing house. Then I entered academia because I couldn't find anything else and I liked teaching. Six years later, I had tenure trouble not for my failure to have published enough but for my teaching. To attenuate the indignity of having to blow my own horn, I wrote an irreverent P & T statement. But then I proceeded to write a whole book about my life. These are some of the ironies and inconsistencies in my life. Of larger significance, though, is this partial irony: I came to America in search of knowledge and freedom; I've found lots of both, but I've also found humbugs galore and new forms of unfreedom. Hence, my joy and gratefulness are tempered by melancholy (see app. 14).

There was one more development in this story. In a valiant attempt to escape poverty in retirement, I ignored my wife's counsel and applied for promotion to associate professor in fall 2004. Although the divisional P & T Committee couldn't spare me its venerable ritual, it did make a positive recommendation, as did the new dean. In January 2005, however, the University P & T Committee upheld its standards and rejected my application, saying that there was insufficient evidence in my dossier that my record was very strong in any of the three areas of teaching, scholarship, and service. Astounded by the surrealism of the whole affair, I couldn't help but feel that my university is more Kafkaesque than the Chinese Academy of Social Sciences. An angry letter of protest was written but not submitted, followed by a meeting with the interim provost and then a sober letter requesting the committee's reconsideration, which was supported by a letter from my dean. In its reconsideration, the committee judged my teaching to be very strong, but not my scholarship or service, hence no promotion. My dean said that he'd help me apply again in the fall, but unwilling to swallow the little pride left and fed up with frustration I declined his offer. (The dean told me that when the University P & T Committee considered my scholarship, someone questioned the legitimacy of *The Journal of Asian Studies*, which carried a glowing review of my 2nd book. "But it's the official journal of the Association for Asian Studies," I protested in disbelief. "If you're ignorant about a journal, can't you just look it up?") What about poverty in retirement? My wife and I will return to China, where we might still be able to live splendidly before falling into permanent serenity.

15. Coda

The above ending was written in 2006, so I should say a few words to bring you up to date.

I survived the tenure ordeal but the School of Interdisciplinary Studies didn't extend its life beyond the 1st decade of the 21st century. For financial and other reasons, the university's president and provost decided to close the school in 2006. The remaining students could finish their degree while the faculty would in time be dispersed to other departments. In fall 2008 I began teaching a course in Chinese literature per semester in the Department of German, Russian, and East Asian Languages, and in fall 2009 the International Studies (ITS) program let me teach an intro course then a 300-level course. Two-and-a-half years later, the ITS faculty decided that I wasn't good enough for them. By then, the old Western had been scaled down from a school to a program. The old faculty had either retired or joined another department except for one other colleague who like me couldn't find a new home and a third colleague who had been an affiliate of another department but who continued to teach in the new Western. From 2012 onward, I've been teaching in the newly designed Individualized Studies/Western Program plus one course in Chinese literature per semester as before. By fall 2020 the other two old Western colleagues had retired, so I became the grandpa in the program. Lucky for me, the director, a mycologist and Milton devotee, has a delightful sense of humor.

After publishing this life story in early 2007, I began reading more classics and some contemporary books I'd skipped since my grad student days. To prepare a course in Chinese satire and one in science and faith team-taught with the program's director, I spent a few years reading more satires both Chinese and Western, science and religion books as well as watching science courses on DVD offered by the Teaching Company. Around 2012 the program director asked me about my research and I said I'd been reading widely and collecting quotes from my reading. One day an idea occurred to me: maybe I could compile a book of quotations from around the world from ancient times onward. That would address the underrepresentation of non-Western sources in typical dictionaries of quotations. A look through major quote books showed that even some classical Western sources weren't given due attention. To quote from my book proposal to a British publisher:

> The largest single-volume general-purpose quote book in print I know of, *Encarta Book of Quotations*, has 25,000 quotes from around the world and "spanning the centuries." But it has no entry from Ibn Khaldûn, the 14th-century Arab historian, widely considered a forerunner of historiography, sociology, economics and demography; nor does it have any entry by Murasaki Shikibu, the Japanese court lady who

> wrote the world's first novel, *The Tale of Genji,* and a diary. Of one of the greatest Chinese historians (many say *the* greatest), Sima Qian (Ssu-ma Ch'ien), whose ten-volume (in a modern edition) history of ancient China have been partially [but substantially] translated into English three times, a measly two entries are included. Even its coverage of Western sources has glaring lacunae: the celebrated Italian scholar Giambattista Vico is missing as is the influential German scholar Johann Gottfried von Herder. The seminal ethnographer Bronislaw Malinowski is nowhere to be seen, nor can one find Bernard Mandeville's *The Fable of the Bees.*

Hence, a decade-long immersion in books of all kinds. In the final several years I didn't spend a single day without working on the collection, including the two times we moved. The result, *Deflating Human Beings: Sources and Quotations from Around the World*, proved too expensive for a university or commercial press, so I chose amazon.com to bring it out. The 1st two volumes were published in 2020 with volumes 3 and 4 out in 2021. Having discovered some errors, I brought out a corrected version in 2022. The collection presents a panorama of the *downside* of the human condition, human conduct, and human nature: vanity, errors, sins, limitations, illusions, vulnerability, misunderstanding, ignorance, self-deception, cruelty and much more, at individual, group, institutional and societal levels. (This is part of the blurb I wrote for the collection.) You may wonder: who do you think you are, trying to deflate human beings? If you've read this far, you already know that the foregoing list and much more apply to me except cruelty. (I've said as much to my students. As a meat eater I cannot say I'm cruel to nonhuman animals without being hypocritical.) As a philosopher more by temperament than by profession, I cannot be Krishna's Truth-lover, who enjoys "equanimity, and charity / Which spieth no man's faults," although I do share his "love of lonely study."

How does one write the author (selector) bio for a book that denigrates self-promotion? By boasting of one's modesty, of course! Or, of being "[un]known for being unknown." I failed to find a publisher for my 3rd and 4th books, so I had to resort to the new technology of print on demand. Those were my 9th and 11th academic failures.

To expose my students in Chinese Satire to more sources, I culled the Chinese satirical quotes from the larger collection and added an appendix of additional sources chosen from what I'd saved over the years as well as those introduced in sixteen histories of and reference works in Chinese literature. This small compilation also came out in 2022.

Teaching continues as before, except beginning in 2022 my reading of student papers stopped being as close: neither my eyes nor my spirit would allow business as usual. Also, at some point I began taking attendance; otherwise, too many students wouldn't come to class. Social media and the COVID-19 epidemic have made things slightly worse.

The last time Haiyan and I went to the movies was to one of the Harry Potter flicks years ago. We left in less than twenty minutes.

I haven't published anything of my own since my life story, and feel there's one more book in me. Back in 1999, in my tenure application I wrote this: "[A]t some point, I would like to write a book à la George Carlin's *Brain Droppings* or one that might be called *Xiuliver's Travels in Modernity*." That book is barely begun. (I may be guilty of other things, but not of high productivity.)

I have an unenviable record in research funding applications. In twenty-eight years, I applied for external research funding twice and for internal research help four times. Only once did I succeed, in fall 1994, when a Miami committee found my project worthy enough.

To mark the milestone of reaching senior citizenship, I stopped renewing my membership in the Association for Asian Studies at the end of September, 2022, and in the International Society for Humor Studies for 2023, retaining only my membership in American Philosophical Association.

In 1994 I was hired at $33,800; by my 28th year at Miami (2021–'22) my pay had been raised to a whopping $68,460. Several years ago, at a year's end party the conversation drifted to faculty pay and I said to my boss that the Princeton poet James Richardson said he considered himself grossly overpaid except compared to his colleagues, adding: When I receive a fund-raising email from the administration, I think to myself: my pay translates to a 50-grand-a-year donation to the university, so I'm good. According to univstats, in 2021, the average salary for Miami's assistant professors was $91,889 ($94,049 for men); that for lecturers, $66,895 ($70,648 for men). (The figures seem too high but see https://www.univstats.com/salary/miami-university-oxford/faculty/.) According to the U.S. Bureau of Labor Statistics, the estimated 2021 median annual income of those with doctoral degrees were $99,268.

After fall '94 Qiyu visited me in Oxford and he remained a sweet boy. I would take him with me when I went to see my students who lived off campus. I'd buy cigarettes and offer one to him and he'd decline. I asked him whether I should find a spouse in this country, in China or in a third country (I was thinking of Russia and had even read a couple of books about Russian women), and he said he had no preference one way or another.

In a few years Qiyu grew into an entirely different person. In 2000 he moved from Minnesota to live with Haiyan and me but not because he liked us better. His mom had been married to a white man for a few years and Qiyu began to regard that man as his father. Haiyan and I helped him through college; we even sent him $12,000 one year when he ran into difficulties in grad school, in spite of the fact that he'd said he'd have nothing to do with us once he finished his schooling. Before he did, he called me on Father's Day without calling me "Dad," but I haven't heard from him for eight years, so he's made good his promise. Eight to nine years ago I emailed him for computer help; he didn't respond. So I stopped bothering him. You may think that I blame American culture for the way he turned out. I do. But I too am to blame: I was an absent father and gave him half of his genes or, according to one source, 49 percent of his DNA. (According another source, "we actually 'use' more of the DNA that we inherit from our fathers.")

What about retirement? I turned 65 in 2022, and I've had a couple of health scares. But Haiyan relies on my health insurance, so having a job looks necessary. For a while she wanted to move to another country such as Thailand, except the Covid-19 pandemic has made life everywhere more difficult. I also need certain medicines that may not be readily available where we'd like to go. Here in Oxford, we have two families of good friends. Plus, we need to support her son in China, who, due to health and other reasons, is chronically unemployed. So now I half-jokingly say that I'll work till I'm 85. Or I may want to stop at 70. Conditions in both China and the U.S. have worsened, but then again, since ancient times philosophers have frequently complained about their own society, worrying that it might be going down the tubes. We'll see. Whatever the future, we'll continue to roam free inside the cage.

Appendix 1: A published record of Grandpa

According to 《起義風雲录》(张仲田等, 山西人民出版社, 1992), p. 459, Grandpa was the commander of the 717th Division (see the photocopy below: his name, 刘又闻, is in the left column, 2nd entry from the bottom up). Yet on both p. 377 and p. 394, the same book says the 144th Division was in Mianzhu, Sichuan in 1949 (north of Mianzhu on p. 377). Division 144 is confirmed by Grandpa's autobiography and his autobiographical tables (in my possession). The book is also wrong about his rank: both his autobiographical tables and autobiography say he was deputy commander, not commander.

起义投诚人员简介 〔459〕

究委员会研究员、北京市海淀区政协常委。

刘 翥 男，1907年生，四川成都人。原四川省第14区少将保安司令，1949年12月在四川江油起义。起义后曾任成都市政府参事。1980年病故。

刘 璋 男，汉族，曾任国民党湖南省政府财政厅代理厅长，1949年8月在长沙起义。已病故。

刘 臻 男，汉族，曾任国民党西北军垦处少将副处长。1949年8月在新疆起义。已病故。

刘一平 原名刘安愚，男，1919年生，汉族，安徽省临泉县人，绥远傅作义部干训所毕业，历任少尉排长、中尉副官、上尉连长、少校营长、中校副团长、上校团长、第35军267师少将师长，1949年1月在北平起义。以后任四野49军独立99师师长、军校教员、安徽省政协委员、常委委员、民革安徽省委会主任委员。

刘人奎 男，1905年生，湖南益阳人。原任湖南省保安独立团少将团长，1949年起义。起义后曾任武汉市市政环卫管理局顾问、武汉市政协常委。1985年病故。

刘又闻 男，汉族，湖南省岳阳市人。曾任国民党第717师 师长，1949年12月在四川起义。已病故。

刘士杰 男，1911年10月生，汉族，湖南省邵阳县人，1927年起历任国民党长沙军分校，湖南新编第8师准尉见习排、连长，第4路军干部教导总队，湘军16师、湘军独立旅、49师、军政部总务处少校分队长、少校参谋、少校营长、中校参谋，东北军官总队第8保安区上校教务科长、主任参谋，第9兵团少将高参、东北总部荣荣支队少将司令。1948年11月在沈阳市投诚。1979年任吉林省人民政府参事。

刘万诚 男，1915年生，回族、河北省泊头市人。起义前任国民党驻绥远部队指挥所少将秘书主任。1949年9月19日在绥远起义。现任包头市政协委员。

刘万泉 男，1918年生，满族，辽宁省辽阳县人。曾任国民党37军208师少将参谋 长，1950年9月参加国民党国防部二厅特务组织，受特工训练后被委任为“东北区军政特派员兼PTL组组 长”，接受派遣回内地进行特务活动。1951年5月15日，刘从香港到深圳后，向我边防公安机关交代了特务身份。广东省公安厅复查认定刘万泉为投诚人员。

刘子仁 男，1900年生，河南永城人。原127军309师少将师长，1949年12月在四川起义。已故。

刘元瑄 男，1909年生于四川大邑县，原任国民党第24军副军长兼第137师 师 长，1949年12月在雅安起义。起义后曾任川西行署委员。

Appendix 2: Grandpa's autobiography

There are two page-fives (Grandpa's pagination error).

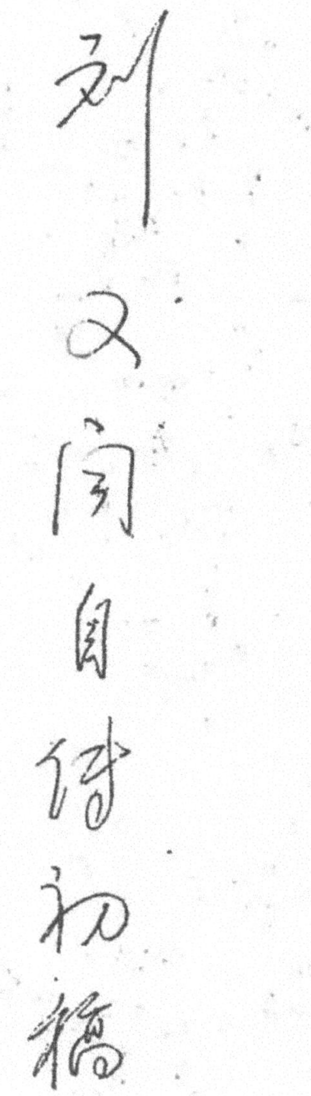

中國人民政治協商會議湖南省岳陽縣委員會稿紙

第 1 頁

刘又闳自传初稿

我现名又闳，曾名郁文，曾用乳名训读，[illegible]，目前仍以又闳二字通用。男性，生于一八九九年十二月，原籍湖南省岳阳县第三区荣新乡[illegible]村，家庭地主成份，个人旧知识分子出身，现在我个人及家庭是依靠[illegible]儿女们生活。以下第一部份，系我家庭主要成员经济情况和社会关系、社会活动；第二部份系我个人读书和工作两个阶段的过程及读书和工作时期所产生的一些问题和谬误。

第一部份

（一）家庭主要成员：过去我家庭主要成员共有十人，即父亲刘学成（农民），母亲胡重阳（家庭妇女），弟刘仲岳（农民），弟媳李秀贤（家庭妇女），侄刘美伦（读书），和我的妻邹韵和（家庭妇女），长女刘淑清（读书），次女刘中坐（读书），子刘美侗（读书）。自长女刘淑清于一九三八年去延安抗日大学毕业回籍，在岳阳、湘阴、平江一带进行地下工作，被人暗杀。母亲胡重阳也于一九四一年十月去世。一九四九年十二月父亲刘学成又因病死。一九五一年三月弟刘仲岳因[illegible]被人检举，于土改中镇压。侄刘美伦[illegible]，现在耕种田地。子刘美侗于一九四八年八月去南京时，因我无力送读，即考入国民党反动政府遗族学校免费求学，一九四九年[illegible]月随校迁往台湾，他的政治立场已经站在反动地位了。次女刘中坐又名静琦，于一九四九年八月已与湖北宜城丁正焕结婚，九年来仍在当地教学校，其政治思想尚

1 9 5　年　月　日

中國人民政治協商會議湖南省岳陽縣委員會稿紙

第 2 頁

不隐人。目前家庭主要成员，祇有我和爱人彭玉明，而他于一九五一年三月也曾参加川北军区妇校学习，对于党和政府，有认识，但私有观念，仍未完全放弃，若祇从其治家一点，还欠积极努力。

（二）家庭以前和现在经济情况：我于一九四九年参加革命前，共有水旱田三石六斗（即现时三十六亩左右）破旧瓦屋四间，我夫妇长期出外，從未过问，到岳阳解放前夕，仅人还欠我百伍十余元，而上述水旱田和房屋，一小部份是在我父親兄弟四人分家时由祖父划出的田分给，另一大部份，相傳係其分宗傳給他，继續受了佃租约四十余年，又先後经营屋叶和南正西叶，及使用长工，并更得助於其连襟王锡朋长期出息借贷，以及我出外工作二十余年中寄回少数薪金的种种剥削所造成，在土改时评我家庭成份为地主，这是适当的。一九五一年实行土改，由政府照顾分配我和爱人彭玉明水田六斗三升，瓦房两间，尚属半通，一九五三年因爱人患病变卖一斗八升，一九五五年又因偿还剩欠之前的旧债，复三斗，此外还剩一斗五升和房屋，本想早日交还政府，另作处理，但以爱人尚须同意，是至一九五六年一月，才和他协商妥当，由我作为全民所有制，一併以之交与[illegible]的行业叶生产合作社作为国家财产。现在家庭经济仅爱人手中尚有金钏一只计重约一两，金戒一个计重约三钱（为我们结婚纪念品）此项金饰，原有戒两三钱，并在一九五二年参加川北军区三反运动中作了交代，后因回乡还乡时路过重庆急需添置衣物，曾换去一两，目前所剩约一两三钱，在一九五三年就已交爱人变卖，他以本年患病，这未许可，舍此以外再无任何财产。

第 3 頁

（三）家庭及个人社会关系：这个问题就以往来说是比较复杂的，而现在都已单纯了。在直系和旁系亲属方面，仅仅只有次女刘申、儿媳刘美伦。刘申生早在湖北宜城明正店粮管所[illegible]职员，常有家书往返，他于一九五五年七月曾回来过见面一次，他对党和政府的培养教育之厚，是深刻理解的。刘美伦从[illegible]在家务农，但对农业生产由劳力和技术不够，她开始担任初学[illegible]工作，但因[illegible]尚未改掉，很难提高生产积极性，过去我们夫妇对她的帮助和教育也已尽了最大努力，但[illegible]收效不大，还是[illegible]，因此一年来就很少联系了。其[illegible]亲友中高[illegible]间关系的在乡下有内兄彭[illegible]（地主）内侄彭华桂（中农）堂弟刘[illegible]（地主）刘春山（贫农），在城内有旧[illegible]胡树基（红十字会工作）朋友杨伯[illegible]（[illegible]二中工作）萧芳祥（[illegible]生产合作社工作）周继勋（[illegible]工作），堂弟刘红山（[illegible]农业社工作），刘有元（[illegible]二一一工厂工作）。他们这些人的成分虽然不同，但对党和政府的政策法令，都有不同程度的理解，即上面所讲的地主分子也能和中贫农一样在农业生产战线上搞得不错，从这里就可以看出他们是诚意改造自己重新做人的。还有在县城的旧任教师和同学孙楠（省人民委员会参事室工作）去年曾有联系，但不经常，我的朋友远在四川、湖北、河南、陕西、南京、北京和浙江等地的，都是同[illegible]的同志，有的已经返乡转业，有的尚在部队服务。自一九五二年[illegible]四川分居联系已告中断，而台湾方面的朋友亦然不少，那些旧军将领更早已断绝关系，即对自己[illegible]去到台湾的究竟也仍然认人去待了。

195 年 月 日

第 4 页

(四)個人社會活動：我少年好勇，喜歡和朋友打架，在爭勝負時，從不示弱，往往不是打破腦袋，便是扯破衣服，因此父母管教極嚴，每次見我闖禍，必在晚上

關着房門將我打一頓，由於這種壓力，也就慢慢地把我征服了。到了成年，

[illegible]

195 年 月 日

[illegible]委员会稿纸

第 5 页

必是进步分子，当时我未参加他的工作，但对他的行动是很表同情的。一九三二年四月，同乡共产党员周佳信被山西军阀局捕押，为了营救他的生命，我和刘[illegible]也曾作过担保。从这些事例说明，自己的思想是有进步基础的。

1920年秋后，我曾随西坡乡有同族私塾先生到樊林，接受大宗山附近的西村南宫道灵子李[illegible]先生家里设坛，招集他的学生和亲友入道信神，并经常来往演说：南宫道不但能[illegible]，完全能够成为[illegible]不死，在修行成功后，就可上西天，成仙佛。当时被这伙煽动的学生和农民就有十几人加入，每晚在家唱道打拳，好像是疯魔似的。我这年轻了，虽然不十分相信神鬼，但在他们的煽动引诱下，也要想看看神鬼为何物，因此就跟着他们进了南宫道，在同他们唱道打拳时，从没有什么神鬼附体，只唱手打，完全是由自己作主。搞了几个月，就[illegible]，以后到樊林又学会道行[illegible]南宫道[illegible]，说[illegible]修成功时，可从那里学习[illegible]上西天。[illegible]我为了[illegible]又跟着他们[illegible]的[illegible]在那[illegible]道行好几天，这[illegible]道和的[illegible]不多，[illegible]西天的说法，到[illegible]看见一个，我认清楚了他们的[illegible]，完全是[illegible]作欺骗[illegible]，[illegible]也[illegible]声明告退了。[illegible]还有很多[illegible]想成仙佛的[illegible]，那里[illegible]不久就被反动军队打散了。[illegible]道行[illegible]上了西天，我[illegible]几天[illegible]觉悟，[illegible]自恨何[illegible]如此。

（此段所写反动情况系写到前页第十七行第七个字前面。）

195 年 月 日

中國人民政治協商會議湖南省岳陽縣委員會稿紙

第 5 頁

第二部分

(一)读书时期，(包括家庭经济情况和个人道德问题)

自一九零八年八岁时开始，即入[illegible]私塾读书。在当时我家庭的经济情况是不够富裕的，在幼年中我只知好玩不知求学，经常[illegible]去赌点铜钱、捉摸子、[illegible]等不好的习惯，耽误功课不少，经常受老师责罚，回家又遭父母打骂，因此父母就[illegible]我也不为所惜，更常去外祖母胡家一住数月，[illegible]一九[illegible]二年我看见一般同时读书的同学，写字作文都比我[illegible]，才[illegible]读书[illegible]很不[illegible]父母[illegible]读，[illegible]努力，而父母[illegible]我[illegible]读书[illegible]，又因[illegible]种田，[illegible]一[illegible]一[illegible]不[illegible]的[illegible]下，我外祖母[illegible]要我去[illegible]读书，一切费用[illegible]由他[illegible]负责，但[illegible]农忙季节，[illegible]我回家帮助[illegible]田[illegible]或[illegible]答。[illegible]读书，对于[illegible]工作[illegible]，[illegible]一九一八年，[illegible]家庭经济[illegible]，[illegible]

1 9 5 　年　一月　　日

中國人民政治協商會議湖南省岳陽縣委員會稿紙

第 6 頁

[illegible]

195 年 月 日

第 7 頁

四十元，在岳陽之初，曾以律費入不肯接受，我就自己拿回了，同時給學校出去岳陽見面，他正要去換送，我也送給銀元八塊，幫助解決困難，這筆意外之財，在當時地理上，應該平均分給同班人員，據為私有，我竟一人獨吞，[illegible]，又不負什麼責。（這件歷史證明不用談到，現在岳陽群益會武陵服務）

一九二二年五月，[illegible]先讀私塾，前通祖時發展，可由譚家亞瑞明借了學費去長沙考入湖南公立甲門學校，原應在畢業後找事工作，選上宣達，誰料畢業就是失業，一切成為空想，特給陳[illegible]歷史，自此即告收局。

（二）工作時期：（包括三次參加反革命工作，三次背叛革命工作和[illegible]以及婚姻家庭的問題）

一九二四年八月 ——— 一九五六年三月

這段工作時間，長達三十三年之久，其中歷史又較複雜，為了系統地寫出情況，特分別為六個階段。

1、失業後參加岳陽西塘地方保衛團隊的歷史階段：（一九二四年八月 —— 一九二六年八月）

從一九二四年六月由湖南公立甲門學校畢業回家，就[illegible]怕長期失業，經常把父母所教的"先找工作"和老師所說的"擇業"的話，念之不忘，認為要達到這個目的，必須快找工作。當這個年代，正是南北軍閥爭城奪地混戰時期，各地土匪乘機蜂起，[illegible]，我們官軍的也層出不窮，[illegible]陷

195 年 月 日

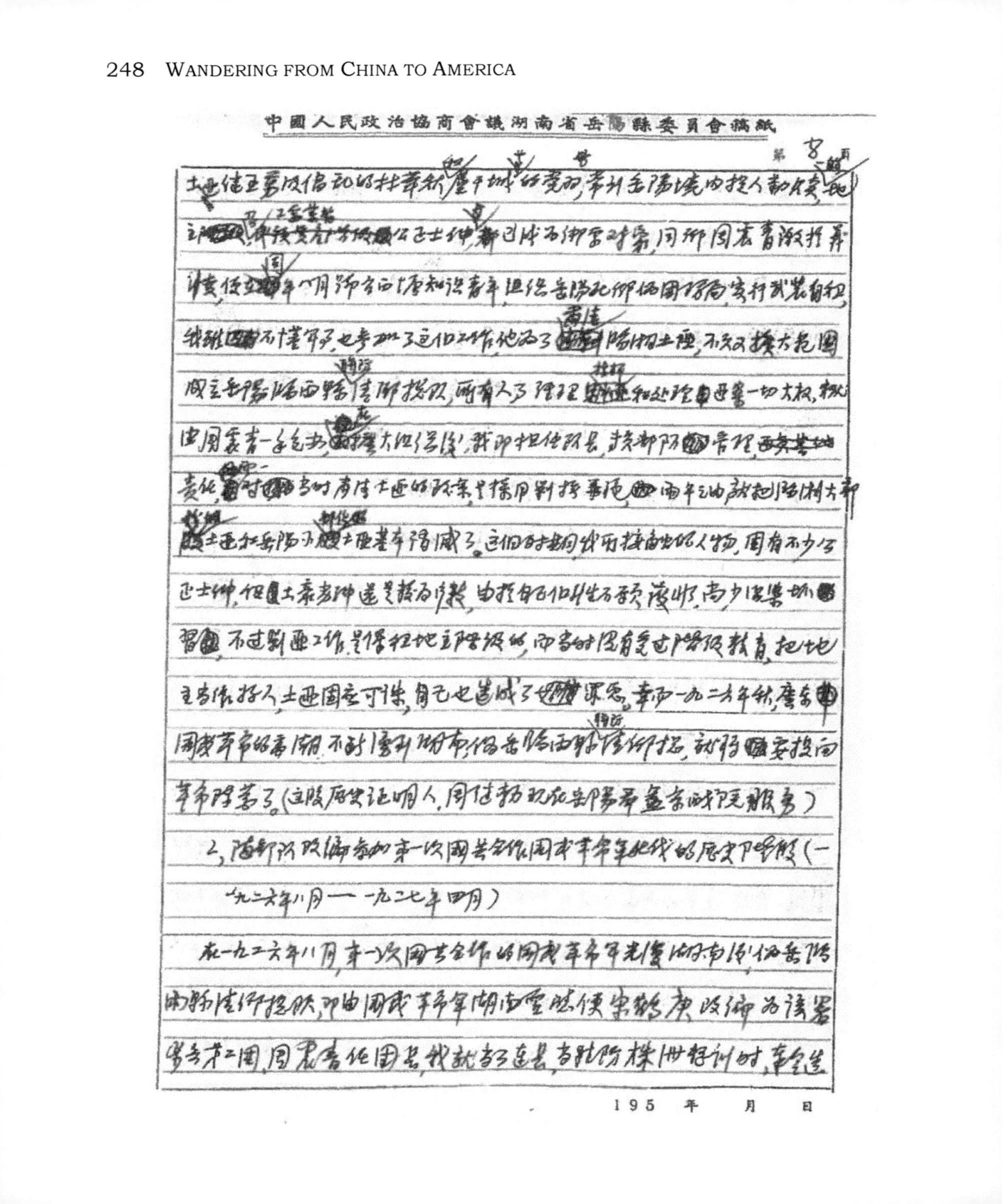

中國人民政治協商會議湖南省岳陽縣委員會稿紙

第 8 頁

[illegible]

二、隋部队改编参加第一次国共合作国民革命军北伐的历史阶段（一九二六年八月——一九二七年四月）

[illegible]

195 年 月 日

中国人民政治协商会议湖南省岳阳县委员会稿纸

第 9 页

机度忌，为了巩固自己的职权，就假造资格，借用原卅年前保留所学叶的名义，欺骗上级。同年十一月，又随部队改编为国民革命军独立第二师贺耀组部步兵第九团，我任营长，并随部队调驻九江待命，因家有事因不能担任正式作战指挥，即调为顾问，团长职务改由陈雨卿接替（这段历史证明人周鸿勋，现在岳阳军区家属院服务）

一九二七年一月，跟着贺耀组师本部北伐，转战江西安徽江苏南京等地，旅团以上的部队，都有共产党的党代表，领导政治工作，开展军民宣传运动，当时指导员记得我们的故事，都是根据北伐军纪律严明的精神，在我们革命武装向北进军途中，群众莫不箪食壶浆以迎，并且帮助带路，帮助运输，敌人虽然得到军阀的抵抗，但一开始战斗，就像势如破竹，一鼓而下安徽，再鼓而克南京，当时这些军阀的反动势力，都在这次北伐战争中土崩瓦解了。这些胜利的得来不是偶然的，是执行联俄联共扶助农工的三大政策，取得群众拥护，和共产党的党代表随同部队进行军民合作宣传教育，仅凭国民党北伐部队的力量发展，而要取得胜利就是不可能的。我随部队进克南京后，独立第二师即扩编为四十军，贺耀组任军长，谷正伦任师长，我[illegible]仍当顾问职，在眼看着马上有军阀将要一鼓荡平而全国统一在即的时候，不料国民党反动头子蒋介石又想独揽萧墙，独霸革命果实，使北伐胜利功败垂成。（这段历史证明人，贺耀组，现在北京全国政治协商委员会服务）

195 年 月 日

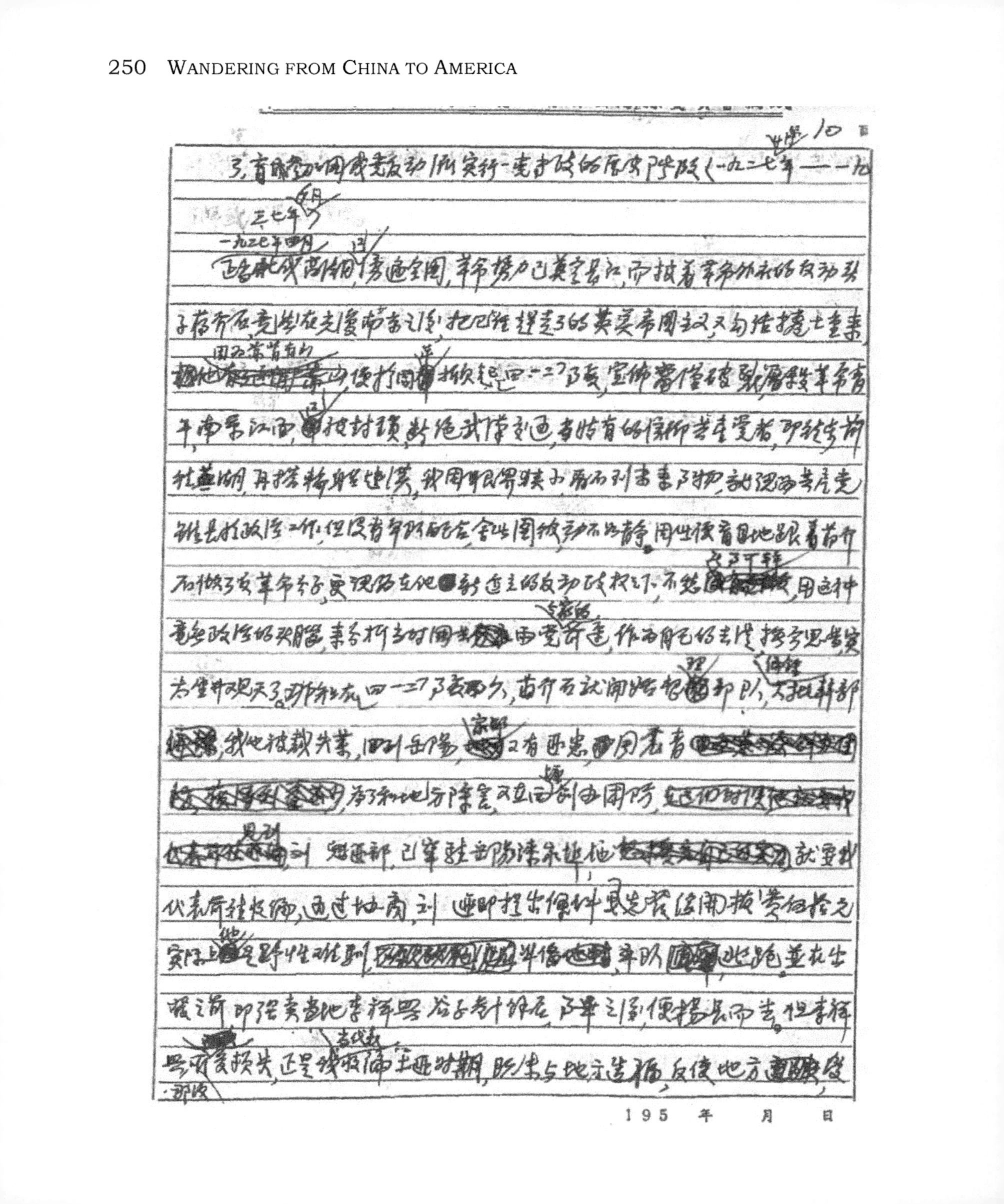

195 年 月 日

中國人民政治協商會議湖南省岳陽縣委員會稿紙

第 15 頁

大队长，他的任务，并负指导学生加强军事训练之责。后来继续革命战，由李励政接充主任，我为第一队之长。一九三六年和一九三七年六月，上海市各大中学校学生又继续在苏州和上海集中训练，[illegible]和[illegible]交通和工作没有实现时，而日本帝国主义，即大举进攻淞沪，因而交通和防御等计划和军事工作，都已提前结束。十二月上海被日寇占领，我才和爱人刘玉明及次女[illegible]乘轮船由香港经广州回到岳阳（这段时间的工作证明人李默庵，现在湖南省政治协商委员会服务）

4. 回家以后继续参加第二次国共合作抗日战争的历史阶段（一九三七年七月——一九四五年八月）

一九三七年十二月，在上海沦陷后，早就知道共产党为了挽救中国危亡，在日本侵略者发动七七事变之先，已和国民党反动派协商合作组成统一战线了。我一九三八年一月回家以后，本来不再外出工作，[illegible]也[illegible]安抗大学[illegible]，[illegible]他[illegible]岳阳湘阴和平江一带去做地下工作，我当时本不想外出活动的思想，也就继续想要外出了。同时在家和友人通往较繁，南京沦陷大批[illegible]费用[illegible]，又日见穷迫，但都欲外出作事，但又感到无路可走，因此我将[illegible]由上海带回的若干枪支，子弹若干颗，送给李[illegible]使用，以为将来外出进行工作时，打下一个可靠基础。同年十月，日寇由武汉侵犯湘北，迫近我家，在这种情况下，又和爱人

195 年 月 日

中國人民政治協商會議河南省[illegible]縣委員會稿紙

第 16 頁

[illegible]

195 年 月 日

第 17 页

[illegible]争执，[illegible]程署长为[illegible]余同卿[illegible]，乃要我

暂时让步[illegible]，在他那种一言可以丧邦的权威下，也就只得[illegible]

[illegible]了。一九四六年二月，各种训练班结业，我由李[illegible]调任军训部国民兵教

育处视察员，兼[illegible]兼任中央兵役巡察团委员，先后到福建河南陕西和四川

各省检阅地方保安团队，国民兵团及各大中学校军事训练，以及各师管区兵

役行政业务，由于自己的贤庸阶级思想作怪，在陕西和福建，惩处过好些人，并在

中央训练团党政班受训时[illegible]集体参加过三民主义青年团，也领过团员证，但未

开过会和做过工作，回想入团时年已四十二岁，国民党还要我们加入

这样盲目乱抓党[illegible]的[illegible]，正在军训部[illegible]对于打抗日战策，

早于一九三零年就有[illegible]，他早倡和日寇汪精卫[illegible]，打的作战全然指向共产党

[illegible]，[illegible]他[illegible]的政策看来[illegible]有[illegible]日的[illegible]，今

天说他是卖国贼[illegible]由来已久了。把他[illegible]比作卖国[illegible]和袁世凯之流恐有过

之而无不及。一九四三年八月，又带职往遵义陆军步兵学校特官训练班受训，以加强

平时练兵和战时打仗指挥[illegible]，毕业后已另找工作，未再回到国民兵教育

处。（这段[illegible]到重庆的历史证明人，李[illegible]，现在河南省政治协商委员会

服务）

一九[illegible]年一月，我在遵义陆军步兵学校特官训练班毕了业，就由同学李[illegible]

调[illegible]四王村的中央步兵学校毕业生调查处军官[illegible]教育组长，指导编

195 年 月 日

第 8 页

判可用勤务兵一名，由于当时物价昂贵，薪水不够维持生活，为了补助开支，就将这个勤务兵空额吃缺了。一九四五年八月，日寇宣布投降，而后军官总队，即奉令撤销，另行成立军政部第一军官总队，[illegible]

我即调任第二大队中队长，帮助(审讯)[illegible]部队编余干部办理复员手续，在这个时候，国民党反共的声浪已经是公开而不宣的秘密了，有(一)次第二大队副队长曾对干部这样说：现在我们对共产党只要三月就可完全胜利，我就当场辩驳：目前共产党的力量已经不是江西时代，如果要和他打仗取胜，恐非三年不可，大家(纷纷地说)我放狗屁，他们(说明)共产党固然不是江西时代，而国民党现在的军队数量，装备(都已)又经过八年抗(战)，富有作战经验，日本人都被打败，难道(对)共产党(和不)什么的当然我还不(明白)日本人是什么人打败的，因此我就不响了。[illegible]

这可是我的现状。共胜先机之处可见一斑。（这段历史说明人民喜爱和平[illegible]）

5，不识时务，随之参加国民党(反动派)反对共产党的历史阶段（一九四五年六月——一九四九年七月）

在一九四五年十月由伪[illegible]中央军校毕业生调训军官总队调任伪军政部第一军官总队后，对共产党第二次和国民党合作打败日本帝国主义的伟大团结，我(还)认识不够，[illegible]

[illegible]因此就不识时务地又随着国民党反动派(的)进行对共产党和(对)人民的内战(的)帮凶，同时还继续贪污吃缺了兵空缺两名作为

思想根源是由西方的立场所决定的。

195 年 月 日

中國人民政治協商會議湖南省岳陽縣委員會稿紙

第19頁

[illegible]自己生活開支始不足。一九四六年五月，因整編搜索隊，以陳仿仿為首[illegible]貪

污的事故，大闹竟規，我就另向編兵役部進行了送信官的工作。同年六月，即由

重慶管區前往河南沁陽整編第十五師武[illegible]庭麟部隊士兵人事。在工

作時未離開河南時，武庭麟曾以同學關係送給我關金伍十萬元，這筆

錢我尚少，但[illegible]容易地[illegible]陷的。[illegible]我在開封南京蘇常[illegible]

中對於這次工作，曾經作過[illegible]整編部隊士兵人事上報五次表冊

[illegible]都被保存辦理[illegible]，証料到了南京國兵役部[illegible]

蘇州第二十九軍官搜索隊受訓，由於憤怒，如此如常，凡在那裡受訓的編餘人員

[illegible]，到処墻上都貼着「此路不通要找毛澤東」的標語，說國

民黨中部腐敗，這些人對於蔣介石的信仰是完全沒有了。我曾當過失業的痛苦，很好

另找出路。同年十一月已請由李默庵將我調到他所主管的南通綏靖第一區

請區政治部主任李超寰（少將編制），名義雖[illegible]，但[illegible]認為

搞錢不能黑心，搞個[illegible]有希望。得[illegible]任李默庵部長報請委了個國防

部試任[illegible]少將，往同國民黨政工改制，李默庵即另調工作，

我因階級沒有升實，且對政工[illegible]所厭，也於一九四七年九月商請保[illegible]量

局局長杜心武設法已經將我調到保國防部之[illegible]派該局服務，因當原

軍官搜索部隊任務未完，故仍在南通搞了一個時期才去南京。（這

段由蘇州軍官搜索隊調動以後的歷史証明人李默庵，現在河南省政治協商委

第29页

黄金服务了。

一九四八年五月，伪测量局成立地图整编处，杜心源又保我充任该处副处长，这是一个测绘技术机关，我所掌握的是处内行政工作和图书训练资料图表的军事管理，在一年的任期内，[illegible]虽处长送给我米或万斤，并按照国防部通案规定凡属部机关都可借金元券[illegible]向伪中央银行[illegible]黄金，我也没有例外的被贯进，这些便宜又何尝不是贪污呢。

同年五月[illegible]子到美国，已由[illegible]参谋部并往南京，但以[illegible]由彭次安正在东方中学毕业，但以入学办法，难于负担，乃将[illegible]到美国作为陪[illegible]，将我的儿子送到伪中央政府[illegible]子弟免费读书，这一[illegible]无耻已极。十二月[illegible]国民党反动派[illegible]淮海会战失败，伪军各机关着届限期疏散，与此同时，伪中央政府也积极的争取迁移广州，因而南京下关搭船他往者，秩序非常混乱，特别是上船时争先恐后而被挤死落水死或挤到江内淹死的，惨状难以形容，在这个时候，我也[illegible]同意人彭玉明和次安到中央由下关搭船前往武昌，就将[illegible]当[illegible]一口，所有比较好的衣服、衣料、物品和个人以往在反动政府服务[illegible]及国民党团证

第 2[illegible] 页

件，新的[illegible]件，和充损失报告（这段历史证明人胡静海，现在湘潭路

人商委五金商业科服务，易遂量现在益阳市三区西塘乡九庙村初小服务）

一九四九年一月，我随伪地图学局迁往广州附近[illegible]五公段，曾去武

昌接爱人彭玉明和侄女刘中真到驻地，经过岳阳，即便道回家省亲，又打

赴粤途中，[illegible]丁冠英[illegible]由衡阳下车[illegible]，见面[illegible]，他[illegible]

提的第三要求就是将侄女刘中生和他的儿子丁正焕即订婚，订婚

时，他又提出意见说目前时局严重，愿意将刘中生留他家[illegible]，我认为

过去和他友谊甚厚，打算又是宗女亲，为了减轻负担应付时局，也就勉

强同意，[illegible]，如果不是自己太穷，就绝不会[illegible]好

女儿的。回到广州去了，人民革命的高潮，国民党上[illegible]大衔头，很

伤心好像共产党已经到了广州城郊似的，同时湖南程潜陈明仁起义

我也对广州国民党大而国民党反动派为了争取干部[illegible]共产党就大

肆造谣说，共产党进入南京时，曾将国民党的军官怎样怎样，怎样屠杀，

[illegible]中又单伪局长决定将伪地图中央政府所有人员以

三分之一东迁台湾，另以三分之二西迁重庆，同年五月，伪地图学局也，也

被撤销，自己就考虑[illegible]，认为赴台既不可能，去渝又非

得计，[illegible]，因而就下决心，想回湖南参

加起义，一则工作可以接近家乡，二则生活也能免得危险，便商请杜心[illegible]

27 頁

[illegible]

195 年 月 日

中國人民政治協商會議湖南省岳陽縣委員會稿紙

第 23 頁

195 年 月 日

中國人民政治協商會議湖南省岳陽縣委員會[illegible]

在閩粵州集一带打擊我們的部隊進行[illegible] 頁

截，退到珠江大橋河底，一面自己又策划組織臨時戰鬥改編重慶行轅

司令楊森也對[illegible]採取[illegible]堅壁清野堅守部署，以緊急措施去作背

城一戰，並說了一套層層築守地方將變化為焦土，一時風聲鶴唳，[illegible]人心

自[illegible]而偽國防部[illegible]對[illegible]組幹部又下達命令凡願意回家的當

發給資遣，如不願意回家而願去[illegible]部隊工作的也隨時照派發給[illegible]費。

我[illegible]這個時候的處境，又和廣州一樣通過自己考慮，決定再下部隊[illegible]

[illegible]十一月下旬，[illegible]國防部人事局又將我

[illegible]派到偽陸軍六十九軍二十四師擔任副師長，當時我往四川三台[illegible]軍

報到，又藉動身之前，借了王西貴[illegible]金子壹兩和[illegible]的金戒子兩個（重約

三錢）準備便道將愛人彭玉明送到四川綿陽等居，作為生活費用（因彭玉

明前夫之子周昭援[illegible]在綿陽[illegible]）[illegible]從綿陽趕三台[illegible]時

周昭援[illegible]回去，[illegible]任鄭[illegible]介紹前往借[illegible]我錢了，

我到三台後，偽軍長胡長青又將我改派[illegible]駐四川江油的一四四師

[illegible]副之際他[illegible]還說，你們部隊的[illegible]

到達江油，偽師長嚴[illegible]正由[illegible]回，隨即[illegible]率領部隊向

川西撤退，相處還算相[illegible]，在行軍途中[illegible]聽說嚴師長是不准打牌的

因為打牌就是打散了，我當時聽了這話覺得很有味道，現在回憶起來它就

是一個典型的唯心主義者了。最可恨得[illegible]的部隊一到安營，士兵就往 百

195 年 月 日

中國人民政治協商會議湖南省岳陽縣委員會稿紙

第 2[illegible] 頁

姓家里倾箱倒箧，柴米油盐鸡鱼肉以及贵重的衣物，都被抢掠一空，纪
律之坏，甚于土匪，当时我想像这样的部队如果不能做到古时所说秋毫无犯
那怕是不准打骂而要打败了。有一次在营部和尹澜洲副军长谈天，问他是否
知道共产党随便杀人？他说：“不，他过去曾在江西剿共，战后被俘，不仅没
有受着危险，反而优待释放，并且共产党[illegible]将会天下，他还较不错。”这是
谣言何必置信。经过这次了解，才把自己的怀疑完全消失。十二月二十三日，部队到
了四川绵竹大炊堰，即奉令停止待命，士兵不守纪律，[illegible]彻[illegible]打家劫舍，[illegible]
[illegible]
[illegible]像这样[illegible]的部队，也就证实和加速了国民党反动派的
灭亡，究竟部队为什么要在绵竹停止待命，而绵竹又非撤退目的地，一般干
部都认为要闯些和共产党作战，但我当时在思想的估计，知道[illegible]蒋介
石[illegible]，损兵败千里，何能言
战，[illegible]，继此起义，就快要投降了。（这段转折历史证明人胡静一现在
湘阴人民委员会服务，[illegible]易季梅 现在长沙省人民委员会参事室服务，邬
绪勤 现在岳阳市三五华村乡[illegible]农业合作社服务）

6、起义后参加中国人民解放军和返乡转业的历史（一九四九年十二月——一九
五六年三月）

一九四九年十二月二十三日，我随一四四师由江油撤退到了绵竹

195　年　月　日

中國人民政治協商會議湖南省益陽縣委員會稿紙

第 26 頁

[illegible]

195 年 月 日

中國人民政治協商會議湖南省岳陽縣委員會稿紙

[illegible]

195　年　月　日

第 28 页

處佈号召部队后，也随时作了传达教育，这付起死回生的良药一吃，部队就从此循规蹈矩了（这段历史证明人陈仿勤现在岳阳第三团兼新乡村新村农业生产合作社服务）

一九五零年一月，随着部队调往四川中江时，西南军区司令部党员黄立陆和苏整两同志[illegible]分任正副团长率领第二工作团先期到达，二月初到七月底止，进行部队改造教育，我在这个学习期间，参加了整编民主运动和自我批评运动，坦白交代了自己的罪恶历史，由于学习有所深入，尚有问题[illegible]来作检查，并参加了战士诉苦大会，[illegible]才认识到旧社会的地主阶级和旧军队[illegible]罪恶之大，[illegible]初步在思想上和他们划清了敌我，划清了界线，同时也自觉地愿意改变自己的旧思想，旧作风和旧习惯，求得脱胎换骨重新做人。同年三月，因爱人彭玉明寄居四川铜梁，得了病，曾请假前往[illegible]探望，不料该县伪指[illegible]当地[illegible]风声静，我正在铜梁街上寻找亲戚，一时得悉伪说土匪攻城，行人乱跑，而我即被当地区政府武装人员扣留了送去加以[illegible]，当经[illegible]由中江寄到铜梁[illegible]，并提出前西南军区第二工作团通行证件，以西风强撤回信，当时得到谅解，第二天该区又将我送往川东行署，听候发落，后经黄主任团长去电证实，才将这回铜梁和中江这一段问题，幸亏出在我党的政策，恐怕就要戴上帽子不得生还了（这段历史证明人陈仿勤现在岳阳第三团新

第 28 页

师以当好农业生产合作社服务）

八月部队进完毕，奉令北上合编，第七兵团大部份干部，都已调转，而去北上的尚有师级以上人员十余人，到重庆军大学习，我只承受的培养由副师调川北军区军官教导团团长，改团革命形势发展，即改编由川北军区负责第三支队支队长，仍任支队长，副行政任第二支队长副中共军政委，在三个月中，造成了热火朝天的学习，打通了学员回家生产的思想，农村经济的恢复也获得助力不少。

一九五一年二月，我奉调川北军区担任参议员兼参议室行政责任，[illegible]部的成员，都是起义部团级以上的干部，在一年零三个月的时期，时打比较大的工作，[illegible]部队训练计划，通过各种教育器材和有规模的图书室，主要是对学员进行思想改造。同年五月，即参加军区直属部队干部运动，重新交代历史，在已假装没有展开前，第一学习镇压反革命分子文件，进一步认识了国民党反动派不甘死亡，已特务已在起义部队中活动时，没有交代[illegible]曾经加入反动的复兴社及时作了交代，放下了思想包袱，认清了反动派面貌。第二学习土地改革文件，并以农民斗争地主一些[illegible]事实，就证实了自己家庭也是地主成份，剥削就有轻重但剥削不能没有，[illegible]在土改之中，[illegible]政策法令和群众意见，低头认罪不停[illegible]。第三，学习抗美援朝文件，明确了美帝国主义武装侵略朝鲜，是企图走日本帝国主义的老路，进一步侵略中国

195 年 月 日

第 30 页

援助蒋介石侵占台湾，目的也是妄想要它打回中国大陆，变中国为它的殖民地，作为倾销市场。因而提高了自己的爱国主义和国际主义的思想，把过去崇美观念变成了恨美仇美观念，认为中国人民只有坚决的抗美国才能援助朝鲜独立，才有收回台湾、肃清蒋介石，才能保障中国土地的完整，不受帝国主义侵略。由于通过这一系列的学习，已消除了自己不少的思想障碍。在正式开始政治运动时，对于自己所犯的历史罪恶又作了回忆，认为在个人方面，好像并没有什么重要问题可以交代了，不过对家庭方面还有些顾虑，可是在已交代的，这次为群众完全交代，觉得有伤体面，由于这种小资产阶级的思想作风作怪，就有所不敢。但又再考虑党的政策和自己的进步，是不容许固执己见，拒不坦白的，经过几天几晚的思想斗争，个人的理性战胜了感性克服了，而毫无顾虑的抱着忠诚老实的态度，把个人及家庭的一些应该交代的罪恶和历史罪恶的历史情况，在当时的很多自述中，重新作了交代，帮助了组织了解了自己，这才不是完全粉碎了旧我，达到了新我，但感到像放下了一大包袱，心情是特别愉快的。在这三个月的改造教育，不仅深刻地明白了国民党反动派的罪恶滔天，而且更自深刻地明了自己的罪恶也是死有余辜，同时又进一步明白了党是对犯罪阶级斗争来教育和改造干部，但是他的用的完全是为了挽救干部，改造干部，只要彻底接受改造的人员，特别是对于犯罪人员，一贯是宽大为怀，不是残害的，人非木石，谁不诚服呢？当然初结束之际，并且对于一般干部的家属，自己动员回去，不计较过去，要人去了去明来历，还要获得同等、专人

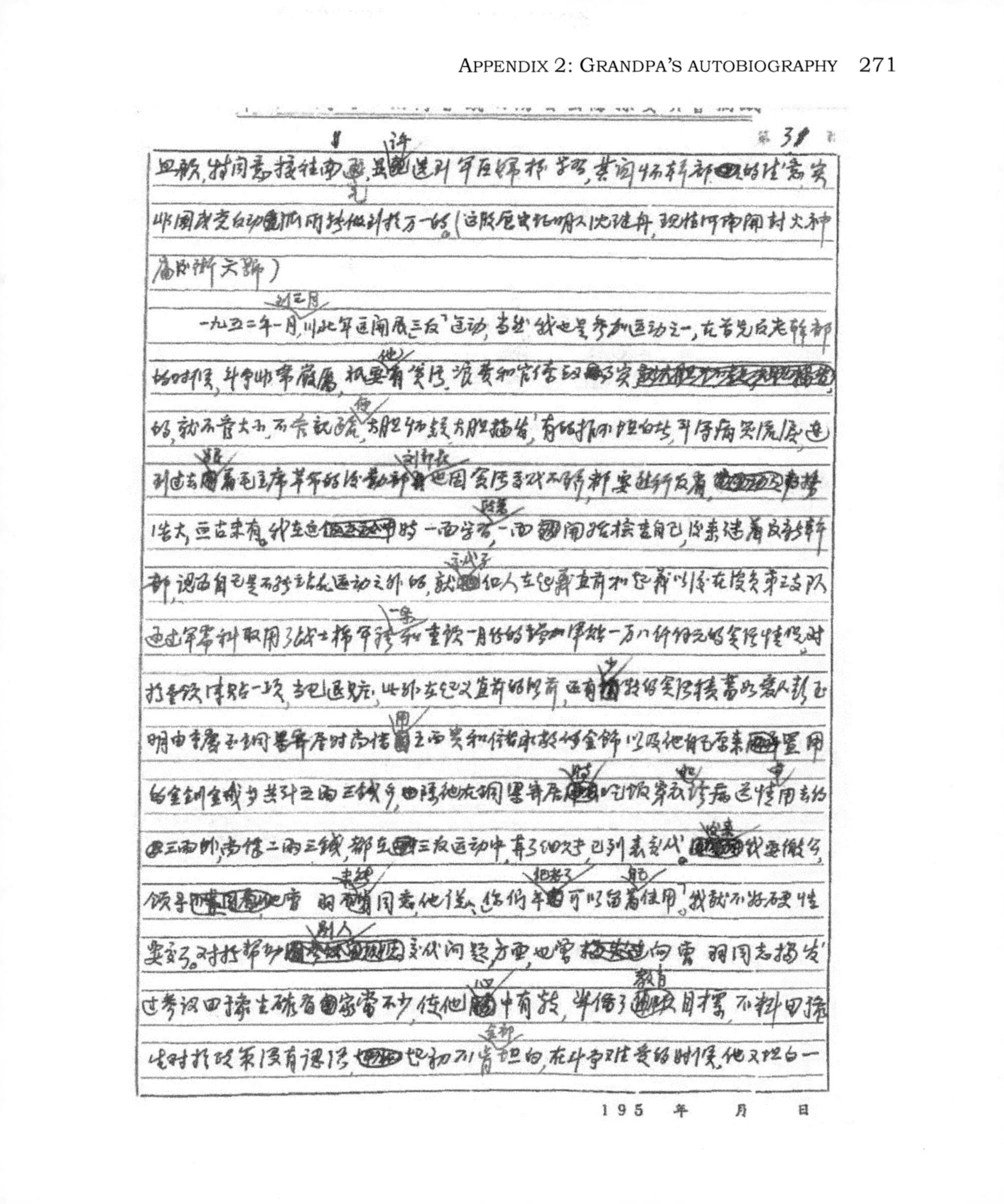

第 31 頁

[illegible]

一九五二年一月，川北军区开展"三反"运动，当然我也是参加运动之一，[illegible]

[illegible]

195 年 月 日

第 52 页

肚，群众见他贪财如命，就大骂阎罗之师，迫使交他的火炉灰和帐篷搜出了金十余两，以及公债券数百万元，师军区处理好该案，还是念他本人是饶了，法律上的责任，我知道党的政策，不是为了黄金钞票，故意害人，而是要把干部的资产阶级思想，改造成为无产阶级的思想，然后才能全心全意为人民服务，这种伟大的教育，就是顽石也要点头了。三反运动后，接着第一，参加了评薪运动，知道部队体制即将改为工薪制度，同时规定了干部的服装庄严和家属的住房水电应由自己负责，我因自己的负担不重，不致影响生活，便须初评时报出自报，每月拟定工薪贰百叁十分，比较参议室同级参议，所报的工薪要低三分之一。第二，参加了整编运动，明确了部队要精兵简政，自己就考虑年愈五十，不宜再担军事工作，首先在会上向应上级师首长愿意回乡转业，对于参议室人员的转业问题，也起了一些带头作用。第三，参加了评级运动，又体会到党对起义人员原来部队的阶级，不想长久给以政治待遇，因而我的评为正团级，以我二十多年的反动，贻误人民事业立功，一旦蒙此优遇，实感惭愧无已。（这段历史证明人阮德真，现住河南开封大钟楼后街大号）

同年六月奉令遣乡转业，路过重庆时，为了急需添置衣物，曾将在王府中交成的金饰向当地人民银行兑换去壹两，并已取得兑换收据。

第 33 页

到邵阳，即向当地政府报到，九月一日承分配邵阳林业公司服务，从一九五二年五月一日起至一九五五年九月底止，先后我担任了收发员、稽查员和营业员等工作，和在门市部收款开票，说话也是有条理的，讲情理，思想很不安定，如果给人[illegible]见，他不笑我是开倒车么？也怕不保证为人民服务任何工作都是光荣的伟大，[illegible]已经懂得他把它作正当，在林业公司几年的劳动竞赛中，我就没有起到什么作用，但把自己能做好工作，都是一贯主动争取的，[illegible]自己[illegible]粗枝大叶的毛病，不是差收不结款，就是结账时有困难，工作虽然主动，而结果是没有做出成绩的，同时不仅如此，并且还犯了错误，即一九五四年八月，我在林业公司门市部工作时，曾[illegible]人民币，由于[illegible]人知道，当就瞒了[illegible]，交由他[illegible]处理，又为了[illegible]这种一念之差，就造成了自己的错误，所以我的个人主义的思想改造，还是没有做到的。

一九五五年十月我调到政协邵阳县委员会任驻会常务委员，在[illegible]的领导下，担任[illegible]代表人士和社会人士的联系教育工作六个月以来，毫无成绩，但对学习和自我改造方面，稍有进步，[illegible]一系列毛主席关于农业合作化问题的重要文献，提高了社会主义的觉悟，加深了对农业社优越性的认识，于一九五六年一月已将自己[illegible]所剩的水田壹亩五分，山地若干块和瓦房两间，[illegible]一样作为全

中國人民政治協商會議湖南省岳陽縣委員會稿紙

第34页

我所有[illegible]借去送给了[illegible]此地正在[illegible]的[illegible]农业生产合作社，特

别是解决了它们急需房屋办社和[illegible]的困难，当地群众，都[illegible]对

我加强社员办社的责任感和鼓舞农民入社的积极性，感到[illegible]

[illegible]的第二，听了[illegible]部长[illegible]，谈[illegible]批评和自我批评的报告，也

[illegible]了我对自我批评进一步获得认识，并在政协所组织的各界代表人

士学习批评与自我批评的第一次动员会上作了中心发言，批判了自己过去

对工作学习和生活上不细致[illegible]的一些错误[illegible]，更揭发了一九

五四年八月在茶叶公司隐瞒[illegible]五万元[illegible]

子的[illegible]

自我批评武器来教育自己，改造自己，还要用这个武器去帮助别人进行思

想改造，[illegible]

所以说[illegible]离开了批评武器是不能成功的

以上所交代的[illegible]问题，都是我个人的具体[illegible]和我家庭的具体

情况，由于[illegible]，年代久，而当时的[illegible]

不实而中肯的，[illegible]

[illegible]

有生之年[illegible]加强自我改造，全心全意[illegible]

完

1956年5月20日完 [illegible]

我下放于一九五八年下放劳动锻炼[illegible] 年 月 日

中国人民政治协商会議湖南省岳阳县委員会

一九五七年　月，随着国家形势的发展，我又参加了伟大的整风反右的运动。在发扬四大当中，自己的认识是进一步有所提高的：第一，通过五八年的反右，肯定了那些右派分子的确是向党猖狂进攻，大肆诬蔑，企图篡夺工人阶级领导权，阴谋资本阶级在中国复辟的。自己在这个运动中也检查了资产阶级思想，认为[illegible]，搞得不好，买肉都要站队，在菜蔬物价方面，并有提高。我不知不觉地也说做了右派分子的言论，通过反右辩论，已明确了是非，对于自己不正确的认识，才得到纠正。在交心方面，我有的是真实情况，有的是戴帽子过关的。我所以要这样做的原因是求戴好帽子以便在今后思想上和工作上很好改造自己，[illegible]公教育。认识了商业部门确有贪污盗窃分子，这种坏人坏事，是挖了社会主义墙脚的。我在这个运动中，也认真地检查了自己的错误，在挪用公款方面，曾通过杨忠安同志挪借了顾客遗失存入现金的钱，两次三角多，买了小菜和馒头，但随时已经归还了。在占小便宜方面又先后两次以人民币壹角和两角，通过杨忠安同志买了小百货店的[illegible]两个。在执行物价政策方面，曾将定价薄扇每把两角和另一种定价薄扇每把贰角壹分的，对外混同出售了，既破坏了物价政策，又影响了党群众关係，这个性質虽是罗大伟同志所做的，但当時我没有及时纠正，从责任来说，我是应该承担的。第三，通过同年的反右倾，鼓干劲运动，我也检查了自己是中[illegible]思想，既怕晚上营业，又怕白天工時延长。去年

第　頁　196　年　月　日

中国人民政治协商会議湖南省岳阳县委員会

八月党支部派我下乡支援双抢，我就向经理反映自己有病不能
去，要求封建党支部没有做到那里需要那里去服从调配，是犯了原则
性的错误的。第四，通过一九六○年的三反运动，揭发了商业部门的贪污
盗窃分子钱来钱去，有的前年犯了去年又犯，有的在三反运动中犯了，三反
运动后又犯，同时也有边反边犯的，例如陈泽武、田清泉等就是典型人
物。我在这个运动中，又重新检查了自己过去没有执行物价政策和贪小便
宜的错误，并交出在门市替朋友买了胶鞋两双，及小百货店经销蒲扇先
已给人的特权思想。在反官僚主义和反贪污盗窃的斗争大会后，自己
的思想认识又大大提高了一步，认清了资产阶级思想，树立无产阶级思想，
应当在运动中吸取经验和教训，绝对服从党的领导，做好党的工具，
更好地学习毛主席著作，只要自己的[illegible]立场，过好了[illegible]，过
[illegible]人就斗，思想才有方向，工作才有进步。我下放商业部门劳动锻炼
已经两年又四个月了，由于年老病多，工作是没有成绩的。但对于小百货店
的营业、验收、统计报表和陈列商品、清洁卫生以及每天上下铺板，
每夜看守铺[illegible]一些工作，一直是主动争取的，虽然有病也是不辞劳苦
的。我的缺点，在劳动纪律上没有完全[illegible]遵守，在义务劳动上也没有
完全参加，比如[illegible]年[illegible]，我就是没有参加了。
今后应当很好改造自己，做一个名符其实的劳动者。

刘[illegible]
一九六一年一月八日

Appendix 3: Grandpa's demobilization certificate

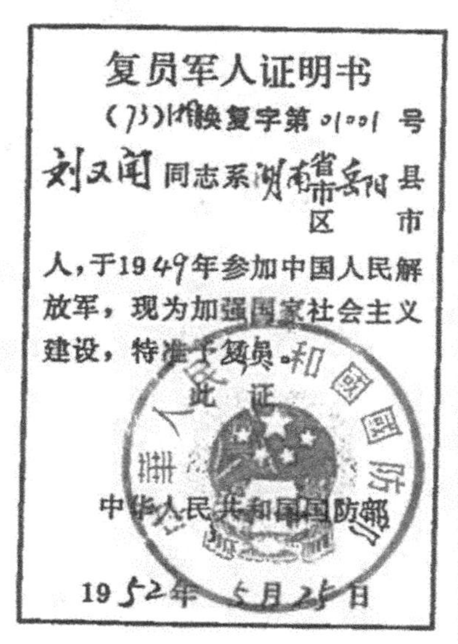

复员军人证明书

(73)湘换复字第01001号

刘汉闻同志系湖南省岳阳县人，于1949年参加中国人民解放军，现为加强国家社会主义建设，特准予复员。

此证

中华人民共和国国防部

1952年5月25日

出生年月 一八九九年十一月

部　　别 川北军区司令部参谋室

职　　务 参议

专业技术

经生活资助粮 1160斤

换发证件机关

一九七三年九月廿日

Appendix 4: A published account of Aunt's activities and death

Aunt's name was 刘淑慎, the book in which her activities and death are briefly described is 《巴陵烽火》(岳阳县人民革命史编纂委员会, 中共党史出版社, 1995).

第二节　革命志士奔赴延安

抗日战争爆发后，岳阳人民特别是广大青年从沦陷区千百万同胞遭受日寇铁蹄蹂躏的血的教训中觉悟到，只有在共产党领导下才能坚决抗战到底，才能挽救中华民族的危亡，个人也才有出路。所以一批批进步知识青年纷纷离开家乡，冲破重重障碍，投奔当时中共中央所在地、全国抗日救亡中心、民主革命的圣地—延安，寻求抗日救国的道路。

从 1937 年 12 月到 1938 年 8 月，岳阳县先后有 20 多人分 5 批奔赴延安。第一批赴延安的革命青年是：赵绿吟(女)、邹泽溥、彭庆旨、黄建忠、毛仁村(女)、刘淑慎(女)。其中赵绿吟、毛仁村、刘淑慎是湖南省立长沙女子学校师范部学生，抗日战争爆发后，她们积极参加长沙抗敌后援会，和同学们一道分头去募款、募寒衣，演唱抗日救亡歌曲，散发抗日传单。她们认为，如今国难当头，再也不能坐下"读书救国了"！一天，赵绿吟从报上看到"国共合作抗日、十八集团军高级参议驻湘办事处代表徐特立先生赴长到任"的消息后，立即偕好友刘淑慎、毛仁村等前往驻在梨头街南方旅社的八路军驻湘办事处，找到了徐特立先生。徐老用浓厚的长沙乡音向他们讲述了抗日的前景和民族的前途，中国共产党的抗日主张，并告诉她们延安抗日军政大学正

135

在招生的消息。徐老的话深深打动了赵绿吟等人的心，抗大招生的消息更使她们激动不已，她们早就向往革命圣地延安，渴望到那里去学习。因此，便向徐老提出到延安去的请求，徐老答应了她们的要求。几天后，在溆浦卢峰中学教书的彭庆旨来到长沙，也准备赴延安参加抗日救亡运动，正巧碰上同乡黄建忠、邹泽溥及赵绿吟、毛仁村、刘淑慎几位具有同感的热血青年，于是，他们6人分头筹借一些路费，于1937年10月底的一个晚上，拿着八路军驻湘通讯处的介绍信，踏上了去延安的征途。

第二批去延安的是在岳郡联立简易师范学校读书的万年和张祖楷。1937年冬，岳阳抗日救亡运动高涨，他俩在进步教师李西谈、许曙升的教育和引导下，认识到"国家兴亡，匹夫有责"，现在民族危急，国家将亡，自己决不能袖手旁观。于是，利用各种机会，参加抗日救亡宣传活动。1938年春节后，万年到青年教师许曙升住处，得知延安抗日军政大学招生的消息后，毅然决定前往。并找到正为学费发愁的同学张祖楷，张即表示愿意同往。李西谈、许曙升两位教师为他俩借了五元钱（银元）。几天后，他俩爬上一列军车，在汽笛长鸣中离开了岳阳。

任凤生（女）、王国雄、李开桂（女）、姚钟隆、彭泽棠、冯治生是第三批赴延安的革命青年。"七·七"事变前，岳阳抗日救亡活动兴起，在县立高小读书的任凤生，在大革命时期入党的教师王养直的教导下，通过阅读揭露和控诉日寇暴行的进步书刊，懂得了一些革命道理，便积极参加学生自

136

任中共岳阳中心县委妇女部长，后调任湘鄂赣特委任妇女干事。1939年6月12日被国民党军逮捕，她始终坚贞不屈，大义凛然，在敌人要下毒手时，放声高唱抗日战歌："枪口对外，齐步向前，不打老百姓，不杀自己人……"。共产党员王国雄和爱人李开桂，1938年8月底毕业后回到家乡参加抗日救亡运动，在"平江惨案"后的恶劣环境下继续坚持革命斗争，由于暴露了身份，夫妻俩奉命撤离，不幸被捕，受尽敌人酷刑而不屈服，两人同时在岳阳就义，还有刘淑慎也在白色恐怖中被国民党反动派杀害了。解放后，岳阳县人民政府追认他们为革命烈士。

第三节　岳阳抗日民族统一战线的建立

1937年7月8日，中共中央通电全国，号召全国军民组成抗日民族统一战线，奋勇抗击日本侵略者。17日，中共中央派周恩来到庐山与蒋介石举行国共合作谈判。8月14日，国民党政府发表自卫宣言。不久，又承认了中国共产党的合法地位，公布国共合作宣言，抗日民族统一战线形成。

1938年春，中共湖南省工委和八路军驻湘通讯处与以张治中为主席的国民党湖南省政府团结合作，建立了湖南抗日民族统一战线。中共湖南省工委派出一批共产党员到各地宣传党的主张，恢复和发展党的组织，开展抗日统一战线工作。同年2月，中共岳阳临时县委建立。国民党岳阳

Appendix 5: Published records of Paternal Grandpa (Ding)

Grandpa told me that my birth father's father, **丁冠英**, had been a fellow student of his in Nanjing and they had arranged the future marriage of my parents. Indeed, my mother was born in 1933 and was married to my birth father in August 1949, before both grandpas had switched sides to the People's Liberation Army. Grandpa said my birth father's father had been Wuhan's garrison commander but the latter's lists of positions in two online sources state that he'd been eastern Hubei's deputy commander. His position mentioned in the only relevant book I've been able to find seems the last one before his uprising. (The book is the same one that has an entry on Grandpa mentioned in app. 1. **丁冠英** is in the left column, the 2nd name from the bottom up. Funny coincidences: both grandpas were stationed in Sichuan at the time of their uprising and both grandpas' names appear in the same location on a page in the above book.)

丁冠英

少将。又名莫群，号廷楷，湖北宜城人。中央军校军官研究班毕业。曾任第 14 军上校代参谋长，1946 年 2 月任中央训练团庐山分团教育处少将副处长，后任鄂 东师管区副司令，1949 年初任第 7 编练司令部干训班少将副主任，同年 12 月 11 日在四川宜宾参加起义。后任解放军西南军区高级研究班学员，1952 年 5 月专业回乡。

[转帖]湖北籍国民党少将名录

1. 丁冠英（19021979）又名莫群，号廷楷，宜城人。中央军校军官研究班毕业。曾任第 14 军上校代参谋长，1946 年 2 月任中央训练团庐山分团教育处少将副处长，后任鄂东师管区副司令，1949 年初任第 7 编练司令部干训班少将副主任，同年 12 月 11 日在四川宜宾参加起义。

(These two webpages no longer exist; however, similar but briefer entries can be found on the Internet.)

〔422〕

解放战争时期原国民党省将级起义投诚人员简介

丁 柏 男，汉族，湖南省益阳县人。曾任江南地下第4军11师副师长，1949年9月在湖南省湘阴县起义。已病故。

丁一安 男，湖南省桃江县人。曾任国民党第七兵团少将参谋长，1949年12月在四川起义。已故。

丁文藻 男，1917年生，汉族，内蒙古人，曾任国民党第12战区工作委员会平津区少将专员。1949年9月19日在绥远起义。已故。

丁冠英 男，1903年生，湖北宜城人。原第7编练司令部干部班少将副主任，1949年12月在四川宜宾起义。1979年病故。

丁鹤羽 男，汉族，曾任国民党新疆警备总司令部卫训组少将副主任。1949年9月在新疆迪化参加起义。已病故。

刁可成 男，1911年2月生，汉族，山东省人。历任傅作义部骑兵三师政治部主任，第8战区干训团驻绥分团政治部副主任，第12战区长官部参谋处情报科科长，第35军政工处处长，华北"剿总"少将督察员、北平自卫总队队副。1949年1月在北平起义，为傅部派出同人民解放军谈判的工作人员之一。起义后，历任绥远省政府参事，内蒙古自治区人民政府办公厅秘书，内蒙古文史馆馆员。

于竹三 男，1908年生，甘肃武威人。原河北省干训团少将大队长，1949年1月参加北平和平解放后曾任甘肃河西盐务局股长、武威县人大代表，政协委员。

于怀安 男，1903年生，山东单县人。原第6军军长，1945年11月在山东滕县起义。起义后历任解放军第35军代参谋长、第103师师长、

Appendix 6: *The Three-Character Classic* as remembered by Grandpa Wang, p. 1

三字经回忆录

第　页

人之初　性本善　性相近　习相远
苟不教　性乃迁　教之道　贵以专　传
昔孟母　择邻处　子不学　断机杼
窦燕山　有义方　教五子　名俱扬
养不教　父之过　教不严　师之惰
子不学　非所宜　幼不学　老何为
玉不琢　不成器　人不学　不知义
为人子　方少时　亲师友　习礼仪
香九龄　能温席　孝于亲　所当执
融四岁　能让梨　弟于长　宜先知
首孝弟　次见闻　知某数　识某文
一而十　十而百　百而千　千而万
三才者　天地人　三光者　日月星
三纲者　君臣义　父子亲　夫妇顺
曰春夏　曰秋冬　此四时　运不穷
曰南北　曰西东　此四方　应乎中
曰水火　木金土　此五行　本乎数
曰仁义　礼智信　此五常　不容紊

装　订　线

(74.2?)

Appendix 7: Grandpa's annotations of the *Illustrated Four-Character Classic for Females*, p. 1

绘图女四字经

第 1 页

名词解释

(註一) 昔日冀臣 其妻不仁：见前给邓付部长取去的材料中

(註二) 孟光举案 希蘭敬夫至诚：〃 〃

(註三) 令女割鼻 为夫守贞：令女姓曹，似是东汉末人，夫死，无所出，父母逼其改嫁，令女誓志自守，初则断发以明心迹，不为父母所谅，遂割鼻毁其容，父母亦为之感泣。

(註四) 董氏封发 为夫远行：似是秦末人，夫将远戍，董氏于夫临行中束其发，令夫亲手封之，直待其夫回家始启其封，十数年来不事梳沐有如是。

(註五) 孟母投机（杼）为子戒識：见前次邓付部长取去的材料中

(註六) ~~谢女道韫 文咏诗成：〃~~

(註七) ~~蔡女文姬 能辨琴音：〃~~ 〃

(註八) 行惠大家 援笔成文：大家（音姑）即曹大家，号班昭，东汉安陵人，字惠姬，班彪女，班固妹，曹世叔之妻。早寡，博学高才，因班固著汉书，八表天文志未及竟而卒，和帝诏昭就东观藏书之所，踵而完成汉书，并令皇后诸贵人以师事之，曹大家还著有女诫七篇。

(74.2.)

Appendix 8: Grandpa's annotations of the *Illustrated Improved Classic for Girls*, p. 1

第 1 页

绘图改良女儿经

名词解释

①
(註一)周姜之母仪：周人尽称扬之。周姜即周太王之妻，文王祖母，周之母仪，周人皆钦[illegible]风。

②
(註二)太姒和之宴子孙甚多广：太姒即周武王之母，姒姓，莘国女。史记周本纪：武王同母兄弟十人，母曰太姒，文王正妃也。列女传：太姒仁而明道，号曰文母；文王理阳道而治外，文母理阴道而治内，太姒教子明德，生育贤行，

装订线

③
(註三)缇萦朝上书而赎父身：缇萦，女，西汉人，其父淳于意犯罪判大辟（将处死刑），自叹"生女不生男，缓急非所益"，萦伤之，即上书汉文帝，愿没为官婢，以赎父罪，帝怜而释。

④
(註四)卢氏不避盗冒刃以卫姑：卢氏不知何时人，夫外出未归，卢氏侍其姑，一夕，盗破门而入，挥刀将杀其姑，卢氏即以身卫姑，身被数刃不肯却，盗叹息而去。

(74·2·)

Appendix 9: Grandpa Liao's poems

予以衰暮之年，欣逢国庆二十五週年，目睹轰轰烈烈的社会主义建设，成就辉煌，国际地位蒸蒸日上，不禁喜跃高谛，偶成七绝八首，以志盛况。

——廖华耕，1974年国庆节，时年八十八岁

人民八亿冠環球，岁岁丰穰乐有秋；
思想言行都一致，主公路线指前途。

其二

建国才过廿五年，辉煌业绩一何妍！
神洲改造翻新样，马列精神别有天。

其三

批林批孔日纵深，极右思潮挖老根；
觉悟提高添干劲，工农生产倍加增。

其四

金融稳定庆繁荣，生活年年逐步升；
内外清偿无国债，国家威望日蒸蒸。

其五

机关企业未区分，男女同工各有营；
事业何曾分贵贱，缘都服务为人民。

第　　页

其六

工农

劳奋斗气轩昂，自力更生好主张；

工作长期无失业，退休养老有规章。

其七

孤鳏寡独叹零丁，往昔穷民痛苦深；

足食足衣今赖党，终身温暖胜亲人。

其八

旧日妓寮曾绝迹，游民消失是真情，

谁能说此非奇迹，今日人寰实罕闻。

Appendix 10: Teacher Liang's evaluation of and advice for me

湖南大学試卷

班别 ________
学号 ________
姓名 ________
評分

修武同志：

"总结"是你一学期来最好的一篇文章，但不是由于我的工作对你真正有所裨益；因为它仍未反映出你已达到的水平。

同学们说你读书最多，平常接触我也发现你的理解力很强，尤其是你在学习上不落框框，不受教师的束缚，能独立钻研，主动地安排时间，你也并不忽视课文练，可是写作总不见显著的提高，我很抱歉。严格地检查起来，你们班上几个读文程度原来较高的同学，进步都不十分显著，与我的传授方法之一般化是有关的。除了我自己再找找其中的底细外，也提几点你今后学习应注意的事项，不过由于所知太少，我对你未必能深知，所提的只是凭过去的经验，据一般情况的猜测，聊供参考

一、你自学了不少知识，是是由于聪明，也由于借的书籍总能自己地看，没有养成苦思深钻的治学习

惯；一看就懂，随手抛开，致学的知处于散乱的情况。不能系统运用。

二、从保密听课的情况看，你有能贪玩，不坚张，表现出学有余力，甚或有时还能兼做其别的事。如果可以两者（或三者）都不失其要领，是优点；资质较高的人也应当努力锻炼"眼观六路，耳听八方"的本领，提高学习、工作的效率。但我有时发现你忽略了要点，而且不是完全自主地分别使用注意力，却像是不能自制的精神涣散。若然，请认真改正，尽量地迅速地培养成持久控制注意力的能力。可先要有分，分段和使用精力的时间开始不宜过长。

三、请回顾一下："四害"书屋，对自己有无消极的影响。记得你们说过：看过的书都不能使你信服，不盲从。不轻信是好的，但不可停止于不信服而陷入虚无。要多想、多读，有比较，有鉴别，最终确定自己的信念。没有信念的人生是空虚的，无意义的。可怕的是些，确定信念不是一朝一夕，或一年半载之功，但要决心去确定；你和同学的关係较好，有些问题可以商讨。建议你们都能够"自由思想，民主讨论，实事求是，追求真理"，使自己的学习、工作、生活与

湖南大学試卷

班别 ____________ 学号 ____________ 姓名 ____________ 評分 ____

祖国的命运，人民的利益发生自觉的关系。

四、语文的学习要不拘于"语文"，你入学后不也读过报纸、刊物、政治理论、历史等书籍吗？那不都是中国的语言文字吗？怎么说"主要是语文课"呢？政治班王一同学在信中写道："如果我出生落地的第一声哭喊是一个叹词，那么我跟语文打交道将近二十年了"，语文是这样看，极到处渗透的地方。以后读有关语文课了，更要注意这一点。你的语文，至少是写作的水平尚有待提高。以前的作业甚至还出现词语的不妥处，也没有引入表达过较复杂的内容。

以上意见有不当处，望通过学习委员告诉我。

谭再 1978.1.7

你若同意，请与仇晓阳交换看看，你们俩的能力以及长处互补，将有好处。

Appendix 11: Haiyan and I getting married in my office building

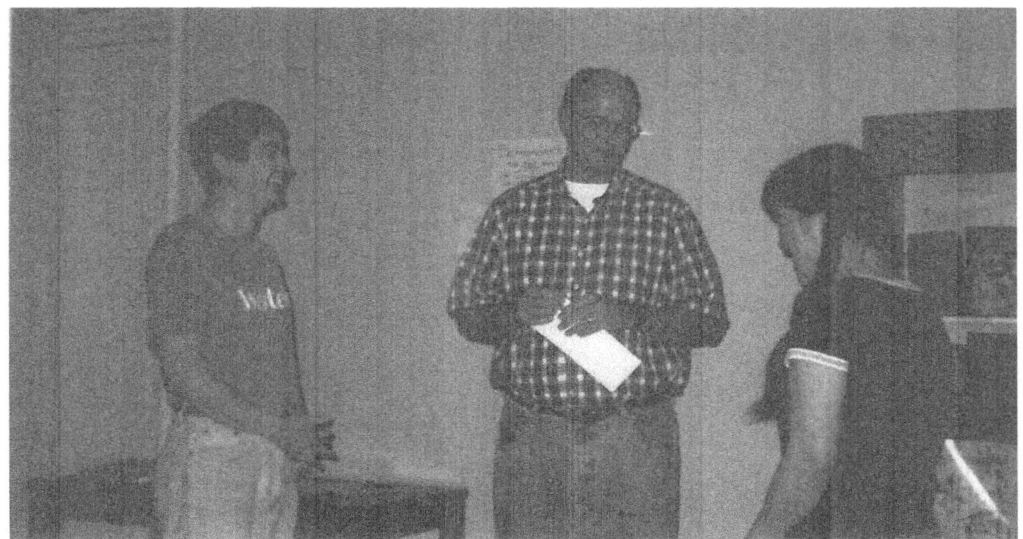

Appendix 12: N. T. Wang's letter to the P & T Committee

The addressee's name has been whited out and initials are used to provide some privacy. There is a typo under (1), where "constructism" should be "constructivism."

COLUMBIA UNIVERSITY
IN THE CITY OF NEW YORK

EAST ASIAN INSTITUTE

October 14, 1999

Professor E. M.
Chair of the Promotion and Tenure Committee
School of Interdisciplinary Studies
Miami University
Oxford, Ohio 45056-1981

RE: XIUWU LIU, Candidate for Tenure and Promotion to Associate Professor

Dear Professor M.

In response to your request to review and evaluate samples of Professor Liu's writings in connection with your consideration for his tenure and promotion I am pleased to submit the following report:

(1) I have read Prof. Liu's Western Perspectives on Chinese Higher Education (Cranbury, NJ: Associated University Presses, 1996) and From Academics to Entrepreneurs: The Founding of a Private Electronics Company in South China (offset). The first study proposes a general epistemic model of "realist constructism" for scholarly cross-cultural inquiry. The objective is to clear up a confusion about the relationship between a cross-cultural study and the studied social reality and to demonstrate, by the use of case studies, how the model can help cross-cultural scholars improve their studies. In constructing the model numerous alternative models and a large body of literature from various disciplines are assessed. In inquiring whether a particular cross-cultural study is fair or distorted, their (i) assumptions, explicit or implicit (ii) emphases and silences (iii) terms translated (iv) points of views represented and (v) evaluation criteria are scrutinized. The second study, based largely on interview, is primarily an empirical account of the birth of a private enterprises in a transitional milieu. The social background and personal aspirations are examined in some detail. Although no formal test of theories is attempted numerous explanations and interpretations throw light on the sequencing of evens and causal connections. The application of the model of the first study in this case is also apparent though not specifically stated.

(2) These two studies are well researched and convincingly articulated. They demonstrate the candidate's scholarly ability and achievements in both theoretical

International Affairs Building   Mail Code 3333   420 West 118th Street   New York, NY 10027   212-854-2592   Fax 212-749-1497 and empirical endeavours. In particular, the breath and depth of theoretical discussions are uncommon even among well-established gurus. The skills exhibited in conducting field studies are exemplary in eliciting truthful and hard-to-get information.

Given the candidate's proven ability and maturity it appears that his tenure and promotion may be overdue. A possible reason for the belated recognition is that interdisciplinary studies require longer time for preparation. Indeed, given the academic emphasis on separate disciplines those engaged in interdisciplinary work are often disadvantaged. It is, therefore, all the more important that a candidate who has invested so much in such a "specialization" and succeeded in demonstrating his worth be promptly recognized.

(3) The candidate's diverse background and many skills have enabled him to tackle virtually any topic in the social sciences. I am impressed by the variety of courses that the candidate has offered in a short span of years. Presumably many of these courses reflect student demand. Looking into the future, it may be useful to allow the candidate to take on fewer courses in diverse fields so that he can devote more time to scholarly writings.

(4) Although the candidate has not made the claim that his work has broader relevance to areas other than pure academic work, two examples may be illustrative of the usefulness of his work. One is the use of international experts in advising governments. My personal experience is that although a foreigner does not know all the intricacies of another country his detachment can be an advantage if he approaches his job as advised by the candidate similarly an outside consultant, not necessarily from a different country, is usually a better adviser for corporate restructuring because, unlike the lieutenants of the chief executive officer, he does not have his turf to protect and can concentrate on the good of the whole, including necessary changes in the corporate culture.

(5) In conclusion, I have no hesitation in recommending the tenure and promotion of the candidate.

Sincerely,

N. T. Wang
Senior Research Scholar,
Director, China-International
Business Project
Columbia University

Appendix 13: My former teacher mentor's letter to the P & T Committee

Personal names have been whited out and initials are used to provide some privacy.

DEPARTMENT OF EDUCATIONAL LEADERSHIP
SCHOOL OF EDUCATION AND ALLIED PROFESSIONS

McGUFFEY HALL ROOM 350
OXFORD, OHIO 45056-1853
(513) 529-6825
(513) 529-1729 FAX

December 22, 1999

E.W.M. Jr., Chair
Promotion and Tenure Committee
School of Interdisciplinary Studies
Miami University,
Oxford, OH 45056

Dear G.

Diversity does not come easy. It does not come easy for the culturally different faculty member who must figure out how much of his/her difference to hold on to and how much to give up. It does not come easy for the students who must take classes from the culturally different instructor and figure out how to succeed in a classroom where the assumptions about teaching and learning may be somewhat different from their own cultural understandings. And it does not come easy to those faculty, like me, who are of the dominant white European-American culture and who must learn how to work with and evaluate the worthiness of our culturally different colleagues. If there is one thing that I have learned in the nearly twenty-five years that I have studied the intersection of culture and education, creating a diverse educational environment does not come easy for anyone. Right now you are embedded in one of those very difficult tasks: What are you to make of the fact that a colleague, whom you and your students have come to like personally, continues to receive below average mean scores on student evaluations—particularly in the area of seminar teaching? Are these scores and the comments of a few students indicative of a fatal flaw in his teaching ability or are they indicative of the kinds of struggles that culturally homogeneous close-knit communities often go through when trying to diversify their culture? This can not be an easy decision for you, but let me try to suggest why you should understand that the apparent teaching deficiencies of Xiuwu Liu may be less the deficiencies of a single individual and more the (not unusual) results of teacher and students struggling to create education given their ethnic differences.

A few years ago I was approached by Dean C. E. to see if I would be willing to serve as a teaching mentor for Xiuwu Liu. Knowing my scholarly interest in culture and education, my long interest in college teaching, my experience as a member of the University Promotion and Tenure Committee, and my extensive knowledge of the School of

Interdisciplinary Studies (having taught in your school for a semester and having had continued association with many of the faculty and students through the years), C. thought that I might be able to help Xiuwu. Though I had never met Xiuwu, I agreed to do what I could. During our association we met regularly and I had the opportunity to visit his classes and he mine. My thoughts following that period are expressed in a letter that is in your file. In that letter I express the belief that Xiuwu was successfully initiating changes in his teaching and as a result was beginning to show improvement, that he had promise as an instructor, and that he had room still to improve. Since I wrote that letter, I had the opportunity to meet a few more times with Xiuwu and to visit one of his seminars as part of a larger study of seminar teaching at Miami University. In that larger study I visited undergraduate and masters seminars throughout the university. This letter draws on my personal conversations with and observation of Xiuwu, my expertise in the area of culture and education, and my recent study of seminar teaching at Miami.

Undergraduate seminars at Miami have a peculiarly American flavor. They are frequently marked by an interaction pattern that might be described as a wagon-wheel pattern in which the instructor is the hub of the conversation and the students form the spots on the wheel where the spokes connect to the rim. The conversation takes place mostly along the spokes and depends on the hub for its motion and for its ability to distribute the conversation along all of the spokes. Faculty throughout the university are frustrated by their inability to remove themselves from the center of the conversation and tend to blame this persistent wagon-wheel pattern on Miami students' lack of intellectual vigor. My analysis does not disagree with this faculty interpretation as much as it places the students' actions within a broader cultural context. I suggest in that analysis that student action in undergraduate seminars is connected with the dilemma created by the American cultural commitment to individualism—the dilemma resulting from the need to *conform to a cultural construct* while appearing to *remain an individual*. The nature of my argument and its implications are far too complex to develop in this brief letter and its importance lies less in the particulars of the argument than in the recognition that something like a seminar is not a culturally universal form of education. In other words, our undergraduate seminars are influenced by our cultural commitment to individualism and are, therefore, peculiarly American.

Our cultural commitment to individualism is not only found in the interaction patterns of our classrooms, but it is found in our tendency to reduce racism and ethnocentrism to individual prejudice. When students express a personal liking for a faculty member while, at the same time, suggesting that he doesn't teach well; we are likely to interpret this as evidence that racism or ethnocentrism are not relevant factors in their evaluation. Our assumption is that if racism or ethnocentrism were involved, it would show up in students' attitudes toward the instructor. But we all know that the real effects of racism and ethnocentrism are found less in the attitudes of individuals than in the institutionalization of our practices. Culture gets built into the very way that we do things and that creates problems for those who are not of the cultural mainstream both students and instructors. We know that, on average, instructors of color and those who are culturally different obtain lower mean scores on student evaluations than those of the mainstream. Why this is so is less clear, but certainly one of the reasons is the way in which some students of the dominant culture react to the (sometimes minor) cultural influences introduced by the culturally different instructor. We should not be surprised to find that many of our students are uncomfortable given unfamiliar cultural expectations and that, as a result, some students evaluate their instructors lower than they might otherwise do. The low evaluations of only a few students can significantly lower the mean score.

The discrepancy between the culture of the students and that of the instructor is one of the dilemmas that faculty who are culturally different must deal with. How much of their difference should they bring with them into the classroom and how much should they leave outside? Certainly they must be expected to make some, even many, adjustments for their American students. To teach at an American university as if it were a Chinese university, for example, is not acceptable. On the other hand, we do not want our culturally different instructors to leave all of their culture outside the classroom. If we were to do that, all we would be left with is education that is culturally the same with instructors who look different but aren't. What we want are instructors who create a learning environment that helps our students adjust to different ways of organizing our world and that engages their monocultural worldview. For many of our students this is not an easy (or even desired) experience.

Is there any reason to believe that the seminar instruction of Xiuwu and his subsequent evaluation by students is colored by cultural difference? I believe that there is. On the one hand, in visiting Xiuwu's classes he impressed me by the way in which he adjusted to American seminar instruction. For example, I was impressed with Xiuwu's willingness to follow students' leads through discussions rather than to try to maintain full control of the direction that the conversations evolved. I was also impressed by his attempt to devise strategies to get students engaged such as assigning responsibility for certain sections to certain students, making connections to everyday American issues, and finding contemporary metaphors for material that was frequently difficult and distant. I was impressed by his willingness to reach out to students, work with them individually whenever necessary and desired, and with his willingness and ability to bring personal narrative into the discussion. All of these are things that suggest a desire to adapt to American educational culture. But I also saw that certain American student expectations violate Xiuwu's cultural integrity and that some of

Xiuwu's expectations for students may have challenged a few students' understanding of good teaching.

Consider the way in which teachers are venerated in Chinese culture. Traditionally in Chinese culture a teacher is so honored that long after the formal relationship has ended students are expected to show honor toward their teachers. Once someone has been your teacher, always that person is your teacher. On the other hand, teachers show respect toward their students by not imposing upon them, by waiting and observing until the student indicates a readiness to learn, by assuming that the student recognizes the intrinsic nature of learning, by only offering the student their best critique, and by speaking obliquely or indirectly rather than explicitly and directly. Good education results only when the student has indicated a readiness and a willingness to learn. It only occurs when the student recognizes the teacher's evaluation is in his/her own best interest and attempts to adjust from that critique. A good teacher should not insult his or her students by underestimating their knowledge or abilities as too explicit instruction certainly can do. Compare this to the American cultural expectation in which a teacher is expected to earn the students' respect before the student will give it. In recent years, the relationship between teacher and student has gone so far as to be described in the language of the market place. The teacher is understood to be the paid provider of a consumer good. American teachers find themselves having to be proactive in their interactions with students. They are salesmen and students understand themselves as consumers. Whereas in Chinese culture the responsibility for initiating learning falls on the shoulders of the students; in recent years American students understand the responsibility for learning falls on the shoulders of the instructor (see Arthur Levine & Jeanette Cureton, *When Hope and Fear Collide: A Portrait of Today's College Student*, San Francisco, Jossey-Bass, 1998). While I believe that Xiuwu has adapted to the American expectation that he, as instructor, has the responsibility to initiate the learning, he is reluctant to take that responsibility as far as many American instructors which appears, perhaps, to relieve students of their own responsibility to learning. For Xiuwu as for other Chinese instructors, students must take charge of their own learning. You can see this cultural conflict in such things as Xiuwu's reluctance to coerce students' reading through assignment of graded homework (students should not have to be coerced to read). It is found in his belief that students should not have to even be told to attend class let alone apply sanctions to those who do not. It is found in his belief that students have some responsibility in moving conversations forward. To define learning as a mere consumer product like a Penguin Classic paperback or a Broadway stage production probably offends all of us, but it offends the Chinese sensibility even more.

In similar ways, Chinese culture emphasizes the value of reflection and thought and respects others, including authors, by listening and interrogating their positions carefully. To fail to question as well as praise a student's comments is to demean that student. To fail to engage in a close reading of and analysis of a text is to demean the author. American culture seems to value action more than reflection and thought ("Just do it!"). Americans tend to interpret close questioning of their comments as interfering with their right to voice their opinion—of attempting to silence them. Of course, most American university faculty find themselves frustrated with the belief of many of their students that reasoned critique is "harsh," but for one who has been educated in China such reactions are not just frustrating, they turn everything upside down. To fail to raise a reasoned critique is to insult the student—not the other way around.

So, yes, I do believe there is reason to think that Xiuwu's mean score on student evaluations is suppressed as a result of his cultural difference and the resistance and confusion on the part of *some* students to those differences. These differences may appear to some American students as unfair and to some American faculty colleagues as unreasonable. To the Chinese eye the practice of American teachers violates good teaching practice. To the American eye the practice of Chinese teachers violates good teaching practice. But, of course, neither the Chinese practices nor the American are inherently good or bad pedagogy. So what are we to expect from Chinese instructors hired to teach in American universities? I would hope that we would expect them to adjust to their American students enough to bring them along, but not so much that they don't challenge them culturally. The reason we want cultural diversity at a university is so that we all learn to adjust when the cultural rules are altered. My first year at Miami, a departing colleague told me, "At Miami, you can look different or you can act different, but you can't look *and* act different." In twenty years I hope that our commitment to diversity has brought us further than that. I hope that at Miami today one can both look different and act differently.

What does this mean to those of us who must evaluate the performance of our culturally different colleagues? Does it mean that any culturally different instructor should be held to a lower standard? Should it mean that we just shouldn't expect the same quality of instruction? No, it does not. We must hold all of our instructors to the same high standard, but it does mean that we might need to re-evaluate what good instruction might be and that we recognize the inexactness of our ability to measure excellent teaching. Specifically it means looking for the meaning behind the evidence that we do have. What is the evidence in the evaluation of Xiuwu Liu? According to the written evaluations, Xiuwu seems to perform adequately or better than adequately on all measures of teaching except one—mean student scores (particularly in the area of seminar teaching). These lower than average mean scores are given some depth by the comments of a few students that suggest that while they like Xiuwu as a person, they found his seminars frustrating and unproductive. Given Miami's official commitment to multiple indicators of performance, the denial of tenure based on a single criterion strikes me as unusual. If we are to deny tenure based on a single criterion (or even a small number of criteria), we must be very confident that that criterion is trustworthy. In this case, how confident can you be that the evidence tells the story accurately? Given my observation of Miami undergraduate seminars, I am not surprised that some students find Xiuwu's expectations "unreasonable" and his seminars "frustrating." They expect a wagon-wheel interaction pattern, while Xiuwu is reluctant to take up with enthusiasm the role of "hub." The question for you is whether or not the education of your students is strengthened by allowing their culturally narrow and resistant expectations to remain unchallenged or whether their education will be strengthened by their being required to respond to Xiuwu's culturally different expectations. My own sense is that if the student evaluations combined with other indicators of teaching practices were significantly and meaningfully below expectations then a negative tenure decision makes sense. But if multiple indicators suggest positive teaching on a wide-range of factors and if the differential between Xiuwu's student ratings and those of his senior, more experienced colleagues could easily be explained as much by cultural differences as by individual teaching abilities then a positive tenure decision makes sense.

Miami University and the School of Interdisciplinary Studies is committed to building cultural diversity. By this we do not mean that we are committed to doing the same things in the same ways only with different looking people at the helm. Having had the responsibility to make decisions such as yours many times, I know that your choice is a difficult one and that you will make it in the best interest of your students and your colleagues in the School of Interdisciplinary Studies. I hope that the thoughts expressed in this letter help you in that process.

Yours,

Richard Quantz

Richard Quantz
Professor
Social Foundations of Education

Associate Director
Center for Education and Cultural Studies

Appendix 14: My response to the dean's annual evaluation of me

In the dean's evaluation of me for 2001 he discussed my teaching, service and lack of participation in conferences. I wrote a response in which I'd said this about faculty meetings: "About verbal participation in Executive Committee meetings, I wish to avoid blarney, or, to adapt the definition of Andrew Greeley and William McCreedy, the tendency to mean not what one says and to say not what one means." I emailed this response to my friend Aili (who was teaching at Iowa State) for feedback and she said she was very concerned about it and asked me to "give the letter some more consideration." So I toned it down by deleting most of my own words (using only his first name's initial below).

May 30, 2002

B.,

Instead of writing a detailed response to your letter of evaluation, I offer the following to show where I am coming from.

Yi-Fu Tuan on teaching and scholarship (*Dear Colleague*, U of Minnesota Pr., 2002) [a front-page feature story in the *Chronicle of Higher Education* from the 1990s called him the most influential social scientist you've never heard of]:

John McCormick relates in *Santayana* that Eliot [president of Harvard] ran into George Santayana in the yard (in 1900?) and asked him how his philosophy class was doing. Santayana replied that his students were making progress through Plato and should soon move on to Aristotle. "No, no, Santayana, what I mean by my enquiry is, how many students have enrolled for your lectures?" (p. 105)

Alexandre Grothendieck, one of France's most distinguished mathematicians, turned down his share ($135,000) of the prestigious Crawford Prize of the Royal Swedish Academy of Science (*Science*, May 13, 1988). Grothendieck gave two reasons for his surprising action. One: as a professor at the University of Montpellier he already has enough to live on. Two: only the passage of time can show whether his ideas are truly fertile. His second reason reinforces my belief that the teaching awards that universities now regularly hand out, under society's pressure, are ill-advised. Immediate evaluations by students cannot be very useful if good teaching—really good teaching—is the imparting of ideas and aspirations that prove fertile months, even years, after the event. (p. 105)

René Dubos, a distinguished microbiologist, was a towering leader of the environmental movement in the 1960s and 1970s. He became somewhat disillusioned, however, late in life—not with the goal of the movement, but with the intellectual preparedness if its ardent young supporters. He even thought that his own multidisciplinary approach to environmental problems was setting a bad example. He put it this way:

> When I retired . . . I was asked to teach in two universities. I seemed to be a big success. But I was a "big success" in a way I found extremely dangerous. The students saw me, at the end of my life, working on very general problems and making observations about every discipline, be it social, medical or scientific. Immediately they wanted to do the same thing, to come to grips from the start with problems on a worldwide scale, without being willing to work before thinking. Yet I'd tell them every day, "I want to stress that for forty years I was the most disciplined microbiologist possible . . ." But they simply wouldn't accept my explanation. I believe that from then on I began to feel that I was a bad influence on them. Because my courses were going too well, I gave up teaching and from then on gave no more courses of that sort. (*Science*, April 17, 1992)

. . . takes pains (and pleasure) in reminding them of the existence of the True, the Beautiful, and the Good. Teaching, in the end, is that simple—and that difficult. (p. 115)

Being "up-to-date" in perspective or theoretical outlook may be essential in a professor of the sciences, but I am not so sure that it is as essential in a professor of the humanities. It may well be that the humanities professor's greatest contribution to his students' education lies in being "out-of-date," in being a creature of his time—a time that no young student has personally experienced—and so provide them with a difference of outlook that cannot be found in "cutting edge" journals or in the discourses of grooving young instructors. In English and cultural studies departments awash with deconstruction and feminist theory, think how refreshing it is for the student to step into the classroom and hear the view of a scholar who is a positivist, or even a Christian humanist! Now that would be exposure to real difference—to another world, another time, another reality. (pp. 115-16)

In old age, the Cambridge classicist F. L. Luca regretted the years he had spent on third-rate literature in order to write and publish scholarly papers. He wished he had spent more time on the great books. Had he done so, his scholarly reputation would have suffered, but the quality of his life would have improved. (p. 110)

To conclude, I mention but a few works that reveal the subtle and not-so-subtle academic careerism in our time: Denise Pope's *Doing School;* David Lodge's *Changing Places* and *Small World;* and John Lukacs's *A Thread of Years,* pp. 452[–]56.

Sincerely,

Xiuwu Liu

(Please file this letter with yours to me.)

(My reading notes on Tuan's book also contained this passage on teaching and student participation:

> When pedagogues commend "participation," they seem to have in mind not a quiet class in which students listen, but rather a noisy class in which they speak out, interrupting one another and the teacher. Yet one certainly participates by listening, and it may well be the more demanding way. Think of monkeys in a tropical forest. They speak out—*do* they speak out! But do they ever listen? Is it even within their intellectual capacity to listen? We human beings occasionally listen, and when we do we recognize the individuality and worth of another. And what is the worth? In large part, it is his or her take on the world. So shut up and listen. (p. 75)

In today's classrooms, the instructor has to compete with cellphones, tablets, laptops and listening devices.)

ibidem.eu